LIGHT ON THE MOUNTAIN

Greek Patristic and Byantine Homilies
on the Transfiguration of the Lord

ST VLADIMIR'S SEMINARY PRESS
Popular Patristics Series
Number 48

The Popular Patristics Series published by St Vladimir's Seminary Press provides readable and accurate translations of a wide range of early Christian literature to a wide audience—students of Christian history to lay Christians reading for spiritual benefit. Recognized scholars in their fields provide short but comprehensive and clear introductions to the material. The texts include classics of Christian literature, thematic volumes, collections of homilies, letters on spiritual counsel, and poetical works from a variety of geographical contexts and historical backgrounds. The mission of the series is to mine the riches of the early Church and to make these treasures available to all.

Series Editor
JOHN BEHR

Associate Editor
AUGUSTINE CASIDAY

Light on the Mountain

GREEK PATRISTIC AND BYZANTINE HOMILIES ON THE TRANSFIGURATION OF THE LORD

Translated by

BRIAN E. DALEY, SJ

ST VLADIMIR'S SEMINARY PRESS
YONKERS, NEW YORK
2013

Library of Congress Cataloging-in-Publication Data

Light on the mountain : Greek Patristic and Byzantine homilies on the
Transfiguration of the Lord / translated by Brian E. Daley, SJ.
    p. cm. — (Popular patristics series, ISSN 1555–5755 ; Number 48)
    Includes bibliographical references.
    ISBN 978–0–88141–467–7 (alk. paper)
    1. Jesus Christ—Transfiguration—Sermons. 2.. Sermons, Greek—
Translations into English. I. Daley, Brian, 1940–.

    BT410.L55 2013
    232.9'56—dc23

2013002958

COPYRIGHT © 2013 BY

ST VLADIMIR'S SEMINARY PRESS
575 Scarsdale Road, Yonkers, NY 10707
1-800-204-2665
www.svspress.com

ISBN 978–088141–467–7
ISSN 1555–5755

PRINTED IN THE UNITED STATES OF AMERICA

For my fellow members,
past and present,
of the North American
Orthodox-Catholic Consultation
ἐν τῷ φωτί σου ὀψόμεθα φῶς
(Psalm 36.9)

Table of Contents

And after six days Jesus took with him Peter and James and John, and led them up a high mountain apart by themselves; and he was transfigured before them, and his garments became glistening, intensely white, as no fuller on earth could bleach them. And there appeared to them Elijah with Moses; and they were talking to Jesus. And Peter said to Jesus, "Master, it is well that we are here; let us make three booths, one for you and one for Moses and one for Elijah." For he did not know what to say, for they were exceedingly afraid. And a cloud overshadowed them, and a voice came out of the cloud, "This is my beloved Son; listen to him." And suddenly looking around they no longer saw anyone with them but Jesus only.

Mark 9.2–8

Introduction

A number of summers ago, I spent a weekend as a guest at the monastery of Chevetogne, in southern Belgium—the famous Catholic Benedictine community devoted to promoting mutual understanding and reconciliation between Orthodox and Catholic Christians. Since its foundation in 1925, this unique monastic community has, among other activities, devoted itself to celebrating the sacred liturgy and the divine office each day in both the Eastern and the Western forms, each regime of prayer attended on normal days by approximately half the monastic community. The rationale for this is the conviction that the most important way to work towards the reunion of the Churches is not simply to talk and study, to run conferences and to practice hospitality, but to pray daily in both liturgical traditions, as a single community of faith.

It was early August, and I was seated next to the Prior for the Sunday evening meal. He asked me how long I planned to stay, and when I told him that I was thinking of leaving the next day, he seemed surprised: "Then you are not going to stay for the feast?" he asked. I looked blankly at him, and he explained, "Tuesday, of course—the Feast of the Transfiguration, August 6; one of the twelve great feasts of the liturgical year in the Eastern calendar!" "Of course," I said, not admitting that I had forgotten. And I decided then and there to stay an extra day and to join in the celebration: an unforgettable experience, as it turned out, with a solemn all-night vigil and a festive Eastern liturgy in the morning, repeatedly and movingly punctuated by the great *apolytikon* or dismissal verse for the feast, which prays, "You have been transfigured on the mountain, Christ our God, to reveal your glory to your disciples . . . By the prayers of

the Mother of God, let your eternal light shine also on us sinners . . .
Giver of light, glory to you!"

This feast has been solemnly celebrated on August 6 by the
Western Church, as well, since early medieval times, and was placed
on the universal Roman liturgical calendar by Pope Callistus III
in 1456; yet for most Catholics, it attracts relatively little attention,
compared with the other major liturgical events of the year, which
celebrate Gospel events in the life of Jesus and of Mary his Mother.
In the tradition of the Eastern Churches, on the other hand, the
commemoration of Jesus' Transfiguration continues to loom large,
as an occasion to commemorate an incident that was understood by
theologians and preachers throughout the early Christian tradition
to provide an essential key for understanding who Jesus really is,
and how his life, culminating in his death and resurrection, brings
to fulfillment God's saving work in history. In the Gospel context,
the Mystery of the Transfiguration of the Lord might be thought of
as the interpretive link between the beginning of Jesus' mission, at
his baptism in the Jordan, and the climax of that mission on Calvary.
It is his crowning epiphany to his disciples, the confirmation of
their incipient faith that he is the Promised One of Israel and God's
Beloved Son, revealed to them even as he "set his face to journey
towards Jerusalem" (Luke 9.51). It stands, then, at the heart of what
we call, in modern Western terms, Christology.

I. *The Transfiguration Account in the Gospels.* The importance of
the Transfiguration episode stands out with special clarity in the
Gospel of Mark. Most contemporary Biblical scholars take Mark's
Gospel to be slightly older than those of Mathew and Luke, which
seem to use it as a textual basis, while adding their own material
and their distinctive interpretive themes. One of the principal organizing themes in Mark is the gradual discovery, by his fellow Jews
and especially by his followers, of Jesus' true identity as the unique
Son of God, sent by the God of Israel to inaugurate his Kingdom
on earth, even in the face of Jesus' apparent failure, rejection, and

crucifixion by the occupying Romans, with the collusion of the leaders of his own people.

So the opening verse of Mark identifies the purpose of the work, even as it identifies Jesus by now-familiar titles: "The beginning of the Gospel of Jesus Christ, the Son of God" (Mark 1.1). In the first several chapters, as Jesus' early ministry of preaching and healing is narrated, his identity remains mysterious; people are amazed by the authority of his teaching and the power of his signs (e.g., 1.27; 4.41; 5.42). In fact, Jesus is concerned to prevent his reputation as a wonderworker from simply spreading by word of mouth (e.g., 1.43; 5.43), though his wishes are usually contravened. Only the demons who experience his power recognize that he is "the Holy One of God" (1.24; cf 1.34), "Son of the Most High God" (5.8). Eventually, at the end of the narrative, as Jesus hangs dead on the cross, with the label "The King of the Jews" ironically tacked over head (15.26), it is the nameless Roman centurion—neither a Jew nor a disciple—standing at the scene, who affirms, without qualification or apparent motive, "Truly, this man was a Son of God!" (15.39)

In the Greek manuscripts, Mark's Gospel ends in several different ways. Most of the longer versions seem mainly to incorporate summaries of the accounts of Jesus' appearances to his disciples that appear in the three other canonical Gospels. The so-called "short ending," contained in the Codex Sinaiticus and other ancient, authoritative New Testament manuscripts, and which many New Testament scholars today consider to be the most likely original ending, appears to stop its account of the discovery of his resurrection abruptly in mid-story. Mary Magdalene and two other women disciples go to Jesus' tomb early in the morning of the first day of the week, find that it is empty, and encounter a young man in white, who informs them that Jesus has been raised, and will meet them and the disciples again in Galilee. Mark reports that at this point the women "said nothing to anyone, for they were afraid." If this narrative does indeed constitute the original ending of Mark's Gospel, then clearly the rest of the story of the disciples' growth to full faith in Jesus and his saving work was not spelled out here. It remained to be told—after the text had been read—in the oral witness of the Apostles, as the conclusion of a process that had only haltingly begun in the Gospel narrative itself: the process of fully realizing what it means to see in Jesus, who had been crucified, Israel's true Messiah and God's Son. But the structure of Mark's Gospel, and the carefully arranged details of the story, are clearly meant to suggest that that real faith in him was already available, in principle, for those who were able to understand the story fully.

In Mark's Gospel, in fact, it is Jesus' disciples, more than any other group, who are depicted as engaged in a continuing struggle to grasp who Jesus really is, and in light of his identity to understand the full significance of his mission. In this context, a key section of the Gospel—situated, significantly, in virtually the exact center of the narrative—is Mark 8.27–9.8, a small complex of events in which the leading disciples, for whom Peter speaks, are depicted as beginning to grasp Jesus' identity, then being shocked by the possibility of his crucifixion, and finally experiencing a revelation of his glory, in the context of God's overpowering proclamation of Jesus' mission as Son—the story of the Transfiguration.

Jesus and the disciples are presented as being at the northernmost limits of Israel, "the villages of Caesaraea Philippi," at the start of the section (8.27). Almost casually, Jesus asks the disciples who the public says that he is, and they report a variety of current rumors: he is John the Baptist, Elijah, one of the ancient prophets returned to earth. He is, in any event, a person of extraordinary power. "But who do *you* say that I am?" Jesus asks them suddenly. A direct challenge to their faith has been issued; and Mark presents Peter as answering immediately for the rest, with a clarity and insight that shocks the reader: "You are the Christ!" (8.29).[1] Jesus makes no attempt here to

[1] In Matthew's parallel text, Matt 16.16, Peter identifies Jesus in still more elaborate terms, seemingly anticipating the revelation of God from on high in the Transfiguration scene shortly thereafter: "You are the Messiah, the Son of the living God." It seems likely that this represents an elaboration by the Matthaean redactor on the text of Mark.

disagree with Peter's identification, but characteristically moves to prevent this title from becoming public before its time: "He sternly ordered them not to tell anyone about him" (8.30).

In all three Synoptic Gospels, this episode of Peter's confession of faith that Jesus is the Messiah is immediately followed by Jesus' prediction of his own coming rejection by Israel. Mark puts it this way:

> Then he began to teach them that the Son of Man must undergo great suffering, and be rejected by the elders, the chief priests, and the scribes, and be killed, and after three days rise again. He said all this quite openly.[2]

The contrast with what has just preceded this text is startling. Jesus has just been acknowledged—timidly, perhaps, but unequivo-cally—to be Israel's anointed King of the end-time, her Messiah, by Peter, who seems to speak for all the disciples; Jesus himself offers no objection to the identification. Yet he immediately insists that the religious leaders of Israel will reject him and put him to death amidst great suffering; his Messianic identity will be denied by the very nation that had, for centuries, longed for a Messiah to come—he will be the Messiah who is crucified. And when Peter, incredulous at this apparent denial of his own confession, rebukes Jesus for making such a suggestion, Jesus criticizes him sharply as a "Satan," a tempter, and suggests Peter is thinking in a purely worldly way (8.32–33). Even if he truly is the Messiah sent by God, Jesus seems to be saying, he will certainly not be the Messiah of popular expectations.

In the verses that follow, Jesus expands his prediction of his own coming conflict and apparent failure into a kind of rule for genuine discipleship, and for preparing oneself to share the eternal life of the Kingdom: every real disciple must somehow imitate Jesus, doing as he does, "taking up his cross" to follow him (8.34). To "save one's life," one must be ready to lose it for Jesus' sake (8.35). To survive before

[2]Mark 8.31–32.

the final, severe judgment of the Son of Man, one must now be committed not to be "ashamed" of him, as the shape of his life is finally determined: not to reject the violent fate that will surprisingly be his, as Messiah, but to affirm it and even to share in it personally (8.38). Following him towards death, Jesus suggests, is the only way to find enduring life (8.36–37). A new paradigm of salvation has begun to be sketched out, which will be of distinctive and central importance for the Christian tradition.

It is at this point that the Synoptics present to us the episode of Jesus' Transfiguration (Mark 9.2–8; Matt 17.1–8; Luke 9.28–36): an unusual and solemn narrative that clearly parallels, in style and many details, the story of his baptism in the Jordan at the start of his public ministry.[3] Jesus leads Peter, James, and John–the three disciples who tend to speak for the rest–'up a high mountain by themselves alone,"[4] and there "was transfigured (*metemorphōthē*) in front of them" (9.2). The word "transfigured" is clearly meant to convey a complete change of appearance, at least. Jesus' clothes became "dazzling white," Mark tells us, and Matthew adds that "his face shone like the sun" (Matt 17.2). The transformation seems meant to suggest that Jesus' form took on the glory and divine splendor of the theophanies at Mount Sinai in the book of Exodus:[5] a sight both terrifying and attractive, which overpowers the senses with its intensity.

Mark next relates that "there appeared to [the three disciples] Moses and Elijah, who were talking with Jesus" (9.4). For the Jewish reader of Jesus' day, Moses and Elijah would have immediately suggested the heart of Israel's Scriptural tradition: personifications of "the Law and the Prophets," who embodied God's historic revelation to their people. More importantly, both Moses and Elijah had,

[3]Mark 1.9–11; Matt 3.16–17; Luke21–22; cf. John 1.33–34.

[4]Although the Christian tradition, since at least the writings of Origen in the third century, identified the "high mountain" of the Gospel episode with Mount Thabor, in central Galilee not far from Nazareth, this identification is not suggested in the Gospels themselves.

[5]Ex 20.16–21; 24.9–11; 33.7–11; 33.19–23.

in their own struggles to carry out God's commands, sought to see God and to talk to God face to face, and for that purpose had climbed to the top of a mountain.[6] Here, at the top of another mountain, somewhere in Galilee, they are now depicted as talking face to face with Jesus.

The implication for the early readers of the Gospels would likely have been that the three disciples here recognized Jesus as communicating God's glorious presence and power in the same way these two representative figures of Israel's past had experienced it: radiating light on a mountaintop, speaking in an intimate yet authoritative way to his chosen servants. Jesus stands here as the heart of a Biblical theophany. And although Peter, looking on the scene, seems to conclude that what he is seeing puts Jesus on the same level as Moses and Elijah, as one of the rare human beings chosen to converse with God—hence his suggestion about "building three tents" there, modeled perhaps on Moses' "tent of meeting" in Ex 33.7–11,[7] a suggestion that Mark and Luke immediately brand as an unreflective idea[8]–God himself suddenly intervenes to give a startlingly different interpretation of who Jesus really is: "Then a cloud overshadowed them, and from the cloud there came a voice, 'This is my Son, the Beloved; listen to him!' "[9] God is identifying Jesus as the bearer of his revelation

[6]Ex 33.17–34.9; I Kg 19.8–18. In the Scriptural accounts, God's giving of the Law to Moses, and Israel's original infidelities, are said in the book of Exodus to have occurred on and before Mount Sinai, in the desert of Sinai (so, e.g., Ex 19.20–23); Deuteronomy refers to the place as "Horeb, the mountain of God" (e.g., Deut 9.8), which is also given in Exodus 3.1 as place of Moses' original encounter with God at the burning bush. Elijah, under persecution for confuting the prophets of Baal, flees Israel and journeys through the desert to "Horeb, the mountain of God" (I Kg 19.8), where he is allowed to encounter the Lord in an experience of silence at the mouth of his cave (19.11–12). It is not clear whether "Sinai" and "Horeb" are two alternate names for the same mountain, are two different outcroppings on the same *massif*, or represent two different traditions on the place of these key theophanies.

[7]Cf Ex 34.29–35, where Moses' face is said to be dazzlingly radiant whenever he talks to the Lord.

[8]Mark 9.6; Luke 9.33.

[9]Mark 9.7. Almost the same words are reported as coming from heaven at Jesus' baptism, in Mark 1.11; Matt 3.17; Luke 3.22.

in a new and unique sense. As God's Beloved Son, he now is the one
to be listened to, the one who speaks God's final word.

After the theophany is over, and Moses and Elijah are no longer
visible, the Gospel writers tell us that the three disciples "saw no
one with him any more, but only Jesus."[10] Their relationship has
returned to its normal shape. And now, immediately after the great
theophany, Jesus begins speaking to them again about his coming
passion and death, as well as about his resurrection, as events that
will happen in the near future.[11] As a result, in the story told in the
ensuing chapters, Jesus moves purposefully through Galilee and
northern Judaea towards Jerusalem, where he knows he will meet
rejection and death[12]—as Luke puts it (9.51), "he set his face to go
to Jerusalem." Disciples, too, and would-be disciples, are called to
share in this new pattern of free, self-emptying service, if they desire
to "come after" Jesus.[13] Significantly, this entire central section of
Mark's Gospel (8.27–10.52), so consistently focused on the paradox
of Jesus' identity and on its implications for genuine discipleship, is
framed by two healings of blind men, whom Jesus empowers to see
clearly (8.22–26;10.46–52); the second of them, Bartimaeus, stands
up immediately and "follows Jesus on the way" (Mark 10.52). The
implication is inescapable: to be a disciple implies joining Jesus on
his own "way" to Jerusalem and to death; and this, in turn, requires
that one be empowered by him to "see" him clearly for who and what
he is–that one recognize in Jesus' coming death not simply defeat
and tragedy, but the mysterious yet essential achievement of God's
saving plan. In this narrative context, the dazzling vision of Jesus
transfigured, conversing with the main representatives of Israel's
encounter with God and acknowledged as Son by God himself, is
the event in the whole story that, more than any other, makes this
recognition, and this fullness of discipleship, possible.

[10]Mark 9.8; cf. Matt 17.8; Luke 9.36.
[11]Mark 9.9–13.
[12]So Mark 9.31–32; 10.32–34.
[13]So Mark 9.33–37; 10.28–31; 10.35–40; 10.43–45.

II. *The Liturgical Celebration.* In the liturgy of both Eastern and Western Christianity, as we have mentioned, this incident from the Synoptic Gospels has long been celebrated as a separate liturgical feast on August 6th. Little is known with certainty about the origins of this observance, but it seems most likely that, like most of the major feasts that took their places in the calendars of the Greek and Latin Churches, the Transfiguration was first celebrated liturgically in Jerusalem and in the Churches of Palestine and Syria.[14] The great historian of early Syriac liturgy, Anton Baumstark, pointed out early in the 20th century that manuscripts of lectionaries from the "Nestorian" Christian Churches—communities of West Syrian or Antiochene background, which sought refuge in the Persian Empire after the Council of Chalcedon (451)—from the turn of the 5th and 6th centuries attest a celebration of the Transfiguration of Jesus on August 6, which suggests the origin of the feast may lie in the general region of Palestine.[15] The Georgian Lectionary of Jerusalem, which is probably based on the liturgical calendar of the Greek Church in Jerusalem from the mid-seventh century, lists Scripture passages for August 6th as specific to "the Transfiguration of the Savior, which took place on Mount Thabor";[16] this is the earliest attestation of such a feast within the Chalcedonian Churches. The homily of Anastasius of Sinai for the feast of the Transfiguration, which we have translated in this volume, probably was originally delivered in the monastery of Sinai itself, a community which would have followed the liturgical customs of Jerusalem, during the last decades of the seventh century, and is the earliest homiletic witness we have to such a liturgical celebration. Homilies for the feast then become more frequent in the

[14] See P. Jounel, "Feasts of the Lord in Ordinary Time," in Aimé Georges Martimort (ed.), *The Church at Prayer* 4 (Collegeville, MN: Liturgical Press, 1992) 97.

[15] Anton Baumstark, *Festbrevier und Kirchenjahr der syrischen Jacobiten* (Paderborn: Schöningh, 1910) 260. Baumstark indicates (261) that an eighth-century Non-Chalcedonian or "Jacobite" lectionary from the eighth century, Vat. Syr. 13, refers to the celebration as the "feast of Mt Thabor."

[16] Ed. Michael Tarchnischvili (CSCO 204–205 [Leuven: CSCO, 1960] 204.27; 205.25)

eastern Mediterranean world, attesting to a growing awareness of
the day as a major event on the religious calendar.

A puzzling question is the original reason for celebrating the
Transfiguration precisely on this date. Baumstark, pointing to an
early Syriac designation of the day as the "feast of Mt Thabor," conjectures that August 6 may commemorate the dedication of a basilica on that mountain in memory of the Gospel event, but there is no
evidence for such a dedication. It seems more likely that the date of
this commemoration is linked to another feast: the celebration of the
glory and power of the *cross* of Jesus on September 14, exactly forty
days later.[17] We know that the dedication or *enkainia* of the Con-
stantinian Basilica at the Holy Places in Jerusalem in 335 was later
commemorated on September 13—according to Egeria, the date on
which the remains of Christ's cross had been found, shortly after the
Emperor had inaugurated the "peace of the Church".[18] The Armenian Lectionary of Jerusalem, which reflects the liturgical calendar
and practices of the Jerusalem Church shortly after 400, relates that
on the second day of that eight-day dedication festival in September
each year, "the venerable, life-giving, and holy cross is shown to the
whole congregation"—presumably for their veneration.[19] Since the
main point of the episode of Jesus' Transfiguration in the Synoptic
Gospels is to make it unmistakably clear that the one whom Peter
had acknowledged as the Messiah of Israel—and who then repeatedly began to predict his own coming rejection and death on the
cross, as central to his own mission and indeed as the central model
of discipleship—was in fact God's "Beloved Son," the one with whom
Moses and Elijah conversed, any liturgical emphasis on the "glory"

[17]See Jounel 97. A number of early Christian writers seem to have calculated
the crucifixion of Jesus as taking place forty days after his Transfiguration, just as his
glorious ascension took place, according to Luke, forty days after his resurrection. See
J. van Goudoever, *Biblical Calendars* (Leiden: Brill, 1959) 251–258.

[18]Egeria, *Travels* 48.2.

[19]*Armenian Lectionary of Jerusalem* (ed. Athanase Renoux: PO 36/2 [Turnhout:
Brepols, 1971] 363). This exposure of the relics of the cross for veneration is the ori-
gin of the feast of the Exaltation of the Cross in both the Eastern and the Western
Churches.

and the "life-giving" effect of the cross in the larger plan of salvation would depend on linking it in memory with the Transfiguration event. And by the common logic of Biblical narrative, such a connection—by which one event follows another not immediately, but after a substantial, if measurable period of time—would easily have been conceived of as a period of "forty days." What the disciples saw, and only barely began to grasp, on the mount of Transfiguration, became painful but life-changing reality for them after forty days of journeying through Galilee and Judaea up to Jerusalem. For the later liturgical mind of the Church, the meaning of the Transfiguration would have become fully clear forty days later, too, in the solemn veneration of the cross of Christ as the locus of salvation.

Exactly how the liturgical feast of the Transfiguration, and that of the Exaltation or Veneration of the Cross, with which it thus seems to be linked, came to be celebrated as major feasts in Constantinople and in the West, is not entirely clear. The early, ninth-century part of the *Liber Pontificalis* attests that Pope Sergius (687–701) brought a fragment of the cross, until then preserved at the Vatican, to the Lateran basilica—the official cathedral church of Rome—on September 14, and adds: "It was blessed and venerated by all the Christian people as the day of the exaltation of the holy cross"[20]: presumably that day was chosen in order to follow the established use of Jerusalem. The original discovery of the relics of the cross in the time of Constantine had itself been celebrated in Rome since the early fifth century on May 3; the new feast instituted by Pope Sergius at the end of the seventh century, which followed the Jerusalem calendar in venerating this cross as the source of renewed life on September 13, was now linked instead to the story of the return of the relic to Jerusalem, and its being venerated in the Basilica of the Holy Sepulchre there, in 629, through the negotiations of the Emperor Heraclius, after it had been captured by the Persian army in their sack of Jerusalem, in 614.

---

[20]*Liber Pontificalis* (ed. L. Duchesne; Paris: E. Boccard, 1955–1957) 1.374.

We have less precise information about the spread of the feast of the Transfiguration. The 11th century canonical and monastic writer, Nikon of the Black Mountain, as well as the early 12th-century Patriarch of Constantinople, Nicholas III, allude in passing to an interruption in the midsummer "Lent" or preparatory fast before the feast of Mary's Dormition—an interruption that had been introduced in the imperial capital in the time of Emperor Leo VI, in the early 10th century, by a new, solemn celebration of the Lord's Transfiguration.[21] Vénance Grumel has argued persuasively that these references do not necessarily mean that Leo himself introduced the feast of the Transfiguration to the Church of Constantinople, but only that he may have elevated its rank, causing it to be celebrated with greater solemnity—even if that meant interrupting a traditional time of fasting.[22] As can be seen in the three homilies by Leo that we have translated in this volume, the learned Emperor certainly was convinced of the central importance of this event in the longer story of salvation in Christ.

In any case, liturgical commemorations of the Transfiguration of the Lord on August 6 begin to appear also in Western liturgical books in Naples and Germanic lands in the mid-ninth century,[23] in Spain and France in the tenth,[24] and in Rome in the 11th.[25] In 1453, to commemorate the victory of Western imperial forces over the Turks at Belgrade on July 22 of that year, Pope Calixtus III instituted it as a feast on the universal Roman calendar, although it had been

[21]See A. Guillou, "Le monastère de la Théotokos au Sinaï," *Mélanges d'archéologie et d'histoire* 67 (1955) 216–258, who cites the Russian codicologist Vladimir Benesević for these sources, and takes them to be suggesting Leo actually brought the feast to Constantinople.

[22]Vénance Grumel, "Sur l'ancienneté de la fête de la Transfiguration," *Revue des études byzantines* 14 (1956) 209–210. Grumel points here to an allusion to a feast of the Transfiguration—albeit on November 27!—in an Evangeliary from Sinai dating from 710 or 755, which may come from Constantinople.

[23]So Jounel 98.

[24]Ibid. The feast was particularly promoted in Cluniac houses during the abbacy of Peter the Venerable (d. 1156).

[25]José Antonio Goñi, *Historia del Año Liturgico del Calendario Romano* (Barcelona: Centre do Pastorál Liturgica, 2010) 92.

celebrated locally in many Churches for some six centuries.[26] As so often happened, what had begun as a usage of the Church in Jerusalem had by now become a central part of the liturgical life of all Christians.

III. *The Homilies.* In this collection, we have translated twenty-three homilies by Greek authors on the Transfiguration of the Lord—all the Greek homilies on this event, from the third through the fourteenth centuries, that are presently available—beginning with Origen, the great third-century interpreter of the Christian Scriptures, and ending with two festal homilies by St Gregory Palamas. About half of the pieces included here are not connected with any liturgical celebration of the Transfiguration, but were either given before the event was celebrated in a liturgical feast, formed part of larger sets of homilies on a particular Gospel, or were catecheses addressed to monks. The rest allude to a liturgical setting, and generally invite their hearers to enter as participants, through the words of the Gospel and the actions of the Eucharist, into the transforming vision of Jesus first shared by his three Apostles on the mountain. All of them, taken together, offer us food for our own meditation, as well as a panorama of the reflections of earlier generations on this centrally significant Gospel story, as it developed through eleven formative centuries.

The earliest writer whose thoughts on the Transfiguration we have translated here is *Origen of Alexandria* (c. 185–c. 253), the towering theologian, apologist, and exegete of the early Greek Church, whose influence on theology and Scriptural scholarship continued in East and West throughout the Patristic, medieval, and early modern periods. Born in a devout Christian family, Origen received a thorough education in classical grammar and rhetoric as a young man, and was also widely read in Greek philosophy. Although he acted as chief catechist for his bishop for a number of years, accord-

[26]Juan B. Ferreres, "La Transfiguration de Notre Seigneur: Histoire de sa Fête et de sa Messe," *Ephemerides theologicae Lovanienses* 5 (1928) 630–643.

ing to Eusebius of Caesaraea,[27] his interest was clearly focused on
using all the available methods of literary interpretation of his time
to uncover the inner significance of the Christian Scriptures, as that
body of writings was received in the Alexandrian Church of his day.
For Origen, the words of the Bible were literally words of life; he
begins the preface to his work *On First Principles*, for instance, with
the statement:

> All who believe and are convinced that grace and truth came
> by Jesus Christ, and who know Christ to be the truth . . . ,
> derive the knowledge that calls people to lead a good and
> blessed life from no other source but from the very words
> and teaching of Christ.[28]

Origen immediately explains that the "words and teaching of Christ"
includes the whole of what Christians of his day recognized as the
Bible, including all the Hebrew Scriptures—in Greek translation—
the four Gospels and the letters of Paul, and doubtless a number of
other writings. In any case, it is apparent that finding God's intended
meaning in the Bible accepted by the Christian community was, in
his view, central to Christian faith and life.

As a result, almost all of Origen's considerable literary output
was Scriptural interpretation and argument, in one form or another.
One of his main surviving exegetical works is his *Commentary on
Matthew*; this originally contained twenty-five books, eight of which
are still extant in the original Greek and several more in an early
Latin translation, which cover, all together, Matthew 13.36 through
27.66. This work seems to have been given originally as a set of lectures, aimed at a somewhat more sophisticated audience than his

[27]Most of the biographical details we know about Origen come from Eusebius
of Caesaraea's *Church History* 6.2–39, which was written some seventy years after
Origen's death.

[28]*De Principiis*, Praefatio 1 (ed. H. Görgemanns and H. Karpp [Darmstadt:
Wissenschaftliche Buchgesellschaft, 1976] 82); trans. G. W. Butterworth (New York:
Harper and Row, 1966).

Scriptural homilies and offering a running analysis of this centrally important Gospel text. Like many of his other works of Biblical interpretation, Origen apparently delivered the *Commentary on Matthew* after he moved to Caesaraea in Palestine, probably around 246. What we have translated here—unlike the other pieces in this volume—is not a separate homily, but the section of Book 12 of the *Commentary* that deals with the Transfiguration event–particularly as it is recounted in Matthew 17.1–9, but commenting also, in the process, on details from the other two Synoptic Gospels.

We have included Origen's reflections on this passage because of his lasting influence on later commentators and preachers, and because his approach to this text is so representative of the Patristic approach to Scripture: his central concern with discovering in every Biblical passage the saving Mystery of the Incarnation; his sense that puzzling details in a verse are best interpreted by connecting the text with other passages in the canonical Scriptures; his practice of looking for clues to meaning both on the natural or psychological human level and on the level of the symbolic significance a thing or event might carry for human salvation—by considering what he calls here both the "literal" and the "tropological" or "mystical" meaning that may be intended by God in Scripture's words. So Origen speculates here on possible reasons why the real-life Peter may have wanted to linger on the mountain with Jesus and his companions, but also reflects on the deeper significance that may be providentially intended in the text by the "six days" that preceded the vision, by the ascent of Jesus and his disciples, the radiance of his garments, the overshadowing cloud. In the process of searching out the text's significance for the community of faith, Origen displays—as always—an astonishing command of the whole content of the Bible and of the possible interconnections among widely scattered passages, as well as a dogged determination not to let any detail in the text go unexplained. More than most ancient commentators, too, he is sensitive to even small variations of phrasing and detail among the Synoptic authors; unlike many modern exegetes, however, he tends to assume that none of these details is narrated without purpose, and that the whole text is intended to tell us about our relationship to God through Christ.

Our second text on this episode is by *John "Chrysostom"* ("Golden-mouthed"; c. 350–407), the great Antiochene exegete and preacher, who reluctantly became bishop of Constantinople in 398; this is Homily 56 of his ninety *Homilies on Matthew*, delivered in Antioch, at the height of his activity there as a pastoral commentator, probably in 390. In many ways, it is a typical example of Chrysostom's approach to Scriptural texts. Lively and simple in style, with frequent questions challenging his hearers to reflect on the event for themselves, Chrysostom's approach to the scene of the Transfiguration focuses mainly on seeking out the human motives, fears, and hopes of the human characters in the story, rather than on the possible symbolic meaning of its material details. And as in many of his Scriptural homilies, his dominant interest seems to be in using the occasion for practical moral exhortation as well as in Biblical explanation for its own sake. So here, after presenting the event itself in dramatic and believable human terms, John leads his hearers to deeper moral reflection by connecting this scene of Jesus' glory on the mountaintop with the eschatological drama of the Last Judgment, when all humanity will gaze on him in the full splendor of his divine person. Here, after some general comments on the moral seriousness the prospect of such a judgment ought to introduce in our lives, Chrysostom reflects at length on the particular cruelty of usury: charging interest on loans to those who need money. Although the connection of usury to the Gospel story of the Transfiguration is tenuous, the sermon as a whole reveals Chrysostom's relentless moral seriousness, and his concern to have the liturgy and the public preaching of the Gospel make a perceptible difference in how the faithful live.

Our third homily is very probably the work of one of Chrysostom's successors in the capital: *Proclus*, who, after being involved in the conflicts surrounding Nestorius in that see in the late 420s and early 430s, himself became Patriarch in 434 and remained in that position until his death in 446. Probably a native of Constantinople, Proclus was known at court for being a powerful preacher, as well as for his devotion to the Virgin Mary. This homily on the Transfiguration, like many Scriptural homilies from the early fifth century, is attributed in some manuscripts to John Chrysostom. However, the main modern scholar of Proclus' corpus, François Leroy, argues on both theological and stylistic grounds that it is Proclus' work. The homily, which presumably dates from the 420s or 430s, is based on the presentation of this Gospel event by both Matthew and Luke, and invites the hearers' meditation in somewhat more grandiose rhetorical terms than one usually finds in Chrysostom. A few themes appear here for the first time, which will appear with some frequency in later sermons on the scene: an attempt to explain why only Peter, James, and John were privileged to glimpse Jesus' glory at this time, as due to Jesus' desire not to inflame Judas—who was clearly not worthy to see it—with jealousy over his apparent exclusion; and the connection of this revelation, assumed by now to be on Mt Thabor in Galilee, with the verse from Psalm 89.12 (LXX): "Thabor and Hermon shout for joy at your name." Like the authentic works of Chrysostom, the homily is lively and concrete, and addressed to the hearers in an engaging way; the author shows a greater willingness, however, than Chrysostom usually does to speculate on theological issues, and it lacks Chrysostom's moralizing tendency.

The next homily we have translated here is *Cyril of Alexandria's Homily 51 on Luke*, the only one of this set of homilies preserved in the Greek original. It is found by itself in a number of Greek collections as an independent piece; but Cyril's full series of sermons on Luke—which are probably his latest series on a whole Gospel and which seem to date from 429 or later, after the start of his controversy with Nestorius—exists completely in a Syriac translation, which enables us to identify this text as part of the whole set. Cyril here connects the Transfiguration scene with Jesus' promise, expressed immediately before it in Mark's Gospel, "There are some standing here who will not taste death before they see that the Kingdom of God has come with power."[29] In Cyril's view, this is precisely what occurs six days later on the mountain: Peter, James, and John see the kingly power of God present in Jesus' person. Cyril also sees clearly the connection suggested in the Gospels between "the Law and the Prophets," represented by Moses and Elijah, and Jesus' coming passion and death, which Luke makes explicitly the subject of their conversation. He takes the fact that "Jesus was found alone" after the vision had disappeared as a confirmation, in Luke's eyes, that neither Moses nor Elijah is signified by the voice from above, identifying Jesus as "Beloved Son." In short, it is a vision which the Gospels—and Cyril—understand as confirming the Christological faith of the Church.

The next several sermons we have translated here are less certain in their date and attribution, although they witness to the importance of the Transfiguration scene to the Greek-speaking Church in the sixth and seventh centuries. The first of these is attributed to "*Pantoleon*, Deacon and Chartophylax"; his place and time of activity are not precisely known, but Maurice Sachot conjectures that the homily may come from the time of Severus of Antioch, in the first two decades of the sixth century.[30] A Byzantine lead seal, dated to the sixth century, exists with the inscription, "Belonging to Pantoleon the Chartophylax," which could conceivably refer to the same person.[31] A *chartophylax* was an ecclesiastical administrator charged with financial records—the kind of position that might appropriately have been entrusted to a deacon. The homily, in any case, is focused on the image of light, and on the change effected by the vision in the viewers, especially in Peter, after gazing on the light radiating from the transfigured Jesus.

[29]Mk 9.1.

[30]Maurice Sachot, *Les homélies grecques sur la Transfiguration* (Paris: Centre Nationale de la Recherche Scientifique, 1987).

[31]For a photograph and date, see *www.arminius-numismatics* (12/191). This seal is apparently in a private collection.

The homily on the Transfiguration attributed to *Leontius, Presbyter of Constantinople*, is probably a genuine work of this sixth-century preacher, who left us a collection of homilies on other major feasts and Gospel events, but whose life is itself unknown. Leontius' works are clearly inspired by the preaching of John Chrysostom and Proclus, to whom some of them have occasionally been attributed; this homily on the Transfiguration story, which appears in the manuscripts as a work of Chrysostom, also shows striking connections in its content with the homily of Proclus we have discussed already.[32] Jesus is said here, for instance, to have revealed his glory only to three of his disciples, although the rest were also deserving of the sight, in order not to make Judas, who was clearly unworthy, envious of the others if he were to be the only disciple excluded from the vision. In any case, if the work is by Leontius the Presbyter, it surely antedates the celebration of the Transfiguration event as a liturgical feast. Sachot, followed by the modern editors Datema and Allen, suspect it may belong to a series of homilies by Leontius on the Gospel of Matthew, which is otherwise lost.

Another homily on the Transfiguration (listed in modern Catalogues as CPG 6947), which appears to come from the sixth century, but whose authorship is not entirely certain, is usually attributed to *Patriarch Anastasius I of Antioch* (558/559–570, 593–598). The author is guided by the versions of the Transfiguration story in both Matthew and in Luke. He begins by reminding his hearers of the need to "take up the cross," as Jesus commands, and to embrace a life of serious asceticism, if one is to receive a favorable judgment from Jesus when he returns in glory at the end of the "six days" of material creation. The story of Jesus' Transfiguration on Mount Thabor, Anastasius insists, is a glimpse of that glorious Jesus of the last days,

[32]The work is identified as a homily of Leontius by Maurice Sachot, *L'homélie pseudo-chrysostomienne sur la Transfiguration* (CP 4724, BHG 1975) (Frankfurt: Peter Lang, 1981); text and French translation: 292–329. Sachot's text has been incorporated into the edition of all Leontius' homilies by Cornelius Datema and Pauline Allen, *Leontii Presbyteri Constantinopolitani Homiliae* (Corpus Christianorum, Series Graeca 17 [Turnhout: Brepols, 1987]).

given us as a pledge to secure that hope. Anastasius is certainly
influenced here by earlier homilists and commentators, especially
Origen and Proclus; his explanation of Peter's proposal to "build
three tents" on the mountain is that this was a scheme to keep Jesus
there, away from the priests in Jerusalem who might endanger his
life. For these three disciples, however, as later for the rest, the voice
of the Father acknowledging Jesus to be his Son soon dispelled all
doubt about the rightness of his way towards the Passion, and made
clear the centrality of the cross in God's saving plan.

Even more uncertain in origin than this homily of Anastasius
is the *Homily on the Cross and the Transfiguration* (CPG 7406),
attributed to an otherwise unknown *Timothy of Antioch* or Timothy
of Jerusalem, whom Dom Bernard Capelle has argued is the author
of five Biblical homilies attributed to various Patristic authors, and
whom Dom Capelle situates somewhere between the sixth and
the eighth century.[33] Lively and colorful in style, and profoundly
theological in content, this homily is based on Luke's version of the
story, and once again shows no sign of being delivered at a festal
liturgy celebrating the Transfiguration. Here the emphasis is clearly
on the importance of the vision of Jesus transfigured for empower-
ing his disciples to take up the "weapon" of the cross in their own
battle with Satan. The reason the Lord has summoned Moses and
Elijah back from the dead to appear with him is to convince the
disciples, by the witness of these key figures of the Old Testament,
that the only way to share in the Kingdom of God is though sharing
in the cross. As an answer to those who might wonder how the three
disciples recognized these ancient figures, the author suggests each
brought with him an identifying symbol as icon: Moses the tablets
of the Law, Elijah the fiery chariot that had taken him up to heaven.
Peter's proposal to "build three tents" is also taken here to be a way
of holding on to the glorious Jesus of the vision, and of preventing
him from fulfilling his prophecy of the coming cross. In reply, Jesus

[33]Bernard Capelle, "Les homélies liturgiques du prétendu Timothée de Jérusalem," *Ephemerides Liturgicae* 63 (1949) 5–26.

powerfully insists that it is only through his full acceptance of the cross that fallen humanity can be restored. The "bright cloud," as Timothy (perhaps inspired by Cyril's earlier homily) reads the story, "overshadowed"—made invisible—only Moses and Elijah; God's purpose in doing this was to make sure that the three disciples would realize that "only Jesus," who was still visible, was God's "Beloved Son." The homily ends with a powerful confession of Jesus' divinity, and of his eternal involvement in the works of God.

A final representative of these sermons of uncertain origin is the one we have simply identified as an "Anonymous Incomplete Homily on the Transfiguration." This work is apparently the final section of a longer piece on the Transfiguration of Christ, first published from a Venice manuscript by Michel Aubineau in 1967.[34] Aubineau suggests a date for its composition somewhere between the seventh and the ninth centuries; there is no hint in the part of the text we possess that this was preached at a liturgy for the feast of the Transfiguration–negative evidence, at least, for placing it sometime before the end of the seventh century. Here, too, Peter's enthusiastic wish to "build three tents" and to try to prolong the vision is the result of his ecstatic experience of joy at Jesus' glory that "bleared his soul's eye" to the vision's true meaning. But the "bright cloud" and the voice from heaven—both interpreted here as terrifying Apocalyptic signs—forcefully lead the disciples back to reality: to "Jesus only," and to the paradoxical, but still more powerful vision of the cross, and of their own share in the way to it.

The earliest extant homily that was clearly given at a liturgical celebration of the Feast of the Transfiguration, on August 6, is the homily of *Anastasius of Sinai* that we have translated here. Little detail is known for certain about Anastasius' career; he seems to have lived during the final three quarters of the seventh century, apparently a monk in Egypt and Palestine for most of his life, and was probably, for part of this time, the higumen or abbot of the

---

[34]Bernard Capelle, "Les homélies liturgiques du prétendu Timothée de Jérusalem," *Ephemerides Liturgicae* 63 (1949) 5–26.

monastic community gathered on the lower slopes of Mt Sinai. A hundred years earlier, hermits living there had complained to the imperial authorities about harassment by wandering Bedouins, and the Emperor Justinian had responded in the 530s or 540s by fortifying the area where the hermits lived and building a central Church for their use, dedicated to the Mother of God.[35] Shortly afterwards, at some time between 548 (the death of the Empress Theodora) and 565 (the death of Justinian himself), the widowed Emperor-theologian caused the apse of the monastic church to be adorned with the famous mosaic depiction of the Transfiguration scene, which is still there and which has served as the iconographic model for most later Orthodox representations of it.[36] This contemplative community on Sinai, built on what was thought to be the site of Moses' and Elijah's face-to-face encounters with God, was quite naturally a place where Christian monks would remember the three disciples' vision of Jesus in the radiance of his Godhead, conversing on another mountain with those two representative figures of the Old Covenant.

Anastasius was a strong, theologically learned defender of the two-nature Christology of the imperial Councils. His *Hodegos* or *Guide* is a kind of miscellany of essays and dense reflections on the controversy over the details and implications of the Christology of Chalcedon, which had been the focus of so much energy and conflict from 451 until the Third Council of Constantinople in 681–682. Among the eight homilies ascribed to Anastasius is this impressive reflection on the meaning of the Transfiguration of Jesus reported by the Synoptic Gospels; the text itself suggests that its setting was a festal liturgy—what the preacher refers to as "the festival of the Mountain"—probably celebrated in full view of the great apse mosaic. As we have mentioned, the celebration of the Transfiguration in the Church of Jerusalem on August 6 is attested

[35]The entire monastic settlement, by now more centralized, was rededicated to the Alexandrian martyr St Catherine in the ninth century. See Andreas Andreopoulos, *Metamorphosis. The Transfiguration in Byzantine Theology and Iconography* (Crestwood, NY: St Vladimir's Seminary Press, 2005), 127–128, with further references.

[36]Ibid. 128–132.

by the Georgian Lectionary from the mid-seventh century; the Sinai community, as we have already said, probably followed Jerusalem's liturgical calendar at this time.

In his eloquent presentation of the Transfiguration story, Anastasius of Sinai emphasizes that the vision is really a foretaste of eschatological fulfilment for the three disciples who witnessed it, an anticipation of the Kingdom of God. What occurs on Mount Thabor brings the promises conveyed on Mount Sinai to fulfillment, linking the two mountains as the "bookends" of the grand narrative of salvation, beginning with Israel's Exodus from Egypt and ending with the second coming of Jesus in glory, to save and judge all peoples. In Anastasius' interpretation, Moses and Elijah are already in glory, already transfigured themselves, and so fully understand the meaning of his earthly life and passion as they converse with him; the heart of the Mystery, as they realize, is Christ himself, "God in human form," whose self-emptying to share in human weakness is the beginning of the final transformation and transfiguration of the whole human race. With all the other mountains mentioned in the Bible, Anastasius invites Mount Sinai, where he stands, and those who live on it, to dedicate themselves to ascetic preparation for the end, and to join in bowing before Mount Thabor, the place of Transfiguration.

Another eloquent early liturgical homily for the feast of the Transfiguration is that of the great preacher and liturgical poet of the seventh and eighth centuries, *St Andrew of Crete*. Born in Damascus around 660 and educated in Jerusalem at the Church of the Holy Sepulchre, Andrew moved to Constantinople in his mid-twenties, where he represented the interests of his Jerusalem community. It was in the capital that he was eventually ordained a deacon, and from there that he was eventually sent to Crete, as metropolitan of Gortyna, sometime between 692 and 715. Both in Constantinople and later on Crete, Andrew came to be known as a profound and eloquent liturgical rhetorician; he is acknowledged to be the inventor of the *canon*, an elaborate form of liturgical poem, thematically focused on the feast being celebrated, which was intended to be interwoven with the Biblical canticles sung in the divine office. Andrew remained in contact with the Church of Jerusalem, and may have had some role in introducing feasts from the Jerusalem calendar, such as those of the Transfiguration and Mary's Dormition, into the cycle of the Church of Constantinople. He died around 740.

This ambitious, theologically dense sermon on the Transfiguration, based primarily on the account of it in Luke's Gospel, invites its hearers to "ascend the mountain" of contemplation, which leads them above earthly realities, and to celebrate the divinization of human nature, which begins—paradoxically—in the "unconfused union" of God and humanity in the person of Christ. The purpose of his sermon, he insists, is to allow human speech to annihilate itself by pointing beyond human rationality and eloquence, in order that those who hear and absorb it may be drawn into the process of transformation themselves. It lays before its hearers, assembled for the Eucharist, a "spiritual banquet," a feast of words and images. Andrew skillfully—perhaps surprisingly—links the "six days" that elapsed between Jesus' prophecy, that some of his hearers would themselves witness the Kingdom of God, and the vision of Jesus transfigured, with the six forms of love he finds listed in Jesus' words of judgment in Matthew 25; to be found worthy of transfiguration ourselves in the final judgment, he suggests, each if us has to practice active charity towards the hungry, the homeless, the naked and the prisoner in this present life. He then identifies Jesus' "garments" in the Transfiguration story with his earthly words and deeds, or with the visible world of created things; in either case, only those whose vision is purified and who stand on the "rock" of faith are able to perceive the Word's hidden radiance under the surface of creation. What is happening on the mountain, in fact, is that those graced with vision are enabled to perceive the divine radiance that belongs to Jesus because of his identity as Son. Unlike some earlier interpreters, Andrew explains Peter's words, "Lord, it is good for us to be here," not simply as expressions of a misguided desire to avoid the coming challenges of the Passion, but as signs of a deep recognition of the eschatological importance of the moment: he recognizes Jesus' glory truly as an anticipation of human fulfillment. Andrew also interprets the "bright cloud" overshadowing the mountain as a figure of the Holy Spirit, implying that it is only by receiving the Spirit ourselves in baptism that we can enter into a full and participative understanding of the Trinity. Andrew concludes his homily with a powerful exhortation to his hearers to allow God to complete in them the work of transfiguration in Christ.

St John of Damascus, an exact contemporary and a countryman of Andrew of Crete, also emigrated to Jerusalem as a young adult, and seems to have spent the rest of his life there as a monk of the community of St Sabas, in the Judaean desert. Gifted with a remarkable ability to synthesize the mainstream Greek theological tradition before him, John is perhaps best known for his concise theological treatises on Christology and for his concentrated summary of the philosophical and doctrinal foundations of Patristic tradition, the *Fount of Knowledge* (*Pēgē Gnōseōs*). But he was also a renowned preacher and liturgical poet, as Andrew was; at least eight of the homilies ascribed to him are today accepted as genuine by most scholars, and while some doubts have been expressed about the authenticity of the homily on the Transfiguration (CPG 8057), translated here, most continue to regard it as a genuine work of the Damascene.[37] It is clearly being delivered at a festal liturgy, possibly in a church in Palestine dedicated to the Transfiguration (see c. 17); its place and date of composition, however, remain uncertain.

The homily is an eloquent, unified work that repeatedly brings together the kind of precise doctrinal teaching on the person of Christ, for which John is renowned, and a moving, poetic exhortation to its audience to live fully absorbed in the Mystery of Christ.

[37]See Dom J. M. Hoeck, "Stand und Aufgaben der Damaskenos-Forschung," *Orientalia Christiana Periodica* 17 (1951) 43, n. 14. Hoeck's pupil, Dom Bonifatius Kotter, the modern editor of the Damascene's works, still expresses some reservations: see *Joannis Damasceni Opera* 5 (Berlin: De Gruyter, 1988) 421, n. 2.

Like Andrew of Crete, John presents his homily as an invitation to participate in a festal banquet, a celebration at which he acts as host, or at least as interpreter and master of ceremonies. The center of the banquet is the Mystery contained in the Person of Christ, on which the Gospel story of the Transfiguration offers us food for reflection. John draws on the classic Christology of Chalcedon and Constantinople II to emphasize that Jesus is, at the core of his person, the transcendent God, the second Person of the divine Trinity. The glory that radiates forth from him on the mountain is not something adventitious, something specially bestowed on him for the occasion, but flows from who and what he is. What is "transfigured" is the humanity he has personally made his own, the "garments" of visible form and audible words that make his divine identity intelligible to creatures. To see this divine glory radiating through Christ's human-ity requires that the disciple follow him, ascend the "mountain" of human virtues, whose unifying center is love; and the promise implied in the vision is eschatological fulfillment, final participation in Jesus' triumph over death, adoption as beloved children of God. John communicates this message by a simple, phrase-by-phrase interpretation of the Gospel episode, unfolding each of its details as conveying this one central Christian message. It is a classic example of preaching that is anchored in the text of Scripture, yet centrally theological.

In this collection, John's work is followed by three homilies given by a celebrated Byzantine Emperor from the turn of the tenth century (866–912), *Leo VI*, who is commonly known as "Leo the Wise"—or perhaps better, "Leo the Learned (Λεὼν σοφός)". A pupil of the Patriarch Photios when he was a young prince, Leo embodied the intellectual energy and breadth of interests typical of his time–a period after the conclusion of the long conflict over the veneration of images, when classical literary, philosophical and theological studies were cultivated in Byzantium with new vigor among both laity and clergy.[38] Although his reign was marked by conflict with

[38]For a thoughtful and wide-ranging presentation of the revival of classical

external foes and political enemies at home, as well as by a long struggle with Church leaders over the legitimization of his four marriages, Leo remained, throughout his reign, an active scholar, a prolific writer and (apparently) a pious Christian. His literary corpus includes a revision of the Roman legal code, several treatises on government and on military tactics, a body of poems, liturgical hymns and letters, and forty-three recently-published liturgical homilies, which he seems to have himself delivered in the Churches of the capital. Three of those homilies were composed for the feast of the Transfiguration, on August 6, which Leo apparently insisted on celebrating with greater solemnity than it had previously enjoyed in Constantinople. Theological and Scriptural learning were a central part of the humanistic revival in Byzantium, and preaching was an expression of both.

Two of the three Transfiguration homilies in his corpus, Homilies 11 and 39, are short and relatively simple. In both, Leo acknowledges the pressure of time, and laments that he cannot fully develop his thoughts on the feast, which he presents—as Andrew and John of Damascus had done—as an occasion when the Christian people are mainly invited to rejoice in the promise of eschatological transformation in Christ. Homily 11 alludes to the daunting effect on the preacher of the presence of a number of learned and eloquent bishops; Theodora Antonopoulou, the modern editor, sees here a hint that this may be a youthful work. On the other hand, Homily 10 is long and elaborate, displaying the full range of the Emperor's classical learning and rhetorical skill. The Emperor's style is lively, original, often challenging to the point of obscurity; in his attempts to engage his hearers conversationally, he reminds us in places of the work of Chrysostom.

Like his predecessors, Leo emphasizes that this feast celebrates "the greatest of visions," and for that reason offers the faithful community

studies in post-iconoclastic Byzantium, see Paul Lemerle, *Le premier humanisme byzantin* (Paris: Presses universitaires de France, 1971), esp. chapters 7 and 8, which deal with the influence of Photios and the reign of Leo VI.

an occasion for the richest celebration possible; the content of the three disciples' vision is nothing less than the promise of our own ultimate transfiguration through participation in the Mystery of Christ. So Leo, like John of Damascus and others before him, urges his hearers, at the start, to "ascend the mountain" with the disciples, an image that here stands for taking on the daunting challenge of contemplating Christ in the full Mystery of his identity. Later on, he reflects at some length on why, in the Gospel episode, only three of Jesus' disciples are allowed to witness his Transfiguration at the start—why Jesus seems to take care to wrap both the event and his own true identity in temporary silence. In the latter part of the piece, Leo also makes a long and learned comparison of the Transfiguration of Christ, as reported in the Gospel, with the many transformations of gods and humans into other visible forms, as reported by Greek myths. Leo's point, despite the literary diversions and artifices, remains consistent: in the Transfiguration of Christ, the disciples witnessed a visible manifestation of the presence of the transcendent reality of God in human flesh, not simply some aesthetic change. The promise of the event is that believing Christians, too, through gazing on the scene and contemplating it in faith with the disciples, will come to share by participation in that same transforming presence.

The next piece we have translated, a homily by the monk *Philagathos of Cerami* for the feast of the Transfiguration, comes from Southern Italy in the early twelfth century, a time when the Latin and Greek Churches in that part if the world were still in *de facto* communion. Philagathos, probably a Greek-speaking Sicilian, was a monk of the Byzantine monastery of Santa Maria del Patir in southern Italy, just outside of the famous Italo-Greek cultural center of Rossano. He was apparently a frequent preacher at the cathedral of Rossano and other local churches, and compiled what came to be known as the "Italo-Greek Homiliary"—a collection of sermons for major feasts, in Greek, by himself and others. Sicily and southern Italy were, at this time, ruled by Normans who had come most recently from the Iberian peninsula; Philagathos seems to have been active mainly during the reign of Count Roger II (1105–1154), a time of prosperity and cultural flourishing in that region.

Unlike most of the other preachers in this collection, Philagathos begins—after the usual invitation to his hearers to join him in celebrating a spiritual banquet and to climb a spiritual mountain—by enumerating a list of twelve questions his hearers might well want to ask about the details of the story: why did it happen "after six days," for instance, why on *this* particular mountain, why before *these* three disciples and not the others? After offering answers calculated to satisfy his hearers' curiosity, all the while deftly connecting this episode with a number of Old Testament images and texts, Philagathos goes on to present a brief interpretation of the Transfiguration story itself, in homely language and with lively imaginative effects, as well as with a few excursions into number-symbolism. He concludes by inviting his hearers to make efforts to move beyond the world of sense-based knowledge, towards a "mystical" understanding of all the details of the story as they reveal the real identity of Jesus and his promise of salvation.

Next in our collection of translations we include two monastic catecheses from the twelfth and thirteenth centuries: apparently not formal liturgical homilies, but instructions for communities of monks that celebrated the feast, and whose lives were shaped by Scriptural prayer and liturgy. The first of these is a brief catechesis by *Neophytos the Recluse* (*Neophytos Enkleistos*; 1134–after 1214), the monk and hermit of Cyprus whose life and practice left a lasting impression on the monastic life of that island. After an early formation in the Monastery of St John Chrysostom on Mt Koutzouvendes on Cyprus, Neophytos travelled for some years through Palestine, then returned to the monastery and asked permission to live nearby as a hermit. Refused at first, by 1159 he was allowed by superiors to withdraw, and he spent the rest of his long life in solitude in a cave. As often happens, however, Neophytos soon became the center of a group of his own disciples, who formed a new monastic community around him known as "the Hermitage" (*Enkleismos*); his catecheses—not all of which have been published—were given to this community, probably in the last decade of the twelfth century and the first decade of the thirteenth.

This brief, simple instruction is on the significance of Jesus' Transfiguration, which the community was clearly celebrating as a liturgical feast on August 6. The homily should be read in the context of the military and religious pressures exerted on the Byzantine Empire and Church in the 1190s, from which, Neophytos seems to say, God has thus far protected his people. This allusion may refer, as to a danger now past, to the Crusader Kingdom established on Cyprus by soldiers of the Third Crusade (1189–1192), and may suggest that the instruction antedates the siege and capture of Constantinople by Frankish invaders in 1203–1204. Neophytos emphasizes that the real theme of the Transfiguration episode is that of the divine light, naturally situated in the person of Jesus, radiating outward into the world to defeat the forces of darkness. For his hearers, this triumph of light is reflected in God's protection of the civil and religious leaders of his people in their own time. Yet to participate in the revelation of this divine light fully, one must "ascend" to a pure life governed by the Gospels and free of the weight of passion. The Gospel story, however, is only a temporary and partial pointer towards the final revelation of Christ in his glory, at his Second Coming. Through our conversion and ascetical practice, we now prepare for that ultimate vision of Christ transfigured.

The second monastic catechesis on the Transfiguration included here is a brief discourse by *Theoleptos of Philadelphia*, a scholarly hermit originally from Nicaea, who was made bishop of Philadelphia in western Asia Minor in 1283 or 1284, and who actively directed that Church, and occasionally led its civil defense against Turkish attack, until his death in 1322. During the years before he became a bishop, Theoleptos was known and highly esteemed as a spiritual director; his monastic catecheses, including this one, probably come from that period in his life, some eighty years after the work of Neophytos we have just discussed.

The context for this instruction is also clearly the liturgical celebration of the Transfiguration on August 6. Theoleptos suggests at the start that the ascent of the mountain by the three disciples should be taken as a metaphor for the labor of the ascetic life; only someone courageous enough to take on this struggle, and to detach himself or herself from the snares of worldly pleasure, will be able to enter contemplatively into the spiritual experience narrated in the Gospel text. To contemplate Christ in his transfigured form, Theoleptos insists, is to enter into the "perfection of pure prayer," which "drives away all thoughts of this present world and forms the whole mind into something radiant" (par. 3). In ascetical practice and the "ceaseless prayer" it makes possible, Theoleptos sees the meaning and the eschatological promise of the Transfiguration feast.

We next present a translation of a longer and more complicated piece, the discourse or treatise of the Byzantine statesman and intellectual *Nikephoros Choumnos* (1250–1255—1327) on the Transfiguration, which seems to have been written for a community of nuns, perhaps around 1315–1316. Born to a wealthy, politically well-connected family, Nikephoros received a thorough humanistic and scientific education, and spent most of his adult life as a civil official, eventually serving as *mesazōn* or prime minister to Emperor Andronicus II from 1293 until 1305. Like his contemporary—and political rival—Theodore Metochites, Nikephoros continued to pursue his intellectual interests and to write philosophical, theological, and literary essays while busy with court politics; this discourse on the Transfiguration is his longest theological piece, and seems to have been widely known and admired during his lifetime. The discourse offers no hint that it was ever connected with a liturgical celebration, or delivered orally at all; although anchored in the Gospel story of the Transfiguration and repeatedly returning to it, it is really an extended meditation on the new covenant of salvation, promised in the Old Law, accomplished by Jesus on the cross, and given validity by the identity of Jesus as Son of God, which is emblematically revealed to the disciples on Mount Thabor.

So, after contrasting the theophany on Thabor with those granted to Moses and Elijah on Mount Horeb, and pointing out the reference to the revelation of God's name to Mounts Thabor and Hermon in Psalm 89 (LXX: 88), Nikephoros challenges those who seek salvation in observing the Mosaic Law to find it instead in the covenant of the cross. Nikephoros then meditates at length on the story of Abraham, comparing the sacrifice of Isaac with God's sacrifice of his Son; he also points to the details of the Exodus story and of Israel's journey to the Promised Land as types of human liberation through Christ. Eventually, he returns to his main point: "[God] gives us the first covenant, in shadows and symbols, as it were, . . . but he gives us the second covenant—the one through which we are all saved—no longer in hidden ways, in signs and wrappings, but now on Mount Thabor, in the radiance of ineffable light: the Father and the Son and the Holy Spirit together, the blessed and almighty Triad" (c. 20). The point of the Transfiguration event is to enable the key disciples to know in advance, before the Passion, who Jesus is, as a constituent member of the Trinity, and so to be ready to find in his cross and resurrection God's final work of salvation. In conclusion, he invites his audience to "ascend the mountain" of ascesis themselves, and through it to be "lightened" of their fleshly preoccupations and made capable of encountering and following Christ as giver of life.

From the late thirteenth or early fourteenth century, in all likelihood, we also possess a brief liturgical homily (CPG 5017) from Southern Italy or Sicily, *attributed* (like many other Greek sermons) *to St John Chrysostom*, but very different from John's authentic work in language and style. The modern editor of this homily, Maurice Sachot, conjectures that it is an Italo-Greek product, probably not much older than the lone manuscript that contains it: Messina, MS San Salvatore 29, dated 1307; like the earlier work of Philagathos of Cerami we have also translated here, it may even have originally come from Rossano, in Southern Italy. The homily begins with an invitation to its hearers to participate in the "mystical banquet" that has been prepared by Wisdom for those who seek her, to which Peter and his companions now lead us in bringing us with them to gaze on Jesus in his glory. The Transfiguration reveals to us who Jesus is, as the divine Son in his undiminished human nature; more important, perhaps, it reveals to us what humanity was originally created to be, before Adam's sin. The disciples are able to recognize Moses and Elijah, the preacher argues, because they hear them speaking with Jesus in words that identify them with earlier Biblical events. After the vision, when they again see "only Jesus," the disciples are able to recognize him—as even later on the cross—in terms of classical Chalcedonian Christology: "they realized that he is true God, and the offspring of the true Father; and also a true human being, a single one who is also double and never confused [in nature]" (sec. 6). The Transfiguration, for this Medieval "Pseudo-Chrysostom," sums up the Church's vision of Jesus.

The next homily in our collection is the work of *Saint Gregory the Sinaite* (c. 1265–after 1337), one of the leading monastic founders and spiritual writers of the fourteenth century. Born on the western shore of Asia Minor between 1255 and 1265, Gregory entered a monastery on Cyprus as a young man, moved on to Mount Sinai (whence his usual sobriquet), then via Jerusalem to Crete, where he was trained in "the prayer of the heart"—a form of prayer focused on the ceaseless repetition of a short formula containing the name of Jesus—which at that time was coming to be widely practiced in many Greek monasteries as the basis of contemplative union with God. Probably around 1300, Gregory moved on to the small skete of Magoula on Mount Athos, where he was sought out as a spiritual director, but eventually was forced by Turkish harassment to flee again, settling in the Paroria or mountainous region near the Black Sea, between the Byzantine Empire and the kingdom of Bulgaria. There he founded as new monastery, dedicated to the Theotokos, which welcomed both Greek and Slavic members, and continued to teach what came to be known as "hesychastic" prayer or "the prayer of Jesus." He died some time after 1337; his biography was later written by his disciple Kallistos, who was Patriarch of Constantinople from 1350 to 1363.

In this discourse—apparently a homily for the liturgical feast of the Transfiguration, published only in 1981 from a single fifteenth-century manuscript on Mount Athos—Gregory seems to be addressing a monastic audience. The homily begins with a powerful invitation to the hearers to contemplate the scene on Thabor in its full implications, to "gaze and listen" (c. 1), and so to gain at least a taste of God's glory. He presents the event as recounting above all an ecstatic experience of God as overpowering light, shared by the three disciples who had accompanied Jesus to the summit. In the process of retelling the story, Gregory distinguishes four "levels" of meaning to be found there: first, the physical events themselves, which are awe-inspiring and remind us of the theophanies of the Old Testament; second, the typological significance of these Biblical events, as they point to the new covenant in Christ; third, the beauty and radiance of the person of Christ, who embodies in his humanity the glorious light of God's nature; fourth, the "divine and spiritual radiance," which always exceeds our comprehension but which, in its very incomprehensibility, is the source of our ultimate blessedness (c. 3).

After reflecting at length on these dimensions and effects of the human experience of God's activity, Gregory turns to the Transfiguration story itself (c. 12). Here again, he emphasizes its ability to overpower ordinary knowledge and sensation: "For when the mind is swallowed up by that ineffable light and comes to exist outside of the everyday world, it is removed from perceiving relationships, and [God] dulls the senses by the light of his power" (c. 13). Because of this ecstatic character, perhaps, the episode is for Gregory—as for several of our other preachers—a foretaste of our own eschatological transformation, "a pledge of the eternal blessedness of heaven," which will itself be a life of unitive contemplation. For Gregory, what is revealed on the mountain, and what will be revealed to us all more amply in eternity, is nothing less than God as God is: the Mystery of God as Trinity—the Father glorifying the Son and revealing his own power and beauty in the Son, the Son glorifying the Father and making him known to the world, the Holy Spirit being poured out as the light in which both Father and Son are recognized for what they are. Gregory reflects here at some length on the Trinitarian shape of God's being, and the Trinitarian mode in which created minds gradually come to know and participate in God (cc. 18–23). In the process, he reflects on the development of our awareness of God's Trinitarian being within the story of creation and salvation (c. 24). Finally, Gregory invites his hearers to offer themselves for the ascent to this vision, and to allow themselves eventually to be transfigured as well, by being adopted as sons and daughters of God with Jesus (cc. 26–27). The homily closes with an elaborate outpouring of praise, and with a prayer for continuing fidelity.

The final author represented in this collection is a contemporary of Gregory of Sinai, *St Gregory Palamas* (1296–1359)—one of the great spiritual and mystical theologians of medieval Europe. Like Nikephoros Choumnos, Palamas came from a highly cultured aristocratic family in Constantinople; a pupil of Nikephoros' rival, Theodore Metochites, he was educated at court during the revival of classical literary and philosophical culture of the early Palaeologan period, and probably had rich opportunities for a successful political career. Instead, Gregory became a monk on Mount Athos in 1316, first entering the monastery of Vatopedi, later transferring to the Great Lavra and still later to the skete of Glossia, where he pursued a more strictly eremitical life and devoted himself, like his namesake Gregory the Sinaite, to the practice of hesychastic prayer. He became known during these years as a spiritual director and guide. After withdrawing, with a number of fellow monks, to the fortified safety of nearby Thesslonica during Turkish raids in 1326, Gregory returned to the Holy Mountain in 1334, and soon began writing treatises and letters on prayer.

Sharp criticisms had been made of this approach to prayer, on the grounds that it claimed to give the practitioner direct, experiential knowledge of the ineffable God; these were most pointedly advanced by the Italo-Greek monk Barlaam of Calabria, who was then staying in Constantinople. Gregory, in responding to Barlaam's critique, came to be recognized as the principal theorist of hesychastic contemplation. In his *Triads in Defense of the Holy Hesychasts*, completed in 1337, he elaborated his famous distinction—based on Aristotelian metaphysics—that while the essence or nature of God must always remain beyond the knowledge and participation of creatures, it is certainly possible for creatures to know and share in God's uncreated, natural "energies": in the operations or active self-manifestations that eternally flow out of God's transcendent being, for the benefit of creatures. The debate between Gregory and Barlaam, hotly contested in Byzantine court circles in the 1340s and 50s, took on the coloring of the political conflicts of the time. Although hesychastic prayer was approved in two local synods in the capital in 1341, a new Patriarch, John XIV Calecas, who opposed it in theory, came to office in 1342 and had Gregory imprisoned. When Calecas was deposed in 1347, Gregory was released, and shortly afterwards was ordained archbishop of Thessaloniki, an office he filled with great pastoral and spiritual energy until his death in November, 1359. His homilies, including this pair delivered during an all-night vigil for the feast of the Transfiguration on August 6 (Homilies 34 and 35) come from his years as archbishop.

Gregory's first homily for the feast (Hom. 34) was apparently given during the night vigil preceding the morning's solemn liturgy. The language, here and in the homily that follows, is simple and direct, probably intended for lay hearers of every background, but the message is an invitation to profound human and spiritual transformation. Gregory focuses on God's action to renew creation by communicating to creatures his own light and radiant beauty. He begins with an invitation to his hearers to join in praising God as he reveals himself in creation, and stresses the importance of doing this in an awareness of the tradition of the Christian Fathers—not in a spirit of idolatry or heresy. The main theme of the Transfiguration story, in Palamas' reading of it, is that of "light on the mountain": the divine light, radiating on the three chosen disciples from Jesus' own person, on the mountaintop of ascetical discipline. Gregory draws on earlier exegetical tradition in interpreting the details of the Gospel story—taking the "six days" mentioned by Matthew, for instance, as separating Jesus' prediction of his Passion from his Transfiguration, as suggesting the history of this present world, and the "eight days" in Luke's version as an allusion to the eschatological "new creation" yet to come.

His central message, however, is that the brilliant radiance suffusing the person and garments of Christ on the mountain is the "uncreated light" or beauty that always issues forth from God's unknowable being. Jesus revealed "the brightness of the divine nature, hidden beneath his flesh" (c. 13); it is the light of the divinity itself, an operation in the created realm that manifests, without ever fully defining, what God is. To perceive it in this world of space and time, one needs "eyes transformed by the power of the Holy Spirit"; yet other blessed humans before the three disciples—Mary, for instance, and Simeon and Anna—shared the same privilege of seeing God in Jesus. The central new blessing of the coming Kingdom will be that all those who are found worthy will share in the Spirit and in the vision—all will be "changed through union with the Word of God" (c. 14). The vision of Christ radiating God's light, in fact, is what Jesus meant when predicting, just before the Transfiguration, "There are some of those standing here who will not taste death until they see the Kingdom of God coming in power."[39] The Kingdom of God, in Gregory's understanding, is essentially this transforming divine light in which, by the power of the Spirit, the three disciples now shared.

In the second of his Transfiguration homilies (Hom. 35), Gregory continues his reflection on the light and glory the disciples saw. He begins by emphasizing that Christ himself is understood by the Church as "the sun of justice" (Mal 4.2), the full revelation in human terms of the holiness to which all are called. Christian morality is essentially to let his "light break forth within us,"[40] to be transformed

[39]Mark 9.1.
[40]See Is 58.8–10.

into bearers of his light. But the central theme of this homily, as it proceeds, is that the light radiating outward from Christ on the mountain was supernatural in character, transforming the ordinary appearances of physical things in its splendor; it is, as Gregory explains, the shining forth of the "inaccessible light, in which God dwells" (c. 10). This light, as an outpouring of God's activities within creation, is unintelligible in human terms; paradoxically, it is darkness to us. So the Gospel story tells us that the mountaintop was "overshadowed" by a bright cloud: God's very light had shown itself impenetrable to the human gaze. At the same time, Gregory insists, this blinding light of God's glory is not God's infinite essence itself, but rather the beauty that radiates from that essence, and that can be shared with creatures, in the measure that God wills; "not only the angels," Gregory writes, "but also holy human beings share in the glory and the Kingdom. But the Father and the Son, along with the Holy Spirit, share the glory and the Kingdom by their *nature*, while holy angels and human beings have a share in this by *grace*, receiving their light from that source" (c. 15). So the life of God's holy people is marked by a yearning to share ever more fully in that divine radiance, which comes forth from, but is not identical with, God's being; "Let the glory of God be upon us," the Psalmist prays[41] (c. 16). The great paradox of salvation revealed on Mount Thabor, for Gregory, is "our own nature, co-existing forever with the immaterial fire of the Godhead" (c. 18). And the real meaning of the Gospel incident and the feast is its invitation both to contemplate this possibility of participated glory and to be open to the transfiguration it requires in us all.

IV. *These Translations.* The Gospel episode of Jesus' Transfiguration, set in the narrative context of the whole story of the discovery of Jesus' identity, of his death and resurrection, and of his role for faith as eschatological Savior, is a prism through which light of many theological colors has passed. What I have tried to offer here

[41]Ps 89.17 (LXX).

is a panorama of the developing interpretation of the event by the classical authors of the Greek theological tradition: translations of the extant commentaries and homilies on the Transfiguration from Origen, in the third century, who laid much of the groundwork for subsequent exegesis of the story, to Gregory Palamas, eleven centuries later, who clearly identified it with the view of the created world and the vocation of the human person that underlies much of the Eastern tradition of mystical prayer. These texts often build on each other, sharing themes and interpretive strategies in a way that underscores the tendency of Christian theologians to see their work as inseparable from a common tradition; yet most of these preachers bring new questions and new emphases to what they discover in the Biblical text and in the corresponding liturgical feast. In discerning their theological trajectory, we come to see more clearly what they understand as the Mystery of Christ.

I have tried to offer here as complete a collection of classical Greek Transfiguration homilies as is presently available. Completeness is, of course, a relative notion, and there are doubtless texts that might have been included here, which I have omitted or missed.[42] My aim has been to give as faithful a rendering of the original text, in intelligible contemporary English, as I can, both in thought content and in literary effect. Sometimes this has made it necessary, in my judgment, to break up long and complicated sentences—in which Byzantine Greek often abounds—and to use the devices of English punctuation more liberally than the editors of the Greek texts themselves have seen fit to do. But I have tried hard not to add to or subtract from the content of the originals, and have indicated by brackets any added words I have thought clarity requires. Where

[42]I have not included, for instance, the brief monastic catechesis for the Transfiguration by Theodore of Stoudios, now edited by J. Cozza-Luzi (Naples: Bibliopolis, 2007), because it contains virtually no reference to the event and its meaning; it seems simply to have been given to Theodore's monastic community on the feast of the Transfiguration. I have also decided not to include translations of the two canons of Andrew of Crete for the feast, or of the canons of John of Damascus and Cosmas of Maiouma, simply because they would have made a long book still longer.

possible, I have used recent critical texts of the originals as a base, and have only used older editions, such as those reprinted in the Abbé Migne's *Patrologia Graeca*, when no adequate modern edition is available. I have added short introductions to each translation, to set it and its author in their historical and theological context as briefly as possible, as well as brief notes to explain obscure passages or identify Scriptural references; neither of these aims at offering substantial theological interpretation. Yet even the texts by themselves, I think, with a minimum of contextual help, can be rich resources for anyone hoping to find spiritual and theological nourishment in his or her quest to know Jesus as the Church through the centuries has come to know him.

The origin of this collection lies in the invitation by my friend Fr John Behr, now Dean of St Vladimir's Seminary, back in the spring of 2004, to put together a set of translations of classical Greek homilies on the Transfiguration of the Lord, to parallel the set I had already translated on the Dormition of Mary.[43] I set to work finding as many examples as I could, and worked on the translations themselves—as a "side" project, mainly in the evenings—during my sabbaticals at the Center of Theological Inquiry in Princeton, New Jersey, in 2004–2005 and 2010–2011. I am deeply grateful to Fr John for his encouragement to start the project, and for his patience in waiting for me to finish it. What has emerged is, I fear, bulkier than that first collection on the Dormition, but I hope it will be equally useful. I am equally grateful to Dr Wallace Allston and Dr William Storrar, the directors of the Center in Princeton, as well as to two different sets of colleagues there, for their support and interest in all my work. I am grateful, too, to my student and graduate assistant at Notre Dame, Ms Han-Luen Komline—herself a graduate of Princeton Theological Seminary—for her friendship and her help in reading through the manuscript during a busy season of exams. Finally, I am deeply grateful to Ms Kate Skrebutenas, the research librarian

[43]*Early Patristic Homilies on the Dormition of Mary* (Crestwood, NY: St Vladimir's Seminary Press, 1998).

at the Princeton Theological Seminary, for her constant kindness, resourcefulness and wisdom during my stays there. Her help makes scholarship seem easy!

My hope in publishing these rich and beautiful homilies in translation is that Christians of East and West may again discover in them a central strand of the theological tradition we share, and that through it we may find deeper unity in our love and worship of the transfigured Christ.

> *Brian E. Daley, S.J.*
> *University of Notre Dame*
> *Second Sunday of Lent, 2012*
> *Feast of St Gregory Palamas*

O Light of light, by love inclined,
Jesu, Redeemer of mankind,
With loving-kindness deign to hear
From suppliant voices praise and prayer.

Thou who to raise our souls from hell
Didst deign in fleshly form to dwell,
Vouchsafe us, when our race is run,
In Thy fair body to be one.

More bright by day Thy face did show,
Thy raiment whiter than the snow,
When on the mount to mortals blest
Man's Maker Thou wast manifest.

Two prophets, that had faith to see,
With Thine elect found company,
Where unto each, divinely shown,
The Godhead veiled in form was known.

The heavens above His glory named,
The Father's voice the Son proclaimed;
To whom, the King of glory now,
All faithful hearts adoring bow.

May all who seek Thy praise aright
Through purer lives show forth Thy light;
So to the brightness of the skies
By holy deeds our hearts shall rise.

Eternal God, to Thee we raise,
The King of kings, our hymn of praise,
Who Three in One and One in Three
Dost live and reign eternally.

10th-century Latin hymn: O Nata Lux de Lumine
Translated by Laurence Housman

ORIGEN OF ALEXANDRIA

Origen, who even in his own time was a center of controversy, was surely one of the formative intellectual figures of early Christianity. Born to a devout Christian family in Alexandria about 185, he lived in an age when the Christian community was never far from the threat of persecution, and lost his own father in the persecution of 202, under Septimius Severus (for Origen's life, see Eusebius, *Church History* 6.2–38). The Alexandria of his day was a vibrant cultural center, with a religiously diverse population. Origen received a strong early education in classical literature and philosophy, but turned his attention in his early twenties to teaching adult candidates for baptism, and later simply to the interpretation of the Christian Scriptures, as they were received in his Church. Along with the Valentinian teacher Heracleon, whom he criticizes extensively in his early *Commentary on John*, Origen can justly be called the first professional Christian Scripture scholar.

Origen began his work of commenting at length on the Scriptures while still living in Alexandria. After moving permanently to Caesaraea in Palestine in 231, he set up his own library, where he and his pupils carried out extensive research in the texts, translations and theological significance of the books of the Bible, as Jews and Christians of his day knew it. Encouraged by his local bishop, he began preaching to the community in Caesaraea on all the books of the Bible—a project he probably never completed—and also composed more detailed commentaries on the text of major Biblical books, modeled on Alexandrian commentaries on classical authors. These seem to have been based on lectures given to students on these books.

Origen's engagement with the Gospel passage on Jesus' Transfiguration, which was to have a significant effect on most later Greek exegesis of the text, is mainly found in book 12 of his *Commentary on Matthew*. He probably began work on this monumental enterprise, which eventually filled twenty-five books, in 246. Part of it still survives: eight books are extant in Greek, and several more in an early Latin translation. Book 12, which comments in detail on Matthew 17.1–9, belongs—fortunately—to the surviving Greek text of the *Commentary*. We translate here the Greek original of the *Commentary on Matthew* 12.36–43.

Commentary on Matthew 12.36–43

(on Matthew 17.1–9)[1]

36 "And after six days" (according to Matthew and Mark), "he took Peter and James and John his brother, and led them by themselves up a high mountain. And he was transfigured before them."

It seems to me not without purpose that those who are being led by Jesus "up the high mountain," and who are deemed worthy of seeing his transfiguration "by themselves," are led up, according to the words we have just quoted, "after six days." For since the whole world—this complete creation–came into being in six days, a perfect number, for this reason I think that the one who overcomes all worldly things by no longer keeping in view "the things that are seen" (for "they are temporal") but now "things that are unseen" and only things that are unseen (for "they are eternal"[2]), is revealed in the statement that Jesus took these particular disciples up "after six days." For if any one of us wishes, with Jesus leading him, to be led by him "to the high mountain" and to be deemed worthy of privately seeing his transfiguration, he must ascend above the six days, so that he may no longer gaze on "things visible" nor any longer "love the world or the things in the world,"[3] nor experience any worldly desire, which is desire for bodies and bodily wealth and the glory of

---

[1]The Greek text on which this translation is based is the critical edition of Erich Klostermann, Griechische christliche Schriftsteller *Origenes X (Leipzig, 1935)* *150–170*.

[2]II Cor 4.18. This whole passage interweaves this text of II Corinthians with the account of the transfiguration of Jesus in Matthew.

[3]I John 2.15.

the flesh, and all that tends to distract the soul and draw it away from the better and more divine things, and to drag it down, and to thrust it, by the deception of this age, into the midst of wealth and glory and the other desires that are enemies of truth. For when one passes beyond the six days, as we have said, one celebrates the new Sabbath, rejoicing on the high mountain at the sight of the transfigured Jesus before him. For the Logos has different forms, appearing to each onlooker as is fitting, and not revealed to anyone beyond what the onlooker can receive.[4]

37   You ask, however, if, when he was transfigured before those who had been led by him up the high mountain, he appeared to them "in the form of God,"[5] in which he existed before, so that he maintains the "form of a slave"[6] to those below, but to those who follow him "after six days" to the "high mountain" he reveals not that form, but the form of God. But hear these words in a spiritual way, if you can, paying attention at the same time to the fact that it is not simply said that "he was transfigured," but with a certain necessary addition that Matthew and Mark have written: for according to both of them, "he was transfigured before them." You ask whether it is possible for Jesus to be transfigured before some with this kind of transfiguration, and at the same time not to be transfigured before others.

If you wish to understand the transfiguration of Jesus before those who "ascend the high mountain privately with him," consider that the Jesus of the Gospels is understood more simply, and known, as one might say, "according to the flesh"[7] by those who have not ascended, through elevating works and thoughts, the "high mountain" of wisdom, but that he is no longer known according

---

[4]This is a familiar theme in Origen's understanding of the Incarnation: the Word makes himself visible and accessible in ways suited to the capacities of each intellectual creature, in order to lead all of them to a vision of God and reality that will ultimately re-unite them to their creator.

[5]Phil 2.6.
[6]Ibid. 2.7.
[7]II Cor 5.16.

to the flesh to those who *have* ascended, but is understood as God throughout the Gospels, and is contemplated, according to their way of knowing, in the "form of God." For it is "before them" that Jesus is transfigured, and not in the minds of any of those below. And when he is transfigured, "his face" also "shines like the sun," so that he might appear to "the children of light,"[8] who have "put off the works of darkness and put on the armor of light,"[9] and are no longer "children of darkness or night"[10] but have become "children of the day," walking "becomingly, as in the day";[11] and when he appears, he shines on them not simply *like* the sun, but in a way that reveals to them that he *is* "the sun of justice."[12]

38 And he is not simply transfigured before these disciples, nor does he simply add to his transfiguration this shining of his face like the sun; "his garments," for those who are led by him up the high mountain by themselves, "became white as light." The garments of Jesus are the sayings and writings of the Gospels, which he has "put on." I think that the things explained about him by the Apostles are the "garments" of Jesus, which become "white" for those who ascend the high mountain with Jesus. But since there are different kinds of whiteness, "his garments became white" as the most brilliant and pure whiteness of all, and that is "light." So that when you see a person not only expounding the divine reality of Jesus accurately, but even making clear the whole text of the Gospels, do not hesitate to say that to him "the garments of Jesus have become white as light."

And when the transfigured Son of God is understood and contemplated in this way, so that "his face became as the sun and his garments white as light," there should immediately appear, to one who sees Jesus in this way, Moses the law, and Elijah—by a figure

---

[8]Eph 5.8.
[9]Rom 13.12.
[10]I Thess 5.5.
[11]Rom 13.13.
[12]Mal 3.20.

of speech,[13] not simply one but all the prophets—conversing with Jesus; for this is what is meant by "speaking together with him." In Luke's version, this is indicated by "Moses and Elijah appeared in glory," and the rest of the passage up to the words "in Jerusalem";[14] if someone saw the glory of Moses, understanding by it the spiritual law, as one with the teaching of Jesus, and the "wisdom hidden in mystery"[15] in the prophets, one has seen "Moses and Elijah in glory," when one sees them with Jesus.

39   Next, since it will be necessary to explain Mark's phrasing, "and in the act of praying he was transfigured before them,"[16] we should say that perhaps it is above all possible to see the Word transfigured before us, if we do what we have mentioned before and ascend the mountain, and see the one who is the Word himself, conversing with the Father and praying to him for those for whom a true high priest would pray to the true and only God. And that he might thus converse with God and pray to the Father, he ascends the mountain. And then, according to Mark, "his garments became white and radiant as the light, in a way that no fuller on earth is able to whiten."[17] Perhaps the "fullers on earth" are those who attempt to be wise in terms of this age, which they consider brilliant and pure, so that they think that even shameful thoughts and false doctrines can be beautified by what I might call their bleaching skill. But the one who reveals his "garments" as "radiant" to those who have ascended, more brilliant than anything their own bleachers' art can achieve, is the Word, offering the radiance of his thoughts in phrases of Scripture that are held in contempt by many—since the garment of Jesus, according to Luke, became white and flashed like lightning.

[13]Literally, "by synecdoche," the figure of speech which refers to a whole by mentioning one of its parts.

[14]Luke 9.30–31: "Suddenly they saw two men, Moses and Elijah, talking to him. They appeared in glory and were speaking of his departure (*exodus*), which he was about to accomplish at Jerusalem."

[15]I Cor 2.7.

[16]Mark 9.2.

[17]Mark 9.3.

40 Let us consider, then, after this, what Peter had in mind when he "answered and said to Jesus, 'Lord, it is good that we are here. Let us make three tents,'" and so on. We must investigate this verse especially, since Mark adds, as if speaking in his own voice, the words, "for he did not know what he was saying," and Luke also says, "not knowing what he said." You will need to establish, then, whether he says this in a state of ecstasy, filled with the spirit who moves him to say these things—which cannot be the Holy Spirit; for John teaches in the Gospel that before the resurrection of the Savior no one possessed the Holy Spirit, saying, "For there was not yet a Spirit, since Jesus was not yet glorified."[18] If "there was not yet a Spirit," and the one who "did not know what he was saying" spoke under the impulse of some spirit, the one stirring him up to say these things was one of the spirits which had not yet been "led away in triumph" on the cross,[19] nor made into a show along with those of whom it is written, "disarming the powers and principalities, [Christ] freely made a show of them, triumphing on the cross."[20] This, perhaps, was the scandal mentioned by Jesus, and the one referred to as Satan in the text, "Get behind me, Satan; you are a scandal to me."[21] I know that this offends many readers, who think that it makes no sense for the one to be blamed who shortly before this was proclaimed blessed by Jesus, because "not flesh and blood, but the Father in heaven" had revealed to him all that concerned the Savior,[22] namely that Jesus was both "the Christ" and "the Son of the living God."[23] But let such a person take his stand on the precise language of Peter and the other Apostles, even when they were beseeching—as if they were still aliens—the one who would buy them free from the enemy and "purchase" them "with his precious blood."[24] Otherwise, let those

[18] John 7.39.
[19] See Col 2.14–15.
[20] Col 2.15.
[21] Matt 16.23.
[22] Matt 16.17.
[23] Ibid. 16.
[24] I Pet 1.18–19.

who want to hold that the Apostles had been made perfect even before the suffering of Jesus tell us why "Peter and those with him," at the time of Jesus' transfiguration, "were heavy with sleep."

But to anticipate a little, and bring something of what comes later into the present narrative, let me raise the following questions: is it possible that someone would take offence at Jesus apart from the activity of the devil, who causes us to take offence? Is it possible to deny Jesus—and that in the presence of a slave girl and a porter and other people of low rank[25]—if there were not associating with the one denying him a spirit hostile to the Spirit and wisdom given to those helped by God to make confession, on the basis of some merit of theirs?[26] Surely anyone who has learned to refer the root causes of sins to the devil, the father of sin, will not say either that the Apostles took offense, or that Peter denied Christ three times before that cockcrow, apart from his influence.

If this is so, it is just possible that the one who was setting everything in motion that might contribute, as far as he could bring it about, to putting obstacles in Jesus' way and to making him abandon his plan—which he so eagerly embraced—to work the salvation of humanity through suffering, even here wants, as it were, to divert Jesus' attention by deception, suggesting that it might be a good thing no longer to adapt himself to human limitations and come down to them, and accept a death for their sakes, but to remain on the mountaintop with Moses and Elijah. So he promised here to "build three tents," one specially for Jesus "and another for Moses and another for Elijah," as if one tent could not contain all three of them—even if they needed to remain in tents and on the mountaintop! Perhaps in this, too, the one causing Peter not to "know what to say" was doing his evil work, not wanting Jesus and Moses and Elijah to be together, but wanting to separate them from each other, under the pretext of "three tents."

[25]Origen seems to be emphasizing the obscurity of the people before whom Peter would deny Christ in order to suggest that Peter was not pressured by anyone in authority to do so; he was preserving his reputation among nobodies!

[26]See Matt 10.17–20.

This, too, was a lie: his saying, "It is good for us to be here." For if it were good, they would also have remained there; but if it is a lie, ask yourself who was putting the lie into circulation, especially since, according to John, "When he speaks a lie, he speaks on his own, because he is a liar and the father of lying."[27] And just as there is no truth apart from the activity of him who says, "I am the truth,"[28] so there is no falsehood apart from the enemy of truth.

Two opposites, then, were in Peter together, truth and falsehood. On the basis of truth, he said, "You are the Christ, the Son of God,"[29] but on the basis of falsehood, "God forbid, Lord—this will not happen to you,"[30] as well as his saying, "It is good for us to be here." But if someone does not agree that Peter said these things under some influence of an evil spirit, but sees his words as the result simply of his own decision, and is asked how he would interpret the texts "not knowing what he was saying,"[31] and "for he did not know what to answer,"[32] he will say that in the earlier passage Peter thought it slanderous and unworthy of Jesus to admit that "the Son of the living God,"[33] the Christ whom the Father had just revealed to him, would be put to death; and in this passage, that when he saw the two forms of Jesus, and saw that his transfigured form was so very different, he was delighted by it and said it would be good to make a longer stay on that mountain, so that he and those with him might rejoice at the sight of Jesus' transfiguration, his "face brilliant as the sun" and his "garments white as light," and in addition that they might forever see in glory Moses and Elijah, whom they had seen in glory this once, and might rejoice at the things they would hear them saying to each other and discussing—Moses and Elijah to Jesus, and Jesus to them.

[27] John 8.44.
[28] John 14.6.
[29] Matt 16.16.
[30] Matt 16.22.
[31] Lk 9.33.
[32] Mark 9.6.
[33] Matt 16.16.

41 But in saying this, we have not yet taken the trouble to search out the figural meaning[34] of what we have examined literally in this passage. So let us next see if perhaps Peter and the "sons of thunder," whom we are speaking about, having been led to the height of true doctrine and having seen the transfiguration of Jesus and of Moses and Elijah, who appeared with him in glory, might have wished to make tents within themselves, for the Word of God to dwell in them, and for his law, contemplated along with his glory, and for the prophecy that speaks of the "departure" of Jesus "which he was going to accomplish";[35] and if Peter, who loved the contemplative life and preferred its delights to being amidst the crowds in all their bustle, may have said—for the sake of helping those who wish [such a life]—that "it is good for us to be here." But since love "does not seek its own benefit,"[36] Jesus did not do what seemed a good thing to Peter. Therefore he came down from the mountain, to those who were unable to go up it and to see his transfiguration, so that they might contemplate him in the way they were capable of receiving. For it is proper to a just person, and to one possessing the love that "does not seek its own"[37] to be "free of all" and to "be a slave to all" who live below, so that he might "gain most of them."[38]

However, someone who does not accept this way of interpreting the ecstasy of Peter, and the activity of the evil spirit in his "not knowing what he was saying," might say that according to Paul, some who "wished to be teachers of the law" did not know what they were talking about; although they were not clear on the nature of the things they discussed, and did not know their meaning, they made strong

---

[34]Greek: "tropologia." This normally suggests a moral interpretation of a Scriptural text, but below, in no. 43 (pp. 64ff), he speaks of this present attempt at exegesis simply as giving the "mystical" meaning.

[35]Cf, Lk 9.31, where Jesus is said to be discussing his coming "departure"—in Greek, his *exodus*—with Moses and Elijah.

[36]I Cor 13.5.

[37]Ibid.

[38]I Cor 9.19.

assertions on subjects of which they were ignorant.[39] Peter, too, [they say,] experienced something like this. For not grasping the goodness of the divine plan with respect to Jesus, or to Moses and Elijah, who appeared on the mountain, he said, "It is good for us to be here," and so on, "not knowing what he was saying." "For he did not know what he said."[40] For if "the wise person will know what comes forth from his own mouth, and wears prudence on his lips,"[41] the one who is not wise does not know "what comes forth from his own mouth," nor is he aware of the nature of his own words.

42 Next after this is the statement, "While he was speaking, behold, a bright cloud overshadowed them," and so on. I think that God wanted to deter Peter from pitching three tents, under which they would—according to his plan—take shelter, and so revealed a single, better (if I may call it so), and very different tent: the cloud. For if it is the function of a tent to give shade and shelter to the one inside, and "the bright cloud overshadowed them," God made a tent for them, as it were, that was more divine because it happened also to be filled with light, as a model of the refreshment that is to come. For "a bright cloud" will overshadow the righteous, who will be at once protected and illuminated and made to glow by it. But what is the "bright cloud" that overshadows the righteous, except perhaps the power of the Father, from which comes the Father's voice, witnessing to the Son as beloved and pleasing, and urging those overshadowed by it to hear him and no other? The Father speaks just as he has always spoken and will always speak, through the expression of his will. And perhaps the "bright cloud" is also the Holy Spirit, overshadowing the righteous and speaking prophetically, working God's purpose in the cloud by saying, "This is my beloved Son, in whom I am well pleased." And I might also dare to say that our Savior, too, is the "bright cloud." For when Peter said,

[39]I Tim 1.7.
[40]Mk 9.6.
[41]Prov 16.23 (LXX).

"Let us make here three tents," one was on his own account,[42] one on account of the Son, and one on account of the Holy Spirit;[43] for the "bright cloud" of Father, Son and Holy Spirit always overshadows the genuine disciples of Jesus. Or the "cloud" that overshadows the Gospel and the Law and the Prophets is "bright" for one who is able to see within its light, according to Gospel, Law and Prophets. And the voice from the cloud is saying, perhaps to Moses and Elijah, "This is my Son, the beloved, in whom I am well pleased. Listen to him!" For they desired to see the Son of God and to hear him, and to gaze on him as he was in glory. But perhaps he is teaching the disciples that the one who is truly Son of God and God's Beloved, in whom he is well pleased—the one to whom one must listen before all others—was the one on whom they were then gazing, who was transfigured and whose face was shining like the sun, who was clothed in garments white as light.

43   After this it is written that when they heard the voice from the cloud, witnessing to the Son, the three Apostles were unable to bear the glory of the voice and the power that accompanied it, and fell on their faces in supplication before God; "for they were very much afraid" at the miraculous character of their vision, and of what was said to them from the vision. Consider carefully, now, whether you can also say this about what is contained in this passage: that when the disciples—who realized that the Son of God had spoken to Moses and that he was the one who had said, "No one shall see my face and live"—saw that the face of the Son of God had become like the sun, and when they grasped, as well, God's testimony about him, they were humbled "under the mighty hand of God"[44] because they could not bear the brilliant rays coming forth from the Word.

---

[42]Origen's meaning in this phrase is unclear. Klostermann, the editor of the text we are using here, suggests emending it to read, "on God's account" (*apo tou theou* instead of *aph' heautou*).

[43]The meaning of the first half of this sentence is obscure; the Greek text may be incomplete or corrupt.

[44]I Pet 5.6.

But after they had been touched by the Word, "they raised their eyes and saw only Jesus, and no one else." For Moses, who was the law, and Elijah, who was prophecy, had become only one with Jesus, who is Gospel—they did not remain three, as they formerly were, but the three came to be one. Consider this, then, as far as the mystical content is concerned.

As far as the bare meaning of the letter is concerned, Moses and Elijah, "having appeared in glory"[45] and having conversed with Jesus, departed to the place from which they had come, perhaps to share the things Jesus had spoken to them with those who had not yet received his blessings, but who would be blessed by him at the time of his passion, when he would raise "many of the bodies of the saints who had fallen asleep,"[46] opening their tombs and leading them to the true holy city, the Jerusalem over which Jesus did not weep, and would there "appear to many."[47]

And after the divine events[48] on the mountain were finished, the disciples came down from the mountain, that they might go to the crowd and assist the Son of God in the work of their salvation. Jesus commanded them, saying, "Tell the vision to no one until the Son of Man is risen from the dead." The words, "Tell the vision to no one," mean something very close to the saying we examined above, "He ordered the disciples not to tell anyone that he was the Christ."[49] So what was said about that former passage can be useful for us also in regard to this present text, since Jesus wished, in the same sense, that the news of his glory not be spoken of before the glory that came after his suffering. For those who heard it, especially

[45]Luke 9.31.

[46]Matt 27.52.

[47]Matt 27.53. For a consideration of this verse, to which Origen alludes, as suggesting many of the Old Testament saints actually rose from the grave in their bodies and entered heaven at the time of Jesus' resurrection, see H. Zeller, "Corpora Sanctorum. Eine Studie zu Mt. 27.52–53," *Zeitschrift für katholische Theologie* 71 (1949) 385–465; also Karl Rahner, "*Assumptio Beatae Mariae Virginis*," *Sämtliche Werke* 9 (Freiburg: Herder, 2004), 202–214.

[48]Greek: *oikonomia*.

[49]Matt 16.20.

the crowd, would have been damaged [in their faith], when they saw him crucified, who had been glorified in this way. Therefore, since his glory in the resurrection was very close to his transfigured form, and to his face that appeared like the sun, he wished that these things only be spoken of by the Apostles at the time "when he had risen from the dead."

JOHN CHRYSOSTOM

Saint John Chrysostom (between 344 and 354—407)—John "the Golden-Mouthed," as he has been called since the sixth century—remains one of the best-known and most popular writers of early Greek Christianity. Born to an aristocratic Christian family in Antioch in the middle of the fifth century, he received a first-class secular education, studying with the well-known pagan rhetor Libanius, among others. As a young man he was attracted to the serious practice of his ancestral faith, was baptized while in his twenties, and attempted first to practice an austere form of Christian asceticism at home with his widowed mother. At the same time, he also devoted himself to the study of the Christian Scriptures, under the guidance of the celebrated Diodore of Tarsus. After spending four years under the guidance of a hermit outside Antioch, and another two as a solitary in the mountains, John returned to the city in 381, weakened in health, and was ordained a deacon soon afterwards by Meletius, bishop of the moderately pro-Nicene faction in the local Church. Ordained a presbyter in 387, John soon became famous as a preacher, commenting serially on many of the books of the Old and New Testament, as well as on various controversial areas of Christian life.

In 397, the Emperor Arcadius had John brought, under deceptive excuses, to Constantinople, where—despite his strenuous objections—he was ordained archbishop and Patriarch of the imperial capital. Always uncompromising in his positions, he made strong efforts to reform the Church's practices and its relationships to the powerful, and to emphasize strongly its commitment to serve the poor and marginalized. As a result of his moral strictness and

penchant for social critique, John earned the enmity of the Empress
Eudoxia and a number of well-connected bishops. Having backed
the cause of several exiled Egyptian monks against their bishop
Theophilus, he faced mounting opposition from many leaders in
Church and state, was deposed and then recalled in 403, and was
finally exiled for good in 404 to a remote spot in the Caucasus, where
he died—a martyr of enforced neglect—in 407.

This homily on the Transfiguration, from Chrysostom's series of
homilies preached on the Gospel of Matthew, comes from the time
of his early activity as a presbyter and Biblical interpreter in Antioch,
probably around 390. It reveals the lively, engaged style of exegetical
preaching that made him so famous as a pastoral guide and exegete:
concrete, direct in its address to his audience, dramatically imaginative in its reconstruction of the Biblical scene. Here as elsewhere,
Chrysostom shows little interest in figural or spiritual interpretation of the events surrounding the Transfiguration; he is interested,
rather, in reflecting on why the various characters in the story may
have acted as they did, what Jesus' motives and purpose were, how
this scene forms part of his wider teaching. As in almost all of his
Biblical homilies, a long concluding section—after the scene itself
has been explained—is reserved for the direct moral application of
the passage to the daily life of his congregation. Here that takes the
form of an impassioned attack on the practice of usury—charging
interest on loans—which he connects with the Transfiguration scene
by interpreting it as a preview of Christ's final coming in glory to
judge all people. Among other kinds of sinners, usurers will not fare
well, John reminds his hearers, before the final radiant appearance
of Jesus.

JOHN CHRYSOSTOM
Homily 56 on the Gospel of Matthew
(Matthew 16.28–17.9)[1]

Amen, amen I say to you: there are some of you standing
here who will not taste death, before they see the Son of Man
coming in his kingdom.

1   Since [Jesus] has said a great deal about danger and death, about
his own suffering and the slaughter of his disciples, so he also lays
these harsh commands upon them. These belong to the present life,
right before them; but the good things belong to promise and expectation—things like people saving their lives who now lose them, or
like his own coming in the glory of his Father, and the distribution of
rewards. And wishing to give assurance even to their sense of sight,
and to reveal what that glory is, in which he is going to come again
(so far as it was possible for them to learn about it), he also shows
and reveals this clearly to them in this present life, so that they will
not grieve any longer either over their own death or over that of their
Lord—especially Peter, in his pain. See what he does: after talking
about Gehenna and the Kingdom—for in saying, "The one who
saves his life will lose it, and whoever loses his life for my sake will
save it,"[2] and "He will give to each one according to his deeds,"[3] he
has signified both of these—in speaking about both of them, then,

[1]There is not yet a modern critical edition of Chrysostom's *Homilies on Matthew*.
We have translated here the Greek text of Frederick Field (Cambridge, 1839), as that
is reprinted in PG 58.549–558.
    [2]John 12.25.
    [3]Matt 16.27.

he reveals the Kingdom to them visually, but not Gehenna. Why is this? If some others were coarser in their understanding, that, too would have been necessary; but since [the Apostles] were honorable and well-disposed, he leads them on with more positive prospects. And this is not the only reason he shows them this vision; it is also that this befitted him better. On the other hand, he does not neglect the other side; there are times when he almost puts the reality of Gehenna before their very eyes, as when he introduces the vision of Lazarus, and recalls the one who demanded the hundred denarii from his debtor, and the man dressed in ragged clothes, and many other images.

"And after six days he took Peter and James and John." Another evangelist says eight days, not contradicting this passage but completely agreeing with it. For the one is referring to the very day on which he had spoken, as well as the one on which he led them up the mountain, but the other only of the days in between. Notice how self-controlled Matthew is,[4] not making any attempt to downplay the role of those who were set over him. John often does this, too, describing with great vividness the praises lavished on Peter. The company of these saints was always free of jealousy and vainglory!

Taking the leaders, then, "He led them up a high mountain by themselves, and was transfigured in their presence, and his face shone like the sun, and his garments became as white as light. And Moses and Elijah appeared to them, speaking with him." Why does he only take these disciples? They were superior to the others! Peter clearly showed his superiority in the intensity of his love; John made it clear by being loved intensely; James, from the answer he gave, along with his brother, "We can drink this cup."[5] And not only from his answer, but also from his actions—among others, those in which he fulfilled what he had said: for he was very troublesome to the Jews,

---

[4]Literally: "Notice what a philosopher Matthew is." To "be a philosopher," in late fourth-century Christian language, normally meant to live a life of self-discipline and consciously cultivated virtue. See below, "Anonymous Incomplete Homily," n. 4.

[5]Matt 20.22.

so much so that Herod thought he would be doing the greatest possible favor to the Jews if he got him out of the way! But why, then, did Jesus not lead them up immediately? So that the other disciples would not have their human sensibilities hurt. This was the reason that he did not even mention them by name, as the ones who were going to ascend with him. For surely the rest would have strongly desired to follow along, to see the form of that glory, and they would have been grieved to miss it. And even though he would show it in a more bodily form,[6] still it was something that roused great longing. Well, why then did he make his prediction at all?[7] So that they [i.e., Peter, James and John] would become more open to contemplative learning, as a result of what he had said, and, filled with more intense longing in counting the days, might be present at the event with sober and anxious minds.

And for what reason does he bring Moses and Elijah onto the scene? One might offer a number of reasons. First this: that since "some" of the crowd "said he was Elijah, others Jeremiah or one of the ancient prophets,"[8] he brought the leading prophets there, so that even from them one might see the difference between servants and the master, and how right it was that Peter was praised for confessing him to be Son of God. But secondly, one may also say something else. People constantly charged him with transgressing the law, and considered him a blasphemer, usurping for himself the glory that belonged to the Father, and said, "This one is not from God, because he does not observe the Sabbath,"[9] and again, "It is not for a good work that we are stoning you, but for blasphemy, and because you, being a human being, make yourself to be God."[10] So, that it might be obvious that both these charges were based on

[6]I.e., at his resurrection.

[7]John seems to be referring here to Jesus' prediction, in Matt 16.28, "There are some of those standing here who will not taste death before they see the Son of Man coming in his Kingdom." He takes this to refer to the three disciples who would shortly witness his Transfiguration.

[8]Matt 16.14.

[9]John 9.16.

[10]John 10.33.

jealousy, and that he was innocent of both of them, and that what
had happened was not a transgression of the law, nor his saying he
was equal to the Father a usurpation of a glory that did not belong
to him, he brought into his presence the shining authorities on
both these issues. Moses, after all, gave the law, and the Jews could
be convinced that he would not stand by and watch it be trampled
under foot, as they suspected, nor would he be conciliatory towards
anyone who was transgressing it and hostile to its giver. And Elijah
was "jealous for God's glory,"[11] and would not himself have stood
by submissively if Jesus were opposed to God, and said he was God,
making himself equal to the Father, yet were not what he said he
was, and not making appropriate claims.

2   One might mention another reason, along with those we have
given. What is that? That they might learn that he has authority over
death and life, and rules both what is above and what is below. So he
brings on the scene both one who is dead and one who never suffered that fate. And the fifth reason—for this is the fifth among all
we have given—the Evangelist himself revealed. What is it? To show
forth the glory of the cross, and to encourage Peter and the others
who were in dread of suffering, and raise their thoughts higher. For
as they [=Moses and Elijah] came to the spot, they were not silent,
but "were speaking," Scripture says, "of the glory that he was to bring
to fulfillment in Jerusalem";[12] the Passion, that is, and the cross, for
that is what they always call it. And it was not only on this point that
he was training them,[13] but on manly virtue itself, which he especially looked for in them. For since he said, "If anyone wants to come
after me, let him take up his cross and follow me,"[14] he brings into

[11]See I Kg. 19.10, 14.

[12]Luke 9.31.

[13]The word Chrysostom uses here, *ēleiphen*, really means "he was anointing
them," which suggests a trainer preparing his athletes for the contest. Some manuscripts change this to *eilēphen*, "he took hold [of them]," but the first reading seems to
fit better with Chrysostom's overall conception of Jesus as the disciples' coach!

[14]Matt 16.24.

their midst men who had died ten thousand times over for God's commands and for the people who had been entrusted to them. Each of them, in fact, in losing his life had found it. For each had spoken boldly to tyrants—the one to the King of Egypt, the other to Achab—and on behalf of an ungrateful and disobedient people; by the very people they were rescuing they were led into mortal danger. Each of them wanted to free the people from idolatry; each of them, too, lacked polish—the one slow and hesitant in speech, the other rustic in manner. Each was very strict about having no possessions; for Moses owned nothing, nor did Elijah have anything more than a sheepskin cloak. And all this was in the Old Covenant, when they had not yet received such great grace in working signs.

For if Moses divided the sea, Peter walked on water, and was capable of moving mountains, and healed all kinds of bodily disease, and drove out wild demons, and worked those great marvels by the shadow of his own body,[15] and brought the whole world to conversion. And if Elijah, too, raised a dead man,[16] they raised thousands, even some who had not been yet thought worthy of the Spirit. He brings them, then, on the scene, for this reason: he wanted his disciples to imitate their ability to lead, their energy, their determination—to become gentle like Moses, impassioned like Elijah, careful guardians like both of them. For the one endured three years of famine for the sake of the Jewish people,[17] and the other said, "If you will take away their sin, take it away; but if not, then blot me also out of the book which you have written."[18] By the vision, he reminded them of all these things. For he brought them [i.e., Moses and Elijah] forth in glory, not that they [i.e., the disciples] might come up to their measure and rest, but that they might surpass it. When they said, for example, "Let us call fire down from heaven," and recalled the example of Elijah doing this,[19] he replied: "You do not know what

[15]See Acts 5.15.
[16]I Kg 17.17–22.
[17]I Kg 17–18.
[18]Ex 32.32.
[19]I Kg 18.36–39.

spirit you belong to!"[20] He was training them in endurance by the difference in the grace that was given. And let no one think we look down on Elijah's example as of little worth; we are not saying that— for surely, he had attained great perfection! But in his own times, when the mind of men and women was less mature, they needed this kind of paedagogy. In this way, Moses too was perfect, yet nevertheless, they would be held to a higher standard than he. "For if your righteousness is not more abundant than that of the scribes and Pharisees, you will not enter into the Kingdom of heaven."[21] For they did not go out to Egypt, but to the whole world—a far worse situation than Egypt! Nor were they simply to argue with Pharaoh, but to spar with the devil, the very lord of evil! The contest set before them was to bind him, and to capture all his armor;[22] and they did this not by splitting the sea in two, but by splitting the depth of wickedness, whose waves are far more terrible, with the rod of Jesse. Look at all the things that terrify people: death, poverty, lack of respect, countless sufferings; they trembled more at these things, than the Jews had formerly done at the sea. Nevertheless, he persuaded them to take on all these dangers daringly, and to cross them, as it were, on dry land in full safety. Readying them, then, for all these challenges, he brought before them the Old Testament's shining examples.

What, then, does rash Peter say? "It is good for us to be here!" For since he has heard that Jesus had to depart for Jerusalem and to suffer, but fears and trembles still for his sake, even after Jesus' rebuke, he does not dare to approach him and say the same thing again, "Far be it from you!"[23] But speaking from that same fear, he again hints the same thing in different words. For since he saw the mountain, its great remoteness and its deserted character, he got the idea that there was a strong prospect of safety here, due to the place itself—and not just from the place, but from his never leaving it to

[20]Lk 9.54–55
[21]Matt 5.20.
[22]Cf. Matt 12.29.
[23]Matt 16.22.

go to Jerusalem. For he wanted Jesus to remain there always; that is why he mentions tents. For if this were to happen, he is saying, we shall not go up to Jerusalem, and if we do not go up, he will not die; it is there, after all, that he said the scribes would attack him. But he does not dare say this outright. Wanting to bring it about, however, he says with assurance, "It is good for us to be here," where Moses and Elijah are present: Elijah, who drew fire down on a mountaintop, and Moses, who entered into darkness to speak with God—no one will have any idea where we are!

3   Do you see the hot-headed lover of Christ? For do not focus on the fact that his manner of coming to Christ's help was not well considered; think instead of how fervent he was, how consumed he was by the love of Christ! After all, here is proof that he did not say this because he feared so much for himself: when [Jesus] intimated to him the death and the attack that lay in his future, hear what he says: "I will lay down my life for you! Even if I should have to die with you, I will not deny you!"[24] And see how willing he is to take risks, even in the midst of danger: when a large crowd surrounded him, he not only did not flee, but even drew his sword and cut of the ear of the high priest's slave. This shows how little he was looking out for his own welfare, but rather trembled for his Teacher.

But now, after he had blurted this out directly, he began to gain control of himself, and taking thought that he might not earn another rebuke, said: "If you will, let us make here three tents: one for you, one for Moses and one for Elijah." What are you saying, Peter? Did you not, just a short while ago, separate him from all his servants? Are you now changing course, and counting him with his servants? Do you see how very immature they were in the face of the cross? For if indeed the Father had revealed things to him, he did not continue to hold on to the revelation, but was shaken by anguish—not just this anguish I have mentioned, but by another one, too, which came as a result of this very vision. The other Evangelists, indeed, make this

[24]Mk 14.31.

clear, and point out that the confused state of his mind, in which he uttered these things, came from that second wave of anguish. Mark, for instance, writes: "He did not know what he was saying; for they were terrified."[25] And Luke, after making him say, "Let us build three tents," adds, "not knowing what he was saying."[26] Then, to make clear that they were seized by great fear, both Peter and the others, Luke says: "They were heavy with sleep; and when they woke, they saw his glory."[27] By "sleep" here he means the heavy drowsiness that had come over them as a result of that vision. For they experienced something like what we feel, when our eyes are dimmed by overpowering brightness. It was not night, after all, but day; and the excess of splendor weighed down the weakness of their eyes.

What happened then? Jesus himself said nothing, nor did Moses, nor Elijah; but the one who is greater than all, more trustworthy than all—the Father—let his voice sound from the cloud. Why from a cloud? This is always how God appears! For "cloud and darkness surround him,"[28] and "he sits upon a light cloud";[29] and again, "he has made clouds his staircase,"[30] and "clouds received him from their sight,"[31] and "the Son of Man is coming on the clouds."[32] That they might believe, then, that the voice came from God, that is where it originated. And the cloud was bright. "For while he was speaking, behold, a bright cloud overshadowed them. And behold, a voice spoke from the cloud, saying, 'This is my Son, the Beloved, in whom I take pleasure. Listen to him.'" For when he threatens, he shows a dark cloud, as on Sinai; for Scripture says, "Moses went into the cloud and into the darkness,"[33] and "the smoke went up like steam."[34]

[25]Mk 9.6.
[26]Lk 9.33.
[27]Lk 9.32.
[28]Ps 97.2.
[29]Is 19.1.
[30]Ps 104.3.
[31]Acts 1.9.
[32]Dan 7.13.
[33]Ex 24.18.
[34]Cf. Ex 19.18.

The Prophet speaks of God's threatening side when he says, "Dark water is in the misty clouds."[35] But here, since he does not want to cause fear but to instruct, the cloud is bright.

And Peter said, "Let us build three tents," but Jesus himself revealed the tent not made by hands. Therefore we find earlier smoke and mist, but here ineffable light, and a voice. Then, that it might be revealed that the voice spoke not simply of any one of the three, but about Christ alone, when the voice sounded those others withdrew. For if it were speaking about just any one of them, he would not remain alone while the other two disappeared. Why, then, did the cloud not cover Christ alone, but all of them? If it covered Christ alone, he would have been thought to have uttered those words. So the Evangelist, to make sure this is clear, says that the voice came out of the cloud—that is, from God.

And what does the voice say? "This is my Son, the Beloved." If he is the Beloved, Peter, do not be afraid. For it was necessary that you come to know his power, and be assured about his resurrection; since you still do not know this, take courage from the Father's voice. For if God is powerful—and powerful indeed he is!—it is fully clear that the Son is powerful as well. Do not be terrified, then, by adversities. And if you cannot yet accept this, consider at least that he is the Son, and that he is loved. For "this," he says, "is my Son, the Beloved." And if he is loved, do not fear. For no one abandons one whom he loves. Do not be disturbed, then; even if you love him ten thousand times more than the rest, you do not love him to the degree that the one who begot him does! "In him I take pleasure." For the Father does not love the Son simply because he begot him, but because the Son is equal to him in every way, and is of one mind with him. So love is bound here by a double, even a triple spell: he is Son, he is Beloved, in him the Father takes pleasure. And what does this mean, "In him I take pleasure"? It is as if he were saying, "I take my rest in him, in whom I take pleasure," because he is in every respect precisely the Father's equal, and there is one will in him and in the

[35]Ps 18.12.

Father; even while he remains Son, he is in every way one with the one who begot him. "Listen to him!" So that even if he wills to be crucified, do not stand in his way!

"And when they heard this, they fell on their faces, and were very much afraid. And Jesus came to them and touched them, and said, 'Get up, and do not be afraid.' And lifting up their eyes, they saw no one, except only Jesus."

4 How is it that when they heard these things, they were so amazed? For earlier, a voice like this sounded above the Jordan, and a crowd was present, yet no one experienced anything like this. And after this it would happen again, when people said that it had thundered;[36] but not even then did they feel this sort of reaction. Why, then, did they fall on their faces on the mountain? Because it was a lonely, high, very quiet place, and his transfiguration inspired terror, and the light was unbearable, and the cloud immense—all of which drove them into deep mental anguish. Amazement came upon them from every side, and they fell down at once in fear and in adoration. But so that the fear might not remain with them long, driving away their memory of what had happened, he immediately resolved their anguish; he was seen alone, and commanded them to say nothing of this to anyone, until he should rise from the dead. For "as they came down from the mountain, he commanded them not to tell the vision to anyone, until he should rise from the dead." For the greater the things were that they reported about him, the more difficult it would then become for the crowds to accept him; and the scandal that came from the cross grew all the greater, in fact, for this reason. Therefore he orders silence—not just by a command, but by reminding them again of his passion, as if almost to give the reason he was ordering them not to speak. For he did not order them never to speak of this to anyone, but "until he should rise from the dead." Keeping silence, then, about what was hard to bear, he revealed only good things. What then? Would they not experience obstacles after this? Certainly! His con-

[36]John 12.29.

cern was simply the time that would come before the cross. For after that, they would be allowed to share in the Spirit, and they would have the voice of signs to come to their help, and all they would say from then on would be easy to accept, since the facts themselves would proclaim his might more brilliantly than a trumpet, and no obstacle such as this could stand in the way of what had happened.

No one, then, is more blessed than the Apostles, and particularly than the three who were granted to be overshadowed by the same cloud as the Lord. But if we wish, we ourselves shall see Christ: not in the same way as they did then on the mountain, but much more gloriously. For he will not come again in the same way.[37] For then, to spare the disciples, he only revealed as much of his glory as they could bear; but he will come later on in the very glory of the Father, not only with Moses and Elijah, but with the immense army of angels, with the archangels, with the cherubim, with those countless throngs. There will be no cloud over his head, but the heavens themselves will be cast down. For just as the attendants draw back the curtains, when judges are about to give public judgments, and reveal them to everyone, so in that day all will see him seated, and the whole of human nature will stand before him, and he will, by himself, pass sentence on them. And to some he will say: "Come, you blessed of my Father; for I was hungry, and you gave me to eat";[38] and to others he will say, "Well done, good and faithful servant; you were faithful over a few things, so I will set you over many."[39] And then, passing an opposite judgment, he will respond to some, "Go into the eternal fire prepared for the devil and his angels";[40] and to others, "Wicked and cowardly servant!"[41] And some he will cut off,[42] and hand over to the

[37]For the opposite prediction, see Acts 1.11.

[38]Matt 25.34. Chrysostom here changes the scene from the Transfiguration to Jesus' description of the last judgment, but stays mainly with Matthew's Gospel. The connecting link seems to be the sight of Jesus in glory: in Matt 25, a vision available not just to three favored disciples, but to all people.

[39]Matt 25.21.

[40]Matt 25.41.

[41]Matt 25.26.

[42]Matt 24.51.

torturers,[43] while others he will command to be "bound hand and foot and cast into the outer darkness."[44] And after the axe has done its work, the furnace will receive them,[45] and what is thrown away from the net will finish there.[46] But "then the righteous will shine like the sun,"[47] or rather even more than the sun. This comparison is made, not because their light will only be as great as the sun's; but since we know nothing brighter than this star, the Gospel wanted to present the future brilliance of the saints in some familiar image. Since it says, when Jesus was on the mountain, that "he shone like the sun," it speaks in these terms here for the same reason. For the disciples showed, by falling on the ground, that the light was greater than this example. But if that light was not immense, but equivalent to the sun, they would not have fallen down, but could easily have endured it. So then, "the righteous will shine like the sun," and far more than the sun, in that time to come; but sinners will experience the ultimate sufferings. In that day, there will be no need for affidavits, no need for cross-examination, no need for witnesses; he will be the one who brings all things to justice, as witness and examiner and judge. For he knows all things with clarity: "Everything lies naked and utterly open before his eyes."[48] No one will appear rich there, no one poor, or powerful, or weak, or wise, or foolish, or slave, or free; but all these masks will be shattered, and there will simply be an examination of our deeds. For in our own courts, if someone is accused of tyrannical acts or murder, whatever it might be, even if he be a proconsul or consul, he loses all rank, and if convicted he is sentenced to ultimate punishment. How much more will this be true in that judgment!

[43] Matt 18.34.
[44] Matt 22.13.
[45] See Matt 3.10 (the preaching of John the Baptist).
[46] See Matt 13.47–50.
[47] Matt 13.43.
[48] Hebr 4.13.

5   But that this may not happen, let us put aside our soiled clothing and put on the armor of light, and the glory of God will enfold us.[49] For what is burdensome about the commandments? What is not easy there? Listen to what the Prophet is saying, and you will realize how easy they are: "Not if you bend your neck as under a yoke, or cover yourself with sackcloth and ashes—not that way will you proclaim an acceptable fast; but loose every unjust bond, untie the knots of coercive alliances."[50] See the Prophet's wisdom! For putting aside and annulling what is burdensome, he believes that we shall be saved as a result of easy actions, showing us that God does not require heavy duties from us, but simply obedience. Next, wanting to make it clear that virtue is easy, but vice a heavy burden, he achieves this through the words themselves. For he says that wickedness is a "bond" and a "knot," but virtue is release, the annulling of all these things. "Tear up every unjust contract," he says, referring in this way to notes for loans with interest; "release the oppressed by forgiving their debts."[51] For that is how a debtor reacts: when he sees his creditor, his mind is broken, and he fears him more than a wild beast. "Bring the homeless poor into your home; if you see someone naked, clothe him, and do not turn your eyes away from your own, from those of your seed."[52]

In a recent homily we spoke about rewards, and pointed out the riches that we can expect; now let us consider if any of the commandments is a burden, or exceeds the power of our nature. But we will not find anything of the sort; rather, it is just the opposite: these commandments are very easy, but the works of vice involve a great deal of labor! For what is more worrisome than lending, and then being concerned about interest and contracts, and demanding security,

[49]Here Chrysostom begins his transition from depicting the scene of Jesus' Transfiguration to exhorting his congregation to practice social justice, especially by avoiding the practice of usury. The connection is our human need to become "transfigured" with Christ, and to reflect his lowly yet glorious appearance in our actions.

[50]Is 58.5–6.

[51]Cf. Is 58.6.

[52]Is 58.7.

and fearing and being upset about collateral, about the principal, about bookkeeping, about profits, about the things pledged? Such is the way we make a living! But those things that seem to our minds to give security are the shakiest of all, and make us suspicious; it is easier, and more freeing from every kind of worry, to be merciful! Let us, then, not make other people's misfortunes into our business, or turn kindness to others into a trade!

Now I know that many will not like hearing these words. But what is the gain in silence? For if I keep silent, and cause no one trouble with my words, I will not be able to save you from punishment by this silence. The result will be the complete opposite: retribution will not only follow for you, but this silence of mine will procure punishment for me as well! What good, then, is the charm of words, when they do not help us to action, but in fact harm us? What gain is there in being comforting in speech and doing injury in fact? In pleasing the ear and punishing the soul? That is the reason we must mourn in this life, that we may not be subject to retribution in the next.

A grave illness, my friends, a grave illness in need of much healing, has fallen on the Church. For those who are forbidden even to store up treasures gained justly from their toil, but commanded rather to open up their houses to the needy, are making profit from the poverty of others, imagining theft to have a respectable face and finding good excuses for greed! Don't tell me about civil laws, since even the tax collector [in the Gospel] obeys civil law, yet nevertheless is punished. And we will suffer the same thing, if we do not leave off afflicting the poor, and misusing their want and need as an opportunity for shameless profiteering. This is the reason you have money: that you may put an end to poverty, not that you may turn poverty into a business! Instead, under the guise of offering others help you make their misfortune greater, and sell human kindness for money. Sell your wares, and I won't prevent you: but trade in the Kingdom of heaven! Don't accept the fat compensation of a one-percent monthly interest for such a virtuous act,[53] but rather the reward of life without

[53]Literally, "an interest of a hundredth part," referring to the legally sanctioned

end! Why are you so poor, so cheap and petty in your thinking, that you sell great things for a trifle—for money that perishes—when you ought to be selling it for the Kingdom that always lasts? Why do you cast God away to gain human profit? Why do you run after the rich man, but harass the poor man? Why do you turn away from the one who will repay you, and make deals with someone who has no concern for you at all? God wants to reward you, while this man will complain if he must return what is yours. He will pay his one percent only grudgingly, but God will give a hundred times more, and eternal life as well. He will pay with resentment and abuse, but God with praise and congratulation. He will bear a grudge against you, but God will weave you a crown. He will barely pay you in this life, but God both here and in the life to come. Is this not, then, the ultimate in foolishness, not to know where real profit is to be found? How many people have lost the principal as well, through demanding interest? How many have fallen into danger because of interest? How many have wrapped both themselves and others in ultimate poverty, through their unspeakable greed?

6 Don't tell me that [your borrower] is delighted to receive it, or that he is grateful for the loan! For this happens through your cruelty.

practice of ancient money-lenders to demand one one-hundredth of the principal per month—or twelve percent a year—in interest. This was enacted as the official standard for interest on loans by the Emperor Constantine in a decree of April 17, 325: see Cod. Theod. I, 33.1. A decree of Valentinian and Theodosius, of October 25, 386, confirmed this as the legal limit: Cod. Theod. II, 33.2. Interest on loans, in other words, was perfectly legal by civil standards; Christian teachers, however, continuing the attitudes expressed in the Old Testament, considered it immoral. (See, for instance, Ex 22.25; Lev 25.36; Deut 15.3; 23.20 [which allows Jews to take interest from Gentiles]; Neh. 5.10–11; Ps 15.5; Ezek 18.8–9; 22.12.) John's criticism here, as also in his *Homily 10 on I Thessalonians*, is that Christians are lending money to the poor—in itself an act of philanthropy, urged by Jesus—only for the profit of the high interest rates their lending promises in return. (As a point of comparison, the annual interest rate charged today by most American banks for credit card loans is normally 18% per annum or higher.) For a discussion of early Christian teaching on taking interest for loans, see Robert P. Maloney, "The Teaching of the Fathers on Usury: an Historical Study on the Development of Christian Thinking," *Vigiliae Christianae* 27 (1973) 241–265.

When Abraham handed his wife over to the barbarians, he contrived that his scheme would be well received; but he did not do this willingly—only out of fear of Pharaoh.[54] So too the poor man, when you do not even consider him worthy of such a favor,[55] is even forced to show gratitude for your cruelty. You seem to me even to be the kind of person who, if you freed someone from danger, would ask him to pay you for the rescue. "Go away," [the lender] says—"far be it from me to act that way!" What are you saying? Freeing him from a great danger, you would not wish to ask for money; but for a lesser rescue, you would show such inhumanity? Do you not see what punishment awaits such an action? Do you not hear, even in the Old Testament, that this is forbidden?[56] "But what is all this talk of riches? I accept interest," he says, "but I give to the poor." That sounds fine, my friend, but God does not want this kind of sacrifice. Do not play logical games with the law. It is better not to give to the poor, than to give from such a source; for you often turn money gained by honest labor into something illegal, through this wicked interest—as if one were to force a good womb to give birth to scorpions.

And why do I speak of God's law? Do you not call it a sordid activity yourselves? And if you judge your business in this way, while you are making money at it, consider what a judgment God will pass on you. But if you want also to ask the pagan lawgivers, hear that to them, too, this kind of activity seems to be the pattern of ultimate shamelessness. For those of high rank, who are counted as members of the great council they call the Senate, are not permitted to shame themselves by earnings of this kind; and it is the law that forbids such income among them.[57] How then can it be anything less than fearful,

---

[54]Gen 12.10–20.

[55]I.e., lending him money, as Abraham "lent" Sara to Pharaoh!

[56]See Deut 15.1–11, where Jews are urged to lend liberally to their fellow Jews, and all debts are to be cancelled every seventh year.

[57]See Cod. Theod. II, 33.3, an imperial rescript of Nov. 23, 397—when John Chrysostom was Patriarch of Constantinople—acknowledging the established principle that those born to senatorial rank (*illustres*) may not legally take interest on loans: apparently a form of *noblesse oblige*. See also ibid. II, 33.4, of June 12, 405 which loosens this restriction, but allows creditors of senatorial rank only to charge

if you do not show the same reverence to the heavenly City that the lawgivers show to the Roman Senate? Do you think heaven is less important than earth? Do you not even blush at the very irrationality of your action? For what would be more irrational than for someone to be forced to plant seed without earth and rain and a plough? This is the reason those who plan to carry on this kind of farming are sowing weeds, which will be thrown in the fire![58]

Are there not many just kinds of business? What about working the fields, tending flocks of sheep or cattle, breeding animals, working with one's hands, tending to one's own property? Why do you go mad and lose your wits, as if you set out to cultivate thorns? Is it that the fruits of the earth suffer from disasters–from hail and rust and thunderstorms? Not from such great disasters, though, as interest leads to! For when misfortunes of the first kind occur, the loss involves what is produced, but the capital—the field—remains intact. But in this case, many have often undergone complete shipwreck as regards the principal, and even before the loss they are in a continual state of anxiety. The money-lender never enjoys his possessions or takes pleasure in them; rather, when the interest is produced, he does not rejoice that income has been realized, but grieves that the interest has not yet overtaken the principal in amount![59] And before this evil offspring[60] is completely delivered, he forces it to give birth itself, making the interest into a new principal, thus forcing the aborted offspring, before their time, to bring forth a "brood of vipers."[61]

6% annual interest on loans—half the ordinary legal rate. In the reign of Justinian (527–565), the allowable interest rate on loans was restricted to 6% per annum for all lenders, and that charged by *illustres* to 4%.

[58]See Matt 13.30.

[59]Chrysostom here echoes Gregory of Nyssa, *Sermon against Usurers* (GNO IX/1, 202.14–203.11; PG 46.447–448).

[60]The Greek word for interest, *tokos*, literally means "offspring." Aristotle had argued that charging interest on loans is unnatural, because money, as a sterile object, cannot generate more money by itself: *Politics* I, 10 (1258b). See Basil of Caesaraea, *Homily 2 on Psalm 14*.3; Gregory of Nyssa, *Homily against Usury* (GNO IX/1, 200.29–201.1; PG 46.443).

[61]Lk 3.7.

That is what interest does, after all. More than those beasts, they eat up and tear apart the souls of the wretched. This is the bond of injustice, the strangle-hold of coercive contracts. For the lender says: I give, not that you may receive, but that you may give back more. God does not command that we receive back what we have given; for he says, "Give to them, from whom you do not expect to receive back."[62] But you demand more than you have given, and you force the receiver to pay out to you what you have not given, as if it were owed. And you think that you will increase your property from such a practice; instead of property, however, you are lighting unquenchable fire!

That this may not happen, let us discontinue the wicked propagation of interest, let us put a stop to this lawless progeny, let us empty out this belly of destruction, and let us only pursue true and substantial profits. And what are these? Listen to Paul as he says, "A great way to make a living is piety combined with self-sufficiency."[63] Let us be rich, then, with this kind of riches alone, so that in this life we may enjoy freedom from want, and may come to the good things yet ahead of us, by the grace and kindness of our Lord Jesus Christ, to whom be glory and power with the Father and the Holy Spirit, now and always and to the ages of ages. Amen.

[62]Lk .6.35.
[63]I Tim 6.6.

PROCLUS OF
CONSTANTINOPLE

Probably a supporter of John Chrysostom during his struggles against imperial and clerical enemies in the first decade of the century, Proclus (d.446) became Patriarch himself in 434. The date and place of his birth are unknown, but he was educated in Constantinople and ordained a lector as a boy. Like Chrysostom, he seems to have been especially well trained in rhetoric and philosophy; unlike Chrysostom, he remained throughout his life the quintessential court ecclesiastic, drawing on ample reserves of tact and political acumen to survive the bitter controversies on doctrine and Church politics of the 420s and 430s and to exercise a moderating influence on them.

In the early 420s, during the Patriarchate of Atticus of Constantinople, Proclus acted as spiritual advisor and unofficial chaplain to the Princess Pulcheria, regent for her younger brother, the Emperor Theodosius II. Pulcheria, a devout unmarried woman, lived in a virtual monastic community with a number of her ladies at court; they cultivated a strong Marian piety, and seem even to have identified themselves personally with Mary. Proclus apparently encouraged them in this, and himself held a high view of Mary and her importance for the Christian life. It was his use of the traditional term *Theotokos*, "Mother of God," for Mary, in the presence of the newly installed Patriarch Nestorius, in the winter of 429, that seems to have sparked the bitter controversy that led to Nestorius' downfall two years later, and also led to further clarification of the Church's understanding of the Person of Christ.

Although living in the capital, Proclus was bishop of the suffragan see of Cyzicus at the time, but was made Patriarch himself in 434, an office he continued to hold until his death in 446. His diplomatic and linguistic skills seem to have prevented the dispute over the interpretation of Christ's person from becoming more acute than it did. A profound and elegant preacher, Proclus has left behind a small corpus of homilies, several of which—like this one—are attributed in some manuscripts to his predecessor, John Chrysostom. For stylistic and theological reasons, however, modern editors and scholars agree in assigning it to Proclus. It is a simple, straightforward meditation on the Gospel narrative, focused mainly on an imagined conversation between the preacher and Peter, the chief witness of the great theophany on Thabor.

PROCLUS OF CONSTANTINOPLE

Homily on the Transfiguration
of the Savior

(Homily 8)[1]

Come, my friends: today let us not hesitate to lay hold of the treasures of the Gospel, that we may, as always, draw from the riches it
so generously shares with us, riches that can never be consumed!
Come, let us again follow the wise Luke,[2] who guides us so well,
that we may see Christ ascending a high mountain, taking along
Peter and James and John as witnesses of his divine transfiguration.
For he says, "*Taking Peter and his companions*," the Lord "*went up
a high mountain*."[3] A high mountain, on which Moses and Elijah
came to speak with Christ; a high mountain, on which the Law and
the Prophets conversed with Grace; a high mountain, where Moses

---

[1]The Greek text for this homily is available among the *spuria* of John Chrysostom, in PG 61.713–716; also in a somewhat different form (under Proclus' name) in PG
65.764–772. For a catalogue of the manuscripts which contain it, see François Leroy,
*L'homilétique de Proclus de Constantinople. Tradition manuscrite, inédita, études con-
nexes* (Vatican City: Bibliotheca Apostolica Vaticana, 1967) 100–107, 149. Although a
good number of early and medieval manuscripts attribute it to Chrysostom, Proclus'
authorship of the homily is also well attested, and Leroy concludes, for stylistic as well
as theological reasons, that it can safely be ascribed to him. For a characterization of
the features of Proclus' passionate, lively rhetorical style, see ibid. 160–172; for a good
summary of the characteristic features of Proclus' theology as well as of his style, see
also Jan Harm Barkhuizen, *Proclus of Constantinople: Homilies on the Life of Christ*
(Brisbane: Centre for Early Christian Studies, Australian Catholic University, 2001)
3–53. For Barkhuizen's translation of this homily, see ibid. 141–148.

[2]Oddly, Proclus' homily follows the text of Matthew's account of the transfiguration more closely than it does that of Luke.

[3]Lk 9.28; see also Matt 17.1.

was, who slew the paschal lamb and sprinkled the doorposts of the Hebrews with its blood;[4] a high mountain, where Elijah cut up a bull in their presence, consuming by fire a sacrifice made in water;[5] a high mountain, where Moses was, who opened and shut the depths of the Red Sea;[6] a high mountain, so that those with Peter, [John,] and James might learn that this is he, before whom "every knee shall bend, of those in heaven and on earth and under the earth."[7]

Now he took only three along, and did not take all, though he did not begrudge the rest a glimpse of his glory, nor judge them to be less worthy; being just, after all, he does everything justly—but thinking of all of them as being undivided in love for each other, he treated them as one. But since Judas, who was to become his betrayer, was not worthy of the divine vision and of that awe-inspiring apparition, for that reason he left him and the rest behind, so that by not leaving Judas alone he might counter any excuse[8] he might later make; but he invited the three along to be independent witnesses of his transfiguration according to the Law, since they brought the rest also with them in spirit. (For he himself says, "Preserve them, just Father, so that they may be one as we are one."[9]) For when Judas saw Andrew, Thomas, Philip and the rest remaining below the mountain with him, not grumbling or complaining or speaking scornfully, but rejoicing, and considering the grace from above as given in common

---

[4]Ex 12.3–7, 21–23.

[5]I Kg 18.20–39. Proclus is referring, in a compressed way, to the story of Elijah's sacrifice, in which he laid a butchered bull on an altar piled with wood, poured water over both victim and fuel, and called on God to consume it by fire; God did so, proving his reality to the Israelites who looked on.

[6]Ex 14.5–31. Proclus' phrase means literally "the complex whole (*ta systēmata*) of the Red Sea." The word *systēma* can also mean a body of troops; in that case, the Greek would have to be emended to read "opened and closed the Red Sea on the troops." But the word also appears with "sea" in Gen 1.14 (LXX), apparently referring to the whole expanse of the sea and what it contains. Proclus probably has that Biblical verse in mind here, in describing the miracle of the Exodus.

[7]Phil 2.10.

[8]I.e., of favoritism on Jesus' part, if he had taken the other eleven but not Judas to the mountaintop.

[9]John 17.21.

to all of them—even those who were absent—he was completely without grounds for complaint, since he had never been denied the sight of any of the miracles. But he had the money-box,[10] and he needlessly took offense at the ointment,[11] and he dared to betray the Master to his enemies.

What does the Scripture say? "And he was transfigured in their presence, and Moses and Elijah appeared, conversing with him."[12] But Peter, excited as he always was about everything, gazing with the eyes of his mind on these two whom he had never known, as they talked with [Jesus], and not rightly appreciating the marvel or the mystery of the divine radiance, called this deserted spot beautiful. From being a fisherman, he rushed to become a tent-maker,[13] crying out to the Savior, "Let us make here three tents, one for you, and one for Elijah, and one for Moses; now he did not know what he was saying."[14]

O Peter, chief and leader of the disciples! Why do you want to rush forward with lowly ideas, and insult godly things with human considerations, and talk of erecting three tents in the wilderness? Do you mean to define the Lord as equal in honor with his servants? Are you eager to raise one tent for Christ, and the same number of structures for the other two? Was Moses conceived of the Holy Spirit, as he was? Did a virgin give birth to Elijah, as the all-holy Virgin Mary gave him birth? Did the Forerunner,[15] as a fetus in the womb, recognize Moses as he did Christ? Did heaven proclaim the birth of Elijah? Or did Magi venerate the swaddling-bands of Moses? Did Moses and Elijah work so many miracles as he? Or drive out spirits

[10]John 12.6; 13.29.

[11]Judas is said to have complained at the expense, in John 12.3–6, when Mary, the sister of Lazarus, anointed Jesus' feet with costly ointment.

[12]Despite his earlier reference to "following" Luke, Proclus here cites Matthew 17.2–3; cf. Lk 9.29–30.

[13]Proclus may be suggesting that Peter, a fisherman by trade, was wrongly trying to assume the role of Paul, the tent-maker (Acts 18.3) and visionary (II Cor 12.1–5).

[14]Matt 17.4; cf. Lk 9.33, where Peter is made to say this as Moses and Elijah are parting from Jesus.

[15]John the Baptist; see Luke 1.41.

from a human "den"?[16] Moses once was angry, struck the sea with his rod, and went across; but your Teacher Jesus walked on the sea with Peter, and made the depths a walkway.[17] Elijah made the widow's flour increase, and raised her son from the dead; but the one who made you from a fisherman into a disciple fed thousands with a few loaves of bread, and stripped Hades bare, carrying off those who had slept there for ages.

Do not say, then, Peter, "Let us build here three tents," or even "It is good for us to be here"[18]—do not say anything that is human, humble, earthly, lowly. "Think what is above, seek the things above," as Paul reminds us, "not the things of earth."[19] How can it be "good for us to be here," where the snake deceived and injured the first humans created, and shut Paradise? Where we have heard that we must eat our bread "in the sweat of our face"?[20] Where we have learned to groan and tremble on the earth, because of our disobedience? Where all things are in shadow? Where all passes away in an instant? How is it good, then, for us to be here? If Christ were leaving us here, why did he share in blood and flesh? If Christ were leaving us here, why did he come down to the one who had fallen, and raise up the prostrate one?[21] If it were good to be on earth, it is to no purpose that you have been called the holder of heaven's keys! For of what use, I ask you, would the keys of heaven be? Since you

[16]This obscure phrase may be a reference to Matt 21.13: in driving out money changers from the Temple precincts, Jesus accuses them of making God's house "a den of robbers." Corroborating this interpretation would be the reference to Moses' anger, which immediately follows.

[17]A play on words may be intended here: "he made the deep (*bython*)walkable (*baton*)."

[18]Matt 17.4; Lk 9.33. Proclus takes Peter's "here" in the broad sense of "here on earth," not simply as a reference to the event of Jesus' transfiguration on Mt Tabor.

[19]Col 3.2.

[20]Gen 3.19.

[21]For a similar image used to explain the purpose of the Incarnation, see also Nestorius' Sermon "against the title Theotokos," a passage in an oration delivered originally in opposition to Proclus' praise of Mary as Mother of God: in the Latin translation of Marius Mercator, ACO I, 5.1.30, ll. 13–20; English trans., Richard A. Norris, *The Christological Controversy* (Phildelphia: Fortress, 1980) 125.

long for this mountain, say goodbye to heaven! If you want to raise tents, give up being the foundation-rock of the Church! For Christ was transfigured, not simply to be so, but that he might show us the transfiguration of our nature that is to come—his second coming, for our salvation, which will be on the clouds, with the voice of archangels.[22] For he is the one who has "wrapped himself in light as in a garment,"[23] since he is "judge of the living and the dead."[24] Therefore he brought Moses and Elijah into the scene, to offer the confirming sign of these figures from ancient times.

And why does the great writer say, "While he was yet speaking, behold, a bright cloud overshadowed them. And behold, a voice came from the heavens saying, 'This is my Son, the Beloved, in whom I am well pleased. Hear him!'"[25] "While Peter was still speaking," he says, the Father spoke in response: "Why, Peter, do you say '*it is good*,' when you do not know what you are saying? Had you not yet been educated, had you not yet learned the safe way of understanding his Sonship, when you said, 'You are the Christ, the Son of the living God'?[26] Have you seen so many miracles, Bar Jonah, yet still you remain Simon?[27] Has he appointed you keeper of the keys of heaven, and yet you have not yet taken off your sailor's tunic?[28] See, you resist the Savior's will a third time, not knowing what you are saying! For he said to you, 'I must suffer,' and you say, 'It shall not be so with you!'[29] Again he said, 'You will all be caused to stumble,' and you answer, 'Even if all will be caused to stumble, I shall not stumble!'[30] And see, now you want to build something for Christ, who along with me 'laid

[22]Matt 24.30–31; I Thess 4.16–17.
[23]Ps 104.2.
[24]II Tim 4.1.
[25]Matt 17.5; cf. Luke 9.34–35.
[26]Matt 16.16.
[27]In other words, despite having received a new name from Jesus (Matt 16.18), he still persists in old ways of thinking.
[28]Matt 16.19; John 21.7.
[29]Matt 16.21–22.
[30]Matt 26.33–34.

the foundation of the earth,'[31] who put the sea together along with me, who established the firm sky, set the ether ablaze,[32] and created all things, along with me, as my craftsman: a tent for the one who is from me, a tent for the one who is in me and with all of you, a tent for the Adam who has no father,[33] a tent for the God who has no mother,[34] a tent for the one who took up a tent of his own choosing—a Virgin's womb! Well, then—since you want to raise up three tents, 'not realizing what you are saying,' I will make use of a bright cloud as a tent to shelter those present, and I will cry out from the highest heaven, 'This is my Son, the Beloved, in whom I am well pleased.' Not Moses and Elijah, but this one! Nothing else, no one else,[35] but this one: one and the same,[36] 'in whom I am well pleased—listen to him!' I have made Moses righteous, but 'in this one I am well pleased'; I have taken Elijah up, but I sent this one into the Virgin, as into heaven, and from the Virgin to heaven itself. 'For no one,' Scripture says, 'has ascended into heaven except the one who has come down from heaven.'[37] From there, then, he came down to earth, from there he 'emptied himself, taking on the form of a slave.'"[38] (For if he had remained what he was, and had not become what we are—if he had not undergone the cross as we

[31]Cf. Ps 102.25; 104.5.

[32]In the ancient conception of the cosmos, the sky was a solid, translucent dome high above the earth; above it was the fiery region of the "ether," which gave light and energy to the stars.

[33]I.e., the human Jesus.

[34]I.e., Jesus as Son of God.

[35]Proclus seems to be alluding to the famous passage in Gregory of Nazianzus' Letter 101, his first Letter to Cledonius, where Gregory characterizes the persons of the Holy Trinity as "not one thing and another and another (*ouk allo kai allo kai allo*), but one person and another and another (*allos kai allos kai allos*)."

[36]The phrase "one and the same" (*heis kai ho autos*), which was to find its way into the Chalcedonian formulation of the person of Christ, as well as the insistence that God the Son and the human Jesus are not "one [person] and another," appears already in Proclus' most famous sermon, on the Virgin Mary: ACO I, 1,1, 106.21–23. This similarity in phraseology is one of the main grounds for regarding this homily, too, as his work.

[37]John 3.13.

[38]Phil 2.7.

do, for our sake, and purchased the world with his own blood—the saving plan of God is in vain, and the ancient words of the prophets remain unreliable.[39]) "Stop, then, Peter! Stop thinking human thoughts, but think those of God.[40] 'For this is my beloved Son, in whom I am well pleased; listen to him!' For I use this phrase about him now the second time: for you on this mountain, and for John at the river Jordan, a phrase about which the ancient prophet truly cried out, 'Tabor and Hermon will rejoice in your name!'[41] In what name? 'This is my Son, the Beloved!' For 'the name that is above every name'[42] is what gives joy."

But you will surely ask, dear friends, "What does this mean, 'Tabor and Hermon will rejoice in your name'?" Learn, then, in a wise way: "Tabor" signifies the mountain where Christ willed to be transfigured and was named Son by the Father's witness, as you have just heard. And "Hermon" is the mountain a little way from the land of the Jordan, where Elijah was taken up, and near to which Jesus willed to be baptized in the Jordan's stream, and was called "Son" by the Father's witness. On these two mountains, the immaculate Father confirms his Sonship, and cries out then, and now for a second time, "This is my Son, the Beloved, in whom I am well pleased; listen to him. For the one who listens to him listens to me;[43] and the one who is ashamed of him and his words, I will be ashamed of him in my glory and that of my holy angels.[44] Listen to him: without simulation, without bad intentions, without limits; seek him in faith, not in the

[39]In this parenthetical phrase, Proclus apparently steps out of the assumed persona of God the Father, and speaks as a Christian believer.

[40]Cf. Matt 16.23.

[41]Ps 89.12. The transfiguration takes place on Mt Tabor; Mt Hermon (in Proclus' Greek: "Hermoniel"; in the Septuagint text, "Hermoniim") is located on the east side of the Jordan, at the southern end of the Lebanon range, and was associated with the river, perhaps because its snow was recognized as one of the sources of the Jordan's water: see Ps 42.7.

[42]Phil 2.9.

[43]Cf. Luke 10.16, addressed by Jesus to the disciples.

[44]Cf. Luke 9.26; Mark 8.38. In these passages, Jesus speaks this phrase, referring to his own future coming in glory as judge.

confines of human speech; go forward in faith, but do not measure the Word with words."[45] For the orator Paul, restraining linguistic excess, but always ready to teach without hesitation, already cries out: "O the depth of the riches and the wisdom and the knowledge of God! How unsearchable are his judgments, and inscrutable his ways!"[46] To him be glory for the ages of ages!

　　Amen.

---

[45] It is not entirely clear where Proclus intends to switch from the voice of God, back to his own voice; clearly it must come somewhere before the final doxology.

[46] Rom 11.33.

CYRIL OF ALEXANDRIA

Cyril of Alexandria, one of the dominant figures in the formation of Christian orthodoxy in East and West, especially with regard to the Church's understanding of Christ, was probably born in the 470s. The nephew of Patriarch Theophilus, he seems to have received a strong education in theological studies, and to have been initiated at an early age into the political and religious dynamics of the Church's life in this busy, highly diverse metropolis. At the death of his uncle in 412, Cyril was elected to be his successor, and remained Patriarch, and thus metropolitan over all the local Churches in Egypt and Libya, until his death in 444.

Cyril is doubtless best remembered for the part he played in the Christological controversies of the fifth century, but the bulk of his writings are concerned with the interpretation of Scripture. His two earliest works, probably, are two massive treatises on the Pentateuch, particularly on its ritual prescriptions: *On Adoration in Spirit and in Truth*, and the *Glaphyra* ("Elegant Explanations"); his lengthy commentaries on Isaiah and on the Twelve Minor Prophets also seem to have been composed during the first decade of his ministry as bishop. His long *Commentary on John*, perhaps his major work on the New Testament, seems to have been finished also by 429, when his controversy with Nestorius began. The latest work of Cyril's on the New Testament we still possess is his set of 156 homilies on the Gospel of Luke, which exist almost exclusively in a Syriac translation; these sermons, brief and more pastoral in character, seem to come from the 430s. The heart of all his Biblical exegesis, in any case, is clearly his focus on the person of Christ as the key to understanding all of the Bible's figural language. His Christological arguments are always grounded in his deep reading of the text of Scripture, but his approach to Scripture is consistently Christological.

Cyril's homily on the Transfiguration, which we translate here, exists in Greek collections of festal homilies as a separate piece; it is only since the discovery and publication of the Syriac version of the full collection by Angelo Mai, and later by other scholars, in the mid-nineteenth century, that it has been possible to place it in its original setting, as the one homily on Luke's Gospel fully extant in the original version. Like Chrysostom's homily on Matthew's telling of the Transfiguration story, Cyril's approach is to explain the details of the narrative in simple terms. As in a number of his exegetical works, there is also, near the end, an undertone of criticism aimed against Jewish interpretation of the Law—a feature that finds its context in the sometimes strained relations between the Jewish and Christian communities in Alexandria in the fourth and fifth centuries. But the sermon's central message is not simply polemics; it is to proclaim Jesus as bringing, in his own person, full eschatological salvation to all of humanity.

Homily 51 on Luke

(= Homiliae Diversae 9)[1]

Those who are skilled in sports delight in the spectators' applause, and they are spurred on by the hopes of prizes to struggle for the victory appropriate to them. But those who long to gain divine blessings, and who thirst to share in the hope promised to the saints,[2] gladly enter the contests that are centered on devotion to Christ. They fulfill the demands of an upright life, not choosing unprofitable timidity or loving unmanly cowardice, but rather showing the courage needed to face every trial; they consider the threat of persecution worth little concern, as they consider it enrichment to suffer for his sake. They call to mind blessed Paul, who wrote, "The sufferings of the present time are worth nothing, compared with the glory that will be revealed in our case."[3]

Come, then, gaze on our Lord Jesus Christ, once again taking such beautifully practical steps to benefit and build up his holy Apostles. For he said to them, "If anyone wishes to come after me, let him deny himself, and take up his own cross, and follow me. For whoever wishes to save his life will lose it; but whoever loses

---

[1]The Greek text of this homily—the only one of Cyril's homilies on the Gospel of Luke completely preserved in Greek—is available, as an occasional homily entitled "On the Transfiguration of our Lord, God and Savior Jesus Christ," in the edition of J. Aubert, in PG 77.1009–1016. The complete set of homilies on Luke is preserved in Syriac; for the Syriac text, edited by J. Chabot, see CSCO 70; Latin translation by R. M. Tonneau, CSCO 140. There is an English translation of the Syriac homilies by Robert Payne Smith (Oxford: Oxford University Press, 1859; republished by Stoudion Publishers, 1983).

[2]Cf. Col 1.5.

[3]Rom 8.18.

his life for my sake, will find it."[4] The command is a life-giving one, fitting for holy people, and a help towards the glory that is above, creating in us the gladness of heart that leads to final enjoyment. For to choose to suffer for Christ's sake is never without its reward, but rather it procures us a share in glory. But since the disciples had not yet received "the power from on high,"[5] it was likely, perhaps, that they would fall victim to human weakness, and get the idea of saying something like this among themselves: "How could one deny himself? Or how, if one loses one's life, will one find it again? What reward would be commensurate to this loss, for those who should suffer it? What gifts might such a person share?"

In order to lead them away from such thoughts and words, then, and to forge the steel of good courage by generating a desire for the glory that would be given them, he says, "I tell you, there are some standing here who will not taste death, before they see the Kingdom of God."[6] Does this mean, then, that the limit of life will be extended so far for them, that they will reach those days after which, at the end of the ages, he will come from heaven, to restore to the saints the Kingdom that was prepared them?[7] Surely this was possible for him—for he can do everything, and there is nothing that is impossible or inaccessible for his all-powerful commands. But by "Kingdom" here he is referring to the sight of that glory, in which he will also be seen at the moment he sheds his light on those living on earth. For "he will come in the glory of God the Father,"[8] and no longer in that somewhat shabby appearance that belongs to us.

How, then, did he allow those who had received this promise to gaze on this wonder? He led three, whom he had specially chosen from among them all, up the mountain, and then was transfigured into an incomparable, godlike brilliance, so that his clothing seemed

[4] Matt 16.24–25; cf. Luke 9.23–24, which is not quite as close to the text Cyril cites here as Matthew's version is.
[5] Luke 24.49.
[6] Matt 16.28.
[7] See Matt 25.34
[8] See Matt 16.27

to glow with the light that had been supplied to it. Then Moses and Elijah, standing next to Jesus, conversed with him about his "passage, which he was going to accomplish in Jerusalem"[9]—that is, the mystery of his fleshly incarnation, and of his saving passion, which took place on the precious cross. For it is true that the law given through Moses, and the teaching of the holy prophets, revealed in advance the Mystery of Christ: Moses suggesting only in images and shadows, as if in a painting, and the prophets proclaiming "in many ways,"[10] that he would be seen in time in a form like ours, and that for the well-being and life of all of us he would not refuse to suffer death on a cross.

The appearance of Moses and Elijah beside him, then, and their conversation with each other, was a divine stratagem for actually revealing that our Lord Jesus Christ had been preceded on his way by the Law and the Prophets, revealed by the Law and the Prophets themselves to be their Lord, in those very respects in which, consonantly with each other, they had foretold him. For what the prophets said is not at variance with what is said by the Law. This, I think, is what is meant by the fact that holy Moses was speaking with the best of all the prophets—and that is Elijah.

But it is possible to read this in another way.[11] Since some of the crowds "said he was Elijah, others Jeremiah or one of the prophets,"[12] he brings here their leading representatives, so that the disciples might see from this the great gap between the slave and the master. And beyond this, too, one could express still another interpretation. For since people constantly were charging him with transgressing the Law, and thought him a blasphemer because he had tried to take over the Father's glory, which did not belong to him; and [since they] said, "This one is not from God, because he does not observe

---

[9]The Greek word for "passage" here is literally "exodus": Lk 9.31.

[10]Heb 1.1.

[11]The next paragraph, from here until "But the blessed disciples felt sleepy for a while," is missing from the Syriac version.

[12]Matt 16.14; cf. Luke 9.19. Again, Cyril echoes Matthew's text more closely than he does Luke's.

the Sabbath,"[13] and "It is not for a good work that we are stoning you, but for blasphemy, and because you, being a human being, make yourself God";[14] so that it might be clear that both these charges were due to malice, and that he was not guilty of either of them, and that what he had done was not a transgression of the Law, or an appropriation of glory that did not belong to him in saying he was the equal of the Father, he brings before the disciples these two who were distinguished authorities on both issues. Moses, after all, gave the Law, and the Jews could conclude that he would not put up with seeing the Law trampled under foot, as they thought Jesus was doing, nor would [Moses] have shown respect to the one who transgressed it, and was an enemy of its legislator. And Elijah was "jealous for the glory of God,"[15] and he would not himself have stood by [Jesus] and obeyed his word if he were opposed to God, and said he was God, equal to the Father—if indeed he were not what he said, or were not making this claim appropriately. One might give another reason, too, besides what has been said. What is that? That the disciples might learn that he has power over life and death, and rules over the upper and the lower world, therefore he presents to them both one who is living and one who is dead. For when they appeared they were not silent, but "spoke of the passage, which he was to fulfill in Jerusalem:"[16] that is, both his suffering and his cross, and along with them also his resurrection.

But the blessed disciples felt sleepy for a while, as if Christ him-self were turning his attention to prayer—for he fulfilled human needs, according to the plan of the incarnation—and then, when they awoke, they became eye-witnesses of his sublime and amazing transformation.[17] Perhaps blessed Peter thought that the time of

[13]John 9.16

[14]John 10.33.

[15]I Kg 19.10.

[16]Lk 9.31. The Greek text in the *Patrologia* has *doxan*, "glory," for *exodon*, "exodus" or "passage," here; I have emended it to fit the New Testament text.

[17]Since he is preaching on Luke's Gospel, Cyril follows here the details of Luke's narrative at Lk 9.32, which—unlike Matthew or Mark—suggests the following sequence: Jesus and the disciples ascend the mountain to pray; as he prays, his face

the Kingdom of God had arrived; so he welcomes their stay on the mountain, and speaks of three tents being built, without knowing what he was saying. For it was not the moment of the consummation of the ages, nor does it belong to this present time for the saints to attain full participation in the hope that is promised to them. For Paul says, "Who will transfigure our humble body, that it might become conformed to his glorious body"[18]—that is, to Christ's. And since the divine plan of salvation was yet in its early stages, and had not yet reached fulfillment, how would it have been fitting for Christ, who had come among us[19] because of his love for the world,[20] to cease willing to suffer for its sake? For he has saved all things under heaven, both by enduring death in the flesh and by rendering it null through his resurrection from the dead. Peter, however, "did not know what he was saying."[21]

Besides, in addition to this astonishing, unspeakable vision of the glory of Christ, something else, too, was accomplished that was useful and necessary for confirming their faith in him—and not only the disciples' faith, but indeed ours as well. For it was granted that a voice was heard from a cloud above them, from God the Father, saying, "This is my Son, the beloved, in whom I take pleasure: listen to him."[22] "And after the voice was heard," Scripture says, "they found only Jesus."[23] What will the stiff-necked Jew say to this, the one who is hard to lead, the unbelieving one, who has a heart that will heed no

and clothes become radiant; Moses and Elijah appear, talking with him; Peter and his companions are "weighed down with sleep," but once they are fully awake they see Jesus and his two Old Testament companions in glory. Peter then proposes to build three tents, and they are suddenly overshadowed with a cloud, and hear the voice identifying Jesus as "beloved Son." Matthew and Mark do not suggest a further revelation of Jesus' glory, beyond that of his initial radiance; but in Luke, the real *transfiguration* of Jesus, which seems to include a transfiguration of Moses and Elijah as well, is apparently a second stage of the event, not further explained in the text.

[18]Phil 3.21.
[19]Reading *epiphoitēsanta* for the Patrologia's *apophoitēsanta.*
[20]John 3.16.
[21]Mark 9.6. This statement is missing in both Matthew and Luke.
[22]Matt 17.5.
[23]Luke 9.36.

warnings? Behold, while Moses is there, the Father commands the holy Apostles to "listen to him." But if he had wanted them to follow the commands of Moses, he would have said, "Follow Moses, keep the Law." Now, however, God the Father does not say this, but while Moses is standing there, and his prophet Elijah as well, he commands [the disciples] rather to "listen to him." And that the truth might not be manipulated by people saying that the Father was, instead, commanding them to listen to Moses, and not to Christ, the Savior of us all, the Evangelist was forced to signify it clearly, by saying, "At the moment the voice was heard, Jesus was found alone." Therefore when God the Father spoke, as from a cloud above, to command the holy Apostles, saying, "Listen to him," Moses was away, Elijah was no longer there, and Christ was alone. He commanded them, therefore, to hear him, for he is himself "the end of the Law,"[24] as well as of the Prophets. For this reason, he spoke to the Jewish people directly, saying, "If you believe Moses, you should believe me; for he wrote about me."[25] But since they continually dishonored the commands given through the wise Moses, and paid no attention in any circumstances to the word given through the holy prophets, they were justly considered aliens, and were deprived of the good things promised to their ancestors. "For obedience is good beyond sacrifice, and a ready ear beyond the fat of rams,"[26] as Scripture says. All this refers to the fate of the Jews; but for us, who recognize his appearing, all good things in every way are available through Christ and from him, through whom and with whom is glory and power to God the Father, with the Holy Spirit, for the ages of ages.

Amen.

[24]Rom 10.4.
[25]John 5.46.
[26]I Sam 15.22.

PANTOLEON

We know virtually nothing with certainty about the author, date, or original setting of this homily. In its literary polish, its lively way of addressing characters in the Gospel story, and the way it goes about explaining Peter's wish to "build three tents" on the mountain of the Transfiguration, it recalls features from the homilies of Chrysostom, Proclus, and Cyril on the same episode, but there is no evidence of direct dependence.

A sixth-century Byzantine lead seal has recently been published, from a private collection, with the inscription "Belonging to Pantoleon the Chartophylax," which may possibly point to the same person; see *www.arminius-numismatics* (12/191). A chartophylax (Lat.: *chartularius*), or "record-keeper," was a high administrative official of the Church in both West and East; his role was apparently to be in charge of financial records, and to preside over some lower ecclesiastical court proceedings. Such a role would have been compatible, at least, with the role of an ordained deacon, and the sixth century would fit well with the literary and theological features of this text.

Whatever his date and circumstances, the preacher was clearly a person with an extensive rhetorical formation, with some knowledge of the Bible. Its narration of the Transfiguration and the events that surround it seems to be based on Matthew's Gospel.

PANTOLEON, DEACON AND CHARTOPHYLAX[1]
Sermon on the Most Glorious Transfiguraton of Our Lord and God, Jesus Christ

The very first sign of dawn's light drives sleep from our eyelids, and when the first grey daylight breaks forth, it scatters the shadows of our dreams. Then every bird that can sing, sitting among the branches before it takes flight, bears witness to the presence of dawn. For by a movement of its own wings it shakes off the silence as it shakes away the vanity of sleep, and in the morning twilight looks forward to the bright sunshine; those who are still sleeping it rouses by its own voice. In the same way, as the light of the Gospel floods the house of the universal Church, let the mist of sluggishness fade like night, and let every vain activity, like a tent pitched in dreamland, be folded up; let the inspired songs of our teachers resound from the highest branches of the pulpit, bearing their own witness to the presence of the heavenly light.

Now the sound the birds make is without significance, yet it raises the sluggish to wakefulness; among the teachers, however, the saying of Paul is full of meaning: "The night," he cries, "is far advanced. The day draws near."[2] What kind of night is far advanced,

---

[1] The Greek text of the homily translated here is found in PG 98.1253–1260. The title of the homily translated here gives it as the *second* of Pantoleon's homilies on the Transfiguration; the one that precedes it in the PG edition, however, is actually Cyril of Alexandria's 81st homily on Luke, and it is not clear whether or not another work actually by Pantoleon is attested in medieval homiliaries.

[2] Romans 13.12.

Teacher of the Church? What kind of day draws near? Is it that we, who were surrounded in something like the murky blessings of night, are moving forward, as from night, towards the light of day? If the change of times has indeed brought to fulfillment a change from evils, the time which has come near to us is now better than that which passed on, and no praise is now due to human nature unless it is transformed from one state to another. "Wait a minute!" he says. "I am not talking about temporal change, but about the dawning of knowledge! And I am waking up sluggards who have been sleeping for a long time!"

For we ourselves were also "night," but now, having put on Christ, we fit better with the appellation "day." "For we were once darkness, but now are light in the Lord."[3] Blessed are you, Christ, through whom the human person has come to be called "light." Blessed are you, Christ, through whom human nature lent a covering to God, and the divine nature has wrapped its outward appearance[4] around human substance. Blessed are you, Christ, through whom punishment is quenched, out of respect for the kinship between the judge and the condemned. Blessed are you, Christ: for you, who are "the true light,"[5] entering into the lamp of humanity, have nourished with the oil of the Spirit the wick of our nature, setting it alight with the brilliant rays of divine glory. You have brought light to creation through a human vessel, setting this little lamp alight, which neither Peter nor James nor John dared look upon with human eyes; but these topmost branches of the disciples' tree, falling on their faces, confessed how inaccessible the light is. For the Lord who spoke from heaven, making them his hearers and gently revealing to them, by the light of his glory, the divinity that was in their midst, willed to have them as his faithful witnesses, so that they might use their eyes to support their hearing, and never cease to cry out, in a loud voice,

---

[3]Eph 5.8, which reads, "For *you* were once darkness . . ."

[4]The Greek word here is *prosōpon*, "face," a word heavy with significance from the fourth- and fifth-century Christological controversies, signifying appearance or an external role.

[5]John 1.9.

through the whole earth: "What has been from the beginning, what we have heard and have seen with our own eyes . . . "[6]

But since our discourse has so opportunely interrupted the story, it is necessary for us to ascend, in our explanation, with the chief disciples, obeying Isaiah as he cries out in a loud voice, "Come, let us go up to the mountain of the Lord!"[7] Let us not climb with great physical effort or with gasping breath, lifting our feet uphill, but rather—equipping ourselves with a leisurely understanding to receive what has been said—let us first of all open the holy books, and then, gazing on the sacred text, we shall grope for the riches hidden within.

"Jesus took Peter and James and John his brother," it says, "and led them to a high mountain by themselves, and was transfigured before their eyes."[8] If you will, let us first examine the reason he took these three only, and left the rest of the Apostles behind. The revelation aroused great fear: prophets came together in an invisible way, a cloud became radiant, clothing shone like lightning, the light from his face surpassed that of both ordinary lights,[9] the Father's voice cried out from the cloud to bear witness that well-pleasing sonship was proper to the Only-begotten. And so that the Mystery might not be blurted abroad in an untimely way through widespread anxiety, he took only those who he knew belonged to him as his most fervent lovers; to whom he gave the command to keep the secret, and not to reveal that terrifying vision until after his resurrection from the dead; whom he invited to this vision of what was to come because they were deeply immersed in their attachment to him, and dreadfully saddened when they heard him speaking in advance of his passion.

Consider, then, how Peter is ill-disposed towards the explanation of these things. When he heard, after all, that it was necessary

[6]I John 1.1.
[7]Is 2.3.
[8]Matt 17.1.
[9]I.e., the sun and the moon, which Genesis 1.14–15 calls "the two great lights."

for Jesus to go up to Jerusalem, and to suffer many things from the chief priests and elders and scribes of the people, and to be put to death,[10] he was immediately stung in his thoughts, and with much feeling attacked what Jesus had said, and boldly contradicted his teacher. For Scripture says, "And taking him aside, [Peter] began to rebuke him: 'Far be it from you, Lord—this shall certainly not happen to you!' " And what did the Lord say? He attacks such concern to spare him as a harmful attitude! "For I do not want to be loved," he says, "in a way that harms my lovers! My suffering will be the means of healing the suffering of the world. Why do you stand in the way of the planting of the cross, when you are ignorant of the fruit that will come from it? Why do you prevent the slaughter that cuts the sinews of death, if you are unaware of the love of God for the world? You love as humans do, Peter! Let the seed be sown, and get ready for the harvest." Saying this, he persuaded the disciple not to utter such demands to his teacher; yet he did not drive grief at his death from Peter's mind, because of the greatness of Peter's love for him. And so that [Peter] might take comfort about his suffering through [expecting] the resurrection, which was not far off, [Jesus] took him and those who equally loved him aside and gave proof of the power of the divinity within him by that awe-inspiring vision. For the Scripture says, "He was transfigured before their eyes. And his face shone like the sun, and his garments became white as light. And behold, Moses and Elijah appeared to them, speaking with him."[11]

The sun of righteousness restrained the cloud of his body, and the ray of divinity shone all around the onlookers. For a cloud is the visible garment of what is invisible. Isaiah knew this clearly; for when he contemplated the Savior's stay in Egypt, he said, "Behold, the Lord is seated on a light cloud, and will come to Egypt."[12] "And behold, Moses and Elijah appeared, conversing with him."[13] For they were never at any time separated from his divinity. And why Moses

[10]See Matt 16.21.
[11]Matt 17.2–3.
[12]Is 19.1 (LXX).
[13]Matt 17.3.

and Elijah, above the whole company of the prophets? Because Elijah was numbered with the living, but Moses is dead, and for that reason, through the presence of both, he revealed himself to them as Lord of the living and the dead, clearly teaching those who were present, by these signs, that he himself has authority over life and death.

But not even with these assurances did Peter cease from his fear—he was not yet made steadfast by the activity of the Holy Spirit. For a while he was overcome by his weak nature; but after this, by his confidence, he showed the power of the Holy Spirit, as blessed Paul says, "So that the excess of the power may belong to God and not come from us."[14] What then does Peter [now] say, since he is still afraid? "Lord, it is good for us to be here. If you will, let us build three tabernacles—one for you, one for Moses, one for Elijah."[15] Since he was not able to prevent the Passion, he schemes to postpone the journey to Jerusalem, not by saying openly what he desires, but lobbying Jesus that by being *here,* they might not depart for *there*—not saying clearly what he wanted, but trying to achieve his goal by what he *was* saying. "Lord, it is good for us to be here,"—rather than to head for Jerusalem! "If you wish, let us make three tabernacles here." Fearing that he might again be reproached, he persuasively added to his first words, "If you will, let us make three tabernacles here": it is better to build here three tabernacles, and not to depart to build, in that place, the one tomb that is awaited!

Truly the Apostle's fear is beyond bounds! So be it. You urge the Master to remain there, O blessed Peter! What else? Do you ask Elijah and Moses to dwell in a tabernacle with him? "Yes," he says. "If, while we remain here, the crowd of Jews attacks us, Elijah's tongue knows how to bring down fire from heaven, and Moses' rod is skilled at drawing from the air a complementary firestorm of hail!" But as Peter is plotting these things, the answer to his plan resounds from heaven: "This," a voice says, "is my Son, the Beloved![16] Why are

[14]II Cor 4.7.
[15]Matt 17.4.
[16]Matt 17.5.

you afraid, O Peter? Why are you trying to rouse up allies against the Jews? This is my Son, the Beloved! Every prophet has whatever power he is able to have through the power of the Only-begotten. Listen to him,[17] without trying to achieve anything further by your own scheming. In him I am well pleased,[18] and he clearly knows my will."

To him be glory, with the Father and the Holy Spirit, now and forever and to the ages of ages. Amen.

[17] Ibid.
[18] Ibid.

LEONTIUS, PRESBYTER OF CONSTANTINOPLE

As with several other authors represented here, we know almost nothing about this Leontius besides his name. Two homilies attributed in the manuscripts to "Leontius, presbyter of Constantinople," appear in Migne's *Patrologia* with the works of the sixth-century scholastic theologian Leontius of Byzantium, but they are clearly very different in thought, purpose, and style from the works of that author. Maurice Sachot, who edited this homily on the Transfiguration (CPG 4724) separately in 1977, argued convincingly that it is the work of a distinct author with a characteristic style, and suggested that besides the eleven homilies attributed to him in manuscripts, a number of others, identified by the medieval scribes as works of Chrysostom and others, should be seen as works of Leontius the Presbyter. In 1987, Cornelius Datema and Pauline Allen produced a critical edition of the eleven homilies associated with this Leontius, and added three others, which they judged clearly identifiable as his work. Most of these homilies are associated with liturgical feasts and major mysteries in the life of Christ. From the theological themes presented, the work of Leontius seems to fit well in the setting of the imperial capital, in the mid- or late sixth century.

So it is no surprise that this homily on the Transfiguration offers no hint that this event is being celebrated at its own liturgical feast. References to a "banquet" at the beginning may invoke a Eucharistic setting, but the word refers to the banquet of Wisdom as contained in Scripture. And the Scripture passage being commented on is not simply the story of the Transfiguration on Thabor, but is largely concerned with Jesus' prediction of his Passion, in Matthew 16.21ff.

The homily may even be part of a series of homilies on one of the Gospels.

Leontius reveals here, as in the other homilies ascribed to him, a vivid and strongly imaginative way of making the Gospel event come to life. He often uses unusual vocabulary, and draws his hearers into serious engagement with the Gospel text by addressing characters in the story, as if all of them were present at the scene. Like Proclus and other, later preachers, he attempts to explain why Jesus showed himself only to Peter, James, and John by arguing that if he had brought all but Judas up to see his glory, Judas might have been able to claim our sympathy, on grounds of discrimination, for his later act of betrayal. In fact, however, most of the homily is concerned with what goes *before* the Transfiguration scene in the Gospels: Jesus' prediction of the Passion, and his assertion that "some of those standing here" would see the Kingdom of God before they died. In this narrative framework, the account of the Transfiguration itself occupies only a few pages of the homily, which is really a reflection on the readiness of the disciples to believe, and on the glimpse they are given, in the midst of Jesus' ministry, of the fullness of salvation that was yet to come.

[LEONTIUS, PRESBYTER OF CONSTANTINOPLE][1]
Homily for the Transfiguration of Our Lord Jesus Christ

(Homily 14)

Christ, our generous host, has set before us again today a banquet-table worthy of veneration: a table not simply to be honored by custom, but recognized as part of our familiarity with God; a table not marked by yearning for earthly delights, but sharing in those of heaven; a table not splendid with Solomon's delicacies, but crowned by God's laws; a table not made blessed by abundance of food, but made solemn by thoughts of God. For what could be richer than Solomon's table, spreading out day by day (as is told us in the Third Book of the Kingdoms) "thirty kors[2] of fine wheat flour, and sixty

---

[1]In the manuscripts, this homily is transmitted as the work of "our holy father John Chrysostom, archbishop of Constantinople," and the rhetorical style certainly resembles Chrysostom's in a number of ways. Maurice Sachot, however, who published the first critical edition of it, has argued convincingly from similarities between this work and other, known homilies of Leontius the Presbyter, that it should be included among his works: see *L'homélie pseudo-chrysostomienne sur la Transfiguration* (*CPG* 4724, *BHG* 1975) (Frankfurt: Peter Lang, 1981); text and French translation: 292–329. Sachot's edition is included in C. Datema and P. Allen, *Leontii Presbyteri Constantinopolitani Homiliae* (Corpus Christianorum, Series Graeca 17 [Turnhout: Brepols, 1987]). Datema and Allen (408–410) argue, following Sachot, that it was originally not a sermon for the liturgical feast of the Transfiguration, which had not yet been established widely, but part of a series of homilies on the Gospel of Matthew. In any case, the extended development of the image of a banquet, with which the homily begins, suggests that it *was* given in a Eucharistic context. The text of the Greek original used here is that found in Datema and Allen, 433–448.

[2]A *kor* was a Hebrew dry measure, probably equivalent to about 120 gallons.

kors of ground barley meal, and ten tender, choice calves and twenty grazing cows and a hundred sheep—to say nothing of deer and gazelles and choice birds."[3] But such a lavish abundance of dishes brought Solomon no benefit, nor did it lead him towards perfect virtue. Just the opposite: by leading him to indulge himself beyond measure, it led him to go mad in the end. But the table of the Lord, richly laid before us again today—a table that is immaterial, infinite, incorruptible, immortal, uncircumscribed, beyond human reckoning—directs us not only towards earthly blessings, but towards heavenly ones as well! For it does not offer us "thirty kors of wheat flour," but lavishes on us the kingdom of heaven, as the yeast in "three measures of barley." [4] Nor does it set out "sixty kors of barley," but the bread of heaven itself; I mean that the Lord Christ rewards believers here with the gift of himself, day after day.

But I am speaking empty words, I think, when I compare Solomon's luncheon, nourishing the senses, with the spiritual table of the Lord. For there we find "ten chosen calves," but here "the Lamb of God, who takes away the sin of the world."[5] There twelve grazing cows; here innumerable martyrs bestowing their blessings on souls and bodies. There deer, adorned with wide-branching antlers; here prophets "judging spiritual things with spiritual gifts."[6] There gazelles struck in the flank with an arrow; here Apostles enlightening the world with divine Scriptures. There a flock of birds, taking flight without rational pattern; here a reverent people frolicking in the Spirit. There a hundred mindless sheep, giving joy to Solomon's household alone; here Christ our spiritual sheep, shared everywhere on earth, yet never knowing decrease.[7]

---

[3] III Kingdoms (= I Kings) 11.1–13 (LXX).

[4] Matt 13.33. The word translated "measure" here—Greek *saton*; Hebrew *tseah*—was one-thirtieth of a kor.

[5] John 1.29.

[6] I Cor 2.13.

[7] All these comparisons are aimed at comparing the limited, material banquet of Solomon with the continuing spiritual banquet of the Kingdom of God. The final comparison seems clearly to point to Christ's Eucharistic presence.

You just heard Christ, the spiritual sheep, himself speaking to the Apostles about the time of his Lordly passion,[8] predicting that in the time of his suffering they will not endure suffering. What does the Evangelist Matthew say? As you have just heard: "Then Jesus began to reveal to his disciples that it was necessary for him to go up to Jerusalem and to suffer many things from the high priests and scribes and elders of the people, and be killed, and on the third day to be raised."[9] Do you see? The Lord's table is being furnished with a dish that has been raised from the dead![10] What does Solomon's table have to compare with this? There all the slaughtered animals were led, without willing it, to non-existence; here Christ, our spiritual sheep, even though he, too, was slaughtered, nevertheless was slaughtered by his own choice, buried by his own choice, rose by his own choice, ascended into heaven by his own choice, and by his own choice "will come in the glory of his Father, to give to each according to his deeds."[11]

"Then he began." The Evangelist does well to begin by saying, "Then Jesus began," for Christ the Lord began to undertake a revelation of a different activity. He no longer speaks to the disciples as little children, but addresses them as full-grown men. He no longer gives them the milk of comfort, but shows them the hard bread of testing. He no longer anoints them with salve, as weaklings, but sprinkles them with the astringent rinse of the strong. And he is right to do so! Just as an excellent teacher, in the beginning of the term, flatters the pupils who are assigned to him, restrains the movements of his head, cultivates a little smile, whispers a few pleasant phrases, finds common ground with those who have made mistakes, but when they have made some advances in instruction then shows a

---

[8]This sentence alone suggests that the present homily is part of a continuing exposition of Matthew's Gospel, not part of a liturgical celebration of the Transfiguration.

[9]Matt 16.21.

[10]Again, the reference is clearly to the Eucharistic presentation of Christ's sacrifice.

[11]Matt 16.27.

severe expression, makes serious threats, dispenses blows—not to do harm but to improve his pupils. So, in the same way, Christ, our all-wise teacher, utters gentle and soft words to his own disciples at the beginning of his proclamation of the Gospel, saying to them: "Come follow me, and I will make you fishers of men and women,"[12] and "No one will harm you";[13] but even when they frequently desert him and fall into error, the Lord Christ is understanding towards them. But when he saw them making progress in their piety, initiated into knowledge of God, gaining assurance in the fulfillment of their signs, morally strengthened by the Father's testimony, fortified by the Holy Spirit's enlightenment, he no longer supports them in their errors, but begins from then on to teach them in sharper words: "If anyone wants to save his life, he will lose it, and whoever loses it for my sake will find it,"[14] and again, "If anyone wishes to come after me, let him take up his cross and follow me."[15]

For the best disciple must necessarily follow after his teacher. Therefore blessed Paul, rejoicing in this teaching, wrote: "With Christ I am nailed to the cross; I live no longer as myself, but Christ lives in me."[16] Hearing these words, blessed Peter also boils up with boundless warmth and resists the Lord's words. For when the Lord says that he must "go up to Jerusalem and suffer many things from the high priests and scribes and elders of the people, and be killed, and on the third day be raised,"[17] Peter hears these wise words, thinks that the one who cannot err was uttering strange things, and takes hold of the Lord—as you have just heard—and "began to rebuke him, saying, 'Far be it from you, Lord—this shall never happen to you!' "[18] You do not know what you are saying, Lord; you are

[12]Matt 4.19.

[13]Luke 10.19. In the text of Luke, Jesus' words are actually: "nothing will harm you."

[14]Matt 16.25.
[15]Matt 16.24.
[16]Gal 2.19–20.
[17]Matt 16.21.
[18]Matt 16.22.

suggesting what contradicts who you are! Will the one who put all the demons together to flight be afraid of the elders of the Jews?

"Far be it from you, Lord—this shall never happen to you!" Will you, who put the sea under your feet and calmed the raging winds, who subdued the raging ocean, fear the high priests in Jerusalem? Will you, who dried up the fig tree with a word, and made the shriveled hand reach out alive again, become worried about human beings?

"Far be it from you, Lord—this shall never happen to you!" Enoch, who had worked no miracle, was lifted up to heaven with his whole body; and will you, who worked so many signs, be covered by a tomb? If death were not afraid of you, how did it give you Lazarus back? If the legion of demons were not afraid of you, why did it beg you, when leaving its human home, to go off into a herd of pigs? If the water did not know who you are, why was it changed into wine at your command, at Cana in Galilee? If Siloam did not recognize you as the creator of the whole world, why did it wash away the clay from the man born blind and grant him the power of sight again, at your command? Did not the Father of lights cry out about you, "This is my Son, the Beloved—listen to him"?[19] So when the Son of God is dead, in whom shall our hope lie?

"Far be it from you, Lord—this shall never happen to you!" Tell me, why does he proclaim a resurrection? No one has ever raised himself to life from death. But if he has been raised by someone else, point that person out to me, so that I may leave you and become his disciple! "Far be it from you Lord—this shall never happen to you!" Did you not exhort us, Lord, saying, "I am the light," and "the resurrection and the life"?[20] When has light been transformed into darkness? When is resurrection covered over by a tomb? When is life choked off by the tombs of the dead? Go on, Lord—go on! "Far be it from you, Lord—this shall never happen to you!"

[19]Matt 17.5.
[20]John 8.12 and 11.25.

What, then, does the Lord Christ do—the all-wise teacher? He no longer shows patience to Peter in his errors, but is angry and upset, calling the one who causes scandal for him a devil, as you have just heard: "Get behind me, Satan,"[21]—the one who has seduced my Peter into unbelief! "You are a stumbling block to me," Peter, "because you are not thinking the things of God, but those of human beings."[22] If I am not put to death, none of you will taste immortality. "You are a stumbling block to me," Peter. If I am not murdered, none of you will inherit the vineyard.[23] "You are a stumbling-block to me," Peter. "For you are not thinking the things of God, but those of human beings." I am the "grain of wheat," according to the very structure of the Incarnation: "Unless the grain of wheat falls into the ground and dies, it remains alone. But if it dies, it produces much fruit."[24] "You are a stumbling block to me," Peter, "because you are not thinking the things of God but those of human beings." If I do not go down to the underworld, no one will set Adam free from slavery. "You are a stumbling block to me," Peter, "because you are not thinking the things of God, but of human beings." If I am not sacrificed, no one will bestow on you a mystical reward. If I am not crucified, Peter, the thief will not enter an open Paradise. "You are a stumbling block to me," Peter, "because you are not thinking the things of God, but of human beings." I came not only to protect the living, but to benefit those who are fallen asleep.

I did not deceive you, then, Peter, when I said, "I am the light" and "the resurrection and the life." Since I am light, Peter, I must "shine on those in darkness."[25] What kind of light does not put darkness to flight? "I am the resurrection," Peter. I must raise up those who have already been overcome. For what kind of resurrection is it that does not raise those fallen asleep? "I am the life," Peter. I must put death to death; for I suffer as a human, and I save as a lover of

[21]Matt 16.23.
[22]Matt 16.23.
[23]See Matt 21.33–46, esp. 38.
[24]John 12.24.
[25]Luke 1.79.

humanity. Now I suffer according to the divine plan, Peter; but not long from now I will come as divine Lord: not showing myself in the form of a servant,[26] but led in triumphal procession by angels, in the glory of my Father.[27] Now I allow myself to be rejected, through the ordinariness of what people see; but after a little while I will judge with authority, through the power of God.

And as a sign that the Lord Christ is beginning this, you have just heard him say: "The Son of Man is going to come in the glory of the Father with his angels, and he will repay each one according to his works."[28] Let Arius block out these present events; he had no fear of the judgment of the Lord, although it pays no respect to persons. If the Lord Christ is under the Father's power, in that he is divine Word and Son, unlike the one who begot him and sharing nothing of his being—as Arius madly suggested—how will he "come in the glory of the Father"? Behold, only the one who shares his substance will come in the Father's glory; for if beings differ in substance, their glory will differ, too, but if their substance is the same, their glory will also be the same.

But the members of the Arian party will say immediately—they leave nothing untried, after all; for having fallen into material thinking, they have but little sense of evil—"The Only-begotten says that he has received this glory from the Father, after begging and praying and pleading for it. For we often have heard him praying with the words, 'Father, glorify me with the glory which I had in your presence before the world began.'[29] If, then, he has received glory from the Father, how is he of the same substance as the Father?" Such are the sayings of Arius!

But did the Lord Christ pray for these things, O Arius, in his role as God the Word or as a human being? If he prayed for this as God the Word, did he lose his innate glory after the creation of the

[26]Phil 2.7.
[27]See Matt 16.27.
[28]Matt 16.27.
[29]John 17.5.

world, in your opinion? For he says, "Glorify me, Father, with the glory I had in your presence, before the world existed." From this it is obvious that here the Lord Christ was praying not in the role of God the Word, but in the role of humanity. For God the Word has innate glory: it is part of his substance, not made by hands, not received, never to be lost. He obtains nothing of secondary or subsequent character. For if he lost the glory that was innately his, as you suggest, how is the Scripture true when it says, "Glory to God in the highest heaven, and on earth peace, good pleasure among men and women";[30] and again: "My glory, and the one who lifts my head";[31] and in another place, "The nations shall see your glory, and kings your righteousness."[32] From these texts it is shown clearly that the Lord Christ said this[33] not in the role of his divinity but in the role of Adam. Listen intelligently! For when the Lord Christ became the second Adam, he also took up the old human being; but the old Adam had lost his glory in Paradise by the deceitful theft of the devil. For this reason, the Lord Christ prayed in the role of Adam and said, "Father, glorify me with the glory which I had in your presence, before the world came to be"—with a power of reasoning that knows the future! And therefore the Father cried out again in a shining voice, and said: "I have glorified, and I will glorify again."[34] I have glorified you, he says, in Paradise; but when the devil changed that glory into ingloriousness, "I will glorify again," transforming ingloriousness on the cross! Here, then, he was praying from the persona of the incarnation, but in the words just before these from the persona of the divinity.

But when you hear this, do not imagine the Son to be two persons, but recognize one God the Word, with his own flesh. If, then, the word of his incarnation was later to come to an end, he was no longer teaching in the persona of the incarnate one but in the per-

[30]Luke 2.14.
[31]Ps 3.4 (LXX).
[32]Isaiah 62.2 (LXX).
[33]I.e., John 17.5.
[34]John 12.28.

sona of divinity, when he said, "The Son of man is going to come in the glory of his Father with his angels, and then he will give to each one according to his actions."[35] What is this "glory of the Father," of which he speaks? The Kingdom: which is not handed on, not circumscribed, beyond time, not achieved by hands. The glory of the Father, after all, is the kingdom of the Son, a heavenly and not an earthly Kingdom!

And to make the point that the Father's glory is the Son's Kingdom, you have just heard the Lord Christ himself saying: "Amen, I say to you that there are some standing here who will not taste death until they see the Son of Man coming in his Kingdom."[36] Do you see that there is a single glory of Father and Son? Shortly before this he said, "The Son of Man is going to come in the glory of his Father."[37] Here it is, "Until they see the Son of Man coming in his Kingdom."[38] So the Kingdom of Christ is his Father's glory, and the Father's glory the Kingdom of the Son. Who, then, will divide what is indivisible? Who will weigh what cannot be weighed? Who will investigate the Father's heart? Who is so mad as to divide mind and reason and spirit? "Amen, I say to you, there are some of those standing here who will not taste death, until they see the Son of Man coming in his Kingdom." Some of the ancient interpreters, considering some tendency or other in the text, understood these sayings of the Lord as pointing to his glorious second coming. Therefore they established that the Evangelist John would not experience death, but would await the glorious coming of the Lord, because the Lord said, "There are some of those standing here who will not taste death, until they see the Son of Man coming in his Kingdom." But his meaning is this—for one must not yield to the imagination, but must speak the truth, especially now when he has prompted even the little ones to speak their minds! Here, then, he is talking not about his second, glorious coming, but about

[35]Matt 16.27.
[36]Matt 16.28.
[37]Matt 16.27.
[38]Matt 16.28.

his transfiguration on the mountain. For when he was transfigured on the mountain, the Lord Christ showed in some small way to his disciples the glory of his invisible divine kingship.

But immediately those who carry around a tongue sharpened for the kill will say: "And if the divine glory of God the Word is invisible, how did he show it to the Apostles? But if it is visible, it is not invisible, and if it is invisible, it is not visible!" Therefore listen intelligently! Here the Lord Christ both revealed to his disciples the glory of his invisible kingly power, and did not reveal it—fulfilling their expectations on the one hand, but sparing them on the other. For he fulfilled their expectations by showing them the divine glory of his invisible kingly power: not in its full greatness, but as much as those with bodily eyes were able to bear. But he spared them, without any trace of malice, in that he did not show them the full glory of his invisible kingly power, lest with that vision they also lose their lives. The witness of this is what the God of all things said to Moses, when he yearned to gaze on him, as the holy text reminds us: "Then Moses answered God and said, 'If I have found favor in your sight, reveal yourself to me so that I may see you knowingly, face to face.'"[39] And what did God say to him? "You are wrong, Moses, in seeking for this. I do not begrudge you the vision, but I am concerned for your safety. No human being who sees God will live!" Here, then, he both revealed himself and did not reveal himself—fulfilling one desire, leaving the other unfulfilled.

And to show that he is speaking not about his second, glorious coming but about the transfiguration on the mountain, and not about John alone but also about Peter and James—for he expressed himself not in the singular but in the plural form when he said, "There are some of those standing here . . ."; he did not say "one," but "some"!—listen to what follows: for I must remind you, not teach you something new! "And after six days Jesus took Peter and James and John his brother, and he went up a high mountain alone, and was transfigured before them, and his face shone like

[39]Ex 33.12–13.

the sun, and his garments became white as light. And behold a voice was saying, 'This is my Son, the Beloved, in whom I am well pleased. Listen to him.'"[40] Do you see that he was speaking not about his second, glorious coming, but about his transfiguration on the mountain?

What did the Lord mean? Let us follow his train of thought, so that, by your prayers, we may not fail to engage the text before us. "And after six days, he took Peter and James and John." But it is possible that someone may say, "Why did the Lord Christ not take his twelve disciples with him as he went up the mountain, but simply Peter and James and John?" Why? Because Judas was not worthy to gaze upon the Lord's glory in such magnitude, with eyes distorted by his plans! But immediately some will ask, "And if this was the reason, why did he not leave Judas alone below, and lead the eleven up with him?" We are not wiser than the Lord Christ. If it had happened that Judas alone was left behind at the foot of the mountain, while the other eleven went up on the mountain to enjoy the same vision, some would probably say that it was for this reason Judas went on to betray and sell the Lord: that he was deeply hurt! But so that nothing like this might be argued, even among us, and that he might have no such excuse, for that reason [Jesus] left him and the eight others below, so that the three might be full sharers in the glory of this vision, but the nine might be called blessed because they believed what they heard. Therefore the Lord said that those who believed on the basis of hearing alone are blessed: "Blessed are those who do not see, yet believe."[41]

In any case, he led only the three up the mountain, Peter and James and John, so that the well-known text might be fulfilled, "Every assertion will be established on the basis of two or three witnesses."[42] The trio of Peter, James and John are the threefold, endless cord of blessedness, while the pair Moses and Elijah are the immove-

---

[40]Matt 17.1–2, 5.
[41]John 20.29.
[42]Deut 19.15.

able pillars of the law. You just heard the Evangelist say, "And there appeared to them on the mountain Moses and Elijah, speaking with him."[43] Why did he set Moses and Elijah on the mountain with him, and why did such a great transfiguration take place, with a radiant cloud overshadowing them and the voice of his Father thundering forth? What was the reason? Because the Apostles thought the Lord Christ was simply a man, not God in flesh. And so, since they considered him to be in substance simply a man, because of the tears he shed as part of God's plan, and his enacted fear, and his prayers and petitions, the Apostles frequently contradicted him, and disbelieved what he said, and were terrified.

And that he might divert them from suspicions such as these, he brought them up the mountain, and briefly opened the door of his Incarnation for them, and showed them clearly what great glory was concealed within him. In any event, he made it perfectly clear to the Apostles that he is "the Lord of all things, in heaven and on earth and under the earth."[44] He lured Elijah down from above,[45] he fished Moses up from below, he set Peter and James and John alongside him from those still on earth: for the whole is known from the extremes! Therefore when Peter gazes on such great glory, and Moses and Elijah standing by [Jesus] like servants and chatting quietly with him, he no longer rebukes [Jesus], but worships—as you have just heard—[saying] "Lord, it is good for us to be here,"[46] and begs him not to go up to Jerusalem. There Pilate and Caiaphas are breathing death, here Moses and Elijah are pointing to resurrection. "Lord, it is good for us to be here; and if you will, let us make three tabernacles—one for you and one for Moses and one for Elijah."[47] Why, O blessed Peter, are you so dominated by fear, so shaken by cowardice, that you are this eager to weave strange tents of willow

[43] Matt 17.3.

[44] Phil 2.10.

[45] The word Leontius uses here, *ixeusen*, suggests the image of luring a bird into a trap!

[46] Matt 17.4.

[47] Matt 17.4.

branches here,[48] putting the Lord on the same level as his servants? No covering is able to receive the one whom the clouds lead in procession! Heaven and earth are full of his glory: the glory of the Father and the Son and the Holy Spirit, now and always, and for the ages of ages. Amen.

[48]Reading here, with Savile's version of the work in his edition of Chrysostom's homilies, *lygadoplektein*, "weave willow branches," rather than the equally unusual *lygidoplektein*, "weave by twisting knots," that appears in one of the manuscripts and is adopted by Datema and Allen in their edition. Leontius seems to be alluding to the Jewish practice of building tents out of branches at the feast of Tabernacles (*Sukkoth*), to commemorate Israel's sojourn with the Lord in the desert.

ANASTASIUS I OF ANTIOCH

This homily (CPG 6947) is one of several attributed to "Saint Anastasius," who today is understood by most scholars to be Patriarch Anastasius I of Antioch. Originally from Palestine, he is said in some ancient sources to have been a monk of Sinai—probably through confusion with Anastasius of Sinai, the Chalcedonian theologian who lived half a century and more later. After having served as ambassador (*apocrisiarius*) of the Church of Alexandria in Antioch, he was appointed Patriarch of the latter Church by Justinian I in 558 or early 559, a time of political and military tension in Western Syria. Throughout his long reign, Justinian had promoted official adherence to the Christological decree of Chalcedon, but had sought for avenues of rapprochement with those who opposed it and clung to what seemed to be the more clearly unitive formulas of Cyril of Alexandria. Anastasius was a defender of the Chalcedonian synthesis proposed by the Council of Constantinople in 553, but was clearly uncomfortable with the position taken by Justinian towards the end of his life in his "Edict to the Romans," in which he seemed to endorse the view that the human nature of Jesus was the perfect nature of Adam before the fall, free from both moral and physical corruptibility: the so-called "aphthartist" position, which prominent Chalcedonians and anti-Chalcedonians alike had rejected.

In 570, however, five years after Justinian's death, Anastasius was deposed by Emperor Justin II because of his suspected opposition to the Emperor's policy of seeking reunion with those who rejected Chalcedonian Christology, and was brought to live in Constantinople. For a few years, he was not permitted access to any books, even to his own earlier writings. Things gradually eased for him, however, and, thanks to the intervention of the future Pope Gregory the Great, whom he came to know personally during the ensuing decade in the imperial capital when Gregory was the papal legate there, Anastasius was restored to his see in 593, and died in Antioch, still Patriarch, in 598. An opponent also of the tritheism of the Alexandrian John Philoponus, Anastasius is the probable author of a number of short treatises and fragments. (See the account of his life and works by Stergios N. Sakkos, Περὶ Ἀναστασίων Σιναϊτῶν [Thessaloniki: University Press, 1964] 44–86.) He also is the author of a number of festal homilies, some still unedited, which probably were given during one of his periods of patriarchal residency in Antioch. Although his authorship of this sermon (CPG 6947) has been questioned, G. Weiss, who has carefully studied the works attributed to Anastasius, concludes that he can find no conclusive argument against his authorship (*Studia Anastasiana* 1 [Munich, 1965] 91–94).

The homily on the Transfiguration is a straightforward piece of moral and narrative reflection on the Gospel passage in Matthew; there is little in it by way of rhetorical flourish or figural exegesis, and no reference to a festal liturgy celebrating the Transfiguration. It does, however, emphasize a classic Chalcedonian understanding of Christ in its exegesis of the words, "This is my Son, the Beloved, (c. 8). It also suggests that the resurrection of the body is, for all human beings, the fulfillment of God's original plan of creation. The homily follows the text of Matthew's account of the incident closely, generally giving simple explanations for the Gospel's words. For an analysis of Anastasius' understanding of the glorified human body in this sermon, see Dirk Krausmüller, "The Real and the Individual: Byzantine Concepts of the Resurrection (1)," *Golden Horn* 5.1 (1997).

SAINT ANASTASIUS:[1]
On the Transfiguration of
Our Lord Jesus Christ
(Homily 1)

1 Our benefactor Jesus, the good teacher who appeared in the world although he is also God, said to his disciples, "If anyone wants to come after me, let him deny himself, and lift up his cross, and follow me. For whoever would wish to save his life will lose it; but whoever loses his life for my sake will find it. For how will a person profit, if he gains the whole world, but loses his soul? Or what will a person give in exchange for his soul? For the Son of Man will come in the glory of his Father with his holy angels; then he will repay each one according to his works."[2]

2 "If anyone wishes to come after me, let him deny himself." That means: let him deny every human concern; and not only that, but, like me, "Let him take up his cross, and follow me." We understand from his own words that Paul did this; not only was he "crucified to the world, and crucified the world to himself,"[3] but he changed the very form of his life, no longer living as himself, moving and acting as a private agent. Rather, he had Christ living and acting in himself. He disregarded himself completely, and putting his own will to death, he subjected himself completely to the will of God. So that, if I might apply titles boldly, Paul would rather be said to

[1]The Greek text on which this translation is based, along with its chapter divisions, is that of the French Dominican, François Combéfis (1605–1679), as reprinted in PG 89.1361–1376.

[2]Matt 16.24–27.

[3]Gal 6.14.

be Christ than to be a living being; for "his life was Christ."[4] So it is necessary that those who want to belong to Christ walk behind him, and follow him. But since most of the time two opposing wills exist in us, the godly and the human, and it is impossible to live without them—or at least without one of them—it is clear that the person who is attached to one of them is distant from the other, and vice versa. Anyone, then who wishes to make his way behind the Lord will hate all human forms of willing; changing the former way of life he practiced, let him follow [Christ] in this way, leaving himself behind, in a certain sense, and transforming all his soul's powers. For if a person truly wants to find his own soul, when it has been wandering among attractions to the foolish things of life and the dream-like fantasies it promotes, he should first lose it, with regard to the life by which he was involved in these things,[5] and he will then find it as a wonderful discovery. To the degree that he has an inclination towards the material world, however, he will not be able to recognize the destructive state in which he exists.

Clearly, he will not need to seek that soul that has been lost, nor will he find it. For as there are two forms of life, there are also two forms of death: one conformed to God, the other conformed to the world. Paul says this clearly, speaking of "living for sin" and "living for righteousness."[6] So there are two ways to lose one's life: one that is reprehensible, the other praiseworthy. And as the person who lives for sin is dead as regards righteousness, so the opposite is true: the one who lives for righteousness is dead towards sin. So the person who follows the inclinations of the flesh walks in the way of flesh, and is lost as far as walking the way of the Lord is concerned. But the one who hates the flesh—the life which is really destruction—and who says powerfully, "I shall walk behind my God!" has turned from the way of destruction, gaining the praiseworthy life in place of what is reprehensible. For to be lost as far as the world

[4]See Phil 1.21.
[5]The Greek text of this phrase seems to be slightly incomplete.
[6]See Rom 6.2.

is concerned is to be found for God, and to be found for the world is to be lost for God.

And what a foolish plan it is to find or gain the whole world, and to have it as one's own possession, but to forfeit or lose one's soul! For what can one give in exchange for one's soul? Or what will a person give as a price to ransom it?[7] No material thing is of equal value with the soul. Only the soul can be considered of equal value with itself—nothing else can ever be thought so. "For the Son is going to come," receiving the power of judgment from the Father, "to give to each person recompense according to his works."[8] Then none of the circumstances of our lives will be able to do us any good; for we will all stand naked before the seat of judgment, deserted by what does not belong to us (and none of what surrounds us here is properly ours!). Books will then be opened to document the investigation, making clear, from what has been imprinted in our consciences, which it is that each of us has preferred to follow: the flesh or the spirit, Christ or the world—and also which form of losing our life we have chosen: that which comes from God, or that which comes from the world.

And when that dreadful, exact investigation takes place, "the one who receives authority to hold judgment because he is Son of Man,"[9] will give appropriate recompense to everyone. "For he will come in the glory of his Father with the holy angels,"[10] the spirits who minister to him; he will no longer be "without form or beauty,"[11] as he now appears in the world, but "more beautiful in appearance than other men,"[12] having changed his own body into a state of incorruptibility, and revealing it as substantially transformed into a spiritual and heavenly body at the time of resurrection. In this we already have a pledge of our own transformation, and of the reshaping of our

[7]See Matt 16.26.
[8]Matt 16.27.
[9]John 5.27.
[10]Matt 16.27.
[11]Is 53.2 (LXX).
[12]Ps 44 (45).3 (LXX).

own bodies. And that we might hold firmly to this invisible hope, he wishes to reveal even now, to a select group of disciples, the transformation that will then occur, "in a moment," as Paul says, "and in the twinkling of an eye!"[13] Therefore he says, "Amen, I say to you: there are some of those standing here who will not taste death until they see the Son of Man coming in his royal power."[14] And how this will happen, we learn from what follows.

3   "And it happened that, after six days, Jesus took Peter and James, and John his brother, and led them up a high mountain by themselves; and Jesus was transfigured before them. His face shone like the sun, and his garments became white as snow. And behold Moses and Elijah appeared, speaking with him."[15] This should not be heard in a frivolous way, nor should the story be taken simply in what its words tell us, as if it revealed its meaning simply by its language; on the contrary, it signifies a carefully articulated introduction to the Mysteries,[16] and a taste of the blessings that are going to exist for us after this life—or rather, not for us, but for the saints. Therefore, six days after making the promise, he fulfills what he had proclaimed to the disciples. The promise was that "there are some among those standing here, who will not taste death until they see the royal power of God,"[17] the power destined to be revealed after the consummation of this coarse material world. Therefore it was "after six days" that he took those who were to know the divine mysteries of the Kingdom before tasting death. After the six days comes the seventh, the holy day of rest, in which it is not possible to work, since God created heaven and earth in six days, and rested on the seventh, and made it holy.[18] So that the promise was made on the first day, and the fulfillment of promise was realized, once again,

[13] I Cor 15.52.
[14] Matt 16.28.
[15] Matt 17.1–3.
[16] The Greek word here is *mystagogia*.
[17] Matt 16.28.
[18] See Gen 2.3.

on the first day.[19] The number six, then, corresponds to this coarse present world, which is put together and made complete from its own days; [the number] is a sign of the process of birth, and has in itself male and female, whose combination brings about bodily birth.[20] But after them comes the seventh day, in due order, "in which they neither marry nor arrange marriage, but are like God's angels in heaven."[21] Therefore the number seven is said to be virginal, like the Sabbath: holy, putting an end to all servile labor, and making everyone remain where they are, each in his own place.

4   After that day had come, he therefore took with him his three chosen disciples. It would not have made sense, after all, that Judas should become a visual sharer in these mysteries. Nor would it, on the other hand, have been right if he alone was left out of the vision, that this might not serve him as a justification of his betrayal, if he were to judge that the others had been chosen before him.[22] Therefore, taking along only the three, "he led them up a high mountain."[23] But what is higher than his glory? And he led them "by themselves."[24] The life apart from material things is a solitary one. And "he led them" upwards from below; this is said not so much in a spatial sense, as in divine one: that is, he made them able to receive the shining of his light in a way far above their powers.[25] Then "he was transfigured before them."[26] Once before, Jesus the Savior was transfigured, not before human beings but before his own

[19]Anastasius seems to mean that the fulfillment of God's promise of life, made at the beginning of creation, was realized in the resurrection of Christ, which took place on the first day of the week, and was the beginning of a new creation.

[20]It is unclear how Anastasius finds a symbolic allusion to the differentiation of the sexes and to procreation in the number six.

[21]Matt 22.30.

[22]For this same argument justifying the choice of Peter, James, and John to be the sole witnesses of the transfiguration, see the homilies of Proclus of Constantinople, pp. 90–91, and Leontius the Presbyter of Constantinople, p. 125.

[23]Matt 17.1.

[24]Ibid.

[25]The vocabulary in this sentence reminds the reader of the Pseudo-Dionysius.

[26]Matt 17.2.

Father, when "the one who was in the form of God did not consider being equal to God something to cling to, and he emptied himself, taking on the form of a servant."[27] At that time, then, he concealed the divine form, being changed by the form of a servant; but now he restores the form of the servant to its natural appearance—not putting aside the substance of the servant, but making it radiant with divine characteristics. "He was transfigured before them," then, showing them that in this way "he will someday transfigure the body of our lowliness, making it conform to the body of his glory."[28] "And his face shone," it says, "like the sun. And his garments became white as snow." This is written, not because he is to be compared with the sun or with snow—for how can the incomparable be compared?—but because among material things nothing is more brilliant than the sun, or whiter than snow; so the author, wishing to establish, in a modest way, the matchless quality of his light and his whiteness, made this comparison by means of things familiar to us. And the radiance of his garments reveals the change that will take place in our bodies. For we became a covering for him, when he wrapped himself in our flesh Perhaps the phrase "his face shone like the sun" hints, in a symbolic way, at the body that belonged peculiarly to him; but "his garments were as white as snow" refers to those who have been purified through him, by his transforming and life-altering power. For this reason, his spiritual garment is likened to snow, since snow itself is something transformed and vaporized–it becomes snow from water. And [to realize] that our nature will be, in the end, what his garment became, let us listen to Isaiah speaking to him by God's inspiration: "I am alive, says the Lord; for you will clothe yourself in all of them, and wrap them around you like a bride's veil."[29]

5   "He was transfigured," then, "and his face shone like the sun, and his garments became white as snow. And there appeared to them

²⁷Phil 2.6–7.
²⁸Phil 3.21.
²⁹Is 49.18 (LXX).

Moses and Elijah, speaking with him."[30] The Apostles became more clear-sighted, since they had been led with Jesus up the mountain, and gradually recognized that Moses and Elijah were then talking with Jesus, having been transfigured along with him. For if they had not been transfigured with him, they would not be talking to him. But "they were speaking with Jesus," according to Luke, "about the exodus that he was to accomplish in Jerusalem."[31] And the disciples heard from them things that they had failed to understand, when Jesus had formerly told them—as when Peter, thinking in a human way, rebuked Jesus for saying that he was going to be killed by men, and on the third day be raised from the dead. Moses and Elijah, then, as I have said, were speaking with Jesus: that is, the Law and the Prophets! When their words come to be transfigured, and the shadows of the Law are removed, then Moses will be believed as the faithful servant who wrote all of this about Christ, and he will present [Christ's] exodus clearly on the basis of his own words—the exodus that he was to fulfill in Jerusalem. But that some people inquire on what grounds, or how and from what signs, the disciples recognized the prophets,[32] does not seem to me to be an appropriate question, or one worthy of investigation. For if they had advanced to such a height as to be thought worthy of a vision like this—a vision that the one who revealed himself to them, transfigured with the prophets, called the Kingdom of heaven—how could they be unable to recognize those who shared that Kingdom with him? Surely, too, the Apostles were prophets; and when prophets associate with prophets, they share one and the same knowledge—especially when Jesus is there, and enlightens the guiding core of their intellects, and forms their minds according to his own divine form.

[30]Matt 17.2–3.

[31]Luke 9.31.

[32]One preacher who raises precisely this question is Timothy of Antioch, in the homily also translated in this collection. If Anastasius is thinking of Timothy here, this would be the only piece of strong evidence we have for dating Timothy to the mid-sixth century. See Krausmüller (n.1) 1–2 and n.3.

"And Peter answered Jesus, and said, 'Lord, it is good for us to be here. If you will, let us make three tabernacles here—one for you, and one for Moses, and one for Elijah.'"[33] Peter perceived what a difference lies between intelligible and sensible things, and he chose the better over the worse. Still, his knowledge of what he saw had not yet become perfect; otherwise he would not have thought about tabernacles in the intelligible world. And perhaps he was still worrying about his teacher, because of the death he had predicted, and the fact that those who had appeared were speaking about it with Jesus. For with one voice they spoke of that "exodus that was to occur in Jerusalem."[34] Perhaps for this reason, [Peter] begged the teacher to remain there instead, and never to give himself to the Pharisees and Scribes who harbored envious thoughts against him. For perhaps he thought that no one who was plotting against him would come up to them on the mountain, and in any case it was impossible to be both in Jerusalem and somewhere else. "It is good, then, for us to be here with Moses and Elijah, rather than to go towards the unholy priests, the murderers of God." But that he was unaware that by sparing the master he would become a block for the salvation of the world, Luke recognizes when he says, "He did not know what he was saying."[35] And Mark says, "For he did not know what he was saying,"[36] nor what he was thinking. Those who had gone up with Jesus took their stand in that high place.[37]

6 "And while he was still speaking, behold, a luminous cloud overshadowed them, and a voice came out of the cloud, saying, 'This is my Son, the Beloved, in whom I am well pleased. Listen to him.' And when

[33] Matt 17.4.

[34] Luke 9.31.

[35] Luke 9.33.

[36] Mark 9.6 (Anastasius uses the word *eipen* here; the Gospel manuscripts give a number of alternatives, but do not employ this word.)

[37] Reading *hypsēlorerō*, rather than *hypsēloteron*, as in the printed text. It is hard to understand what Anastasius intends to add to the narrative by this sentence, unless he means "they took their stand" in a moral or psychological sense: they refused to move with Jesus towards the cross.

the disciples heard, they fell on their face and were much afraid. And Jesus came forward and touched them, saying, 'Awake, and do not be afraid.' And when they opened their eyes, they saw no one, except only Jesus."[38] While Peter was still speaking words of affection towards his teacher, a luminous cloud from above overshadowed them, and a voice came out of the cloud, correcting Peter, and perhaps also his fellow disciples, who wanted the same thing as he did, and were asking to remain on the mountain, that they might not think any thoughts opposed to the beloved Son, but might listen to him and follow his will. For that is what works the salvation of all people. But we must investigate from similar sayings in Scripture how we must understand this cloud. For we find Moses, too, entering into the cloud, when it covered the mountain in the desert of Horeb; and it is attested that he entered into the darkness where God was.[39] Then also, at various times, when the cloud again covered the tent of meeting, God was heard speaking to Moses also there. And further, a pillar of cloud went ahead of the people, dewy by day and lit by fire at night. Isaiah, too, prophesies that the Lord would come to Egypt on a light cloud.[40] Again, we hear also of Solomon that when he had built the temple and consecrated it, a cloud filled the building, and the priests were unable to enter and carry out their sacred ministries, because of the appearance of the cloud.[41] It is possible to gather these texts and more from the whole Scripture, to establish and clarify this idea before us, and to know what the cloud was that overshadowed those who had appeared, along with the visionaries, when the voice was heard that said, "This is my Son, the Beloved, in whom I am well pleased. Listen to him!"

7   We are to understand that these clouds mentioned in Scripture are related to each other—or rather, we must not hesitate to say that they are all one thing. We should not think that the cloud is some vaporous exhalation from the earth, or an evaporation of water, or some

[38]Matt 17.5–8.
[39]Exod 24.18; Num 16.43–45.
[40]Is 19.1 (LXX).
[41]II Chron 5.13–14.

condensation from the air, or anything airy at all, which is produced from bodily substance; rather, we should think of it as a knowledge of the divine nature, made accessible to us and reaching down to us, which it is more appropriate to call, as David does, [God's] "splendor."[42] For since a grasp of the divine substance is beyond the power of those creatures who come to be and decay, it appears to us in ways that are possible, and in things that are less than divine but are close to it, just as God has spoken to us also through the prophets. So when we hear[43] a man saying, "I am the Lord your God," we do not believe that the man—let us say, Isaiah—is God, but that the one speaking in him is God. Therefore, even if the voice, when it was heard, was the sound of a cloud, still it is clear that it was principally the Father's voice, who was bearing witness to [Jesus'] sonship, through a rational nature that was close to him, and that had sounded out like thunder.[44] For there are also clouds of a lower kind, which put forth a sound and are willing speakers of the Word, as in the text, "The clouds gave forth a voice."[45] And they are enjoined not to pour rain down on the vines bearing clusters of grapes—the bodily house of Israel.[46] I say these clouds are the prophets, who rain down the word, and who water those who need something to drink. But this cloud surpasses all of them, and puts them all in its shadow—we might almost say, it takes provident care of them all.

"This," then, the voice says, "is my Son, the Beloved, in whom I am well pleased. Listen to him!" It does not say, "my Son, who is well loved,"[47] but rather: "the Beloved."[48] The one who is the

[42]E.g., Ps 144.3f. The word here is parallel to "glory".

[43]Along with the original editor, Combéfis, we read here *akouontes*, "hearing," for *akouontos*, which would have to be taken as modifying "a man saying."

[44]Anastasius' idea seems to be that God had spoken here, testifying to Jesus' sonship, by the medium of an angel, who was himself using the cloud as a material instrument. This same idea is proposed by St Augustine in *De Trinitate* III to explain the theophanies of the Old Testament.

[45]Ps 76.18 (LXX).

[46]Is 5.6.

[47]Greek: *ēgapēmenon: "one who is loved."*

[48]Greek: *agapēton:* "one who is loveable"—i.e., who should be loved, the Beloved one.

Beloved is also loved; for the Beloved, surely, is this way by nature, but what is [simply] loved, is not so by nature, it seems, but in virtue of someone's good pleasure.[49] The Son, then, being one individual, is both: Beloved Son and (if I may put it this way) a son loved by good pleasure, since he took on himself something of a different substance from what he was, and that which was not of the same substance was taken up in order to reveal a single hypostasis. The Father, then, revealed the otherness of the Son to us in his testimony: not separating what had been united (for how shall what God has unified be split apart?), but teaching the union of things that are different in nature, and pointing to him who is composed into one from these—his Son Christ the Lord, one Beloved Son, whom all creation finds pleasure in worshipping, and to whom [it delights] to listen.

8   When the Apostles heard this magnificent sound, "they fell on their faces," submitting to the voice that had sounded from on high, "and they were extremely afraid."[50] Perhaps it was because of their previous unbelief, when they realized that they were thinking in a way opposed to the good pleasure of the Father, by trying to prevent the death of the Son, through which salvation was being prepared for all people, according to the ancient plan of the Father. But when they had become terrified, and were lying on the ground, "Jesus drew near, touched them, and said: 'Get up, and do not be afraid.'"[51] For it belonged to no one else to put that panic and fear to flight, but only to the Son, who always commands those who draw near to him to take courage.

9   In obedience to his word, they raised their eyes, which had been bleared, perhaps, by fear. "And raising their eyes, they saw

---

[49]I.e., the one who loves another takes pleasure in that person, whether or not that pleasure is justly derived. Anastasius is playing here on the distinction between the quality of being "loveable" or "dear," which is signified by the same Greek word—*agapētos*—as the English word "Beloved," and the fact of being the object of someone's choice. This distinction is not easily captured in modern English.

[50]Matt 17.6.
[51]Matt 17.7.

only Jesus."[52] This was as far as the mysterious revelation of the Kingdom of Heaven had advanced. "And as they were coming down the mountain, Jesus commanded them, saying, 'Do not tell the vision to anyone, until the Son of Man has risen.' "[53] But why did he prevent them from disclosing what they had seen, and tell them not to reveal the mystery of the resurrection to anyone? Because it was necessary, first, that "the firstborn from the dead"[54] should rise, making the resurrection credible by his action; after that, the common resurrection of all would be made known through witnesses. For who would have believed what was said, if those recognized as Apostles did not believe it? Peter, after all, thought what was being said about the death of the Savior to be blasphemy, until he heard the voice sounding from above, bearing witness to the "Beloved Son" and commanding obedience to him. For the voice said "Listen to him"—consider everything said by him to be a firm law! It was necessary, then, for him to command the disciples to keep what they had seen to themselves, until the time when he should go ahead of them to defeat death in hand-to-hand combat, so that those who heard might not form a habit of disbelieving what was told them [by the Apostles]. For after the resurrection of the first-born [from the dead], they spoke out boldly, making public the resurrection of all people, and their transformation from clumsy bodies into spiritual ones: teaching everyone that just as "Christ, risen from the dead, will not die again, and death has no power over him,"[55] so he will configure us to his glory, and transform our bodies into something spiritual and incorruptible.[56] And if "we walk in newness of life,"[57] "we shall be taken up in the clouds to meet the Lord in the air; and thus we shall always be with the Lord,"[58] to whom be glory and strength, unto the ages of ages. Amen.

[52]Matt 17.8.
[53]Matt 17.9.
[54]Col 1.18.
[55]Rom 6.9.
[56]See Phil 3.21.
[57]Rom 6.4.
[58]I Thess 4.16.

TIMOTHY OF ANTIOCH

Almost nothing certain is known about the author of this homily, or his place of origin or date. It is ascribed in its two extant manuscripts (Vat. Gr. 1633 [10–11 c.]; Kosinitza 28 [12 c.]) to "Timothy of Antioch." Dom Bernard Capelle has argued persuasively, from a careful analysis of the style and language of the texts, that the author is also the author of four other published Greek homilies on Gospel incidents, three of them ascribed to Athanasius, and one to "Timothy, presbyter of Jerusalem" ("Les homélies liturgiques du prétendu Timothée de Jérusalem," *Ephemerides Liturgicae* 63 [1949] 5–26). From Christological themes, as well as from the colorful, idiomatic quality of the Greek style, Capelle and a number of colleagues whom he consulted place these homilies in the early Byzantine period, somewhere between the sixth and the eighth centuries. An attempt by Maurice Sachot to claim this homily for Leontius, Presbyter of Constantinople, has not generally been accepted.

This sermon on the Cross and the Transfiguration is, it seems, simply a homily on the Gospel passage, and shows no signs of having been given as part of a liturgical celebration of the feast. The preacher is apparently reflecting primarily on Luke's narration of the event, beginning (as Leontius' does) with Jesus' prediction of his Passion. Timothy's main concern, however, in the last paragraphs of the homily, is to emphasize the Orthodox understanding of the divine person of Christ, which he carefully distinguishes from the conceptions of the Arian tradition. The number of this work given by the *Clavis Patrum Graecorum* is CPG 7406.

TIMOTHY OF ANTIOCH

Homily on the Cross and the Transfiguration of Our Lord Jesus Christ[1]

The trained soldier is fortified with many different kinds of armor, when he sets forth into battle against foreign troops; following his master, the Roman Emperor, he is bound on all sides by protective gear, eager to keep himself safe against the enemy. That is what the earthly soldier does; but the trusted disciple who loves Christ and wants to follow after his heavenly King in the state of his innermost soul, can devastate the whole troop of demons with one single quiver of arrows. But if the quiver of the cross can conquer the army of the demons, it is certainly clear that it surpasses the whole storm of foreign forces that rages against us; so the prophet says, "I was ready, and was not shaken,"[2] and in another place, "He regarded me as a chosen arrow, and hid me in his quiver."[3] So Christ the Lord, without beginning and eternal, the King who knows no end, and who in the moment of his incarnation revealed his cross as the unconquerable weapon for those who want to obey his commands, even now speaks his word of exhortation to us, as you have just heard in the Gospel according to Luke: "If anyone wishes to come after me, let him deny himself, and take up his cross, and follow me."[4]

---

[1]The sole edition of this homily, translated here, is that of the learned German Jesuit controversial theologian, Jacobus Gretser (1562–1625), who edited and translated many Patristic and medieval works during his years as professor at Ingolstadt. The text is reprinted in PG 86.256–265.

[2]Ps 118.60 (LXX).

[3]Is 49.2 (LXX).

[4]Lk 9.23.

What are you saying, my friend? The spiritual soldier, who wants in the depth of his soul to come after the heavenly King, does not need many arms? "If anyone will come after me, let him deny himself, and take up his cross, and follow me." What an amazing state of affairs! The cross had not yet been constructed by the Jews,[5] and yet the trophy of the cross was being revealed to the faithful. O, the universally nourishing work of the cross: rooted in this age of grace in the sight of a vision, yet sketched out beforehand, in the age of the Law, in the experience of God's help and in the figure of Moses! And that even prior to the age of grace, the victorious work of the cross was sketched out long ages beforehand in the figure of Moses, is a point one can prove with immediately plausible arguments.[6] Joshua,[7] the son of Nave, as you well know, when he drew up his forces in military array against the enemy, and saw by comparing the Israelites and their enemies that the enemy exceeded Israel in number and was stronger in the ability to fight, pointed this out to Moses and said, "Servant of God, Moses, pray that the enemy will be destroyed, because our opponents are stronger than we."[8] Send up your prayers, for genuine petition to God is stronger than arrows! What, then, did Moses do, when he had been granted a revelation from the Holy Spirit? How did he bring it about that the enemy was turned back? Going up onto the wall,[9] he did not bend his knee or bow his head, he did not cry out with his voice, but he stretched out his hands, lifted his head, and formed the shape of the cross; thus when Moses stretched out his hands and formed in advance the

[5]The preacher seems to ignore the fact that crucifixion was a distinctly Roman method of execution, and that the Gospel accounts and other ancient sources do not suggest that the Jewish people themselves were directly involved in constructing it or in carrying out Jesus' execution.

[6]Timothy uses an expression here, *artizēlō logō*, which is unknown elsewhere in classical Greek. His style is, in general, full of colorful, often unparalleled expressions.

[7]In the Greek of the Septuagint, his name is "Jesus."

[8]Exod 17.12.

[9]Timothy seems to imagine Moses sitting on a city wall or fortification, rather than on a mountaintop, as suggested in Exodus.

shape of the cross, he signified to those around him that it is not the secret movement of the lips, but the form of the cross that won the glory of victory. And what happened then? While Moses held his hands extended, Joshua, son of Nave, overcame the enemy. Only when Moses, in his human weakness, grew tired and dropped his hands, the enemy overcame Israel; so when those standing by realized that it was this bodily pose that brought victory, they set two men there, Aaron and Hur, under Moses' hands—Aaron from the Israelite ruling class,[10] Hur representing the kingly house. For the cross must be controlled by sacred and royal power. When, then, the enemy were turned back according to this sign of the cross, and a mighty victory had been won, God said to Moses, "Write this down for me as a memorial for future generations!"[11]

Thus the Lord, too, in his Incarnation, defeated the tyrant by the cross. The first human being, Adam, caused death to grow from moist wood. The Lord, through dry wood, made life to sprout again, furnishing his faithful ones the invincible weapon of the Cross, just as he said a few moments earlier: "If anyone wishes to come after me, let him deny himself and lift up his cross, and follow me."[12] Jesus said this, before all others, to his own disciples. For he knew they were cowardly before the resurrection, timid in spirit, overcome by human emotions; they considered only this present life, full of light and enjoyment, to be the true one, but never considered rebirth to another life, superior to this present one. Therefore when the Lord wanted to show them that the reborn life is more wonderful than this present life, he fulfilled it before their eyes.

For they had just heard him say, "I must go down to Jerusalem, and suffer many things and be killed, and on the third day rise."[13]

---

[10]Timothy may mean by *archē* here the priestly leadership of Israel.

[11]Exod 17.14.

[12]Lk 9.23. In contrasting the "moist wood" of Adam's tree with the "dry wood" of the cross, Timothy seems to be alluding to Jesus' words to his distraught women followers, on the way to Calvary, in Lk 23.31: "If they do these things when the wood is green, what will they do when it is dry?"

[13]Cf. Lk 9.22.

When the Apostles heard this and took it in, they conversed in bitter words with each other, and said, "These are new commands from the Teacher! He is speaking in figurative language to us when he says, 'I must go up to Jerusalem and be killed.' Where will our hope be grounded? It seems as if we have followed him in vain, left our boats and our nets and the care of our households in vain! We felt like immortals, convinced we were disciples of one who raised the dead, and now our hope has been turned around! He must be speaking figuratively when he says to us, 'It is necessary for me to be killed, and on the third day rise.' If he will be raised after three days, why must he also die? And why does he hand himself over to his enemies? If he will be raised from the dead in three days, these are empty words! Who has ever risen from the dead? Elijah was taken up, and did not reappear; Moses died, and is covered with earth in an unknown grave, where he still remains. Yet no one was found to be more powerful than he while he was alive, [no one more celebrated for his deeds.][14] Neither of these men has found an equal. And is our master going to be betrayed, as he tells us, and that to undergo a violent death—and will he be raised after three days? He is deceiving us, like ignorant bumpkins! Nothing of what he has said is going to happen!"

Because of this harsh attitude of the Apostles, the Lord, who was completely certain of the future, did not leave his disciples swimming in the tidal wave of unbelief. Rather, he quickly brought them to certainty, while the Apostles were still on earth, still in the body, and revealed to them the divine power of the resurrection, which bodily eyes could not bear: setting before them Moses and Elijah, who were dead, as the disciples reckoned in their minds—adorned in unapproachable glory—and discussing in their own normal voices the event of his crucifixion in Jerusalem, so that [the disciples] might remain steadfast, supported by what they saw and heard. And that this might happen, they heard the Lord saying to them just

---

[14]The phrase in square brackets is supplied from Gretser's Latin translation; the Greek text, published in the *Patrologia*, seems to have omitted some words.

before this, "Truly I say to you"–O, the great goodness of the Lord! He swears an oath to those who are wavering!—that is, with an oath I say to you; to the degree that you do not believe my words, I now assure you: "Truly I say to you, there are some of those now standing here, who will not taste death until they see the Kingdom of God." What kind of kingdom? The glory to be inherited by the faithful, after their departure from here—the glory that is to come!

What does the Evangelist say? "After these words, about eight days passed."[15] The Lord's assurance came quickly, he soon granted what they yearned for. "For Jesus took Peter and James and John, and went up a mountain to pray. And while he was praying, the form of his face changed, and his garment became white like lightning. And behold, two men stood beside him, who were Moses and Elijah. And appearing in glory, they spoke about his departure, which he was going to accomplish in Jerusalem."[16] What departure? The suffering on the cross, the contempt he suffered there, the beating appropriate for slaves, the salvation of the thief on his right. To whom did they speak? To those around them: Peter and James and John. They were saying to them: because you do not obey the Lord, trust us, at least, who are his servants! "But Peter and those with him were weighed down with sleep. And then, waking up, they saw his glory, and the two men speaking with him. And Peter said to him, 'Master, it is good for us to be here. Let us build three tabernacles—one for you, one for Moses, and one for Elijah—not knowing what he was saying! And while he was saying this, a cloud came and overshadowed them; and they were afraid when they entered under the cloud. And behold, a voice came out of the cloud, saying: 'This is my Son, the Beloved, in whom I am well pleased! Listen to him.'"[17]

What do you say, my friend? See what great assurance the Lord Christ offered only eight days later, in his own person, to those who are still living on earth in doubt, letting the inaccessible beauty of his

[15]Luke 9.28.
[16]Luke 9.28–31.
[17]Luke 9.32–35.

own divinity appear to them—not in its full greatness, but as much as the unruly eyes of human beings were able to bear. In the same way, he set Moses and Elijah before them, blooming more brightly than in their former lives, conversing with him about the coming indications of his cross. Their purpose was that the Apostles might understand that, in their opinion, death never rules over the just, and that they should hate this present life, according to the saying that derives from God, "The just live forever, and their reward is in the Lord, and their hope is with the Most High, for they will conquer in the struggle against their enemies."[18] As a result, Peter was encouraged by the sight, and from that point was changed from sorrow to joy, gazing at his Master and his inaccessible glory, as he was accompanied by Moses and Elijah. And how did they know that it was Moses and Elijah? From the signs: for Elijah stood there with his chariot, and Moses carried the stone tablets.[19] And why was it necessary that he brought up only these three, but none of the prophets except Moses and Elijah? And why was it these three, and those two? That the saying of Paul might be fulfilled, "In the name of Jesus every knee will bend, of those in heaven and on earth and under the earth."[20] From those under the earth he led Moses up; from those in heaven he brought Elijah down; from those on the earth he established Peter and James and John.

After that, Peter—changed from sorrow to joy—approached the Lord and said, "Master, it is good for us to be here. Let us build here three tabernacles, one for you, one for Moses, one for Elijah."[21] "From what is taking place, we understand now the unconquerable glory of your Kingdom. Why then do you alarm us by saying, 'I must go up to Jerusalem, and be killed, and on the third day rise?' Why

[18]Wisdom 5.16.

[19]The author seems to imagine the scene iconically, with the main characters each carrying with them some major symbol from the Biblical narrative concerning them. Elijah's chariot is, of course, the fiery chariot in which he was taken up to heaven, while Moses' tablets are the two stone plaques on which the ten commandments were engraved by God's finger.

[20]Phil 2.10.

[21]Luke 9.33.

do you offer yourself to your enemies for death? It is good for us to be here. No one will dare to come up here—neither one of the high priests, nor any of the numerous crowd. And if they come up, they will arrive as witnesses against themselves. For you have here those powerful commanders of the armies, Moses and Elijah! Elijah will make fire come down from heaven on them, and Moses will send them all to suffocate in a tomb, as the Pharaohs did! 'It is good for us to be here. Let us now make three tabernacles, one for you, one for Moses, one for Elijah.'"

But the Lord said to him, "What are you saying, Peter? Have you decided to construct three tabernacles? Do you treat me in the same way as them? Do you make the master equal to the slaves? You offer an opportunity for blasphemy to Arius and Eunomius,[22] in wanting to make my dwelling place with creatures! Shall I dwell here, even though it is outside my Father's bosom? I come along with my humanity, but I am not circumscribed in my power, which has no beginning! What are you thinking of, Peter? Will you attempt to do what you have not learned? You learned to weave nets, and now will you make me dwell in a tent? Shall I obey your will, or shall I save the world? Shall I remain here? And who will raise Adam from his sleep? Who will set Eve free?[23] Who will redeem the world? Do you care only for yourself, but nothing for the whole universe?" This is why the Evangelist, making apologies for Peter, writes, "He did not know what he was saying!" And he was pardoned, because he spoke without understanding.

[22] By the end of the fourth century, Arius of Alexandria, who argued that the Son or Word of God was the first of creatures, formed by the unknown God to be the mediator of creation, had been almost universally recognized as one of the arch-heretics of Christianity. Eunomius, bishop of Cyzicus from the 350s, attempted to recast Arius' position in more rigorously philosophical arguments, but was himself branded a heretic, as well, by the Cappadocian Fathers and at the Council of Constantinople in 381. From here to the end of the sermon, Timothy is mainly concerned to oppose all forms of Arianism.

[23] The image of Jesus redeeming Adam and Eve by his obedience unto death is sounded by Irenaeus (AH 3.19[?]), and is poignantly and dramatically developed in a late-fourth-century sermon on Jesus' descent into the realm of the dead, ascribed to Epiphanius of Salamis (CPG 3786; PG 43.440–464, esp. 461–464).

So when the Lord had rebuked Peter, Peter—I imagine—replied: "Why, Lord, did you, in your great adaptability, accept the role of dwelling in a tent, even before the time of grace? Did you not enter Abraham's tent? Did not the Patriarch receive you as guest? Did he not prepare a calf for you? Did he not bring you everything you desired? Did you not reward him with the gift of a blessing?" And the Lord said to Peter: "The story is true: I went into Abraham's tent, and when I went in I stayed there. But think of his faith and knowledge, and of the victory of Abraham. He recognized me with two angels; but surely he did not prepare three tents? Surely he did not class me with my servants? Did he not prepare a single table to receive the Lord? Imitate Abraham, and so make your tabernacle!"

What does the Evangelist say? "And behold, a bright cloud over-shadowed them."[24] Whom did it overshadow? Moses and Elijah. And why? To make the Apostles sure in what glory they had come to share. And they were afraid when they entered under the cloud; the Apostles trembled when they encountered this overpowering glory. And after they entered into it, the Father's voice was heard from above, saying, "This is my Son, the Beloved."[25] Consider the Father's voice, and how he kept it from being confused [with earthly voices]. For while Moses and Elijah were present, he did not say, "This is my Son, the Beloved," so that the Apostles might not form strange thoughts and think it was one or the other of them; but after they had become invisible, then he revealed his true Son, saying, "This is my Son, the Beloved."

Let the Jews come to him, let people from every heresy come, let those who adulterate the divinity come, and let them hear the voice of authority: "This is my Son, the Beloved, in whom I am well pleased." He is unique; he is not as the Greeks thought, in their confusion, when they thought of many gods. This one, whom I reveal to you from heaven—not the one whom the foolish Jews have expected. This one, who is of one substance with me, his Father, in

[24]Luke 9.34.
[25]Luke 9.35.

every way—he is not like those whom some heretics have reduced to a slave! This one pre-existed along with me, before the ages. This one put the world together by his Spirit. This one shaped Adam, when he and I together planned to make human beings. This one took mud from the earth and formed the human person. This one transported Enoch in a marvelous way from human company. This one is seen and understood. This one exists with me, and stands on the mountain. This one has walked in your company, and is not separated from the one who begot him. This one is without time, without beginning, without successor, eternal, unchangeable, incomprehensible, ineffable, beyond thought. This one is; he did not come to be, he was not created. He is by nature, not by grace. He is, without having his being in time. He is, for he also was and existed before. For I did not become Father in time, but I always exist as Father. And if I am always Father, then this one is always Son,[26] and the Holy Spirit also always is—who is adored along with me and with the Son, and glorified along with us, always and to the unending ages of ages. Amen."

[26]Here Timothy summarizes an argument developed at length by Athanasius, especially in his three *Orations against the Arians*: to speak of the God of Israel as Father already implies that he is in a relationship of generativity towards the Son.

Anonymous Incomplete Homily (7th-9th Century)

This fragment—apparently the final part of a homily on the New Testament story of the Transfiguration of Christ, of which the opening is missing—appears on two leaves that form part of a miscellaneous manuscript now in the Biblioteca Marciana in Venice: Venetus Marcianus, Append. II, 17 (*olim* Nanianus 38): see discussion in Elpidio Mioni, *Codices graeci manuscript divi Marci Venetiarum* I/1 (Rome, 1967) 101. This part of the manuscript was copied in the ninth century, and first published by Michel Aubineau in 1967. This brief text is followed, in the manuscript, by the beginning of a homily for the feast of the Exaltation of the Cross, ascribed to Pantoleon, "presbyter of the monastery of the Byzantines," a fragment already published in PG 98.1265 B3—C3; it is possible that this is the same Pantoleon, called "deacon and chartophylax," who is the author of the other homily under his name that we have translated in this collection. Aubineau considers the possibility of suggesting an author, but comes up with no satisfactory conclusions. The unknown preacher is clearly a person of considerable rhetorical fluency, although his mannered style tends to overstatement and is not always clear in meaning. There is no indication in the text that it was given at a liturgical celebration of the feast; Aubineau conjectures a date of composition somewhere between the seventh and ninth centuries.

An Incomplete Greek Homily
on the Transfiguration[1]
(Seventh or eighth century?)

... [John the Baptist], whom, because of this outspokenness, Herod had arrested and beheaded with the sword.[2] The one who will precede the glorious second coming, Elijah, will signal the one who is to come: rightly rebuking those who remain faithless until the consummation of the world, and challenging the raw violence of the tyrant, laying the Antichrist's plan bare and bringing the mystery of human sin into view by his own witness, signaling the climactic contest of the race, defeating the impious one by a noble effort of resistance, and indicating the glorious presence and true coming of Christ. For these reasons it is appropriate that Moses and Elijah stood next to the Savior in his transfiguration, together amazed at the manner of his passion and his "exodus" in Jerusalem.[3] Peter—the one who was always boiling with love for Jesus, always quick with his tongue because of the inner longing that saved him—gazed upon the mountain shrouded with clouds and raised high above daily human activities, an unreachable place filled with blessed light; he saw there an appropriate place to cultivate the

[1]The Greek text of this present work, which lacks a beginning in the manuscript, was first published by Michel Aubineau, "Une homélie grecque inedite sur la Transfiguration," *Analecta Bollandiana* 85 (1967) 401–427.

[2]The preacher here seems to be referring to the story of John the Baptist's execution, in Mark, where Jesus identifies John as Elijah, returned to accomplish his eschatological mission. It could also be a reference to the Apostle James, drawn from Acts 12.1–2; but the point here seems to be to explain the presence of Elijah on Mount Thabor with the glorified Jesus.

[3]Luke 9.31.

philosophic life,[4] separated from the tumult of the crowd and from disturbance. Honeyed moisture drizzled down upon [the mountaintop], and life-giving drops from the highest heavens fell as rain; it shone more brilliantly than snow—for what he saw was an image and outline of the coming Kingdom. So Peter, as he reflected on it in the midst of our daily life, considered the mountain a place full of happiness, brimming over (one might say) with much blessedness, especially since it was free from all care, and from the chance fate experienced by the disordered multitude, and from the ruin that people endure every day who risk living in the villages and fields and cities. At that moment, as he gazes on Jesus shining as brightly as the sun, no longer despised by the mass of humanity, and probably surrounded by the beautiful spectacle of the powers on high, and as he sees the prophets standing by him, those most suited to be his companions, he says to Christ: "Lord, it is good for us to be here,[5] in this place where we see your glory, radiant with a pure and unadulterated flash of splendor; for down below, everything is overflowing with gloom and depravity. The cloud of ignorance, hung before us without any order, blears the soul's eye with its density; we are hampered, bound by the great evil around us, and are not permitted now to gaze on the true splendor of the Kingdom, nor can we now understand its worth—being overwhelmed, one might say, with the material aspect of being human. So, then, by right of discipleship, let me pose the question: 'Give us permission, and we will make three tabernacles—one for you, one for Moses, and one

[4] In his homily on the Transfiguration scene in Matthew's Gospel, John Chrysostom has already pointed out Peter's "philosophic" inclinations, which come to light here. Since the rise of the monastic movement in the fourth century, *philosophia* primarily referred to purposeful ascetical practice: see Anne-Marie Malingrey, *Philosophia. Étude d'un groupe des mots dans la littéterature grecque, des présocratiques au IVe siècle après J.-C.* (Paris: Klincksieck, 1961). Pierre Hadot has shown, more recently, that ancient philosophy always was understood to have a largely practical purpose, freeing young minds, by carefully structured "spiritual exercises" of reflection and self-criticism, to pursue virtue and civic service: see his *What Is Ancient Philosophy?* (trans. Michael Chase; Cambridge, MA: Harvard, 2002), and *Philosophy as a Way of Life* (trans. Michael Chase; Oxford/New York: Blackwell, 1995).

[5] Matt 17.4.

for Elijah."[6] For we should not build one for all three—it is not right for the Master to dwell in a single tabernacle with his servants!"

Peter said this as in a vision. But a "bright cloud" suddenly moved over them,[7] and he ceased his words, as he offered[8] to make a tabernacle on the mountain for the immaculate King, [the Lord] of uncircumscribed power. Even as he spoke his faltering words, a voice from heaven terrified him, more powerful than thunder and lightning, which said: 'This is my Son, my Beloved,[9] who is so despised by [all of] you, who for your sake has put on himself such limitation, and who out of love for the world has appeared in human form." And when they heard this testimony, those who were with Peter fell face down on the ground in fear, beating their breasts and shaken by great confusion. For the whole heaven emitted a brilliant, radiant sound as of a waterfall, so that the whole space of the mountains around them was overwhelmed as by an earthquake, rocked by the divine sound; and the foundations of the mountains were shaken along with the rocks themselves, so that the Apostles, agitated by the breath of the Spirit, kept close to the ground, terrified at the strange voice and unable to bear the brilliance of unlimited light.[10]

So the Savior took pity on them, as they were cast into a state of trembling; he took them by the hand and raised them up, saying, "Do not be afraid[11] when you hear the words of the immortal voice, and catch a glimpse of the Kingdom, as in an image or a holy picture. For this is a testimony to your progress, the reward of virtuous souls, which you have gained by your virtuous way of life, as a pledge of renown. For see, as he said who spoke of old,[12] I myself, in fact, said

[6] Matt 17.4.

[7] Matt 17.5.

[8] Reading *prospherontos*, agreeing with *Petros*, rather than the manuscript's *prospheronti*.

[9] Matt 17.5.

[10] The author describes the Apostles' experience in dramatic, vivid terms reminiscent of the Apocalyptic tradition. He seems to understand the event as the beginning of the Kingdom of God.

[11] See Matt 17.8.

[12] It is not clear to whom Jesus is supposed to be referring here—perhaps Moses

to you only yesterday: 'There are some of those standing here who will not taste death until they see the Son of Man in his glory.'[13] Arise, let us go from here[14] to the struggle we have undertaken, to the conclusion of the divine plan! For the one you see shining in glory, and attested by the Father's voice, is the one you will see handed over into the hands of the chief priests, and being put to the trial of blow and insults, and coming once again, after his death, in glory."

These were the Savior's words to the disciples then, and today these are the trustworthy contents of their teachings to us. If we believe them, they will join us together within the immortal ramparts of his Kingdom, in Christ Jesus our Lord, to whom be glory for the ages of ages. Amen.

or Elijah in the Old Testament, perhaps God, who has planned from the start of human history to send his Son as redeemer.

[13]Matt 16.28.

[14]See John 14.31.

ANASTASIUS OF SINAI

This homily (CPG 7753) is one of eight surviving homilies ascribed to Anastasius of Sinai, the seventh-century monk and writer better known for his eclectic collection of essays and sources intended to be a handbook to orthodox faith, and known as the *Hodegos* or *Guide*. Little is known of Anastasius' life, beyond that he was a learned defender of Chalcedonian Christology, who lived for a time in several monastic communities in Egypt and Syria. He was a monk, and later abbot, of the monastery on Mt Sinai during the seventh century, then dedicated to the Theotokos and re-dedicated in the ninth century to St Catherine of Alexandria. The historian Procopius, writing in the mid-sixth century, describes the foundation of the Sinai Monastery by Justinian, in *De Aedificiis* 5.8.1–9. Through its associations with the theophanies experienced by both Moses and Elijah, Sinai is a location closely linked with the Gospel story of Jesus' transfiguration.

This homily is the earliest witness we have to a liturgical celebration of the feast of the Transfiguration of the Lord, and dates apparently from the second half of the seventh century. The Georgian calendar of Jerusalem, which represents the liturgical celebrations of the Church in Palestine in the middle of the seventh century, already lists a feast of the Transfiguration of the Lord for August 6; Anastasius' homily was apparently given during an early celebration of that feast. The celebration was adopted throughout the Eastern Empire, at the latest by the time of Emperor Leo the Wise (886–911); soon afterwards it was gradually integrated into the calendar of the Western Church as well. Here Anastasius not only emphasizes the importance of the Transfiguration event as a revelation of Christ's identity as Son of God and Savior, but he also sees in it the beginning of a transformation of all those who know him in faith into a sharing of his divine beauty.

In the apse of the monastery church on Mt Sinai, there is a large mosaic of the Transfiguration scene, whose inscription allows it to be dated between 548, the year of the death of the Empress Theodora, and 565, the year of her husband Justinian's death. This scene was very likely before the eyes of Anastasius' hearers as he preached this sermon. Both this famous mosaic representation of the Mystery of the Transfiguration, and the liturgical celebration at which the Mystery was commemorated, provide the indispensable context for Anastasius' preaching. For details of the history of this famous mosaic icon, and for an analysis of its symbolism, see Andreas Andreopoulos, *Metamorphosis. The Transfiguration in Byzantine Theology and Iconography* (Crestwood, NY: St Vladimir's Seminary Press, 2005) 127–144. See also John Elsner, "The Viewer and the Vision: the Case of the Sinai Apse," *Art History* 17 (1994) 81–102, for a captivating reflection on the spiritual and visual effect this mosaic must have had on worshippers in the late Patristic era.

ANASTASIUS,
MONK AND PRESBYTER OF SINAI
Homily on the Transfiguration[1]

By our holy Father, Anastasius of Mount Sinai: an oration on the holy Transfiguration of Christ our God, delivered on this Holy Mountain on this very day.

"How terrible is this place,"[2] I will cry out on the Festival of the Mountain,[3] joining myself to the Patriarch Jacob; for like him, I see a ladder, as it were, reaching its way from earth to heaven, with the ladder supported[4] on the ridge that crowned the mountain; so, gripped by amazement at the vision, I cry, "How terrible is this place! This is nothing else but the house of God and the gate of heaven!"[5] This is the gate from which the Father bore witness from above, the gate in which Christ, the sun of justice, shone forth; the mountain on which

---

[1]The Greek text of this sermon has been edited critically, if in a provisional way, by A. Guillou, in an article treating more broadly of the Sinai monastery and its theological history: "Le monastère de la Théotokos au Sinaï," *Mélanges d'archéologie et d'histoire* 67 (1955) 216–258; text of homily: 237–257. The text, however, seems not to be in a good state, and the text of some passages is uncertain.

[2]Gen 28.17.

[3]By referring to the liturgical celebration as "the Festival of the Mountain," Anastasius seems to be connecting Mount Tabor with Mount Sinai—the place of the event itself and the place of the liturgy—at the very beginning of his homily. The comparison of other Biblical mountains, as places of promise, with Tabor, as a mountain where fulfillment is revealed in Christ, continues through the first several paragraphs.

[4]Reading *estērigmenēs* for *estērigmenēn*, as printed in Guillou's text. It is significant that Anastasius puts so much emphasis, here at the beginning of his sermon, on Jacob's ladder. John Climacus (= John "of the Ladder"), as a hermit in the Sinai desert in the late sixth century, had written his classic work on the spiritual "ascent" to God by the "ladder" of ascetical and spiritual practice and was elected abbot of the monastery there, probably several decades before Anastasius took that role himself.

[5]Gen 28.17.

the stone cut from the mountain was revealed;[6] the mountain which the angels celebrate in song; the mountain about which the prophets speak; the mountain which the holy singer proclaims; the mountain enlightening fishermen; the mountain making the foolish wise; the mountain about which David cried out when he said, Christ has "led them to his holy mountain"[7]; the mountain which your right hand founded; the mountain fat like cheese;[8] the mountain which God has been pleased to make known, and to dwell in it.[9] Because of this mountain "the mountains leap for joy and the hills rejoice,"[10] because of it "the valleys are covered, the glens burst into bloom."[11] This mountain the torrents adorn; the rivers clap their hands for it,[12] the seas honor it; the clouds thunder their approval, the birds voice their praise for it. This mountain is the place of mysteries, this is the place of the unspeakable; this rock is the rock of hidden things, this summit is the summit of the heavens. Here the signs of the Kingdom are shown beforehand, here the mysteries of the crucifixion are communicated in advance; here the beauty of the Kingdom is revealed, here the descent of the glorified Christ's second coming is anticipated. On this mountain, the brilliant radiance of the just is shown in shadows; on this mountain, the good things to come are presented in image, as if they were here. This mountain proclaims the coming rapture of the just in the clouds,[13] by means of the cloud that surrounds it; this mountain shapes today, without any deception, the process of our own being shaped and conformed to the image of Christ.

Today he forms the image of the earthly man into the image of heavenly beauty, and transfers it to Mount Thabor. Therefore I am

[6]Dan 2.34.

[7]Ps 42.3 (LXX).

[8]Ps 67.15–16 (LXX). This is the way "the mountains of Bashan" is translated in the LXX.

[9]Ibid.

[10]Ps 113.4, 6 (LXX).

[11]Ps 64.13 (LXX).

[12]Ps 97.8 (LXX).

[13]I Thess 4.17; cf. Matt 24.30–31.

justified in saying again, "How terrible is this place; this is nothing else but the house of God and the gate of heaven"[14]—and properly so! Today "Thabor and Hermon shout out together,"[15] and call the world to the fullness of joy. The land of Zabulon and the land of Naphthali[16] make festival with one voice, and lead the dance for all people under the sun; Galilee and Nazareth dance today, and begin a rural celebration; Mount Tabor rejoices in the festival, too, and by renewing all creation, draws it towards God. For today the Lord has truly appeared on the mountain; today the old nature belonging to Adam—once made in the image of God, but dimmed to resemble the shapes of idols—is transformed in shape once again, transfigured to its ancient beauty in God's image and likeness. Today, on the mountain, an aimless, idolatrous nature that had wandered into the mountains[17] has been altered, never to change again, and now sparkles with the shining brilliance of the divinity.

Today, on the mountain, he who was wrapped in those sad, depressing garments of skin has put on a divinely-woven robe, "wrapping himself in light as in a garment."[18] Today, on Mount Thabor, the joyous state of the coming city and kingdom has appeared, in a way that preserves their secrets. Today—miraculously—on the mountain, the heralds of the old and the new covenants have come to stand on both sides of God, having become the recipients of wondrous mysteries. Today on Mount Thabor, the Mystery of the cross, working life through death, has been sketched out. Just as on Golgotha, [he stood] "between two living creatures,"[19] conformed to a cross, so here he stands between Moses and Elijah in a way conformed to God. The present festival reveals another Sinai—or rather, a mountain much more precious than Sinai in its miraculous

[14]Gen 28.17.

[15]Ps 88.13 (LXX).

[16]Matt 4.13–16; cf. Ps 67.28 (LXX).

[17]Anastasius seems to be referring to the Old Testament convention that the sanctuaries of the pagan gods were in "high places" in the mountains.

[18]Ps 103.2 (LXX).

[19]Hab 3.2 (LXX); cf. Mark 15.27 and par.

reality, surpassing those symbolic, shadowy visions of God with divine revelations that are closely modeled on them.

Just as types were sketched out there that anticipated later realities, so on this mountain truth appears. There we encountered mist,[20] here the sun; there darkness, here a cloud of light; there the Law of the Decalogue,[21] here the eternal Word who exists before all words; there fleshly riddles, here divine things. There, on the mountain, the tablets were broken because of impious behavior,[22] here hearts are made wise for their salvation. Then water came forth out of the rock of unbelief,[23] but now the spring of deathless life bubbles forth. There a staff put forth shoots,[24] here the cross bursts into bloom. There a quail comes down from above[25] to presage punishment, here a dove comes down from above to promise salvation; there the Hebrew Mary[26] plays her cymbal in a mystic sign, here the Lord's Mary brings forth her child in a divine way.[27] There Moses loosed the sandal from his feet,[28] anticipating the end of the Law's worship; here John does not loose it,[29] clearly confirming the bond of union between God the Word and our mortal, skin-covered nature. There Elijah hid from the face of Jezebel;[30] here Elijah gazes on God, face to face.

[20] See Ex 19.16–18.

[21] Ex 20.1–17. "Decalogue" means literally "ten words" or "ten sayings."

[22] Ex 32.19.

[23] Num 20.2–11.

[24] Num 17.8.

[25] Lit. "mother quail" (*ortygomētra*). See Ex 16.13; Num 11.31–32; Ps 104.40 (LXX). The "punishment" Anastasius is referring to is the Lord's anger at the people's thoughtlessness and greed, which led to a plague immediately after they had eaten the quails God had sent down upon them: see Num 11.33–34.

[26] I.e., Moses' sister Miriam, in Ex 15.20. Both she and the mother of Jesus share the same Hebrew name, Mariam.

[27] At the time of Anastasius, the monastic settlement on Sinai, with its Church, was dedicated to Mary, Mother of God.

[28] Ex 3.3.

[29] Adding *ou*, "not," to "here John loosens"; this is missing from Guillou's text, but needs to be there to maintain the sense. See Luke 3.16.

[30] I Kg 19.1–18.

Mount Sinai did not open up the land of promise for Moses, but Thabor led Moses into the land of promise. For reconciliation with God and the forgiveness of the charges against us came to belong to human nature through Jesus; the co-eternal Word of God the Father wanted to show that humanity had been cleansed of the serpent's venom, which had been emptied against him, and he revealed this Mystery to his disciples on Mount Thabor. For when, wishing to put before them his words about the Kingdom and his second, glorious coming, he spoke words of prophecy (and perhaps they were imperfectly disposed towards what had first been said to them about the Kingdom, and were exclusively focused on the things they idly considered in their own minds), he wanted to convince them from present experience of what was to happen, he mysteriously worked a revelation for them on Mount Thabor, as in an image. [It was] a prophetic preview of the Kingdom of heaven, as if he were saying to them: "So that the passage of time may not, perhaps, create unbelief in your hearts, 'Amen, I say to you'—quickly, immediately—'there are some of those standing here and listening to me who will not taste death before they see the Son of Man coming in the glory of his Father.'"[31] And revealing once again that action is for him simultaneous with his willing, the Evangelist says that "After six days, Jesus took Peter and James and John and led them up a high mountain by themselves and was transfigured before their eyes, and his face shone like the sun, his garments became white as light, and behold, Moses and Elijah appeared to them, speaking with him."[32]

These are the divine prodigies behind the present festival; what we celebrate here, on this mountain now, is for us, too, a saving Mystery. This sacred initiation into the Mystery of Christ, this public solemnity, gathers us together. So that we might come inside the ineffable sanctuary, and might enter the place of Mysteries along with those chosen ones who were inspired to speak God's words, let us listen to a divine, most sacred voice, as it seems to invite us from the peak of the

[31]Mark 9.1; Matt 16.28; Lk 9.27.
[32]Matt 17.1–4.

mountain above us, inviting us with strong words of persuasion and saying, "Come, let us go up to the mountain of the Lord,[33] on the day of the Lord—in the place of the Lord and in the house of our God." [Our hope is] that, bathed in a vision of him, flooded with light, we might be changed for the better and joined together as one; and that, grasping hold of the light in light, we might cry out: "How fearful is this place! This is nothing other than the house of God, this is the gate of heaven!"[34] This is the place towards which we must hasten, I make bold to say, since Jesus, who dwells there and who has gone up to heaven before us, is our guide on the way.[35] With him, let us also flash like lightning before spiritual eyes, renewed in the shape of our souls and made divine, transformed along with him in order to be like him, always being deified, always changing for the better—leaping up the mountain slopes more nimbly than powerful deer,[36] soaring higher than spotless doves, lifted up to the summit with Peter and James and John, walking on clouds with Moses and Elijah—so that the Lord might say of us, as well: "There are some of those standing here who will not taste death until they see the Son of man coming" to them "in the glory of his Father."[37]

Let us run forward boldly and brightly, then, let us enter into the cloud—this one becoming Moses and that one Elijah, this one James and that one John! Be lifted up like Peter, to a vision, a mental image, of God; be changed by a good and holy transformation, leave the world behind, depart from the earth, abandon the flesh. Let go of this creation, and go over to the Creator, to whom Peter, in his ecstasy, says, "Lord, it is good for us to be here."[38] How right you

[33] Is 2.3.

[34] Gen 28.17 (LXX).

[35] The word Anastasius uses here for "guide on the way," *hodegos*, is also the title of his most famous work, a collection of documents intended to serve as a handbook of orthodox belief on the subjects of Christ and the Trinity.

[36] The Greek text here is not entirely clear, and is marked with oboloi by André Guillou, its editor. Anastasius may be referring to antelopes or mountain goats, such as are found in the Sinai desert; see Ps 103.18 (LXX).

[37] Matt 16.28 and par.

[38] Matt 17.4 and par.

are, Peter! Truly it is good for us to be here with Jesus, and to remain with him for endless ages! What could be more blessed, more lofty, or more precious than this, to be with God and to be like God in form—to be in the light? So then, let each of us, who has received God in his heart, and who has been transfigured into that divine form, say in our joy: "It is good for us to be here, where everything is full of light, where there is joy and good spirits and exultation, where everything in our hearts is peaceful and calm and free from conflict, where God is to be seen. Here, in the heart, he makes his dwelling with the Father, here he comes close to us and says, 'Today salvation has come to this house;[39] here all the treasures of eternal blessing are gathered along with Christ and stored away; here the first-fruits of all the coming ages are stored, their images sketched out as in a mirror.'"

Peter tasted some of this within himself, and bounded for joy in his soul; he exulted, and left worldly things completely behind. For he perceived in himself a kind of divine enlightenment, a mysterious surge of energy; he perceived a certain strange, unaccustomed joy, a divine leap of exultation. He saw, insofar as he was able to see them, natures and forms and bodiless ideas, better than one can normally perceive. He saw the beauties of incorruption and freedom from passion, and the flashing glory of immortality. He saw sparks of the divine sunshine of the regeneration to come—all of them indistinctly, as in a kind of dream: the kingdoms and civilizations of a world beyond us; the extraordinary beauty of our inheritance, its glory; the conditions and blending of things, the things that rejoice our hearts, the comprehension and enlightenment; the things that cause a good spirit; the gifts that will come and will remain; the eternal joys, the intoxication that needs no wine; the deathless life, the music of the mind; the mystic festivals, the celebrations that bring us to God; the joy of being richly blessed, in the land of the living, with the Kingdom of heaven.[40] So Peter, who holds the keys

[39]Lk 19.9.

[40]This long list of the joyful, glorious aspects of Christian eschatological hope

of the Kingdom where these things are found, opened the door and entered into its divine vestibule. With his spiritual eyes enlightened and opened, he saw, as much as it is possible to see, those dwelling-places and tabernacles on high; he saw the porches where there is no grief, the spouses betrothed to Christ, the unwedded bridegroom;[41] he saw the couches[42] of the incorruptible and endless banquet, he saw the thrones of invisible glory, he saw the crowns woven of the stuff of immortality, he saw the undying torches, he saw the springs flooding forth light, he saw those delicacies that never fail. And as if he had touched them with a finger and tasted them, the leader of the Apostles was moved completely in soul towards all that was there: he was completely altered in his whole heart, completely left his normal way of life, passed over completely towards God, was completely beside himself, was completely filled with light and stupefied with divine wine,[43] was completely possessed by glory, astonishingly and ecstatically overcome by the truth. He received the ability to forget this world and the things within it completely, and cried out to his Master with that blessed, celebrated phrase, "Lord, it is good for us to be here—not realizing (as Scripture puts it) what he was saying."[44]

Peter, the rock of faith, speaks to Christ, the rock, on this rocky mountaintop. Along with the chief spokesmen of the New Covenant, Moses was also there, that divine steward of the Mysteries, who articulated the Old Law; along with Elijah the Thesbite, he sped through the sparkling upper air from Sinai to Thabor, as from power

sketches out some of the "sparks of the divine sunshine" Anastasius envisages as elements of heavenly bliss.

[41]This phrase, "unwedded bridegroom," echoes the often-repeated phrase of the famous *Akathistos* hymn addressed to Mary, which was probably composed around the year 500 and was doubtless well known by Anastasius' time: "Hail, unwedded bride!"

[42]Reading *anakliseis* for *anaklēseis*, as given in the manuscripts and Guillou's edition. Anastasius is clearly portraying the details of the heavenly banquet.

[43]Taking the reading of MS E here (Cod. Parisinus Graecus 1504, of the 12th century).

[44]Lk 9.33. Anastasius interprets the Gospels' comment that Peter did not know what he was saying as a sign of mystical ecstasy.

to power. Moses, then, entered the land of promise as if he were summoned from some exile, the receiver of the law coming up to[45] his Lord on Mount Thabor, bearing the tablets of the law; the servant stood before his master in ecstasy, since he was gazing on divine power in human form. So he left his human consciousness behind, gazing on as those signs from heaven, which had distantly pointed to Christ, now were transformed into the actuality of truth. He was present in an exalted state, already tasting of what he had longed for from of old. He was present, standing at the right of the right hand of the Most High, a traveler arriving quickly from afar. As once he had gazed on the bush, speechless and entranced by the Lord's presence, so now he gazed again on a bush, living and green in the analogous fire of God's presence in ensouled flesh. So, as he comes close to it on Tabor, he no longer says, "I will cross over and see this great sight."[46] Now he is crossing over from bodily life, crossing from the time of the Law, crossing from types, crossing from shadows, crossing also from the letter—leaving Egypt behind, crossing the Red Sea, coming through the darkness, as well; leaving Horeb behind, crossing over the rock, too, passing through desert places, crossing the land of Amalek; crossing by the Ark, leaving even the tabernacle behind, letting go of circumcision; passing beyond the Jordan, going through Gebal,[47] passing by Jericho; leaving behind the temple, leaving behind sacrifice, crossing through the shadows, leaving behind blood, crossing through the slaughter of a bull,[48] crossing beyond the cherubim,[49] passing beyond what lay before and going even beyond the second law,[50] and the veil and covering and hanging of the prophets. "Now I see you who truly are and who eternally are,

[45]Reading *hēkōn*, "coming to," with manuscripts BDE, rather than *hēmōn*, "our," as Guillou prefers.

[46]Ex 3.3.

[47]Ps 82.8 (LXX).

[48]Emending *biou*, "events of life," to *boos*, "bull". Anastasius here is speaking about Christ as offering a contact with God that surpasses the temple liturgy sketched out in the Torah, ascribed to Moses.

[49]I.e., the two gold cherubim fixed as sacred ornaments to the top of the ark.

[50]I.e., the ritual prescriptions of Deuteronomy, which means "second law".

who are with the Father—you who say on the mountain, 'I am the one who is!'[51] I see this great vision: you who have long lain divinely hidden from me, now revealed as God. You are no longer hiding your face, but I see you face to face and my soul is still preserved![52] I see you, whom I have longed to see from of old, as when I said, 'May I see you and know you!'[53] For your revelation is eternal life. I see you, no longer from behind, as I bow myself down to Sinai's rock, but clearly appearing before me on the rock of Thabor; I no longer hide myself, as a human being, in the face of the rock,[54] but I see you as the loving God, hiding yourself in my form; your right hand no longer covers me with its shadow, for you are the right hand of the Most High, revealed to the world. For you are the mediator of old and new—God of old, yet newly human! You are the one who once revealed your name, invisibly, on Mount Sinai, and now are visibly revealed, transfigured on Mount Thabor. For you love to enlighten us, as the heavenly, exalted one from the eternal mountains:[55] from the holy, heavenly powers, or from the mountains of the prophets and Apostles and holy churches, whose foundations are in those holy mountains of yours, from which you have heard me! Crossing over the Law's forms of worship, now I see you in this great vision!

"You are the one who was prefigured on Sinai, and are now witnessed to and proclaimed by God on Thabor as Son. You are the one who once came down on the bush, and who swallowed up Pharaoh's power in the abyss;[56] you are the one who, with a word, made the Sea stand still that blushed red with restless waves—you stopped the world's sea of blood, shed for idols. You are the one who changed a rod, lifeless by nature, into a serpent in public view, and by it destroyed the magicians' tricks.[57] You are the one who gave the

[51] Ex 3.14.
[52] See Ex 33.20.
[53] See Ex 33.13–18.
[54] See Ex 33.21–23.
[55] See Ps 42.3 (LXX).
[56] A reference to the story of Israel's crossing of the Red Sea in Ex 15.
[57] Ex 7.8–13.

chance to breathe freely again to a people journeying on foot across a waterless desert; you revealed a rock to be capable of changing from dry to wet and from wet to dry—for you constantly form and transform our lack of form and shape for the better, by your unchanging power of transformation. Therefore you came from above to humanize and raise to life the human nature that here had lost its humanity by sin, and to raise up the tent of Adam, who had fallen. You are the new tent, planted in truth for all humanity through incorruptibility and immortality; you are the true temple, son and God of David, the father of Solomon—you who set up and founded the temple in the heavenly Jerusalem on high;[58] you are the genuine altar of atonement before the Father, on behalf of the sins of the world. You are the true washing-basin, the Savior whom the Law's basin anticipated in symbol; you are the incorruptible ark of the covenant, establishing our peace with the Father; you are the bread without leaven or seed, free of the yeast of sin; you are the true paschal Lamb, who saved the people from Egypt and the hostile forces of our bitter enemy Pharaoh, and from the nations." (So when he was waiting for you on the mountain, Moses said, "Show me your glory"—let me truly come to know you, reveal yourself to me—"if I have found favor in your sight."[59]) "For nothing in the world is more delightful to me than to see you, and to be filled with your glory, your beauty, your image, your light, your speech, your revealed presence–when your dwelling has been unveiled before men and women, which once you foreshadowed to me in Mystery.

"Therefore I adore you, I praise you, I sing to your name, because, crossing now over the darkness of the Law, I have seen this great, truly great vision. How is it that you, who said to me on Sinai, 'No human being can see my face and live,'[60] have now appeared on

---

[58] Anastasius' reading of the elements of Israel's Temple worship suggests the typological approach of Hebrews 4.14–10.18.

[59] Ex 33.17. Here Anastasius seems to forget that the passage he is developing is spoken by Moses himself, in the first person. But he quickly returns to that literary device.

[60] Ex 33.14, 17–18.

earth in flesh, face to face, and have associated with human beings? How is it that you, who are by your nature life and life-giver, are moving resolutely towards death? How is it that you, who are higher than the highest beings, are moving lower than the lowest, and making your way straight towards the dying? And what then, O Master, can the great mystery of your death really be? Surely you are eager to appear even to those who have been dead for ages; surely you wish to take charge even of our ancestors in Hades; surely you are hastening to loose Adam from his troubles. All of these things, Lord, you prefigured for me in the worship prescribed by the Law. Therefore I now eagerly loose the sandal—the inner intention—from the Law's feet: 'for the place where I am standing is holy ground,'[61] holy land and land of promise. You spoke to me about them in promise long ago, O Master, at the bush: '"Loosen the sandals from your feet"—the law—and cease walking and moving forward; "for the place in which you are standing still" and have ceased your movement "is holy ground": my presence on earth, originating in heaven, and my way towards Hades through death on the cross.'"[62]

According to Luke, Moses and Elijah spoke with Christ about all of this on the mountain, discussing "the exodus" of his soul from his body, "which he was going to accomplish in Jerusalem"[63] in the suffering of the Cross. And Elijah and Moses paid attention, the Lord taught, the disciples listened, the Father spoke from above, the cloud covered them, the mountain flashed forth light, the peak was

[61] Ex 3.5. Anastasius offers here an elaborate exegesis of Moses' gesture of removing his sandals at the burning bush. Origen and his admirers had seen this as an ascetical symbol: removing the "dead skin" of leather, a sign of the garments of mortality in which the fallen Adam and Eve wrapped themselves, in order to stand firmly on the renewed earth of the resurrection; see *Commentary on John* 6.1; *On Pascha* 37; see also Gregory of Nyssa, *Life of Moses* 2.22, 201, 208; *Commentary on the Song of Songs* 11 (ed. H. Langerbeck; GNO 6 [Leiden: Brill, 1976] 329.17–330.2). Anastasius changes the focus of the image, from Moses to the Law he represents and interprets; in removing his sandals of skin, Moses is releasing the Law's inner meaning from the tradition of its external observance.

[62] At this point Anastasius seems to give up on his attempt to address the transfigured Jesus through the mouth of Moses, and again takes up his own narrative voice.

[63] Luke 9.31.

wreathed in smoke, the rocks glowed with fire, the mountaintop was shaken, angels circulated around them, and portrayed on the spot, in symbolic anticipation, all the events of his second coming. And just as one, peering down from heaven, might survey all at once, in a single blink of the eye, everything on earth: I mean the lands, the mountains, the fields, the seas, the rivers, the springs, human beings, cities, villages, plants, animals, creeping things—in a word, every creature on earth—so also at that moment on the mountain, as their spiritual eyes were opened, the disciples saw, in a single vision, as much as they were able to see (or rather, even more than they could see) of the coming Kingdom of heaven. So that just as if they were seeing heaven spinning around and the sun darkened, the moon eclipsed and the stars falling,[64] the earth shaken and the graves opened, angels issuing forth and archangels blowing trumpets[65] and thrones set out and a river of fire drawing us away, the books opened[66] and everyone standing together in terror and confessing their sins, the Apostles at that moment were terrified by their vision. And not being able to bear it, they fell on their faces, as Luke tells us,[67] so that they were overcome by amazement and sleep—the perishable nature of their bodies not being able to gaze on incorruptibility, nor their mortal bodies able to bear, as they needed to do, the contemplation of immortality. That is why I think, myself, that perhaps Moses and Elijah, at that time, were already there in some better kind of body. They were in glory, as Scripture says, on the mountain without fear or disturbance; but the disciples fell down, overcome by some sort of heavy sleep or fainting. For Luke says, once again: "Peter and the disciples were weighed down by sleep."[68] And again, Matthew says, "When they came down from the mountain, Jesus gave them a command, 'Do not tell of the vision to anyone, until the Son of Man has

[64]See Matt 24.29–30.
[65]I Thess 4.14–16.
[66]See Rev 4.1–2; 5.1–7.
[67]Actually this detail comes from Matt 17.6.
[68]Luke 9.32.

risen from the dead'"[69]—do not tell of the vision to anyone, until [you can say] on Mount Thabor, as Moses fittingly declared, "I will cross over and see this great vision for myself!"[70]

For what is greater or more awe-inspiring than this: to see God in human form, his face shining like the sun and even more brightly than the sun, flashing with light, ceaselessly sending forth rays, radiating splendor? To see him raising his immaculate finger in the direction of his own face, pointing with it,[71] and saying to those with him there: "*So* shall the just shine in the resurrection; so shall they be glorified, changed to reveal this form of mine, transfigured to this level of glory, stamped with this form, made like to this image, to this impress, to this light, to this blessedness, and becoming enthroned with me, the Son of God." And when the angels then on the mountain heard what Christ had said, they trembled; the prophets were struck with wonder; the disciples fell faint; creation rejoiced when it heard of its transformation from corruption to incorruptibility; the mountain was filled with delight, the fields were joyful, the villages sang songs of praise; the nations came together, the peoples were exalted; the seas chanted hymns, the rivers clapped their hands; Nazareth cried out, Babylon sang a hymn, Naphthali[72] celebrated a festival; the hills leapt, the deserts bloomed, the roads helped travelers along; all things were unified, all things were filled with joy.

[69] Matt 17.9–10.

[70] Ex 3.3. Some words seem to be missing from the Greek text at this point. Anastasius' point seems to be that on Mount Thabor, as at the burning bush on Mount Sinai (which was also represented above the main Sinai mosaic of the Transfiguration), Moses leads God's people to faith in God's active presence on earth by "crossing over to see" God's present radiance for himself. To see this, however, one must already live in a transformed, glorified body, such as will be ours in the resurrection. This idea is developed in the paragraph that follows. For an explanation of the depiction of Moses in the mosaic, see Andreopoulos 128–132.

[71] This is an interesting detail of Anastasius' narration of the Transfiguration story. It may have been suggested to him by the iconography of the mosaic itself: Jesus' right hand is raised in front of his chest in blessing, three fingers pointing upwards towards his own face.

[72] In the traditional tribal lands of Israel, Mount Thabor—just west of the southern end of the Sea of Galilee—would have been at the southern extremity of the land occupied by the tribe of Naphthali.

And I, too, stand today joyfully on this holy peak, this mountain, lovingly celebrating; stretching out my hand, I cry out in a loud voice from this mountain, inviting all the mountains to worship God: Mount Ararat, Mount Gilboa, Mount Sinai, Mount Paran,[73] the mountains of the North, the mountains of the West, Mount Lebanon, the mountains of the South, the mountains of the Islands, the other mountains: worship Christ our God, bowing your peaks towards Mount Thabor! And so that many other mountains might skip for joy as well: mountains of the Jordan, mountains of Hermon, mountains of Greece, Mount Olympus, Mount Gebal,[74] Mount Arnon,[75] mountains of Epirus, mountains of Gilead, Mount Sion, Mount Golgotha, Mount of Olives—join in the songs of praise and in the joyful celebration of Christ on Mount Thabor with a single voice, singing to him together and saying: "Hail, O creator of all things, Christ our Lord, divinely born bearer of light, you who gave shape to all creation together, and who form it into something better still! Hail, Mary, living mountain of God, holier than all the saints: you who formed Christ in flesh without transforming him—Mary, country woman of Nazareth, God-bearer, Virgin Mother! Hail, holy town, sacred dwelling of God: Nazareth, before all cities and all places the first of all cities! Hail, O icon of the heavenly Kingdom, holy, all-holy Mount Thabor: beautiful with a loveliness beyond all mountains! Hail to you, too, O nearby Jordan: most divine and precious of all rivers: in your waves of joy—in your forbidding waters—you revealed, as did John the Forerunner, the rebirth that comes from God! Hail to you, too, Sea of Tiberias: at once small and yet more famous than all seas; when you were trodden upon by those dry and holy feet, you were also made holy! Hail, 'land of Zabulon and land of Naphthali, road to the sea, Galilee of the Gentiles,'[76] first

---

[73]Deut 33.2. The Greek text here reads "Mount Ekpharan," but there is no mountain by this name mentioned in the Bible. The text of Deut. 33.2, however, reads, "The Lord comes from Sinai, and hastens from (*ek*) Mount Pharan."

[74]Ps. 82.8 (LXX).

[75]See Num 21.21, 28: "the heights of the Arnon."

[76]Matt 4.13–16.

to reveal that first great light, which comes from the Father of lights! Hail, sacred gathering on the mountain of holy priests and high priests, wisely bearing the form of Christ in place of Melchisedek, and offering sacred service![77] Hail, gathering of virgins and monks equal to the angels, imitating the contemplative way of life of Elijah the Thesbite! Hail, children of Christ! Hail, boast of all the faithful peoples of the Church: for this present festive celebration is a time of joy and happiness, in which God's people has come together for this brilliant Feast of God's Mountain! Dance with one soul and one voice with the angels, move in a circle with the stars; proclaim the word with the Apostles, lead the way with Moses, cry out with Elijah; reveal the truth from the peak, thunder from the cloud, bear witness from heaven, shout from the mountaintop, trumpet forth from the rock; invite Nazareth, call Galilee together; make your festival brilliant, deck yourself with speeches of praise, shine out with lamps, skip with the mountains, dance with the maidens, resound with the sea, serve the people with the Jordan;[78] walk up on the mountaintop, celebrate on Mount Thabor with Christ, the universal King—the true God, our Lord Jesus Christ![79] For to him be glory for the ages of ages. Amen."

[77] Anastasius now begins to address the liturgical assembly before him: priests, monks, the faithful. Sinai is now the "mountain of priests" and monks.

[78] Anastasius may be thinking of the Jordan's "service" as the place of John the Baptist's preaching, and of Christ's baptism.

[79] In this final, rhetorically powerful sentence, Anastasius takes up all the details of the Gospel story in a tightly woven picture of liturgical celebration, in which Mount Sinai, where his audience sits before the icon of the Transfiguration, becomes one with Mount Tabor, Sinai's theological counterpart and the setting of the Gospel narrative, in joyful veneration of the Mystery of Christ. So the story of the Transfiguration itself is subtly transformed into a model for the Christian mission and for salvation. See Andreopoulos 138–139.

ANDREW OF CRETE

This is one of a number of elaborate homilies for liturgical feasts given by St Andrew of Crete, the bishop of Gortyna in the early decades of the eighth century. According to his ninth-century biography, Andrew was born around 660 in Damascus, and was educated in Jerusalem at the monastery of the Holy Sepulchre. He was sent as a representative of that community to Constantinople about 685, where he remained, working as the administrator of an orphanage and a hostel. He was ordained a deacon in the imperial capital, and may have been archdeacon of Hagia Sophia before being appointed bishop of Gortyna on Crete, and metropolitan of that island, at some time between 692 and 715.

A powerful artist with words, Andrew is known both for his festal discourses, such as this, and for his liturgical poetry. He is thought to be the inventor of the *canon*, an elaborate set of thematically co-ordinated hymns sung in the liturgical offices of a major feast in place of the fifteen Biblical canticles that were usually chanted. During the reign of the usurping emperor Philippicus Bardanes (711–713), who supported the monothelite position on the person of Christ, Andrew apparently made public statements favorable to that cause, which had already been recognized as a departure from orthodox faith by the Third Council of Constantinople (680–681). He later renounced that position, however, and his famous "Great Canon," still used by the Orthodox Churches during the Lenten season of preparation, may have originated as his own expression of repentance for flirting with unorthodox Christology.

A beautiful lead seal, now in the museum in Heracleon, Crete (No. 514), may commemorate Andrew's tenure on that island as metropolitan. It bears a fine head of St Titus, patron of Crete and venerated at Gortyna, on the obverse; and on the reverse, a cross surrounded by the metrical inscription, "Christ, save Andrew, metropolitan (*proedros*) of Crete." Although some scholars have dated it to the 13th century on stylistic grounds, Stephanos Xanthoudides, its original publisher, and the sigillographer Vitalien Laurent have both argued for an eighth-century origin, and see it as the actual seal of St Andrew, the only known metropolitan of Crete by that name. The versified inscription would fit well with Andrew's poetic career. See S. Xanthoudides, "Molybdinai Boullai ek tēs Krētēs," *Epetēris Hetaireias Vyzantinōn Spoudōn* 2 (1925) 44–48, esp. 47; and V. Laurent, *Corpus des Sceaux de l'Empire Byzantin* V/1 (Paris: CNRS 1963) 464–465.

Andrew is reported to have died on the island of Lesbos on July 4, 740. Although we do not know the date of this homily on the Transfiguration, it is clearly given at a celebration of the divine liturgy on the feast commemorating that event, probably in either Constantinople or Gortyna. The celebration of the feast on August 6, first attested for Jerusalem in the mid-seventh century, apparently had spread widely through the Church of the Eastern empire in the century that followed, and seems to have been universally accepted in the Greek-speaking Church by the end of the ninth century. A dense and deeply engaging work, both in thought and in style, this homily suggests that the author was familiar with the writings of both the Pseudo-Dionysius and the defenders of Chalcedonian Christology in the sixth and seventh centuries, and perhaps even with the Trinitarian thought being developed by his contemporary, John of Damascus.

ST ANDREW OF CRETE
On the Transfiguration of Christ our Lord
(Sermon 7)[1]

All of you who, by taking off the cloak of irrationality because of the
Word's self-emptying,[2] have raised up your minds from the earth
and learned to think "the things that are above,"[3] come now—if you
trust me—as I spread out before you a spiritual banquet of words:[4]
let us ascend with the Word today, as he goes up the high mountain
of the Transfiguration! Let us take off the material, shadowy life
that we wear, and put on "the robe woven from above as a single
whole,"[5] made beautiful in every part by the rays of spiritual virtue.
Christ himself, the pure goal of life, the supernatural Word of the
one who begot him, the one who came down from above for our
sakes and became a poor man in our flesh out of love for humanity,
wishes us—who are already purified in life and mind, who have been
given the spiritual wings of sincere thoughts—to make this ascent
with him. This is clear from the fact that he takes with him chosen
Apostles to be nearer in their relationship to him than ever, and leads

---

[1] The Greek text for this homily has not been critically edited, and shows some
mistakes and omissions, as published. We use, as the only available text, the seven-
teenth-century edition of François Combéfis, as it appears in PG 97.932–957.

[2] Andrew begins his homily with a play on words: to recognize the self-emptying
of the Logos in the Mystery of the Incarnation is to take off the veil of *alogia*. Divine
reason, in the flesh, makes even fleshly minds reasonable.

[3] Col 3.2.

[4] Here, as in his first homily on the feast of the Dormition of Mary (1.7), Andrew
depicts himself as host at a banquet, inviting the members of his congregation to join
in an intellectual, liturgical, and artistic feast. The resonance of such language with
the Eucharistic context is unmistakable.

[5] See John 19.23.

them up the high mountain. What is he going to do, what is he planning to teach them? By revealing to them the glory and radiance of his own divinity, more brilliant than lightning, he had, a little earlier in a mystical way, transformed the nature which had once heard the words, "You are earth, and to earth you shall return";[6] now he will reveal it in full view by his transfiguration.

This is what we celebrate in our feast today, then: the divinization of nature; its change for the better; the displacement and ascent of what conforms to nature, towards what is above nature. How and from where does this great and supernatural grace come to us? Surely in that the Godhead, which incomparably surpasses all mind and reason, has overwhelmed what is human by the Word. And God has done this by making what is anointed—according to the unwavering and underived tradition of the Mystery—precisely that which the Anointer is, and sharing [with him] his very name.[7] Only the otherness of the Unmoved is preserved immoveable in this Mystery, because of the unconfused union, according to which the more perfect element dominates.[8] To put it more precisely, the ineffable act of divinization offers this perfectly true demonstration of itself: the union and identity, in one real individual, of the elements that have come together, which we know has happened in a supernatural way from the very deepest structure of the Mystery. I am speaking here of what touches us, about the pure synthesis and substantial presence of the Word here below, for our sakes: his second birth, without a Father, from a Virgin Mother. So, according to

[6]Gen 3.19.

[7]Andrew seems to mean that the one whom Peter has just recognized as "the Christ" (Matt 16.18) is also recognized in the same verse as "Son of the living God," an identification of Jesus with the Father that is about to be confirmed in the Transfiguration scene by a voice from heaven. It is in his humanity that Jesus is "anointed" with the Spirit who makes God's presence real; but this scene shows that the person who receives this anointing in his humanity is actually himself God the Son.

[8]In speaking of the "unconfused union," in which the divine person of the Word makes the fullness of human nature his own, without annihilating it, Andrew echoes the understanding of the Christology of Chalcedon that came to dominate sixth-century Orthodoxy.

the infallible guidance by the theological writers into the mysteries, this great gift comes forth to us as from an ever-flowing spring, a limitless grace of unalloyed deification.[9]

This the angels wonder at; to this the archangels sing hymns of praise. And all the spiritual world of supra-mundane beings feasts immaterially on this wonder, offering the clearest and most indisputable witness of the Logos' love for us, which surpasses our understanding, and whose infinite and indefinable breadth, which cannot be grasped by our contemplation—the incomprehensibility of God's being—offers us the beginning of still greater contemplation as we ascend. We ourselves want now to praise this Mystery, too, but are not able to do it in the appropriate measure. What am I saying? Praising God in full measure is beyond even the angels, who beheld the first rays of his brilliance, and ceaselessly circle around the Godhead, which rules over all things. So it surely surpasses what the divine Jeremiah calls "the prisoners of earth,"[10] those on whom the darkness of this miserable and wretched and heavily burdened body bears down. Often we are not permitted to form even a vague image of those blessed intelligible visions, since our intelligence is dominated by its attraction towards sensible things, and therefore our hearts find it difficult to desire what is ultimately desirable. Nonetheless, since it pleases God when we do what lies in our power—even if we are condemned by necessity to lag far behind doing what is appropriate, because the Mystery is beyond all our powers of expression and contemplation—we must not be afraid of making the attempt, nor shrink from honoring by our words what is above all words.[11] That

[9]In this dense passage, Andrew presents the Christological significance of the Transfiguration: it is a revelation, in the person of the Word made flesh, of the divinization offered through him to all who share his human nature. It is a glimpse of the destiny of redeemed humanity.

[10]Lam 3.34 (LXX).

[11]In this sentence and the next, as he tries to define more clearly the aim of his sermon (*logos*), Andrew deftly plays with terms having to do with *logos*: "word," "speech," or even "reason." His intention is to speak about the limits of speech itself, and about this miraculous revelation which enabled the disciples to gaze on what speech can never describe.

would be neither praiseworthy nor holy. And this is the goal of our oration: to show by words that what we praise is beyond the powers of language, so that when our speech reveals its own powerlessness in comparison to what it honors, it will have achieved its purpose. In utter defeat, then, it would be rightly crowned, having legitimately achieved success by being conquered.[12]

But let us move on to our subject—rather, let us eagerly move up the mountain! How long, after all, shall we delay in the foothills of our discourse, gazing in wonder at the beauty of the ascent before us, when it is possible to ascend ourselves with those who have been raised up by the Word[13] and have been judged worthy of higher things? [When it is possible for us] to be illuminated by the cloud ourselves, and so to have our own eyes blinded, to leave the realm of what is visible and intelligible and yet to be initiated, by an excess of light, into what is above human power—provided, of course, we are first purified of all material attachments? It is now possible [for us], too, to listen to what is said, even by that blessed voice that reaches us from the Father, as it bears faithful witness to the divinity of the Only-begotten, and clearly presents to us their substantial identity. So that this may happen, come—let us examine, as far as possible, with the guidance of the Spirit, what lies beyond the powers of most of us to contemplate; for it is only with the Spirit's help that reason gazes beyond perception. Guided by the Spirit, then, let us revel in mystical knowledge of what has come to pass in the Transfiguration of the Lord. For I know myself that the purpose of the Transfiguration has this in view, and that the Mystery invites us to sing its praises in this way. For it wants us to understand the depth of what has been accomplished here, and in knowing what is said here, to

---

[12]Reading *enikēthē* for the Patrologia's *enikēsen*, which seems to make little sense here.

[13]Combéfis, who first published the text of this oration, prefers to read *hyperartheisi tō logō*, rather than *epartheisi tō logō*, as his manuscript indicates (and as appears in the Patrologia): "raised up beyond themselves," rather than simply "raised up." This seems to be what Andrew means here, but it is not clear that he expressed his idea with this word.

absorb the grace of the story more effectively by imitating the one who is transfigured—a grace that works this same marvelous and strange Mystery also in us.

What, then, is the Gospel story? I think it would be good to lay the foundation there of our ritual vision or festival, or whatever we are to call it—for I am overcome in tongue and mind by the greatness of this grace! Matthew introduces the Lord speaking to the disciples this way: "Amen I say to you, there are some of those standing here, who will not taste death until they see the Son of Man coming in his kingly power. And after six days Jesus took Peter and James and his brother John, and led them up a high mountain by themselves, and was transfigured in their sight. And his face shone like the sun, and his garments became white as light."[14] And Mark speaks more or less with the same words as Matthew, and is happy to be like him in words and ideas, since he is inspired in soul and formed in understanding by the same Spirit.[15] Even if he seems to differ slightly on one small detail or another of the scene, this still does not amount to opposition or conflict with him or any of the other [authors]. For when they either recount the same deeds faithfully, in slightly different phrasing—if I may philosophize a bit about them in a general way—or when one or the other, or more than one, hand on what perhaps has been left out by this or that Evangelist, they may perhaps seem to disagree, but are not in the slightest real opposition to each other. So that not all of them together, nor any one of the four, has written down in order everything that the Word has done in the ineffable, fleshly plan of God—the Word who is called flesh, yet does not cease to be God; even so, the four have a single goal, which is the truth, and in a comprehensive way reveal the meaning of the whole through the parts. This often occurs through the agreement and harmony of the Spirit's sayings with each other—often, too, in the

[14]Matt 16.28–17.2.

[15]Like most ancient authors, Andrew assumes that the evident similarities in text between Matthew's and Mark's Gospels are due to Mark's imitating Matthew, and not (as most modern critics assume) the other way around.

manner of the limbs in a single body, which maintains the integrity of the whole undamaged, for the sake of structure and unity. A witness to the truth of what we have said is not just what is recounted by them individually, or found only in some of them, but what the great John says when he reaches the end of his Gospel: "There are many other things that Jesus did, so that, if they were written down one by one, I do not think the world itself could contain the books that would be written."[16]

The same thing will be said about Luke, as well, who writes, as he narrates the grace of the Transfiguration, "It happened that about eight days after these sayings, Jesus took Peter and James and John, and went up to the mountain to pray."[17] "It happened," he says, "that about eight days after these sayings . . . " What are you doing, revealer of hidden mysteries? Why do you say, "It happened that about eight days after these sayings"? And what should we do, since Mark and Matthew agree with each other as if speaking with one mouth, saying: "And after six days, Jesus took Peter and James and John his brother, and he led them to a high mountain by themselves, and was transfigured in their sight"? "Yes," says Saint Luke, "nothing of what I and they have said is more unified and harmonious, seen as part of the whole, than this. For truly what has been expressed by us and by them is in agreement, and has the same meaning. They, after all, omitted the day on which what was soon to be accomplished was predicted by the Logos to all the disciples together; and again, they omitted the day on which the Logos would mysteriously bring to fulfillment what had been foretold. And they clearly counted six days occurring between the two—the first, I mean, and the last, or rather, day one and day eight. But if you connect the two, and join the beginning and the end to what lies between, you will incontrovertibly have what you seek, and you will see the agreement among our words, the unifying beauty of the truth shining out more brightly and more purely than the sun."

[16]John 21.25.
[17]Luke 9.28–29.

But since I have verbally sketched out for you the attractive form and pleasing unity of Scripture, as it appears to us according to Luke's teaching, come, now—let me dare to break into hidden places, and reveal the brilliance of mysterious sights hidden within the text, a brilliance that outshines the visible meaning as much as the intellectual realm is both more hidden from us, and more sustaining for us, than what appears before us. First, though, dear initiates of the Word, fellow lovers of all that is good, be purified along with me in ear and mind, by the Spirit who purifies and enlightens all things, so that the Logos might be one with you, as with his own, and might reveal more perfect realities to those inexperienced in the instruction of holy signs.[18] What are we saying, brothers and sisters? What is this spiritual banquet and contemplation of words, to which we invite you today, and which we have been found worthy to enter along with the Spirit?[19]

The number six, say the experts on these things, is the only perfect number within the first ten [integers], because it consists of and is completed by its own parts. "Christ, the Wisdom and the Power of God,"[20] the Logos who is above all goodness, "the only Son, who exists turned towards the Father's bosom,"[21] in six days created all that appears before us, as well as the human person, consisting of the immaterial soul and the matter of the body. And clearly we can count six forms of love, than which no good thing is higher or is even its equal; in response to them, [the Lord] takes generosity towards the needy as directed towards himself. For when he balances mercy against mercy for the merciful, and offers the reward of blessedness in the life to come, as the great giver of gifts, he says to those already

---

[18]Echoing the language and style of the Pseudo-Dionysius, as well as of the earlier Greek tradition of mystery religions, Andrew speaks here in the language of initiation into solemn rites that reveal religious truth inexpressible by ordinary language. Here, his intention is to penetrate more deeply into the significance of the numbers six and eight, beyond a simple explanation in terms of time-reckoning.

[19]Once again, Andrew suggests that he is the host at a spiritual banquet of words and images; see n. 3 above.

[20]I Cor 1.21.

[21]John 1.18.

judged worthy to stand at his right, "Come, you blessed of my Father, inherit the Kingdom prepared for you from the foundation of the world. For I was hungry, and you gave me to eat; I was thirsty, and you gave me to drink; I was a stranger, and you received me, naked and you clothed me, sick and you visited me, I was in prison and you came to me."[22] Since, then, the forms of love are so many and of such kind, as Truth himself clearly cries out to us in the Gospels, and since the love of God is confirmed by the love we show to our neighbor, that person is shown to be worthy of the blessedness we hope for, who has a genuine desire directed towards this love. "From these two commandments the whole Law and the Prophets depend,"[23] as Scripture ordains in the Gospels. From this it is clear that love is something that embraces all other goods, the highest of the blessings revealed in Holy Scripture; and there is no form of virtue, through which a person is made God's own and joined to him, and inherits the glory and Kingdom above, which does not depend on love and is not included within it, joined to it and protected within it by the ineffable structure of things. So that love alone, working itself out through its own six parts, constitutes the most perfect and purest kind of practical philosophy among the human race, the goal of which, they say, is the good, which is God himself. And beyond this, it joins the human person in an incomparable way to God, by enkindling the fire of our knowledge of him.[24]

But to what purpose have we said all this? I say that if one wishes to be lifted up on to the mountain of lofty contemplation with the Word, as a disciple, and to see the unapproachable glory of that Kingdom, and be counted worthy of his visible and spiritual self-manifestation as God, when one hears Christ proclaiming to us beforehand that his Kingdom will not be long in coming—for that is the Transfiguration, in which the unchangeable one has illuminated

---

[22]Matt 25.34–36.

[23]Matt 22.40.

[24]Literally, "by enkindling the fire of theology." *Theologia*, in classical Greek philosophy and early Christian theology, means the ability to speak and think of God, an ability rooted in personal knowledge and experience.

what is ours, what has been taken on for our sake, more brightly than the sun—then he will nourish and give drink to Christ, who hungers and thirsts for the salvation of all. Or to put it another way: through those in need, one receives him who dwells in all those who receive him by faith; one receives him when he is a stranger, clothes him when he is naked, cares for him when he is ill, and does not pass him by when he is shut up in prison—for one is driven on strongly by the yearning to do good for others. And through this laudable greed for virtue, one will not stop at mere appearances, nor will one limit one's benevolence towards the benevolent Lord by a mere external kindliness. So, I dare even to say, if one considers carefully the words, "Whatever you have done to one of the least of my brethren, you have done for me,"[25] and goes, as well, more deeply than appearance allows to become aware of the sufferings of souls, then one would consider the appropriate remedy, and give rational beings, originally formed to reverence God, "a place of shelter in a green pasture," and would nourish them "by the water of repose."[26] And [a disciple] would surely lead with joy into his own home, however humble it might be, anyone who has left his own country to dwell in a foreign land, and who has become a vagabond by his alienation, out of reverence[27] for the one who became a stranger for our sakes. He would lead him from an earthly and isolated life, and transport him to the festal assembly of the saints in heaven that links us together—to the "citizenship" of Paul and of all who fear the Lord.[28] But seeing his neighbor stripped of his father's wealth[29] and taking off the robe of immortality that he might have chosen, he would take pity on his nakedness and clothe him again, putting on him a godly and blessed way of life. And what of the one who is

[25]Matt 25.40.

[26]Psalm 22.2 (LXX). Andrew here applies Jesus' words in Matthew 25 to "spiritual works of mercy" as well as corporal ones.

[27]I follow here the emendation of Combéfis, who reads *aidestheis*, which suggests the one who receives the stranger reveres the incarnate Son, rather than *aidesthenta*, which connects the reverence with the stranger himself.

[28]See Phil 3.20.

[29]See Luke 15.12–14.

"weak in faith,"[30] and still shows a childish mind concerning practical judgments? Would he pass him by silently? Surely not! He would call him back as quickly as possible to the health he yearns for, and with words of truth would put unreasonable weakness to flight, and restore his natural reason to its proper original state. And he would point out to reason the emotions and our sensuality—those twin horses of the passible part of our soul—by reasonable argument, and give them wings, and a new start in the spirit, towards what is right.[31] Going beyond this, he would approach the one who is held back by the darkness of ignorance, who is prevented from seeing the light of infallible knowledge, and taking a thoughtful stand in a dark place, he would break the bond of ignorance, letting the Word illuminate the person's reason like an angel's. He would lead that person to the light of a free way of life in Christ, a life no longer "held captive by the yoke of slavery,"[32] nor prevented from making its way towards the beauties of heaven by the power of the understanding.

And he will reveal all these ways of acting, and others like them, in the appropriate form and manner, and guide us in our souls by the beacon of love—and will do so in two ways. For since we are twofold, constituted of soul and body, the form for showing care for others is also twofold; and all of us, as human beings, need this double care—even if one person needs more, the other less—as long as our faculty of choice is subject to change, and as long as matter bears in itself a principle of disorder and inconsistency, or is subjected to attacks and misfortunes from outside sources. We must act, then, with special benevolence towards each other, so that we might benefit ourselves, in other ways, still more. For an act of kindness, directed to the person receiving the gift rather than to oneself, returns more lavishly still upon the person who performs it, and so generosity changes places through the act of generous receiving.

[30]Rom 14.1.

[31]For the original context of this familiar Platonic metaphor for internal conflict and its resolution, see Plato, *Phaedrus* 246a-254e.

[32]Gal 5.1.

In giving this way, the human being quite clearly imitates God; but imitation is a means of acquisition, and acquisition leads to likeness, which is the highest of blessings.

Do you see how great the fruit of loving your neighbor is? In this way, thrusting aside all servile fear, along with the evil burden of the passions, through the perfect six days of the commandments,[33] purifying oneself as far as possible for higher things, and being made perfect in love, one is blessed with the reward of virtue and the infallible knowledge of the realm of time and the natural, through the contemplation of nature[34] made available in the Spirit. Knowing that the material and visible world, which came to be in six days, is the type of what lies far above perception, one will see the invisible clearly through the visible, transposing the beauties of perceptible things harmoniously into the luminous loveliness of the spiritual world. And so one will have creation guiding his intelligence towards its own source. As a result, through both types of activity—the ascetical, I mean, and the contemplative—after one has reached perfection in them both (a perfection signified by the six divine commandments and also by the six days in which the visible world came to be), one will be able to understand clearly what is the mystery of the eight days.[35] And that this is all laid open to us in the mystical teaching of Luke one can recognize, it seems to me, from what is contemplated

[33]Here and later in this paragraph, Andrew refers to Jesus' urgent commands to love actively, as expressed in the judgment scene of Matt 25, as the "six commandments."

[34]The "contemplation of nature" (*physikē theöria*) is understood, in the classical ascetical theory of the early Church, to be the second step in a person's growth towards the grace of contemplating God. One must begin by the purification of desire and the gradual acquisition of control over the "passions" or distorted attractions towards things in the world; one grows then into a deep understanding of the meaning of creation as God's gift, and one ends by a unitive awareness of God himself that goes beyond ideas and images.

[35]In the Origenist tradition of typological exegesis, the "eight days" of the Christian week points to a new creation, adding to the six days in which Genesis 1 reports the creation of the present world, and the seventh day of God's rest, an eighth day of transformation, which is already realized in the resurrection of Christ on the first day of a new week.

and what exceeds normal perception.[36] What I am saying is that those who share in true knowledge, free from flesh and the world as far as that is possible here in this life, will be taught the forms of the world to come by the various trials they have experienced here. But all of this serves only as a prologue to the glory and grace that will be revealed to the clear-sighted on the mountain. When they climb the mountain with Jesus and come within the cloud, then they will be found worthy of a much clearer and loftier mystical vision of all that has been spoken of before, through the garments of the Word that have been made white as snow and brilliant as the light, as symbols begin to give way to the truth.

But the garments of the Logos, according to the spiritual mode of contemplation, would be those things in which he is wrapped and by which he is revealed. And this is somewhat paradoxical! By the one form of figural explanation, it seems to me, they signify the things said and done by the Savior in this life—a life that is spotless and undefiled; a life shown forth to the world through the divine history of the incarnation, but not comprehended by it; a life incomparably free of all wickedness, which has naturally become the cause and model of all our purity and holiness. When the one who is above all substance truly came to share our substance, and became substantial in a super-substantial way, he associated with us in the flesh. He is the one who shone forth, to an overwhelming degree, on the mountain. He did not, at that point, become purer or more exalted than himself [in his human body]—far from it! But he became what he was before, for those perfected disciples who were initiated into higher things and could contemplate him in truth. And those words and deeds through which that way of life took its form, by which the depth of the Word's divine plan concerning us is revealed as without limit, can be understood, not without good reason, in terms of the garments of the Savior. Or else those things[37]

---

[36]Supplying a preposition meaning "from" (perhaps *ek* or *para*), which seems to be missing in the Greek text.

[37]Presumably, Jesus' words and deeds, as mentioned in the previous sentence.

would be signified through the garments by the purifying work of the Spirit, shining as radiantly as light, through [Jesus'] utter purity and supreme radiance.

The garments of the Logos might be understood in another way, too—a way not unworthy of the Spirit—as the magnificence and sumptuousness of the things brought forth into existence by the Word himself, and especially as Holy Scripture. The first of these [= the beauty of the world] reveals the invisible, uncontainable one as creator, the cause immaculately hidden within creation; the second [=Scripture] reveals him as loving to move and dwell in the world in symbols, ineffably revealing himself to those worthy of the Spirit. Both [= the created world and the Scriptures] are made pure and radiant by the Spirit, and continue to be revealed by their purity—for those who love divine things and are given to contemplation—as "such that no fuller on earth could whiten them."[38] "For the Spirit searches all things," Scripture says, "even the depths of God."[39] So then, through his garments, the Logos, who is hidden inside them, reveals himself, and sends forth the light of knowing him: to those, namely, who have been perfected in spirit like Peter, James and John. One person, like Peter, may be firmly anchored in the rock, the foundation that faith offers, and may carry on his back the structure of the Church; others, like the "sons of thunder," may be entrusted by the Word with the mystical vision of God's highest nature, because they share a hard and unshakeable foundation of immoveable rock. The one, I think, signifies the depth, the other two the breadth and height of faith, which equally surpass, in every direction, all limitlessness, by the sheer inconceivability of the Mystery.

These, then, are the Savior's garments; this is how they radiate light. But what of his face, which shone so brightly? What of the impossible beauty, higher and more precious than all things loveable, which for those who gaze on it is established as a pledge of ceaseless rejoicing—to the degree that what is revealed seems to be

[38]Matt 9.2.
[39]I Cor 2.10.

comprehended? What mind or reason can see or express the hidden, more divine mystery, always incomparably new? For if his garments are such because of the brilliance that gushes forth from within, what must the glory be that is wrapped and hidden by these garments, something beyond our powers to see and know? If, then, this were to happen by itself, if he were to take all covering away, how should I describe it? But that which was revealed through his holy robe alone, the robe he had prepared for himself from a Virgin's blood and mystically wrapped around himself through the Spirit, which is how they saw his glory revealed—who will gaze upon it? There is nothing, nothing at all, of the things we can contemplate in creation that will grasp the excess of its brilliance! For even if nothing in the world is without a share in the Good, still not all of it is shared in an absolute way. Rather, as much as is accessible to the participants comes into their possession, in whatever way it can; and this comes about, through the highest Goodness, by flashes of unlimited grace and brilliance, coming forth and being poured out on all things. A demonstration of what I am saying would be that blessed, much celebrated feeling that came upon the Apostles on the mountain, when the inaccessible, primordial light transfigured its own flesh, and radiated, beyond the power of any substance, its own excess of surging light.

They could not endure the radiance coming forth from that spotless flesh—brilliance that welled up from the divinity of the Word, which had hypostatically united himself to the flesh and shone through it in a way beyond nature—but fell on their faces. O marvel! In a complete departure from their natural functioning, they were overcome by heavy sleep and by fear, and shut off their senses; they ceased from all intellectual movement, and completely lost all awareness of themselves. So, in that divine and invisible darkness, above all light, they mingled with God. By not seeing at all, they received the true gift of vision, and made progress in experiencing, without knowledge, an excess of knowledge; so they were led to share in a wakefulness higher than all intellectual attention.

Strangely, in the strangeness of the event itself, wakefulness turned into sleep—or rather, sleep became wakefulness; this very absence of cognitive perception made credible a knowledge that lies above nature.

Who might be able to give me words as powerful as I wish? Who can be exalted in a way worthy of this mystery? What mental movement can look simply at this sight and not immediately be smothered as a result, drawing back before such an inaccessible wonder? David, that royal and prophetic instrument, recognized this by the Spirit, I think, from afar, and cried out with inspired voice to the God of all things, "Thabor and Hermon will rejoice in your name!"[40] That they would rejoice, he foretold. But what, and of what kind and greatness, the Mystery of the Transfiguration actually would be, at which Thabor and Hermon would rejoice, he honored by silence[41] as something unspeakable and inconceivable, something that would be known in its time by experience itself—God willing—to those worthy of it.

Since our words have come this far, it seems to me—as I grope for words—that I should try also to explain in my discourse what Peter said, when he had nothing of his own to say, but—being seized upon by the Spirit—spoke from an excess of joy. For in his joy, and under the spell of the revelation of light and the vision of divine things that had supernaturally filled his soul, Peter became completely inspired. He could not explain his feeling in words, yet he could not endure that this grace should simply flow away in silence; so he spoke words that were not—as some might suppose—words of ignorance or foolishness. Rather, he found words to express the effects and fruits of that ineffable guidance, the work of God within him. What did he say? "Lord," he said, "it is good for us to be here."[42] Why do you say that, Peter? "Because, freed from the disturbance of public pressure,

[40]Ps 88.13 (LXX).

[41]This phrase, by now almost proverbial, is used by Greek theological writers since at least Gregory of Nazianzus, and is employed by Maximus when he speaks of the eschatological fulfillment that still stands beyond our expectations.

[42]Matt 17.4.

and purified in soul and sense by distance from the crowds, who move and speak in every possible way, we are able here, Lord, to share the unbroken enjoyment of your ineffable divine appearance. And what could be better than this? What could be more desirable, what could be lovelier, for anyone with sense? And therefore, if you are willing, Lord, let us build three tabernacles here: one for you and one for Moses and one for Elijah! For it is good that both the dead letter of the Law, which is signified by Moses, and the living law of [created] nature, which is represented by the living prophet, here be brought into their resting place next to you, the Word who have become human and made your resting place among humans: the true source of rest; the Lord of life and death, for whom all the saints are alive—even though they suffer natural death, in the separation of the parts that make up the human person; the King of all things, the one who holds them together, their cause. And our purpose is that, filled with the light of that inaccessible source from which you have enlightened them, they[43] might themselves make you visible to the world: the Word who dwells in them and walks in them. They will put off their former life, and receive only your grace, which comes to fullness in your Spirit and your divine fire, according to the Gospel's exclusionary decision; grace that is exalted, immaterial; grace that never ends or grows old or decays, but that, in the limitless way grace acts, always advances, and is lifted up to what is greater and more divine, by the burning heat of the Spirit."

But let us enter now within the cloud, and examine what the message of the cloud might be, so that by examining, as far as our powers allow, those who appear in the cloud talking to Jesus, in the meaning hidden deep within these things, we may not stay far away from the significance they all reveal. The shining cloud, then, from which the voice of the Father came forth, piercingly proclaiming who the transfigured one was and whence he came, is the dove who shortly before descended on the Jordan—the Holy Spirit, coming down from above in the form of a dove and remaining on him who

[43]Presumably Andrew is referring here to Moses and Elijah.

was being baptized, the one who would "baptize," according to John's witness, "in spirit and in fire".[44] In him [= Jesus], if we may put it this way, the Spirit has his endless dwelling-place, because the hypostases abide in each other. And we are persuaded to think this about the cloud, because we have the great Apostle as our teacher even in these things, when he writes to the Corinthians, "I do not want you to be unaware, brothers and sisters, that all our ancestors were under the cloud, and all crossed through the sea, and all were baptized into Moses in the cloud and in the sea."[45] He is referring figurally to the Spirit by the cloud, and to water by the sea, from which and through which the spring of baptism flows—or better, he is speaking of the great and beautiful gift of our being begotten of God. For it is not possible that the Father should be mirrored in the Son, or the Son in the Father, except in the Holy Spirit, who proceeds from the Father, and who loves to dwell substantially in, and repose on, the Son—since he shares the same substance with them, and the same throne, and the same honor.[46]

Here, then, as in the Jordan, the same Mystery of the Trinity is revealed: held together in the supremely unified, utterly single, utterly timeless reality of the Godhead, and expressed by means of the same words. And I will add, too, that it is revealed also in action here, for anyone who investigates the story in a godly way, and passes above the bounds of creation by the guidance of the Spirit. This is the reason why those chosen Apostles, who were illuminated by the cloud and deprived of all the activity of sight by the light of the Lord's

[44]Matt 3.11.

[45]I Cor 10.1–2.

[46]Andrew expresses here the classical Greek conception of the equality and mutual indwelling of the three hypostases of the Trinity, before Eastern and Western approaches to the Mystery became divided more sharply by the controversy over the term "Filioque" in the Latin creed. The Spirit is said to "proceed" from the Father, language warranted by John 15.26; but the single divine substance shared by all three hypostases enables Andrew to speak also of the Spirit as "loving to dwell within" the Son "in his essence" and as "reposing on him," presumably not just in the event of his baptism as the Incarnate Word, but in their eternal relationship of unity and distinction.

face, who were judged worthy to become eyewitnesses of the Transfiguration on the mountain, came to be far removed from all visible
things and even from themselves: so that they might be instructed,
through unseeing and unknowing, in the Mystery—super-substantial by sheer excess—that lies beyond all affirmation and negation,[47]
[instructed] by the manifestation of the Word and the overshadowing of the Spirit and the voice of the Father, borne down from the
cloud above them. Moses and Elijah came to be under this cloud
and were seen conversing with Jesus, and hinting in advance at his
"departure" through the cross. The former, as I have said earlier,
indicates the written law, the latter the law of nature. So that the
Word who is proclaimed through both of them "in manifold forms
and many ways,"[48] to use the Apostle's words, might be recognized
as the maker of the one law and the fulfiller of the other; and that
he might impose himself on the one law as its blessed completion,
and renew the other in the Spirit, since it had already grown old and
diminished, among rational creatures, by the force of unreason;[49]
and that he might gather both of them in to himself, and show that
they do not differ in any respect, in him, from each other. They both
become invisible, hidden in the sun of the Gospel—or rather, filled
with light and lifted up to the heights by it; and, if I may speak of
something still greater, they both are gathered into one with the very
sun itself, exchanging their identity with what is above them, wholly
overcome! And blessed is the one who, at the touch of the Word
made dense in flesh, made subject to our sense-perception for our
sakes, has received knowledge of what is revealed in mystical symbols, and does not despise grace, thereby proving himself unworthy

[47]Following the emendation suggested by Combéfis, which reads *theseōs*, "affirmation," for *theiōseōs*, "divinization." Andrew here echoes the radically apophatic
approach to knowledge of God promoted in the liturgical theology of Dionysius the
Areopagite.

[48]Heb 1.1.

[49]See the opening sentence of the homily: for Andrew, the purpose of the Logos'
glorious manifestation of himself on Mount Thabor was to restore the full functioning of human reason (*logos*) by the vision of God's own Logos or Reason in human
form.

of the Spirit; but who rather considers him (Christ) to be the unique law—and does not simply consider him so, but makes himself, by the illumination of the Spirit, to be like [Christ], as he shares our way of life in a new way, by a law which is both divine and human. For he has become human, and so shares our present life; and he has introduced into our pattern of life the gift of sharing with us a way of life above this world. If we accept the gift, our human life is revealed as fertile in the things of the Spirit, since it has laid aside the sterility caused within it by sin. For this reason, then, humans from now on dance with the angels, praising God together with them and saying, "Glory to God in the highest places, and peace on earth, good will among men and women."[50]

Here you have, my beloved, the message of the Mystery; even if much that we hope for is still missing, still it is not outside what lies in our power. And you may hope for a still higher and more mystical promise from the Word himself, who for your sake bore flesh and endured the cross. If you accept it, you can treasure it up within yourself with all eagerness, as an inexplicable, unspeakable word, trusting in the Word until he himself, the Lord who suffered in flesh, conquers death in you and raises you from the dead; and by raising you, as one who had been killed by sin, he will make you divine in the Spirit. "There is a time for everything,"[51] we are told by both Solomon and the Truth!

Knowing this, my fellow human, never convict yourself of being unworthy of grace, or forfeit the heavenly life, which is free from all strife, through laziness in how you live here. Rather, drive out all laziness from your soul and shake off your attraction to material things; become, in every fiber of your being, the pure devotee of better, heavenly things, and receive in the Spirit the pure and blessed

---

[50]Luke 2.14. Andrew here accepts the reading of the *koinē* family of manuscripts, a text form which was dominant in the Antiochene and Byzantine Churches from the fifth century on. The form " Peace on earth to those men and women whom he favors" seems to be a slightly older reading, and is the one chosen by St Jerome for his Latin Vulgate translation.

[51]Eccl 3.1.

gift of sharing the life of the Word, whose outcome is divinization and the enjoyment of ineffable blessings. As a result, true virtue, shaped and stamped by all the virtues, will be revealed in you; and in your steady contemplation of what is, truth will be unveiled.[52] Through your wisdom, Wisdom itself will become known, in which "all things have come into being";[53] it is the cause of all things, and is hymned and honored as the bond that holds together everything in the realm of becoming. To put it simply, may God be glorified in you through both these things, virtue and contemplation: God, who is contemplated and adored as Trinity, and who is the chief and purest goal of virtue and contemplation. Because of him, all other things exist; the goal itself has no cause!

The things that have been given to you, then, my fellow human, are great; so are those that are yet to be given, as you walk on your way to God. The things that the mysterious God has worked for your sake surpass all mind and reason. Do not collapse, then, under the power of laziness; do not be unaware of yourself, or thrust aside the gift that has been given. Show reverence to your call, and do not appear to be unmindful of how much you have been blessed, or complain when you discover that salvation is sheer gift. Leave the things of earth to the earth. For what do you have in common with earth? "Let the dead bury their dead,"[54] the Scripture commands. Quite clearly, all things corruptible and passing are dead, and cause death in those who honor them. Therefore "the dead bury their dead," if through their relationship to what is corruptible they are deprived of true life, and if they gain this reward from their relationship to passing things: to be named as those who have become dead—and what could be more wretched than this? Stripping yourself, then, of

[52]In this final section of his sermon, a passage of earnest moral and ascetical exhortation, Andrew emphasizes the double goal of human life as practical virtue and contemplation of the truth of God, represented in the Transfiguration story by Moses and Elijah, both of whom are overshadowed and transformed by the Holy Spirit and so allowed to recognize Christ as he is.

[53]Col 1.17.

[54]Matt 8.22.

all that flows and passes away—or rather, yourself thrusting aside, by deliberate choice, all the things that will be extinguished along with this fleshly life—accompany the Word and do not turn aside; he has emptied himself for your sake, after all, and put on a form alien to himself, and bears you completely, along with all that is yours, that he might consume in himself what there is in you that is inferior, and completely free you from sin. Walk with Christ, who walked the world for your sake; do not give up, do not stand still in your journey, overpowered in your mind by any thought. But go up with him who ascends into heaven; there transplant your heart and your life.

It is good for you to come to be with God. There will be the festival of the saints, there the surpassingly brilliant sound of people in celebration. Above all, as you fight the good fight, hold on to fear and longing, so that you may be helped by the one not to fall into arrogance, when you glory in the greatness and beauty of virtue, and be inflamed and moved upwards by the other, lest you look down—by some inner weariness[55]—on progress and advancement towards what is truly good. Rather, preserve this divine love[56] for what is beyond this world, unyielding and unsullied forever. For that beloved object, which all your longing reaches out to grasp, is without beginning and without end. This is its limit: to be completely unlimited and boundless. May we now be judged worthy to have its breeze always in our sails, moving us onwards. And when we pass on from here, may we mingle purely with the very object of our longing, by the grace and kindness of our Lord Jesus Christ, through whom and with whom be glory, honor and strength to the Father and the Holy Spirit, now and always and for the ages of ages. Amen.

---

[55] Andrew here uses the Greek word *koros*, a term famously associated with Origen's attempt to explain how intellectual creatures originally became "bored" with their union with God in love and turned away to pursue their own egocentric ends.

[56] Andrew uses the term *erōs* here, suggesting a love characterized by physical longing and need.

JOHN OF DAMASCUS

John of Damascus (c. 680–750) was a monk of the Palestinian monastery of St Sabas for most of his mature life, probably migrating to Palestine from Syria in the first decade of the eighth century. This homily, clearly intended to be part of the liturgical celebration of the Transfiguration of the Lord on August 6, may have been delivered in the church on Mount Thabor itself, which seems to have been built between the fourth and sixth centuries (see c. 16 and n. 87 below). The place and date of the homily's composition remain uncertain. For a theological analysis of this homily, as "a kind of audible icon," in the contemplative tradition of Greek commentary and preaching reaching back to Origen, see Andrew Louth, *St John Damascene* (Oxford: Oxford University Press, 2002) 234–243. It is catalogued in the *Clavis Patrum Graecorum* among the works of John of Damascus, as CPG 8057.

John is primarily known in the later Christian tradition of both East and West as an unusually apt and precise synthesizer of earlier mainstream Christian tradition—a skill manifested in his great dogmatic summary, *The Fount of Knowledge*, as well as in his shorter doctrinal treatises, especially on Christological subjects. He was also highly regarded in antiquity, however, as a liturgical poet and preacher; a number of his *canons* have become classic contributions to Eastern liturgy, and at least eight of his festal homilies—of high rhetorical finish and profound theological content—form a central part of his legacy.

The most recent editor of the Damascene's works, Dom Bonifatius Kotter, points out, in his introduction to the text (*Joannis Damasceni Opera* 5 [Berlin: De Gruyter, 1988] 421), that one important eleventh-century manuscript, Coislin 107 (now in the Bibliothèque Nationale in Paris), refers to the John who delivered this sermon as "monk and presbyter of Antioch, from Damascus". This reference to Antioch, Kotter suggests, may simply be an allusion to the patriarchate to which John's native Church of Damascus belongs. Still, Kotter points to a certain uneasiness among some twentieth-century scholars about assigning the sermon to John, on stylistic grounds, and confesses that "doubts have occasionally occurred to me, too, that here the same author is speaking as that of the other, genuine homilies" (421, n. 2). On the other hand, Kotter's mentor, Dom J. M. Hoeck, OSB, insists that "the homily is through and through typical of Damascene, both in content and in language," and criticizes his more skeptical scholarly colleagues for expecting that the eighth-century monk's thought and style should be incapable of normal development and variation: "Stand und Aufgaben der Damaskenos-Forschung," *Orientalia Christiana Periodica* 17 (1951) 43, n. 14. In any case, the text reveals the theological precision for which John is famous, and movingly exhorts its listeners to commit themselves to following the transfigured Lord on his journey.

BLESSED JOHN,
PRESBYTER OF DAMASCUS
Oration on the Transfiguration of Our Lord and Savior Jesus Christ[1]

1   Come, let us hold a feast, community beloved of God! Come, let us celebrate, along with the heavenly powers, to whom celebrating is dear—for they have come here to celebrate along with us! Come, let us raise up a cry with the resonant cymbals of our lips! Come, let us dance about in spirit! Who is invited to the celebration, the festival? For whom is this gladness and joy? For those who fear the Lord, for those who worship the Trinity, for those who reverence the Son and the Spirit as eternal along with the Father, who confess in soul and understanding and mouth a single Godhead, recognized without division in three hypostases; who know and confess Christ as Son of God and God, one hypostasis known in two undivided and unconfused natures, and in their natural characteristics.[2] For

[1]The Greek text on which this translation is based is the recent critical edition of Bonifatius Kotter, OSB: *Joannis Damasceni Opera* 5 (Berlin: De Gruyter, 1988) 436–459. The text of this celebrated homily previously appeared in the first complete edition of the Damascene's works, by Michel Lequien, OP (Paris 1717; Venice, 1740), which is reprinted in Migne's *Patrologia Graeca* 96.545–576.

[2]Here, right at the start of his sermon, John weaves into his solemn invitation to join in the feast a description of the confession of Trinitarian and Christological orthodoxy in which its meaning and joy is grounded. Only if one realizes who God is, for Christian faith, and who Jesus is, can one begin to grasp the great Mystery on which the day's liturgy invites his hearers to meditate. Reaffirmations of classical conceptions of God, as three and one, and of Christ as a single hypostasis or individual existing in two complete natures, run through the homily.

us there is gladness, all sorts of festive rejoicing. For us Christ has brought the festival to its full meaning; "for there is no rejoicing for the impious."[3] Let us thrust aside the mist of all the grief that shadows our mind, that will not allow it to be lifted up on the heights. Let us despise all earthly things, for our citizenship is not on the earth! Let us stretch our mind up towards heaven, from which we have received a Savior, Christ the Lord.[4]

2   Today the abyss of inaccessible light, today the boundless outpouring of divine radiance shines on the Apostles on Mount Thabor. Today Jesus Christ—a reality and a name that is dear to me, truly the sweetest and most attractive of names, exceeding all notions of sweetness—is recognized as Lord of the Old and New Testament. Today Moses, the leading figure of the Old Covenant, the divine lawgiver, is presented on mount Thabor to Christ, who authored the Law, as to his Lord; he gazes on Christ's divine work, which had long been represented in mystical figures—for I would say myself that this was the significance of "the back parts of God"[5]—and he sees the glory of the Godhead clearly, while sheltered in a hole in the rock, as Scripture says. But the rock is Christ, God who has become flesh, the Word and the Lord, as the divine Paul has expressly instructed us: "For the rock," he says, "was Christ,"[6] who opened a kind of tiny cave, as it were, in his own flesh, and from it flooded those in his presence with boundless light, stronger than any powers of vision.

Today the chief of the New Covenant—the one who proclaimed Christ as Son of God most clearly, when he said, "You are the Christ, the Son of the living God"[7]—sees the leader of the Old Covenant[8] standing next to the lawgiver of both, and hears [Moses] announcing

---

[3]Is 48.22 (LXX).

[4]Cf. Lk 2.11.

[5]Cf. Ex 33.22f. Ancient Biblical commentators had many interpretations of this puzzling passage.

[6]I Cor 10.4.

[7]Matt 16.16.

[8]I.e., Moses.

clearly, "This is the one who is, the one whom I foretold would rise up, a prophet like myself: like me, a human being and the leader of the New Covenant, but above me, as my Lord and Lord of all creation, the one who established both covenants, for me and for you—the Old and the New." Today the virgin of the Old Covenant proclaims as Lord, to the virgin of the New, the one who is a Virgin from the Virgin.[9]

Come, then: let us trust the prophet David, and "Let us sing, sing to our God, sing to our king, sing that God rules over all the earth—let us sing with understanding!"[10] Let us sing with joyful lips, let us sing with mental understanding, sensing the taste of the words. "For the throat tastes food, but the mind discerns words,"[11] the wise man says. Let us sing also in "the Spirit who searches all things, even the unspeakable depths of God themselves,"[12] seeing in the light of the Father, by the light of the Spirit who sheds light on all things, the 'unapproachable light'[13] who is the Son of God. Now things that cannot be gazed on have appeared to human eyes: an earthly body radiating the brilliance of divine splendor, a mortal body pouring forth the glory of the Godhead. "For the Word became flesh,"[14] and the flesh became Word, even if neither of them departed from its own proper nature.

O wonder, exceeding all understanding! Glory did not come upon this body from outside itself, but from within: from the super-divine Godhead of God the Word, made one with it in hypostasis, by an indescribable ordering of things.[15] How can what is unmixed be mingled, and still remain unconfused?[16] How can utterly diverse

[9] Apparently Peter, Moses and Jesus are all identified here as virgins.
[10] Ps 46.7–8 (LXX).
[11] Job 12.11
[12] Cf. I Cor 2.10.
[13] I Tim 6.16.
[14] John 1.14.
[15] John is here playing with the Greek word λόγος, which means both "word" and "reason" and "structure " or "order," in a way untranslatable in English.
[16] John is referring to the two substances or natures in the person or hypostasis of Christ, which—in the dogmatic formulation of Chalcedon—are confessed to

realities come together as one, and still not depart from the proper structures of their natures? This is the drama of the hypostatic union: the things united form one individual, one hypostasis, while their union preserves them in indivisible difference and unconfused hypostatic unity; the duality of natures is preserved through the unchanging incarnation of the Word and the permanent divinization, beyond all understanding, of mortal flesh. Human qualities belong to God, and divine qualities belong to a human being, in the mode of mutual exchange and the unmixed interpenetration of both in each other—of a literally hypostatic unity. For he is one, who eternally is one thing and later became the other.

3   Today things that cannot be heard are heard by human ears; For the visible human being is attested to be Son of God–unique, beloved, of the same substance [as God]. The witness cannot deceive, the proclamation is true; for the very Father who begot him utters the proclamation himself. Let David stand as witness, and strike the lyre of the Spirit that speaks God's words; let him sing the message now, more clearly and precisely, which he foresaw of old, as from a great distance, with purified eyes: the coming of the Word of God to us in flesh, as something yet to be, when he said, "Thabor and Hermon will shout for joy in your name."[17]

Hermon,[18] on the one hand, had rejoiced earlier, hearing the name of Son clearly witnessed for Christ by the Father, when the Forerunner, the connecting link between the Old and the New Testaments, proceeded to baptize him at the Jordan: the treasure hidden in the desert, shining like light in darkness; the 'inaccessible

remain unmixed, while being fully possessed by a single individual or agent, God the Word.

[17]Ps 88.13.

[18]Expanding on this allusion to Ps 88.13, John identifies both Mt Thabor and Mt Hermon as places where Jesus is "named" or revealed as Son of God, by a voice from heaven. This depends on his connecting Hermon with the River Jordan, where Jesus was baptized and first publicly designated as God's Son. Since the headwaters of the Jordan are in the foothills of Mt Hermon, north of the Sea of Galilee, the connection makes sense.

light'[19] that escapes the notice of the near-sighted, commissioning John to make itself publicly known, when, in the midst of the Jordan, that light established the water of forgiveness, purifying the world without itself needing to be purified. When thunder sounded from heaven in the Father's voice, the one baptized was attested to be his 'beloved Son,' and the one so named was pointed out by a dove, as if by the finger of the Spirit.[20]

Now Thabor, too, rejoices and is glad: the divine, holy mountain, the high mountain, now rightly shines out no less, in glory and brilliance, than it does in its physical height; for it contends with heaven in its beauty! Just as the angels are not strong enough to hold their gaze fixed on him in heaven, so on this mountain the chosen Apostles see him radiant with the glory of his Kingdom. On this mountain the resurrection of the dead is confirmed, and Christ is revealed as Lord of dead and living: summoning Moses from the dead, bringing down Elijah, still alive, as witness—that fire-breathing charioteer who long before had driven his team up the path to the skies. Here, in this moment, the chief prophets make their proclamation, indicating the Lord's "departure" through the cross.[21] Therefore the mountain skips and rejoices, imitating the frolicking of sheep,[22] when it is allowed to hear this same witness to the Son coming from the cloud—which is the Spirit: Christ, the giver of life, attested to by the Father. For this is "the name above every name,"[23] over which Thabor and Hermon rejoice: "This is my Son, the Beloved!" This is a cause of rejoicing for all creation, this is a prize for humanity, a boast that will never be taken away! For the one to whom this witness is borne is a human being—even if he is not merely this!

O joy, bestowed on us beyond all imagining! O blessedness here, beyond hope! O gifts of God, overcoming our desires! O graces, not

[19] I Tim 6.16.

[20] See Matt 3.13–17 and parallel passages.

[21] John uses the word "exodus," with which Luke describes the main content of the conversation between these two Old Testament figures and Jesus (Lk 9.31).

[22] Cf. Ps 113.6 (LXX).

[23] Phil 2.9.

given simply in response to modest demands! O generous giver, who have made a supernatural magnificence your own! O grace, befitting not so much the receiver as the giver! O mysterious covenants! O you who grant power and take on weakness! O you who reveal the human being as eternal, in that the eternal one begins to exist bodily as a creature! For if the human person is divinized, in that God is humanized, and the one God himself is revealed as also human, then the same individual, being human, is eternal in divinity, yet still, being God, begins to live in his humanity.

4   In ancient times, on Mount Sinai, smoke and darkness and a windstorm and terrifying fire covered that peak, and proclaimed the lawgiver as inaccessible; he revealed his back parts in a shadowy way, and showed through his own creatures that he was the best of creators. But now all is filled with light and radiance! For the lawgiver himself, the creator and Lord of the universe, comes down from his Father's breast, without leaving his own rightful identity, or even his place near the Father's heart; he has lowered himself to the level of his servants and made the servants' form his own,[24] becoming human in nature and form, so that the uncontainable God might be available to men and women, revealing through himself and in himself the brilliance of the divine nature.

Formerly, in a unified show of his own graciousness, God established humanity: he breathed the breath of life into the one newly formed of earth, gave him a share in a better existence, honored him with his own image and likeness, and made him a citizen of Eden, a tablemate of angels. But since we darkened and destroyed the likeness of the divine image by the filth of passions, he who is compassionate has shared with us a second communion, more secure and still more wonderful than the first. For he remains in the exalted height of his own divinity, but takes on a share of what is less, divinely forming humanity in himself; he mingles the archetype with its image, and reveals in it today his own proper beauty.

[24]Phil 2.6f.

"And his face shone like the sun"—for it was identified hypostatically with immaterial light, and therefore *became* the sun of justice;
"but his garments became white as snow:"[25] for his garments were
glorified as clothing, not by union—by a relationship, not by [unity
of] hypostasis.[26] "A bright cloud overshadowed him,"[27] sketching
an image of the Spirit's flame. This is the way the divine Apostle
speaks, using the sea to convey an image of water, or a cloud that
of the Spirit. But everything is full of light, and more than brilliant,
for those who are capable of receiving the light, and are not soiled
in soul by a stained conscience.

5   Come, then, let us also imitate the obedience of the disciples;
let us eagerly follow Christ as he calls us; let us shake off the swarm
of our sufferings; let us confess the Son of the living God without
shame. And to become worthy of the promise, let us withdraw to the
peak of virtue, which is love, and there let us become observers of
his glory and hearers of unspeakable things. For truly blessed, as the
Lord said, are the eyes of those who see what they see, and the ears
that hear what they hear, which many prophets and kings desired to
see and hear, and did not attain to their desire.[28]

Come, then, let us open up the meaning of the divine sayings, as
much as possible; let us set a table for ourselves as honored guests,
and let us direct all our hunger towards divine things. Let us set a
table that befits our hunger, a table of heavenly words, richly flavored
with the grace of the Spirit—not spiced with the effete wisdom of
Greek arguments, since we have not been particularly initiated into

[25]Matt 17.2, 5; cf. 28.3.

[26]A somewhat obscure sentence. John understands the "garment" of Christ to
be the human flesh which the Son "put on" as his own in the Incarnation. His human
body here begins to radiate the divine glory which naturally belongs to his own
hypostasis or person, as Son of God. So his own "face" (which is the root meaning
of *prosōpon* or "person") acquires no additional glory on Mt Thabor, but this glory
now becomes visible to his disciples for the first time in the flesh with which he has
"robed" himself.

[27]Matt 17.5.

[28]See Matt 13.16f.

their knowledge, but with the wisdom of the one who gives to stammerers a tongue clear in speech, which relies on grace.

6   In Caesaraea Philippi—this is Paneas, once widely renowned among cities, which was named after the Emperor Philip, and called Dan in holy Scripture; David, the Bible says, numbered the people "from Dan to Beersheba"[29]—the Master, with his servants, came and dried up the flow of blood of the woman with a haemorrhage. There he raised the young daughter of the leader of the synagogue;[30] there he gathered the first synod of his own disciples, and using a certain rock as a kind of spontaneous teaching-chair, the rock of life asked his disciples, "Who do people say that the Son of man is?"[31]

It was not because he was unaware of human ignorance that the one who knows all things asked this question, but because he wished to dispel it with the light of knowledge, as it lay like a kind of dark fog over their inner eyes. And they replied that some declared him to be John the Baptist, others Elijah, others Jeremiah or one of the prophets. For when they saw such a depth of miracles, they surmised that one of the ancient prophets had been raised from the dead, and afterwards was deemed worthy of such great grace. This much is clear: "Herod the Tetrarch heard of Jesus' reputation," Scripture says, "and said to his servants, 'This is John the Baptist; he has been raised from the dead, and for this reason the powers are at work in him.'"[32]

In an attempt to disperse this suspicion and to bestow the true faith on the ignorant as a kind of gift—the most excellent gift of all—what did he do, since all power lay in his hands? As a human being, he raises a question; but as God, he secretly bestows wisdom

[29]II Sam 24.1–2. John is particularly precise about identifying the site of Peter's confession geographically, probably because he is preaching to a Palestinian audience. The contemporary name for Caesaraea Philippi, at the northern extremity of Israel, is once more its original name, Paneas.

[30]Matt 9.20–25.
[31]Matt 16.13.
[32]Matt 14.1.

on the one first called, the one first to follow, the one whom he, in his own foreknowledge, had marked out for the dignity of leadership in the Church. As God, he inspires him and speaks out through him. What was his question? "But you—who do *you* say that I am?" And Peter, inflamed with burning eagerness and borne along by the Holy Spirit, replied: "You are the Christ, the Son of the living God!"

O blessed mouth! O richly privileged lips! O soul that speaks of God![33] O mind inspired by God, worthy of sharing divine mysteries! O instruments, on which the Father plays his song! "You are truly blessed, Simon, son of John"—the one who cannot lie has revealed this to you! Not flesh, not blood, not human intelligence, but the heavenly Father has shown you this divine, ineffable formulation of God's ways![34] For no one recognizes the Son except the one who alone is known by him: the Father who begot him, and the Holy Spirit, who understands the depths of God.[35]

This is the upright, unshakable faith, on which—as on a rock—the Church is established; you have been rightly named for it![36] The gates of hell—the mouths of heretics, instruments of demons—will attack it, but not overpower it; will assault it in arms, but not conquer it. Their blows have been, and will be, a weapon of fools! Their tongues will grow weak and will be turned against them. The one who resists the truth contrives evil against himself. He [Christ] acquired it [the Church] by his own blood, and he entrusts it to you [Peter] as his most trusted minister. Protect it by your prayers, steady and firm against the waves! Our confidence is firm that it will never be overturned, never be shaken, never be conquered. Christ has spoken, through whom heaven was made firm, the earth was set in its place and remains unmoved. "By the Word of the Lord the heavens were established,"[37] says the Holy Spirit.

---

[33]Literally: "O theological soul!" Until the end of chapter 6, John apostrophizes Peter, who has expressed so clearly the faith of the Church.

[34]Literally: "this ineffable theology."

[35]See I Cor 2.10.

[36]I.e., Simon receives now the name "Peter".

[37]Ps 32.6 (LXX).

But we pray that the deluge might be tamed, that the force of chaos be broken, and that a peaceful calm, without disturbance, might be bestowed on us. We must petition Christ for this, the Church's spotless bridegroom, who designated you to hold the keys to his Kingdom, who bestowed on you the task of strictly binding and loosing, whom you—with divinely blessed mouth—have truthfully proclaimed the Son of the living God!

O divine events, beyond description! He called himself "Son of Man," and Peter—or rather, God speaking in him—proclaimed him "Son of God." For he is really God and a human being; he is not named son of Peter, or of Paul, or of Joseph, or of any father, but "Son of Man." For he has no father on earth, who has no mother in heaven!

7   Wishing then to confirm his words in deeds, and knowing what he would do, the almighty "Wisdom and Power of God,"[38] " in whom all the treasures of knowledge are hidden,"[39] said, "There are some of those standing here who will not taste of death, until they see the Son of Man coming in his Kingdom."[40] Now if he had said this about just one person, meaning "There is someone among those standing here," we would have supposed him to be suggesting the same thing as in the phrase, "If I wish him to remain until I come, what is that to you?"[41]—which is said about John the Theologian, meaning that he would remain without tasting death until the second coming of Christ; and so, indeed, some very wise people have understood the saying. But since the text indicates that there were several who would see him, and since in fact the event itself followed, it does not leave much room for those who wish to understand the significance of the text in this way.

"There are," then, "some of those standing here," it says. Why does he say "some," and not "all"? Are not all disciples and Apostles?

[38]I Cor 1.24.
[39]Col 2.3.
[40]Matt 16.28.
[41]John 21.22.

Were not all called in the same way, and did not all follow? Did not all receive an equal grace of healing? Why, then, were not all judged similarly worthy of this vision that is beyond seeing? Is not the Lord free of personal preferences? All were disciples, but not all were blinded by the sickness of greed. All were disciples, but not all had lost their sharpness of vision to the bleary humor of envy. All were disciples, but not all were betrayers. All were Apostles, but not all were led by despair to tie their necks in a noose and to try to correct one evil by another. All loved Christ, but only one was a lover of money. This was Judas Iscariot, who alone was not worthy to gaze on the divinity. "Let the wicked man be brought to a halt," Scripture says, "lest he see the glory of the Lord."[42] He alone, then, was let go from the company of the others because, being more envious and malicious, he was inflamed to ever-greater madness.

It was fitting, surely, that those who were going to become witnesses of his sufferings later on should gaze on his glory. For this reason he takes the leading Apostles with him to be witnesses of the glory and divinity that were properly his: suggesting by the number three the sublime mystery of the Trinity, and also since "on the word of two or three witnesses every assertion shall be established."[43] In this way, he reserves for the betrayer the future charges of betrayal, and reveals to the Apostles his own divinity. For if he looked at Andrew, he would not have said that he would be led to betray his Lord for money by the excuse of not sharing the vision. For this reason, Andrew remained below, with all the rest of the apostolic band—distant from him in bodily space, but one with him in the bond of love, staying below physically but following the Master in the yearning and the affections of their souls.

8 "And after six days," Saints Matthew and Mark proclaim to us;[44] but the ever-wise Luke says, "It happened about eight days after these

---

[42]Is 26.10 (LXX).
[43]Deut 19.15.
[44]Matt 17.1; Mark 9.2

things were said . . ."[45] Appropriately and truly, eight and six days are announced by the heralds of truth! There is no contradiction in what is said, but rather high agreement, supported by the same Spirit—for "they are not the ones who are speaking, but the Spirit of God is speaking in them."[46] "For when the Paraclete comes," Jesus says, "he will teach you and remind you of everything."[47] Those, then, who said "after six days" subtracted the end-units—I mean the first and the last days—and counted those in the middle; but he who counted eight days included middle and end in his number. People are used to counting either one way or the other.

And six is understood to be the first perfect number. For it is completely made up of its own parts: three is half of it, two a third, and one a sixth; when multiplied together, they constitute it perfectly. That is why the specialists in these matters have named the number six "perfect." But also, in six days God brought about, by a word, the sum total of all the things we see. It is fitting, then, that those who gaze on God's glory should be perfect, too, since it is beyond all things, alone surpassingly perfect and prior to perfection. For [Christ] says, "Be perfect, as your heavenly father is perfect."[48]

But as for eight: it conveys the symbol of the coming age. For this present life is bounded by seven ages, and the coming life is called the eighth age, as the great Theologian Gregory says when explaining the dictum of Solomon that we should give a share to the seven—the present life—and another to the eight, which is the life to come.[49] It was necessary, too, that on the eighth day the things that belong to the eighth day should be revealed to the perfect. For as the truly divine interpreter, holy Dionysius, says, thus the Lord will appear to his perfect servants, in the same way that he was seen by

[45]Lk 9.28.

[46]Matt 10.20.

[47]John 14.26.

[48]Matt 5.48. Half of the principal manuscripts consulted by the editor have the correct reading of the Gospel, "*your* heavenly Father."

[49]Gregory of Nazianzus, Or. 44.5, explaining Eccl 11.2.

the Apostles on Mount Thabor.[50] Here you have the reason for the numbering of the days.

9   But why did he take along Peter and James and John? Peter, because he wanted to show him that the witness, which he [= Peter] had truly borne, was now confirmed by the witness of the Father, and to make credible his [= Christ's] own statement that the heavenly Father had revealed this to him [= Peter]; and also because he [= Peter] was the chief,[51] and had received the rudder of the whole Church. James, because he was to die for Christ before all the disciples, and so would drink his [Christ's] cup and be baptized into his baptism, for his sake.[52] And John, as the virgin-theologian, the purest instrument, that he might gaze on the timeless glory of the Son; he would thunder out, "In the beginning was the Word, and the Word was with God, and the Word was God"[53]—which is why he is nicknamed "son of thunder."[54]

10   Why does Jesus lead the disciples up a high mountain? Holy Scripture figurally names the virtues "mountains." Now love is clearly the summit and high fortress of all the virtues, for perfection is defined in this way. For if anyone should "speak with the tongues of men and angels," and "if he should have faith so as to move mountains and know all mysteries, and hand over his body to be burned, but not have love, he becomes an echoing piece of brass, or a loud-sounding cymbal," and is reckoned as nothing.[55]

It is right, then, for those who have left the dust to dust, and who have risen up above this lowly body, to be borne up towards the highest, divine region of love, and so to contemplate what lies beyond

---

[50]Ps.-Dionysius, *On the Divine Names* 1.4.

[51]See Matt 16.17.

[52]See Mark 10.39. For the report of his martyrdom, see Acts 12.2; Eusebius, *Church History* 3.5.

[53]John 1.1.

[54]Mark 3.17.

[55]See I Cor 13.1–3, from which these phrases are taken.

sight. For the one who has come to live in love's highest degree stands, in a sense, outside himself, and knows the invisible; flying above the darkness that covers this bodily cloud, he comes into the soul's bright upper atmosphere, and gazes now more clearly than before on the sun of justice. Even if he is not able to be filled completely by the sight, still he prays privately; for the mother of prayer is rest, and prayer is the manifestation of God's glory. [56] For when we shut down the senses and enter into union with ourselves and God, and—freed from the steady revolution of the external world—come to live inside ourselves, then we shall clearly see the Kingdom of God in ourselves. For Jesus, who is God, declared that "the Kingdom of heaven," which is the Kingdom of God, is "within you"![57]

Slaves are accustomed to pray one way, the Lord in another. For slaves approach the master by beseeching him in fear and longing; and prayer serves as a sponsor for the mind in its journey towards union with God, nourishing it and strengthening it by its own power. But that holy mind that is united to the Word of God in his hypostasis—how does it pray? How does the Lord come to our help when we beg him to do so? Clearly, by taking on our person, by training us, by leading the way in our ascent to God through prayer; by teaching us that prayer is the established guide towards attaining God's glory; by showing that he is not a rival to God, and reveres his Father as source and cause of himself; and by bestowing on the flesh the possibility of making its way through its own nature, so that it might

---

[56] The word John uses here, ἡσυχία, rest or peace, seems to be an allusion to the practice of "hesychastic" prayer, based on the continuing repetition of a short Biblical word or phrase, promoted by St John Climacus, the monk of Sinai who died in 649, a century before the death of John of Damascus. This kind of prayer, which is believed to set the heart at peace and to allow the person praying to "center" himself or herself in an awareness of God, continues to be a central part of monastic spirituality in the East, and is used by Christians in many parts of the world, as well as by other religious traditions. For both John Climacus and John Damascene, the practice of contemplative prayer was, in turn, the first step towards human awareness of, and participation in, the glorious "energies" of God—a theme that came to be heavily emphasized by Byzantine spiritual writers in the medieval period.

[57] Luke 17.21.

be strengthened and trained through it, and might be initiated into possessing the better things; and in addition to this, that he might entrap the tyrant, who carefully watches to see if he is God—for that is what the power of his miracles proclaimed![58] In this way, he mingles human qualities everywhere with divine ones, so as to hide the hook with a bit of food![59] For so the one who wanted to entice humanity with the hope of divinity[60] was himself justly lured by the appearance of flesh. If someone were to see him [Jesus] at prayer, radiating light, they would recall that Moses' face, too, shone with glory. But Moses was glorified externally, the glory being bestowed on him from without; while the Lord Jesus did not possess the radiance of glory as something acquired, but as coming from the brilliance of the divine glory that was naturally his own.

11   But let the Prophet David teach you what [Jesus'] prayer of invocation is, as he makes it clear in these words: "He will call upon me, saying, 'You are my Father, my God—the protector who saves me.'"[61] "Father," that is, of God the Son before the ages, who radiates forth from the substance of the one who begets him; "God and the protector who saves me," in that [the Son] has been made flesh and made human, has renewed our nature in himself, and has raised it to the ancient beauty of the image, bearing in himself the common face of humanity.[62] Therefore [David] added, "And I will establish him as my first-born."[63] For the one who, like us, shares in flesh and blood

---

[58]In this remarkable passage, John attempts to summarize what Jesus has revealed in the way he prays, and how he teaches his disciples to pray.

[59]For this familiar Patristic metaphor of God's "hiding" his divinity by his humanity, to entrap the devils into laying hold of him, as a greedy fish might grab a hook baited with food, see also Gregory of Nyssa, *Catechetical Oration* 21 (GNO 4.56.23–24); 24 (ibid. 62.8–13).

[60]See Gen 3.5, where the serpent promises Eve, "You shall be as gods, knowing good from evil," if she and her husband eat from the tree of knowledge.

[61]Ps 88.27 (LXX).

[62]For a similar conception of the effect of the Incarnation in restoring humanity to its original beauty, see Athanasius, *On the Incarnation* 14, 20.

[63]Ps 88.28.

is called "the first-born among many brethren."[64] As God the Word, he was always Son, and did not come into being at a later point; he is said to have been born later, however, as a human being, so that what is proper to sonship might remain unchanged in him. For when he himself became flesh, and the flesh became Son of God in its proper existence, because of the hypostatic union, he is said to have *become* this himself: being in a godly way, becoming as a human being.[65]

12   When he led up Mount Thabor, then, those who were conspicuous for their lofty virtues, "he was transfigured before their faces."[66] He who is always glorified in this way, and who radiates with the brilliance of the Godhead, was transfigured in the presence of his disciples. Begotten without beginning from the Father, he possesses without beginning the natural splendor of the Godhead, and did not acquire either being or glory at some later point. He is from the Father, surely, but he continues to possess the brilliance of glory as his own, without beginning and apart from time; and although he was made flesh, he remains who he is, in the same divine radiance. His flesh, therefore, is glorified at the very moment when it comes from non-being into being; the glory of his Godhead becomes also the glory of his body. The one Christ is both realities: of the same substance as the Father, and naturally one with us, part of the same race.

If, then, the holy body never existed without a share in the divine glory, but because of the genuinely hypostatic union was always

[64]Rom 8.29.

[65]John here borrows the now traditional language of Cyril of Alexandria for speaking about the union of the divine and the human in Christ—language canonized at the Second Council of Constantinople in 553. The *hypostasis*, or concrete individual being, of Christ is one, because of the "literal union" (ἄκρα ἕνωσις) of the divine and human realities, which has taken place. The result of this is that divine characteristics can legitimately be predicated of the man Jesus as his own, and human characteristics can be predicated of the second person of the Trinity. This practice—often used as a test or even a challenge in the early Church, to prove an individual's acceptance of the Church's Christological faith—is usually referred to as "the exchange of characteristics" or (more technically) the "communication of idioms."

[66]Matt 17.2.

enriched in a perfect way by the glory of his divinity, so that the glory of the Word and that of his flesh are one and the same, still the glory present in the visible body had not been revealed to those who could not take in what even angels cannot see—to prisoners of the flesh—and it counted as invisible. He was transfigured, then: not taking on what he was not, nor being changed to what he was not, but making what he *was* visible to his own disciples, opening their eyes and enabling them, who had been blind, to see. This is what the phrase means, "He was transfigured before their faces"; he remained exactly the same as he was, but appeared in a way beyond the way he had appeared before, and in that appearance seemed different to his disciples.

13 "And his face shone like the sun":[67] he who with great power led the sun on its way, who formed the light before the sun, and later crafted the sun, as a vessel of light, to be its lamp. For he himself is the true light, eternally generated from true and immaterial light—the hypostatic Word of the Father, the shining forth of his glory, the natural stamp formed from the individuality of God his Father.[68] This was the one whose face shone like the sun!

What do you say, Evangelist? To what will you liken that which is truly incomparable? What will you set beside that which really has no peer–to what will you compare it? The Lord who shone, with a household slave? The unendurable, inaccessible light, with this sun that flashes forth, gazed on by all? I[69] am tempted to say that I will not make comparisons, nor draw parallels to that which alone is unique, the ray of divine glory that is beyond compare; but speaking out from within the bonds of flesh, I must use as a model the most beautiful and radiant of bodies. It is not completely like him—for it is impossible to form an image of uncreated being within creation,

[67]Matt 17.2.

[68]See Heb 1.3.

[69]For the rest of this paragraph, John seems to be speaking in the person of one of the Evangelists, allowing him to explain what he means by comparing Jesus' radiant face with the sun.

without serious inadequacy. Still, just as the sun is one, yet has two substances–that of light, which came into being earlier, and that of the body which followed it in creation[70]—but the light remains uniform without division through the whole body, and while the body remains contained in itself, the light spreads over all the bounds of the earth; so too Christ, being "light from light" without beginning, came to exist in a time-bound, created body, yet is one "sun of justice,"[71] recognized in two undivided natures.

The holy body, after all, is circumscribed—for as it stood on Thabor, it did not extend beyond the mountain; but the divinity is without place, being in all things and beyond all things. And the body "shines like the sun": for the shining forth of light originated within his body. Every property of the one, enfleshed God the Word came to be held in common, those of the flesh and those of boundless divinity; but their common claims to glory are one thing, and the reasons for recognizing common sufferings are another. The divine reality dominates, and shares some of its proper light and glory with the body—remaining without any share of passibility, even amid [Jesus'] sufferings. So "his face shone like the sun," not that it was less brilliant than the sun, but because this was how much the onlookers were capable of seeing. For if he had showed the full radiance of his glory, how could they have failed to be consumed by it? "His face shone like the sun"; what the sun is among perceptible things, this God is for the intelligible world.

"And his garments became white as light."[72] For the sun is one thing—the spring of light, which cannot be looked at steadily; but the light that reaches the earth from it is something else, for it is seen, through the action of God's wisdom and generosity; we look at

---

[70]Ancient cosmology assumed that the sun, the planets and the stars are living beings—large, intelligent, spherical animals—whose assigned role is to contain the light which had been created earlier, and to shed it on the earth, as well as to "mark the months" by their movements (see Gen. 1.14–18). See Alan Scott, *Origen and the Life of the Stars* (Oxford: Oxford University Press, 1991).

[71]Mal 3.20.

[72]Matt 17.2.

it, so that we might not remain completely without a share in good things. But here, his face shines more clearly than the sun, and his garments are white as light, made brilliant through the imparting of the divine light.

14   When these things had been accomplished in this way, so that the Lord of the Old and the New Testament might be revealed as one, and that the mouths of heretics—whose throats are an open tomb—might be stopped, and the resurrection of the dead might be made credible, and the one to whom witness was being given might be credibly identified as "Lord of living and dead,"[73] Moses and Elijah stand, as servants, alongside their Lord in glory, and are observed by their fellow servants as conversing with him. For it was right that when they saw the glory and freedom of access accorded their fellow servants, also worshippers of God, they should be amazed at the loving adaptation of the Lord to their needs, and should become all the more eager and courageous with regard to their coming struggles. For the person who knows the outcome of his labors might easily dare to struggle. Yearning for the reward usually drives us towards generosity in bodily risks.

For just as soldiers and boxers and field laborers and merchants take up their hard work with great eagerness, and face the waves of the sea and wild beasts, and pay no heed to pirates, so that they might lay hold of the prize they long for—and the more they see those who labored before them feasting on their gains, so much the more they are spurred on to endure their labors—so spiritual infantry and spiritual boxers and spiritual field-workers and merchants do not yearn for earthy gain, or lust after the good things one can see, when they gaze with their own sight on the things stored up in

[73]See Acts 10.42; cf. also the opening lines of Gerard Manley Hopkins' poem, "The Wreck of the Deutschland":

> "Thou mastering me
> God, giver of breath and bread,
> World's strand, sway of the sea,
> Lord of living and dead . . ."

expectation, and see those who have labored before them enjoying the luxury of the good things they hope for. They will be fitted out all the more energetically for contests where they are not ranged against human opponents, and do not "fight as beating the air,"[74] or lead oxen under yoke to plow the field and with them cut furrows in the earth, or beat back the tossing waves of the sea, but they fight against the rulers of darkness, and struggle by being beaten, and gather wealth by stripping it away, and thrust the rudder of the cross against the triple waves of the world and the wicked spirits that stir them up, and drive out howling, grasping beasts by the power of the Spirit, and sow the word of religious reverence in human hearts like plowed furrows, gathering an abundant harvest for the Lord. But let us return to our passage once again.

15   Then Moses probably answered in reply: "Hear, O spiritual Israel," what the visible Israel has not been able to hear; "the Lord your God is a single Lord."[75] For God is recognized as one, in three hypostases. There is one substance of Godhead: the Father who bears witness, and the Son to whom he witnesses, and the Spirit who overshadows him. This is the one now witnessed by the Father, "the life of men and women."[76] People without knowledge see him, hanged up on a cross, and do not believe in their life. Then Elijah responded: "He is the one whom I gazed on long ago, in bodiless form, in the gentle breeze of the Spirit";[77] for "no one has ever seen God"[78] as God is in his nature. And what he saw, he contemplated in the Spirit. "This is how the right hand of the Most High has changed";[79] this is "what eye has not seen and what ear has not heard, what has never entered into the heart of a human being."[80] "In this way"—in the age

[74] I Cor 9.26.
[75] Deut 6.4.
[76] Cf. John 1.4.
[77] See 3 Kg 19.12.
[78] John 1.18.
[79] Ps 76.11 (LXX).
[80] I Cor 2.9.

to come—"we shall always be with the Lord,"[81] seeing Christ radiant with the light of divinity.

16 Why does Peter, who has now become a spectator of this divine revelation, say to the Lord, as if inspired in spirit, "It is good for us to be here"[82]? Who would take darkness in exchange for light? You see this sun—how beautiful and lovely it is, how sweet, how desirable, shining and radiant; you see life—how sweet and desirable it is, how everyone clings to it, how everyone would do anything so as not to throw it away. How much more do you think light in itself, from which all life shines forth, is desirable and sweet? How much more pleasant and delightful is life itself, from which all life has its source and is shared, in which all of us "live and move and have our being"[83]? Not all the sweetness there is, nor all the yearning—there is no reason or desire that can calculate the measure by which it surpasses what we know. It supersedes all comparison, and is not subject to any measurement. For how could we measure what is uncircumscribed, ungrasped by our process of reasoning? This light takes the prize of victory over all nature. This life has overcome the world.[84] Why, then, should not one good thing be distinguished from another? What Peter says is not foolishness!

But since all good things come in their own good time—"for there is a right time for everything,"[85] Solomon proclaimed—it was necessary that this Good not be limited only to those who were there, but that Goodness be poured out on all who believe, and that it journey with them, so that there should be many who share in its benefits. And this is what cross and suffering and death would bring to fulfillment. It would not be good for the one who by his very blood bought free his own creation—the reason for which he became flesh—to remain here. If all of you had remained on Mount

[81] I Thess 4.17.
[82] Matt 17.4.
[83] Acts 17.28.
[84] Cf. I John 5.4.
[85] Eccl 3.1.

Thabor, the promise made to you would never have come to its fulfillment—for you would not have become the keeper of the keys of the Kingdom, Paradise would not have been thrown open for a thief, the haughty tyranny of death would not have been defeated, the kingdom of Hades would not have been made into a fallow field,[86] Adam would not have been rescued, Eve would not have been redeemed, the patriarchs, prophets, and just ones would not have been released from the innermost parts of death's realm, nature would not have been wrapped in incorruption![87]

If Adam had not sought after divinization before the right moment, he would have gained what he yearned for.[88] Do not look for good things before the time, Peter. The time will come when you will obtain this vision unceasingly. The Master has appointed you as housekeeper not of tabernacles, but of the Church throughout the whole world. Your disciples, your sheep, which the good chief shepherd has put into your hands, have brought your words forward to realization by building the tabernacle for Christ—and for Moses and Elijah, his servants—in which we celebrate this feast today.[89]

Peter did not say this because of some calculation, but by the inspiration of the Spirit who foretells what is to come. "For he did not know what he was saying,"[90] the divine Luke tells us. And Mark adds the reason: "They were terrified!"[91] When Simon uttered these

[86]See Is 33.23.

[87]John alludes here to the ancient tradition, found as far back as Irenaeus, *Adversus Haereses* III, 23, that Adam and Eve were rescued from the realm of death, along with the saints of the Old Covenant, when Jesus entered Hades and broke down its doors. See also the famous 13th-century mural of this scene in the monastery Church of Our Holy Savior in Chora (the *Kariye Djami*) in Constantinople.

[88]For this interpretation of the sin of Adam and Eve—that it was a question of seeking the kind of knowledge that they would eventually have shared as God's gift, but seeking it before they were ready to receive it—see Gregory of Nazianzus, Or. 38, "On the Theophany."

[89]This remark may indicate that the Church in which John is preaching this homily is on Mount Thabor in northern Palestine. At least it seems to be dedicated to the Mystery of the Transfiguration.

[90]Lk 9.33.

[91]Mk 9.6.

words, "Behold, a bright cloud overshadowed them," and the disciples were seized with even greater fear, as they gazed on Jesus, the Savior and Lord, now inside the cloud with Moses and Elijah.

17 In ancient times, the one who gazed on God[92] entered into the holy darkness, having received a hint that the Law was a shadow; listen to Paul when he writes, "The law held a shadow of things to come, not the truth itself."[93] After that, "Israel was not able to gaze on the glory of Moses' face, which was passing away";[94] "but we, with faces uncovered, reflect the glory of the Lord, being transfigured from glory to a greater glory, as if led by the Spirit of the Lord."[95] For this reason a cloud, not of darkness but of light, overshadowed them. The "Mystery hidden from all ages and the generations is revealed,"[96] constant and eternal glory is shown forth. This is the reason, surely, that Moses stands alongside Elijah, completing the appearance of the Law and the Prophets. The one whom the Law and the Prophets proclaim, this Jesus, is discovered now to be the giver of life. And Moses represents the whole company of those holy ones who had long ago fallen asleep, but Elijah the company of the living; for the transfigured one is "Lord of living and dead."[97] Moses has entered into the promised land[98]—for Jesus, the giver of the inheritance, has brought him in; and what he once saw in figures, today he gazes on in the clearest light. This, then, is what the brightness of the cloud suggests!

[92]I.e., Moses—see Ex 33.18–20; 34.6–8.
[93]Heb 10.1.
[94]II Cor 3.7.
[95]II Cor 3.18.
[96]Col 1.26.
[97]Acts 10.42.
[98]Because he had doubted in following the Lord's instructions at Massah in the desert, years before, Moses came to the edge of the Promised Land—the mountains across the Jordan from Jericho—but he was not allowed to enter it himself, and died still a wayfarer. See Deut 32.48–52.

18   And a voice came from the cloud, saying, 'This is my Son, the Beloved, in whom I am well pleased. Listen to him!'"[99] The Father's voice has come from the cloud of the Spirit: "This is my Son, the Beloved," this is the visible man, the one who is[100] and who is also seen, the one who became man only yesterday, who moves humbly among you, whose face now shines upon you. This is my beloved Son, who is before the ages; who has come forth eternally and time-lessly, only-begotten, alone from the alone, from me his begetter; who always exists from me and in me and with me, not a moment later in his existence. He is from me as from his Father and cause, begotten of my substance and hypostasis, and therefore "of the same substance."[101] He is begotten in me, inseparably and without com-ing forth from me; he exists with me as a complete hypostasis, not an "uttered word" poured forth into the air[102]—and therefore he is the Beloved! What Son is beloved, as the Only-begotten is? In him I am well pleased! For by the good pleasure of the Father, his only Son and Word has become flesh; by the good pleasure of the Father in his only Son, he has worked the salvation of the whole world; by the good pleasure of the Father in his only Son, he has welded into unity the connections between all things. For if the human person is of his nature a "little world"[103]—bearing in himself the connect-ing link of all that is, visible and invisible, being both the one and the other—then surely the Lord and Creator and Ruler of all things is well pleased that a connection of divinity and humanity should come to full reality in his only Son, of one substance with himself,

[99]Matt 17.5; Luke 9.35.

[100]Greek: *ho ōn*. In icons of the Lord, this title—reminiscent of God's name for himself in Ex 3.14—is traditionally given as an identifying label, inscribed in the nimbus that surrounds Jesus' head.

[101]This adjective, *homoousios*, was of course one of the most contentious terms of the creed of Nicaea (325), and has remained for orthodox Christians a central norm of right faith in Jesus.

[102]John refers here to the distinction found in Justin, *Second Apology* 8, 13, based on the Stoic theory of a cosmic Logos or principle of order, between a "Word" that is present as ordered knowledge within the mind of God, and a Word that is "uttered" to be an active principle of shaping the world.

[103]Literally, "a microcosm."

and through this all creation might be linked as one, "so that God may be all in all."[104]

"This is my Son," "the shining-forth of my glory, the stamp of my hypostasis,[105] through whom I have also made the angels," through whom the heavens took solid form, the earth was set in place; this is the one who "bears all things by his word of power"[106] and by the breath of his mouth—the Spirit, who is the source and guide of life. "Listen to him!" For the one who receives him receives me,[107] the one who sent him—sent him not as Lord and Master, but as Father. As a human being he is sent, but as God he remains in me, and I in him.[108] Whoever does not honor my only, beloved Son, does not honor me, the Father who begot him. "Listen to him!" This is the final goal of the Mysteries you celebrate, the meaning of the Mystery itself.

19 What happened next? He sent Moses and Elijah back to their own places, and is seen alone by the Apostles; and so they come down from the mountain, saying nothing about what they have seen and heard to anyone. For that is what the Lord commanded them. I will tell you what the reason and the purpose of this was: he knew, I think, that the disciples were imperfect, for they had not yet received a perfect share in the Spirit. It was so that grief might not fill the disciples' hearts, and that he might not drive his betrayer into a frenzy of envy.

Come, then, let us bring our discourse to an end with a bit of advice.

20 From all that has been said, may you always bear in your hearts the loveliness of this vision; may you always hear within you the Father's voice: "This is"—not a slave, not an elder, not an angel—but

[104] I Cor 15.28.
[105] See Heb 1.3.
[106] Ibid.
[107] Mk 9.37.
[108] See John 6.56 (spoken of the relationship between the one who receives Jesus in the Eucharist and Jesus himself).

"my beloved Son; listen to him!" Let us, therefore, really listen to him, as he says, "You shall love the Lord your God with your whole heart."[109] "You shall not kill"—but you also shall not be angry with your brother without reason.[110] "Be reconciled with your brother first, and then go and offer your gift."[111] "You shall not commit adultery"—but you also shall not let yourself be excited by someone else's beauty. "You shall not swear falsely"—but you shall not even swear at all; "Let your speech be 'Yes, yes!' and 'No, no!' What lies beyond that is an invention of the Evil One. "[112] "You shall not bear false witness." "You shall not commit fraud"—but "give, too, to the one who asks of you, and do not turn away from the one who wants to borrow,"[113] and do not prevent someone from taking what is yours.[114] "Love your enemies, bless those who curse you, act uprightly towards those who hate you, and pray for those who threaten and persecute you."[115] "Do not judge, so that you may not be judged."[116] Forgive, and you will be forgiven, so that you may become sons of your Father, perfect and merciful as is your Father in heaven,[117] "who makes his sun rise on the wicked and the good, and makes rain fall on the just and the unjust."[118]

Let us observe these divine commands with total concentration, so that we too may feast upon his divine beauty, and be filled with the taste of his sweetness: now, insofar as this is attainable for those weighed down by this earthly tent of the body; but in the next life more clearly and purely, when the "just shall shine like the sun,"[119]

[109] Mk 12.30. In the rest of this paragraph, John skillfully weaves together the central moral code of Israel, summed up in the Ten Commandments, with Jesus' intensification of them in the Sermon on the Mount. Moses and Jesus teach here as one!

[110] Matt 5.21.
[111] Matt 5.27f.
[112] Matt 5.33f.
[113] Matt 5.42.
[114] Luke 6.29.
[115] Luke 6.27f.
[116] Matt 7.1.
[117] Matt 5.45.
[118] Matt 5.48.
[119] Matt 13.43.

when they shall be released from the body's necessities, and shall be imperishable, like angels with the Lord, at the time of the great and radiant appearance of our Lord and God and Savior from heaven, Jesus Christ: with whom may glory be given to the Father, with the Holy Spirit, now and to the endless ages of ages. Amen.

EMPEROR LEO VI
("LEO THE WISE')

The Byzantine Emperor Leo VI (866–912), known since his own time as "Leo the Wise"—perhaps better translated "Leo the Learned"—is one of the most complex figures in the early medieval history of the Eastern Roman Empire. Officially acknowledged as the second son of his predecessor Basil I, "the Macedonian," Leo himself seems to have believed that he was actually the son of Basil's predecessor, Michael III, an indecisive ruler and an alcoholic, whom Basil, then his chief advisor, had assassinated when he was only 27. Basil married Michael's mistress, Eudokia Ingerina, who was Leo's mother, before Leo was born. Despite long-standing hostility between them, Basil made Leo co-emperor in 870, when he was only four, and Leo succeeded Basil as sole Emperor in 886, when he was just 20.

Always eager for a male heir, Leo's first marriage, to the devout Theophano Martinakiou, a relative of his mother, was unhappy, and she bore him only a daughter who died in infancy. Theophano died in 895 or 896, and in 898 Leo married his long-term mistress Zoe, who was already married and whose husband had only recently died. But Zoe herself died a year later, leaving only an infant daughter. In July of 900, Leo married Eudocia Baiane, who died in childbirth, too, with her child, the following April. Finally, in September of 905, Leo's new mistress, Zoe Karbounopsina, bore him a son, who would eventually become the Emperor Constantine VII "Porphyrogenitos," and who presided over one of the most brilliant cultural revivals in Byzantine history. Although such a series of liaisons and remarriages—even when both persons were widowed—was canonically highly irregular in the Byzantine Church, Leo pressed to have his fourth marriage, to Zoe Karbounopsina, recognized as legitimate; despite the strong opposition of many in the clergy, he successfully appealed to the other major patriarchs of the Pentarchy, and the marriage was eventually approved by them in March of 907.

As with England's Henry VIII six centuries later, Leo's marital problems made him highly controversial at court and in the Byzantine Church. Despite these difficulties (also like Henry VIII), Leo was generally acknowledged in his time to be a successful administrator, and was certainly a man of intellectual substance and accomplishment—hence his traditional nickname. In his reign, the academic and cultural revival that had begun a few decades earlier, in the time of Patriarch Photios (858–867, 877–886), took firmer root and was to affect Byzantine religious and civil life for almost a century. Leo had been a pupil of Photios as a young man, although on the death of Basil, who had been Photios' imperial patron, he immediately deposed the Patriarch for the second time. A thoroughgoing humanist, Leo undertook an exhaustive revision of the legal code, wrote two treatises on military tactics and several other works on the organization of government offices; he also composed poetry, liturgical *kontakia* and hymns, a body of letters (most of which are lost), and some 42 homilies, which he apparently wrote and delivered himself at liturgies, both at the Church of Hagia Sophia and at other important Churches in the capital. These were composed for some of the major feasts of the liturgical calendar, as well as in honor of some of Leo's favorite saints, and often show a high, if somewhat showy, level of rhetorical finish and theological erudition.

Two later Greek writers on the liturgy—the 11th-century monastic leader and canonist, Nikon of the Black Mountain, and Patriarch Nicholas III of Constantinople (1084–1111)—tell us that people had begun, during Leo the Wise's reign, to interrupt their preparatory fast for the feast of the Dormition on August 15 in order to celebrate the Transfiguration on August 6. Some have seen here evidence that Leo himself introduced this feast, originally celebrated in Palestine, to the Church of Constantinople; but as Vénance Grumel has pointed out, it could simply mean that the older Palestinian feast, already observed in the capital, now came to be celebrated with greater solemnity. (See V. Grumel, "Sur l'ancienneté de la fête de la Transfiguration," *Revue des études byzantines* 14 [1956] 209–210.) In any case, both these notices and Leo's three homilies indicate an awareness by the learned Emperor of the importance of this Gospel event.

For a discussion of Leo's life and achievements, with further bibliographical information, see Theodora Antonopoulou, *The Homilies of the Emperor Leo VI* (Leiden: Brill, 1997), esp. 3–51.

A Homily by Leo the Emperor, on Christ the Eternal King, When [Christ's] Garment Began to Shine, on Thabor, with the Sparks of Divinity, and He Appeared Miraculously Transfigured

Homily 10[1]

Who might lead me up to the mountain of Jesus' Mysteries, and show me what has been accomplished in him today? Who will give clarity to my eye, and allow me to enjoy this greatest of visions? Or if the Spirit lifts me up and kindly clarifies my vision, shall I attempt the ascent, and arriving—as far as possible—at that place high enough to provide a commanding view, shall I see "darkness set upon my flesh as his hiding place,"[2] and revealing himself from there as through a curtain? Shall I see heaven, shining with the bloom of light and illuminating my body mingled with clay, bringing to light once again the splendor of my original beauty, in a way above all reason? Christ shines forth the rays of his glorious form, on the mountain of his own proper glory. Who would not agree that he rejoices in all obstacles, to focus on one thing alone: to ascend there? The "stamp of his glory"[3] revealing [Christ's] proper beauty, adorns his earthy substance. Who would not desire to feast on a beauty such as this?

---

[1]Lei VI's homilies were critically edited, for the first time, by Theodora Antonopoulou, as volume 63 of the *Corpus Christianorum, Series Graeca*: *Leonis VI Sapientis Imperatoris Byzantini* (Turnhout: Brepols 2008). This is the edition we have used in making this translation.

[2]Ps 17.12 (LXX).

[3]Heb 1.3.

Jesus, God and human, one from two, by stripping away one of the elements of which he is composed and by transforming the other,[4] shines forth in an indescribable way on Thabor. Let us press on, then, to learn the dimensions of the Mystery. Let us climb the mountain, and join in contemplation, and let us be changed along with him, and radiate light along with him. Let us share, too, in the brilliance and the magnificence of him, who did not consider it an unworthy thing to share in our poverty. Let us gaze on the hidden riches of the one who, "for our sake became poor with our poverty."[5] Let us look on the one who saw the lovely imprints destroyed, which he had imposed with his immaculate hand on the earth, and when he saw it—O what depth of mercy and goodness!—could not bear to see the great work of his wisdom reduced in such a way to uselessness; but moving on towards a new creation, better than the first, formed not from clay according to the image of the craftsman, became himself like his creation and made what was unformed his own, by this ineffable appropriation and formation renewing the original marks of his own image. Bringing this now to its completion on Thabor and, by the radiance of his divinity, highlighting what he had taken on with what seemed like sparkles of color, he reveals, as in a lightning flash, rays like those of the sun.

O mingled vision of terrifying and delightful things! Heavenly glory gradually takes the place of splendor radiating from the earth. Dawn viewed from the earth hides that to be seen in heaven—the dawn of Jesus my God, "beautiful beyond all others"[6]—since, out of sympathy towards the one who has become deformed, he bears our likeness, and since, because it is not yet possible to enjoy his

---

[4]Leo here summarizes a decidedly Cyrillian version of the classical Christological formula of Chalcedon, which spoke of the single *hypostasis* or individual substance of Christ being "recognized *in* two natures," not simply as being formed *from* two natures. The suggestion here is that he "stripped himself of what was divine," in becoming visible, and at the same time altered the outward form of his human nature.

[5]II Cor 8.9.
[6]Ps 44.3 (LXX).

beauty due to the malice of the unworthy, he will be seen to have "an unworthy and deficient form."[7] Malice will no longer restrain itself, nor will it hide in the corner, twisting its intentions, nor will it be satisfied by putting forth menacing lips, or set a limit to wickedness there, but—as if it wished to give proof of this wickedness—it moves on to the works of bloodshed. Soon a disciple, exchanging benevolence towards his master for silver, will be revealed as his betrayer; and Pilate, trying to avoid having a part in bloodshed, will wash his hands, but will nevertheless hand over to death one who he knows is suffering unjustly. Another moment in time will witness these things acted out, another Scripture passage will make them its theme.

But for now, let us go up with the Master as he climbs the mountain, and share with him in the Mysteries accomplished there. Let no one be left behind by his own choice, nor remain inactive because he is too lazy to climb; for [Christ] does not want anyone to remain below, but wants us all to ascend and to be initiated into the Mystery he experiences. Let eyes feast on this sight, which until today even the sun has not witnessed. Let them gaze on the one who is "wrapped in light as in a cloak,"[8] radiating light from his garments, and illuminating his earthy covering with sparks of immaterial light. Let us stand and participate in the choicest words of the disciples and the prophets, and let us become sharers in these delights with them.

Those are present here who now experience within the confines of the concrete what they formerly were introduced to as represented symbolically: God associating with the creature, for his salvation, not from the height of his own glory, nor engraving laws on tablets with his finger, but in an incomprehensible way writing out his entire self as on the tablet of his flesh, and there giving us his saving law. They saw what is impassible mingled with matter, and matter aflame with divine fire without being consumed[9]—the presence of God formed as if from a light breeze,[10] gently and noiselessly communi-

[7]Is 53.3.
[8]Ps 103.2 (LXX).
[9]Cf. Ex 3.2.
[10]Cf. I Kg 19.12.

cating through flesh. But some see here the shadowy ordinances of ancient times, while the disciples see how great and important their Teacher's rank is, and are instructed by that.[11]

For it was necessary not only that the King reveal the others[12] in their splendor, removing the corruptible elements of their bodies like filthy rags, and clothing them with the fresh wholeness of first creation, and so make his Kingdom known, but also that he should reveal himself to them, shining in his royal, hitherto invisible robe of glory. It was necessary, too, that the divine glory be seen as it is, insofar as human vision can grasp it, vision that now belongs to our hard servitude, but which will in the future share in the redemption that is to come; and [it was necessary] that God give grace to those who are to be sent out on mission to this degree—even if the vision of glory should not be bestowed on all who will be sent. By an excess of modesty, he wanted to pass by some unnoticed, and in his benevolence he wanted to spare those who would shed his blood. So, it seems, in order that the event should not be learned about by everyone (yet still he does not wish that what is offered to the knowledge of many should remain simply beyond our powers of speech), and that envy should not further inflame and weigh down those who have learned something about this; and perhaps to instruct us, too, not to look towards self-promotion or to set high value on human glory, but to conceal in unawareness great achievements—things whose exposure might motivate honor from those men and women who find honor in things not inconsiderable in themselves; and that, at the same time, freedom might be restored by God's gracious plan, and the people might be set free from the depths of its wretchedness—[now] mortal eyes share in God's glory face to face, as far as they are capable.

Peter, first leader of the Apostolic chorus, and the pair who call Zebedee their father, are found worthy of this awe-inspiring vision.

[11]In the dense, rather circuitous paragraph that follows, Leo seems to be trying to explain why the Son revealed his glory to three of the disciples, but not to all.

[12]I.e., Moses and Elijah, who had left this world long before.

For when the moment of his Passion was about to reveal before their eyes the lowly state of his actions, as the Teacher struggled and flowed with sweat and begged "that the cup might pass,"[13] they will be protected by the greatness of these present events, so that they might not be affected by what would happen at that time, or forget them, as they transfer their attention to what is going on in front of them and remain focused on those things; [God willed] that they might have a memory from now on of the dignity of him who would be tested by humiliation, based on these other, supernatural visions, and might take a firm stand on the peak of the divine considerations to which they have ascended, not be drawn down and immersed in the humiliation of what God has deliberately designed.

Now the Father's witness is proclaimed from above, so that later the placement of the Son with evil-doers might not cause suffering to his own followers, for whom he voluntarily comes to undergo suffering; so, having gazed on those who now stand alongside him—the one having flown down from heaven to stand by him, the other finding in the grip of death no obstacle to being present with him[14]—they might remain immersed in what they had seen when they should see him seized by wicked men and brought before a judgment seat, not forgetting the might of him who undergoes the conspiracy.

How delightful Peter is! What sweet words he utters! In every situation, he surpasses the rest in enthusiasm for his Teacher, in every situation he seems to exceed his fellow disciples in eagerness for him, to hang on him more than the others, to breathe nothing else but him.

"Who do you say that I am?" Peter seizes the answer, becoming the mouth of the whole group. And if he hears Jesus predicting his suffering, he will not receive what he says, but disagrees and is not

[13]Matt 26.37–38; Mk 14.36; Lk 22.42–44.

[14]Leo reflects here the common assumption, based on Deuteronomy and II Kings, that while Moses had died and had not yet been raised, Elijah had been taken up bodily into heaven.

hesitant to contradict him, in the heat of love's spell. He sees his Lord flashing the light of splendor, and holds on tenaciously to the spot in which he has gazed on the Lord's beauty like a lover. He does not want to budge from there, but loves the moments they have spent there, so that he might always be able to mingle with the beauty of the one for whom he yearns. For his eager words about the "tents" had this in mind,[15] since he imagined the things they had seen would remain if they all were to stay on Thabor.

It is a fine desire, Disciple, but it moves beyond the intent of your Teacher! Though he is pressing on with other concerns, he reveals what you now see—but you seem to be letting your reasoning stretch towards something else. As the time for ascending the cross draws near, he, as the One from before the ages, works your welfare here in advance; but you are fleeing from those very things, because of which this vision of those before you is being given.

But Peter speaks here for a while about tents, and about wanting to stay on the mountain. What shall we say in answer? How shall we speak to him who is transfigured? What shall we say? Let us magnify the one who is incomparable in his greatness. Let us exalt him, whose humiliation has raised us up. Let us give glory to him who has released us from our inglorious past, the one who was counted among slaves, without departing from his own majesty, preserving unchanged what he was from the Father, even as he appeared before us as one who had come into being from a virgin womb. His transfiguration and radiance now reveal the brilliance of which the earthly creature will be found worthy, when "God will stand in the midst of the gods,"[16] judging who is worthy of his glory and of divinization. Now the Mystery of this day here forms a harmony with all we have said;[17] as with the Lord's Resurrection our own resurrection is inaugurated, so also with his Transfiguration the glory of those who will

---

[15]Matt 17.4.

[16]Ps 81.1 (LXX).

[17]Here Leo makes his first direct reference to the liturgical feast of the Transfiguration.

be divinely changed is announced by way of prologue—bestowed by the loving Lord, in his limitless goodness, on those worthy of the gift even before they receive it, so that they might not only receive it with joy, but also might delight beforehand with a holy joy, at knowing now how great is the grace and blessing that awaits them.

This is what the Lord's Transfiguration today means to me. As I await transformation, this is given to me by way of a pledge.

Would you like us to recall the tricks produced by the jugglings of Greek atheism?[18] Shall we speak of the transformations that they ascribe to their own gods? The point is not that our festival acquire greater solemnity—for no additional brightness can come to the sun out of darkness—but because it is certainly possible that we who celebrate in a godly way might be established as devout and solemn by revealing dishonorable things, so measuring rather our own honor and in consequence demonstrating the true state of things. Let us say—or rather, let them tell us, who lead on parade things worthy of darkness and turn them into cause for celebration—on the basis of what events, and with what transformations, their gods provide them with witness of their own divinity.

Now let [the god] be a bird, now a piece of gold, now let him moo—easily ready to become anything, as an ill-motivated love changes and reshapes him. Let one [god][19] melt into a flowing river, stung by the gadfly of love for Tyro, so that as his beloved swims in him he might steal an opportunity for intercourse. Let Artemis, too, appear as a doe, that she might release the gods from a dreadful threat, which Ephialtes and his family were about to undertake, if

---

[18]In the next several paragraphs, Leo compares the Transfiguration of Jesus, as presented in the Gospels, with stories of the transformation (*metamorphōsis*) of various humans into animal and other forms in the classical myths. Unlike Jesus' transfiguration, these reputed changes were all responses of the gods to their own passions, or to acts of sexual indiscretion by fellow gods. This unique feature of the present homily attests to the renewed interest in classical literature among learned Byzantines in Leo's day, at the start of the tenth-century "Renaissance."

[19]Poseidon, the sea-god, fell in love with Tyro, the daughter of Salmoneus; she was enamored of the river-god Enipeus, so Poseidon disguised himself as the river, that she might throw herself into his arms.

the doe had not escaped and so prevented danger, when she stirred them up to hunt her; actually, after their revolt against the gods, they destroyed each other with the arrows they had meant for her.[20]

Let someone delight, too, in the foolishness of Derketo,[21] the Syrian goddess, who was transformed from being a human into being a fish, and is thought by those people to be a god; she differs from the gods who became serpents in the way she was transformed, in that she did not change form as they did, out of wicked motives and in order to carry out shameful acts, but that she might find encouragement in the midst of the shame that habit had imposed on her, by fleeing the race that had given her a consciousness of shame.

Let the gods give humans, too, a share in this kind of glory, so that they might make us marvel as well as notice their kindness. Now let Callisto be changed into a bear, for the sake of the all-temperate Zeus;[22] let Io now be transformed into a heifer, and let Argos, of whom she was jealous, watch over her as her cowherd;[23]

[20]Leo seems to be alluding to a version of the late story about the giant Titans, Ephialtes and his twin brother Otos, otherwise only known from the fragments of the second-century collection, the *Genealogiae* or *Fabulae*, attributed to the Latin writer Hyginus. According to this story, Otos and Ephialtes had conspired to assault heaven by piling mountains on top of each other. Ephialtes had wanted to subdue and marry Artemis, if they succeeded, but—in order to protect the community of the gods—she disguised herself as a doe when they were out hunting, and ran between them. Each aimed at her, but they ended up shooting and killing each other.

[21]A middle-Eastern fertility goddess, sometimes known as Atargatis. She was associated in non-Greek mythology with orgies, and was venerated at Hierapolis and at Ephesus; she is often referresd to in Greek and Latin literature simply as "the Syrian goddess (*dea Syria*)". In one version of her story, she fell in love with a shepherd boy and became pregnant by him. Overcome with shame, she ran away and fell into a pool. The gods transformed her into a fish.

[22]Callisto, in Ovid's Latin version (*Metamorphoses* 2.405ff.) of the tale, was loved by Zeus, who came to her disguised as Artemis. When the real Artemis discovered Callisto was pregnant, she sent her wandering; Hera then changed her into a bear. When her son Arkas, out hunting fifteen years later, spotted her and was ready to kill her with his spear, Zeus put them both in the heavens, as the Great Bear and Boötes the "bear-watcher."

[23]In the traditional form of this legend, Io, daughter of Inachos, was a priestess of Hera in the land of Argos in Greece. When Zeus became enamored of her, Hera became jealous, and Zeus changed her into a heifer. Hera then asked for the heifer, and placed Argos Panoptes, who had eyes all over his body, to watch her. Hermes

and let Argos be removed by Hermes—for the lover of a roaming animal had no way of bestowing the blessing of descendants on the heifer—and so let her be led off to Egypt, and there be honored as divine. On the other hand, let the cowherd be transformed into a bird, and let his feathers witness to his unsleeping care by being decorated with images of eyes!

Let them count the varied transformations of Proteus,[24] and Tereus' hoopoe and nightingales and swallows,[25] if they wish, and dolphins who were fishermen,[26] and Diomedes' birds,[27] on whom they say, because of whatever fates captured them, the gods took vengeance by giving them such a form in exchange: to be counted among four-footed beasts or birds or fishes rather than being recognizable as humans. And there is nothing shameful about showing reverence to such creatures, whom those [pagans] seem to be reverencing, as long as whatever divine characteristics they share in, and through which they also share it with others, do not come to be abominations in those permanently endowed with reason.

managed to kill Argos by lulling him to sleep, upon which Argos was changed into the first peacock. Meanwhile, Hera sent a gadfly to drive Io mad and to start her wandering. She eventually came to Egypt, where she regained her sanity, and bore Zeus a son named Epaphos. She was thought then to have been honored by the Egyptians under the name of Isis.

[24]Proteus, a Mediterranean sea-god, was thought able to change himself at will into many different forms.

[25]Tereus, king of Thrace, married Procne, daughter of Pandion. He fell in love with her sister, Philomela, and raped her; when Procne discovered this, she killed Itys, her son by Tereus. When he prepared to kill the two sisters in revenge, he was transformed into a hoopoe, and the sisters into a swallow and a nightingale, respectively. See Plutarch, *Theseus* 19.

[26]In the seventh Homeric hymn, to Dionysos, the god is posing as a handsome young fisherman. He is captured by pirates, who leap overboard when they discover he is a god; they become dolphins, but later belief argued this is the reason dolphins are generally friendly to fishermen.

[27]One of the notable heroes on the Greek side in the Trojan war, Diomedes wounded Aphrodite in the course of battle, and as a result was condemned to wander around the Mediterranean for a time. While visiting some islands in the Adriatic Sea off the east coast of Italy (according to Strabo, *Geography* 7.1.9), he encountered there a flock of sea birds who were friendly to Greeks but hostile to Italians; they were apparently his fellow soldiers, who had been transformed into birds.

We will allow the Greeks to chatter amiably about such things and to say even solemn things about them; dishonor is honorable to them, after all, and what is shameful a subject for serious consideration! But let us, for ourselves, speak only of divine things in religious terms, being transformed and radiating light along with him who today shines forth on Thabor; let us ascend, in mind and soul and in all our senses, above the shadowy mutiny of sin, as far as it still remains possible for those weighed down by clay to be lifted up, and be marked with the sign of light—with which someone else before us was also signed, who foresaw the events of this day and sang in praise, "Thabor and Hermon will rejoice in your name!"[28] What did he mean by this, besides wanting to express the greatness of the Mystery, for the sake of whose grandeur he ascribes a share in perception even to lifeless things, so that they, too, are moved by this delightful vision to rejoice?

Perhaps, too, [David] is hinting about other mountains, such as are mentioned elsewhere as "leaping."[29] Which ones? Those belonging to peoples once lifted up in evil intent, and those also who had had a part in Israel, in whom the rough and uneven ways of the heart have been leveled by the watering of the Gospel and have received the seed of the Gospel; together let them "rejoice in his" great "name."

But now, O Blessed One [=David], the happy vision you saw and sang about in advance has come as a visible reality upon us, who at this moment rejoice in these things; you bring your own joy to the festival, and share in our rejoicing, or rather you now have still more, to the extent that the joy belonging to "your loins"[30] reaches us, and that you saw in advance this present event. Come, now: appear and celebrate the festival with us, do not delay in running forward to what stands before us, do not willingly be left out of the feast, since you, too, are a fellow actor and fellow celebrant in that

[28]Ps 88.13 (LXX).
[29]Ps 113.4.
[30]Acts 2.30. The reference is to Christ as descendant of David.

realm where the one activity is ceaseless celebration! Surely if you sang out beforehand the sweet reality of these things you only saw in vision, now that they have established that sweetness in fact, run, prepare to gaze along with those who here feast on the sweetness, and experience it with them!

For one, then, whose presence clearly seems so much to be expected, it is impossible that he not be with us. We, too, must celebrate in a worthy and truthful way the greatest of events, and also, in an honorable way, those who have come to share invisibly in the festival.

Let the mind set its feet on the height of contemplation, and—leaving behind the things by which our imaginings drag us downwards, towards the fatal forces crawling on the earth—let it ascend along with the Word, and enter the cloud to draw close to him, taking its stand there with Moses and Elijah. Let the eyes, enlightened by the radiance of the face of God, be directed towards one thing alone: the beauty that is truly loveable; and let them turn away from those other things that lead the senses astray. Let the hearing resound with the witness of the Father, and when he tells us to follow the commands of his Beloved, let him be heard with reverence, and let whatever else is being said of a more mystical nature be heard as well, so that not only the Lord is an object of wonder because of his divine greatness, but also that the wonder of his extreme humiliation might be combined with it.

Let us be drawn into the mystery of the rash act of ignorant men, and of the Lord's patient readiness to suffer; and let us praise him for his inconceivable plan of redemption on both grounds—because of what we see [here], and because the mystery is announced by those who foreknew it that one so glorious will suffer for our sake.[31]

Moses and Elijah announce this Mystery, made known by them in ancient times, and now made known again. Let us listen to them,

---

[31] An obscure allusion, it seems, to Luke's assertion (9.31) that when Moses and Elijah appeared alongside Jesus, they were speaking with him "about his Exodus, which he was about to accomplish in Jerusalem."

as they recount it to us, who are present alongside him as ministering to their Lord, present to make clear, also, what he will undergo at the hands of ungrateful slaves. For the disciples, who have become witnesses of such momentous events, must for now understand what is going to happen, so that they might follow their Teacher as he undergoes these things, and not be distracted toward some other purpose; from the greatness of what they have seen, they must accept what is hard to believe—especially Peter, who was stirred more deeply [than the rest] by the warmth of love's spell, and so contradicted the words of the Teacher.

But let us now become participants in the sacred rites, and have a share in this sacred spectacle,[32] now seeing him radiating light on a mountain and under a cloud who will later shine forth in incorruption from a tomb; whom "the congregation of sinners"[33] will buffet and spit on, but before whom Death, the tyrant over creatures, will tremble, as it sees him—whose robe is now radiant and later will be dipped in bloody gore[34]—standing forth in judgment of wrongdoers.

Since we have been initiated into these realities beforehand, when they actually come to pass let us admire him no less for the weakness he will then display than for his present splendor; [when we see him] bearing utter contempt with unmurmuring patience, for the sake of which we now see him in glory; having grounds for honoring him when he is in dishonor, in the witness we now hear borne to him; grounds for worshipping him when he is condemned, when arrogant sinners lay violent hands on the "Beloved Son,"—if you will, the heir of his Father's Lordship—and when the twin lips of madmen spit out ugly-sounding spite against the Only-begotten, and include the Lord with slaves, the creator with creatures, and meddle with the

---

[32]Leo here uses the language of the Greek mystery-religions, who practiced the initiation of members into their cult groups by rites of purification that included the viewing of sacred objects. In this final section of the homily, Leo rightfully emphasizes that the reason for Jesus' transfiguration, in the Gospel narrative, is to give a context for understanding the saving meaning of his coming passion and death

[33]Ps 25.4 (LXX).

[34]Rev 19.13.

being of him who "gives existence to the ages," attempting to define his depths and the structure of his being in monstrous terms. In these events let us see the greatness of him against whom the insults of "sharpened tongues"[35] have been let fly, let us hold fast to those words through which the Father witnesses that this is truly his Son, let us abominate their murderous intentions and the foolishness of their syllogisms, let us stand firm alongside him who is elevated above all honor, let us retain this which the Lord has given, beyond all we could give him in return[36]—his good pleasure; and not departing from this, let us abandon one thing only: those who, in their madness, rebel like the giants against the Most High. I think David foresaw this, when he said that those whose wickedness deceives itself "are out of their minds," and in their madness are "all liars."[37] In that day, they will see the punishments stored up in return for their arrogance, when the one against whom they now conspire will be seated on his own throne, to change his patience into judgment against those who held his goodness in contempt.

And we, as we are transformed in this present moment along with him who is transfigured, and as we, too, become radiant, so also, by that splendor that is going to be revealed in the worthy, in other ways and through our efforts to preserve a sincere love for each other,[38] let us be eager to be transformed even through these things, and to become radiant along with him; let us always be mindful of God's affection for humanity, and keep in mind the actions that it pleased the Beloved Son to share in for our sakes: the cross and death; let us follow him in these things step by step, since he tracked us down as we wandered along the distant ways of destruction, and found us, and lifted us up on his shoulders,[39] lest we find ourselves in a place that is far from his lot and his splendor.

[35]Ps 63.4 (LXX).
[36]See Ps 115.2 (LXX; = Ps 116.11 Hebrew).
[37]Ibid.
[38]Cf. Rom 3.8; 2 Pet 3.1.
[39]Luke 15.5.

O life and light and splendor, in whom we know the undivided Light that is the Father, and through whom we know the light that shines out with you, the all-holy Spirit; O Word and human being, the one of which you eternally are, the other which you became afterwards, out of compassion for your creation—you have dispersed the mist of our earthy darkness with your brilliance, and have enlightened the mind that guides us, by your guiding Spirit. Give us the grace now to care well for the great inheritance you have given us,[40] in a way that is profitable both for us and for them. And when the moment arrives for you to loosen the bond of our days and to judge the matter into which you have breathed life, may you grant us to enjoy a share in your sweet loveliness, transfiguring us into that ancient beauty in which we were formed by your hand, but which we adulterated and rendered useless by passions.

[40]Leo is referring to the people of the Christian Empire, whose care is his responsibility.

HOMILY 11

A Homily of Leo, King in Christ the Eternal King, on the Divine Glory Laid Bare before Us on Thabor and Illuminating with Its Own Brilliance Our Human Formlessness

Every festival aimed at our salvation injects a certain indescribable joy into the souls of those who love God. But this present feast so infuses sweetness into our circle, and so brings about a divine inspiration in those it affects, that despite the many things that turn our tongue aside to silence, this day subjects us to none of them, but establishes us, on the basis of our words, in communion with you, our excellent listeners.

And yet, not to mention all the other considerations, there is such competition within a gathering of priests of God, gathered together as this one is—people senior to me in the ability to speak persuasively—that I seem not to be up to the task; yet even so, as I say, I have been so stirred up to try my wings today that I am not deterred from the contest, but set myself in the midst of this festival of words. But enough prologue; time will not endure a longer delay.

Come, then, chosen people of God,[1] in our discourse let us lay hold of Mount Thabor, that mountain on which Jesus came forth as God, revealed the brilliance of his own divinity; by redesigning his own human formlessness, which comes from passibility, in order

[1]See Ex 29.5; Titus 2.14.

to reveal its archetype, he now shines forth with a kind of ineffable brilliance. Let us gather in company with John and Peter and James. There is, at least, no Judas here; let it not happen that, in order to avoid him, we must abandon this blessed spectacle!

Would you like our homily to be a little daring? Let us not bow to the ground as we gaze on that light beyond any radiance we know; rather, let us be rekindled as by a life-giving source of light, let our eyes become sharper, our vision less blurred; let us not reject the miracle, but let us gaze on it in an attitude of identification, based on a reverent boldness. For those who gaze on him in this way, our "sun of justice"[2] will not blear our eyes, but as strongly as our reverent longing reaches out to him, so much does he communicate of his own brightness.

Moses and Elijah will be there with us. How delightful—how delightful it will surely be, to listen to their conversation, when humans preserve the divine image, unmarked by disfiguring blemishes. Moses is the one who "saw God face to face";[3] Elijah the one who bound up heaven with his tongue,[4] who gave proof of our race's original immortality,[5] who still is honored with immortality and holds the reins of heaven. We shall be enfolded in the radiance of a bright cloud; we shall also hear a voice. May it be possible to receive ears worthy of such a voice, which will reveal the Beloved clearly.

Do you see the brilliance of this feast? Doesn't it make sense for me to cast away all my fear of competition and enter this sacred theater of words? Let us listen to God the Father as he bears witness, "This is my Son, the Beloved, in whom I am well pleased!" How much benefit and nourishment we can draw from these words!

The Father, for our sakes, "did not spare his Beloved Son,"[6] "through whom he made the ages."[7] For the sake of whom? Of those

[2]Mal 4.2.
[3]Ex 33.20.
[4]I Kg 17.1; 18.41–45.
[5]II Kg 2.11.
[6]Rom 8.32.
[7]Heb 1.2.

who had become enemies to him, who had voluntarily chosen the tyrannical rule of sin, who had skipped away from his kingly rule, or in a spirit of competition had nursed a grudge against him. The Father "did not spare his Beloved Son:"[8] [did not spare] his Beloved for the sake of those who had angered him, [did not spare] the King for the sake of pitiable wretches, [did not spare] the powerful one for the sake of the weak, [did not spare] the creator for the sake of clay and dust. Why the human race? Not only do we fail to love those who hate us; we turn away from those who love us! But God the Father "did not spare his own Son,"[9] so that while we were enemies he might make us friends;[10] we ourselves, on the other hand, often do not think twice about driving those into enmity whom we ought to consider dearest friends.

But our discourse here has departed a little from its course, and has plucked a kind of blossom as a by-product of this present feast; it has led us slightly away from fulfilling our purpose—or rather, that of "the great God, our King Jesus Christ."[11] We must bring it back, then, to the place where it began. Peter, the foundation and spokesman, will speak: "Let us set up three tents." These are words of overflowing joy, words of a benevolent heart that loves the Teacher and puts forward the desire to withdraw far from the plots of those who oppose him.

Still, this is a kind of love-charm on Peter's part, as the saving text reminds us: "He said this, not knowing what he was saying."

I wish time allowed us to finish our discourse; for in that way I would be able to supply you lovingly with delightful nourishment from the present argument, and you would also come to know further, in our homily, that divine madness that drives us on. But since time will not allow itself to be extended in parallel both with our homily and with the sacred celebration of the mystical banquet, our discourse yields to those Mysteries—for that is the holy

[8]Rom 8.32.
[9]Rom 8.32.
[10]Cf. Rom 5.7–8.
[11]Cf. Titus 2.13. The text of Titus reads "of the great God, our Savior . . ."

way—and makes itself compact, adding only this for your benefit: O people of God, let us not think about tents built here below, but as we have shared in contemplation on Thabor, so let us be led up in our preaching to the tents of heaven, making ourselves light on the wing of virtue; we seek dwelling-places there, so that we might feast more purely still on the outpouring of light that comes forth from God in Christ Jesus our Lord, to whom be glory and power for the ages. Amen.

HOMILY 39

A Homily by Leo, King in Christ the Eternal King, When What Was Assumed Began to Shine Forth with the Sparks of Divinity on Thabor, and Was Seen Miraculously Transfigured

Since this is a brilliant and divine festival, and we are disposed to share in its brightness, come, let us add to its brilliance by our words, since there is nothing that makes festivals bright as much as this. It will be as concise as possible, since neither length of time nor abundance of hearers now permits us to speak at length.

Christ today is the one who reveals this divine light, and shines forth ineffably. Let us shine along with him, transfigured, as far as possible, by the light of God. Christ, on the mountain, makes the glory that is inaccessible available to the disciples. Let us be lifted up to the height of contemplation, and let us join them in gazing on the Mystery.

Let no one waste time on lowly, earth-centered considerations, but to the extent of each one's power let us be lifted in our desire towards this great vision. Let us be raised to the heights of the Spirit. For it is impossible for those who want to look from the viewpoint of lowly and humble things to see the divine glory. For this reason, then, my Jesus enchants the disciples on the mountain by revealing the magic of his own splendor. O Mystery mingled from sweet and dreadful events! O mixed delight of participation, inviting us to enjoy it, yet preparing us also to tremble in awe at its realization.

[The disciples say:] "What is this, Lord? Have you brought us together to delight in your beauty and so to be happy, or almost to die of fear? We are deprived of joy in the things by which you frighten us, but you allow us to delight in the blessings you bestow on us."

[Jesus replies:] "You are grieved, but you have received comfort from on high. Do you hear resounding, 'This is my Beloved Son, in whom I am well pleased'? I am of the same substance as the one who gave me being. I radiate outwards his glorious light, which did not shine on Moses when he longed for the sight of God's face; for, although [God] said it is impossible for a human being there to receive this vision, still he granted, as a consolation for this desire, to one who had purified his vision by much fasting, a vision—very dim, at that—of his back parts."

So, then, in this life the eye that is involved in seeing mortal things is not capable of enjoying the glory of what is uncreated. But the disciples fell face-down on the ground—for the place of mortals cannot receive immortal light; but Moses and Elijah, since they had moved beyond the bounds of mortal humans, stood and conversed [with him], being judged worthy of enjoying him more clearly. Moses and Elijah, the two summits of history before grace, whom heaven miraculously served—raining bread down for the one to feed a hungry people, obeying the other when he commanded it to withhold the rain, so that those who cultivated impiety might perish of hunger. Today the Lord, wrapped in a bright cloud—and perhaps this is a type of his pure and virginal conception from our stock, in which he wraps himself and mingles with us as befits a servant—speaks informally, one might say, with them about the murderous plot that has not yet overtaken him: people will dare to hand over the Beloved of the Father to death—O audacity that has no reason!—casting bloody hands on the one from whom they received those hands' very existence!

So great an act of insolence was undertaken by them, to their own destruction. But to us, God's riches have been given through his death: new creation, new birth, immortality, "for those who are begotten not of corruptible seed,"[1] as the text says, "but by water and the Spirit,"[2] and who "by being made like him in his death" have received a share "in the likeness of his resurrection."[3]

What do you say? Do we resist the impulse of Scripture, or will you yield freely to the moment?[4] By your silence, you seem to be showing signs of resistance! But since this seems to be so—since the moment does not seem ready to let us invent other, more divine and sacred words, let us now cease this word of exhortation, and turn instead to the sweet, all-encompassing sensation that comes from praising God. It is right to feast on this at every moment, but especially in God's house, since "in his house, everyone utters praise."[5] And may it be that we, too, in sending forth glory and praise, may seem pleasing in his sight now and for all ages! Amen.

[1] I Pet 1.23.
[2] John 3.5.
[3] Rom 6.5.
[4] Leo seems to be referring obscurely to the invitation, implied in his interpretation of the Transfiguration passage, to undertake a serious program of ascetical "ascent" and mystical training. He concludes that the majority of his congregation is not yet ready to begin such a process. The alternative, for the moment, is simply to join in the liturgical praise of the transfigured Jesus.
[5] Ps 28.9 (LXX).

Philagathos of Cerami

Philagathos, monk of the Byzantine monastery of Santa Maria del Patir, just outside of Rossano in Calabria (the "toe" and "instep" of the boot of Italy), is one of the best-known Greek homilists of the early medieval Byzantine world, and is the author or compiler of what is known as the "Italo-Greek Homiliary." His family name appears in the manuscripts as Kerameus (as was that of his contemporary Theophanes, archbishop of Rossano in the mid-eleventh century, with whom he has occasionally been confused); this suggests that he was a native of the town of Cerami in the province of Enna in north central Sicily, some forty miles northwest of Catania. Philagathos, whose baptismal name was apparently Philippos, was born sometime in the late eleventh century, probably of a Greek-speaking family, before or during the reign of the Norman Count Roger I (1071–1101); he died sometime in the middle decades of the twelfth century. Roger II (1095–1154), Count Roger's younger son, became count of Sicily in 1105, expanded his rule in 1127 to include Apulia and Calabria—until then ruled by other members of his family—and declared himself king of Sicily in 1130.

Roger II's reign was a time of great cultural richness, which drew together artistic and literary traditions from the classical Greek and Roman world, as well as contemporary Arabic and Norman elements. Philagathos himself seems to have had an outstanding Greek literary and theological education; his homilies are modeled not only on Patristic sources, but make use of pre-Christian Greek rhetoric and show knowledge of classical authors. They mainly celebrate feasts and episodes from the liturgical cycle, and are widely distributed in Byzantine manuscripts. Philagathos is known to have preached in many of the major churches and cathedrals of the kingdom of Sicily, and in the presence of Roger I and William I, the two predecessors of Roger II; he also seems to have been a regular preacher in the cathedral of Rossano, where the manuscripts say this homily was originally given, doubtless on August 6th. (See Vera von Falkenhausen, "The South Italian Sources," in Mary Whitby, ed., *Byzantines and Crusaders in non-Greek Sources: Proceedings of the British Academy* 132 [London: British Academy 2007] 95–121, esp. 103–104).

Philagathos' monastic community, Santa Maria del Patir in Rossano, was founded in the late eleventh century by the monk Bartholomew of Simeri (c. 1050–1130). Rossano, an ancient center of Greek ecclesiastical life, was only a few miles from the Gulf of Calabria, and had been conquered by the expanding Norman forces in 1060. The monastery of Patir, with easy access to the outside world, quickly became a center for artistic and literary activities in the Byzantine tradition at the turn of the twelfth century. It possessed a celebrated icon of the Virgin Hodigitria, which had been sent from Constantinople as a gift to Bartholomew from the Emperor Alexios Komnenos, and which was supposed to have miraculous powers. In a homily for the "Sunday of Orthodoxy," celebrating this icon (Hom. 41; ed Scorso, Hom. 20), Philagathos asserts it had been painted by St Luke himself; see also the reference here, in section 1. On the monastery of Patir, see Pierre Batiffol, *L'Abbaye de Rossano. Contribution à l'histoire de la Vaticane* (Paris: Picard, 1891), 2–10; on the Hodigitria icon, see ibid., p. 7.

This homily speaks in simple, vivid language about the details of the Gospel episode, and begins by asking twelve questions Philagathos suspects may be in the listeners' minds about those details when they hear the story. After offering concise answers to all of them, Philagathos goes on to develop a more spiritual interpretation of the Transfiguration, exhorting his hearers to rise above the level of sense-knowledge in order to contemplate Jesus as he really is, and to share in the promise of salvation in him.

HOMILY 31
On the Saving Transfiguration
Preached in the Pulpit of the

Archiepiscopacy of Rossano[1]

1   What a shepherd might feel, seeing his flock flourish around him, gathered together in a lush, well-tended, and wide-spreading pasture (for as he sits on a high rock, looking around at the flock gathered before him, it gives him joy and pleasure, and he sings pastoral songs)—that is what I feel about this present celebration.[2] For when I see my people, this flock so beloved of God, eagerly taking refuge in the sacred fold, where the image, not made by hands, of our all-holy Lady is hung, I rejoice and exult, I hasten to begin my role as teacher, and to lay before you the mysteries of this present great feast.

2   I am eagerly drawn, then, to look after my flock; but I feel like some low-class host, ambitious to entertain many high-ranking guests at table, but unable—because of poverty—to delight them

[1]The Greek text of Philagathos' Homily 31, which is translated here, is that of the critical edition of Giuseppe Rossi Taibbi, *Filagato da Cerami: Omelie per i vangeli domenicali e le feste di tutto l'anno* (Istituto Siciliano di Studi Bizantini e Neoellenici: Testi 11; Palermo, 1969) 206–220. An earlier edition, by the Sicilian Jesuit scholar Francisco Scorso [Paris, 1644], along with Scorso's notes, is reprinted in the *Patrologia Graeca* 132.1020–1048, as by the archbishop Theophanes Kerameus, Homily 59.

[2]Philagathos begins his homily by invoking the traditional setting of pastoral poetry, as found in the elegies of the Greek poet Theocritus, and in Vergil's *Eclogues*, which recreated the same genre in Augustan Latin. Theocritus, who flourished in the third century before Christ, was himself probably a native of Syracuse in Sicily; hence the pastoral genre is particularly germane to Philagathos' Hellenistic heritage.

with sweet treats and a dazzling array of foods. Still, having together besought the Divine Mystery with our prayers, that our souls might be illumined by the divine light that today shines on Mount Thabor, "Come, let us go up to the mountain of the Lord,"[3] as Isaiah and Micah urge us; and let us follow, as much as we can, him who "makes us climb to the heights,"[4] as Habakkuk says, so that we, too, might come in our imaginations to the top of the mountain, and there gaze on the glory of Jesus. For there, as Habakkuk also prophesies, "His javelins issue forth like light, and his face is like a flash of lightning."[5]

3   Let us investigate[6] why the Transfiguration happened, and what this strange appearance means; and also why it did not happen earlier, but near to the Passion; and then, why this strange event did not take place with many people gathered there to watch, so that the miracle might have many witnesses, as surely the other miracles did—giving new life to the dead and sight to the blind and strength of limb to the paralyzed. 4. After this, let us investigate why it was not on the plain, but on the mountain that [Jesus] reveals his appearance in this way; and why he does not bring all the disciples along, but left the nine behind and led up only the three; and if three had to be there, why was it not others, but Peter and the sons of Zebedee. And if it had to be, for some mysterious reason, that this apparition should take place on a mountain, why—since there are many mountains in Palestine—he bypassed Sigor and neglected Carmel, and also left behind the mountains of Galilee and Samaria, and did not even go up the Mount of Olives, but chose, among them all, Mount Thabor. And what did the presence of prophets mean? And why was it not

[3] Is 2.3; Micah 4.2 (LXX).
[4] Hab 3.19 (LXX).
[5] Hab 3.11 (LXX).
[6] Here, before starting to reflect on the passage, Philagathos presents his audience with a set of twelve questions about the Transfiguration story, which he then proposes to answer. This gives the homily a somewhat academic character, but seems calculated to rouse the hearers' interest in the episode as something mysterious and challenging.

others, but Moses and Elijah that he set beside him? And how did the Apostles recognize that this is who they were? For since they had not seen their faces before, it must have been difficult to recognize them, suddenly standing beside [Jesus]. 5. And if Moses alone was able to come up from the realm of the dead, and Elijah came down from above, why did it not seem enough for just one of the disciples to join them from the earth? And beyond this, why, when the Son was transfigured and the Father bore witness to him from on high, does Scripture not record the Holy Spirit, who exists inseparable from them; for the "Spirit-fighters"[7] raise this difficulty to us, in their desire to alienate the Paraclete from Father and Son. And now that we have laid out this list of twelve questions, come—with God's help we shall clarify some answers to them, as far as we can!

6   Why, then, did the amazing Transfiguration occur? The reason was this: the time of the Passion was drawing near, and the conspiracy of the Jews was becoming stronger, and God's intervention on our behalf was going to reach its end, and the cross had already been planted; and so that the disciples might not suffer the same malady that the Jews did, and be mentally overwhelmed in their time of suffering, and might not look on the one they had formerly confessed, by Peter's tongue, as Son of God, and consider him to be a mere man when they later saw him hung up as a condemned criminal, he strengthened them by this miraculous apparition, so that—when they would see him betrayed and in agony and praying

[7]The "Spirit-fighters" or Macedonians (so named after Patriarch Macedonius of Constantinople), were a faction in the debates of the late fourth century over the doctrine of the Trinity; they were willing to affirm that Father and Son are "of the same substance," as the Council of Nicaea had affirmed, but thought of the Holy Spirit as a creature of Father and Son—perhaps as a created state of holiness or enlightenment in the lives of believers. The Council of Constantinople in 381 was called together, among other reasons, to affirm that the Spirit is a distinct hypostasis who shares constitutively and inseparably in the same infinite divine essence as Father and Son. It seems unlikely that any followers of this heresy were still active in southern Italy and Sicily in the twelfth century; Philagathos is probably referring to them simply as representatives of a classical heresy concerning the Spirit.

that the cup of death might pass and dragged into the courtyard of
the high priest—they might think back on their climb up Mount
Thabor, and realize that he who had been surrounded in the glory of
divinity, and attested as beloved Son of God, had not been betrayed
to death against his will.   7 If they should see his face slapped and
spit upon, let them no longer be scandalized, since they had stored
in their memories his brilliance that outshone the sun. If they were
to see him clothed in purple as mockery, let them affirm him to be
the one who, on the mountain, was "wrapped in light as in a robe."[8]
If they should see him fixed on a scaffold between two criminals,
let them recognize him here as Lord, standing in majesty between
Moses and Elijah. If they should know him as a corpse, hidden away
in the earth, let them remember him overshadowed by a brilliant
cloud. These are the reasons, then, for which the Transfiguration
took place. And perhaps, too, since the Savior urged them to pay
no heed to the body, saying, "If anyone wishes to follow after me, let
him deny himself,"[9] but it still seemed difficult to deny oneself and
to choose a shameful form of death, he showed his disciples of what
glory they would be found worthy, if they imitated his passion. For
the Transfiguration was nothing else but a foretaste of the last day,
when the just will shine in glory with God.

8 Why, then, did this not happen in the beginning, but just before
his passion? In the beginning [of his ministry], the disciples were
still imperfect, and were not ready to receive a vision such as this. In
their simplicity, surely they would have considered this event simply a magic trick. For this reason, when they had received a deeper
experience of who he was, when they had confessed him to be Son
of God, then at last they were found worthy of a higher revelation.
And there was another reason, too: since, with the reckless passing
of time, forgetfulness takes out of our minds the images they have
received by our sense of sight, therefore he does this not long before

[8]Ps 103.2 (LXX).
[9]Matt 16.24.

his passion, so that they might not forget the miracle, but might retain what their eyes had seen.

9   The divine Transfiguration does not take place in the presence of many people. For the eyes of the uninitiated were not capable of receiving a vision such as this, if Isaiah, seeing a faint image of it, called himself a miserable man.[10] Do you not recall how, long ago, Moses ventured onto Mount Sinai alone, since the people were not capable of gazing on such great glory?[11] And if the Hebrews were not strong enough to gaze on the glorified face of Moses unveiled,[12] how then could they have been capable of seeing the divine glory itself? The restoring of sight to the blind, the cleansing of lepers, the raising of the dead to life—all these were endurable sights for all the people; but even to see a dim glimpse of the glory of God is only endurable for "the clean of heart," according to the Lord's word.[13] For if the bleary eye cannot endure the brilliant rays of the sun, but becomes dark when it is dazzled by the light, what would souls blinded by faithlessness and sin have suffered, if they had gazed on the rays of the divinity? Would not their bodies have fainted, rather, with amazement, their life-giving spirit failing at the miraculous vision, since a human being cannot even bear the sight of an angel? This was the reason that the wondrous event did not happen in the midst of a crowd, but in private.

10   Nor did he take along all the disciples, since Judas, the most avaricious disciple, was among them, and it was not right that the light of divinity be seen by blemished eyes. For how could the soul of a betrayer, the soul that loved money, who set such snares against his Master, have gazed on this divine vision? For if the three chosen disciples, with their clear consciences, cowered with fear and

[10]Is 6.5.
[11]Ex 19.20–24.
[12]Ex 34.35; cf. II Cor 3.13.
[13]Matt 5.8.

fell headlong on the ground, and just escaped being melted away because they could not bear that fire, what would the betrayer have been likely to feel? The wicked man is prevented, then, from seeing the glory of the Lord, as Isaiah knew in advance and solemnly prophesied: "Let the sinner come to a standstill, lest he see the glory of the Lord!"[14]   **11** But perhaps someone will say, "Why, then, did he not leave Judas alone behind, and take the others along? Not all of them were unworthy, surely, as that one was!" But if that happened, the betrayer would have had an excuse for his evil deed, as if it were not through love of money that he devised his plot, but in the desire to get even for an insult. The Lord cut off all excuses, and left his assailant without any pretext, so that what he did might be seen to be the simple choice of a bad conscience.

12   The ascent up the mountain was a symbol of the need felt by anyone who intends to become a participant in the divine mysteries, to leave behind any sympathy with what lies below, and to be raised up onto the mountain of high ascent in one's thoughts. So, in general, God is represented as revealing divine visions on mountains. In ancient times, he ordered that Abraham's sacrifice be offered not in the plain, but on a mountain;[15] and Lot, when he was fleeing from the Five Cities, which had been reduced to ashes, would not have been saved if he had not run up a mountain.[16] When God spoke his words to Moses, and revealed the mystery of the Burning Bush, and entrusted to him the leadership of the people,[17] he did these things on a mountain; and when he also revealed to him the symbolic form of the tabernacle,[18] and conversed with him as a friend, face to face,[19] and engraved the tablets of the Law,[20] he performed

[14] Is 26.10 (LXX altered).
[15] Gen 22.2.
[16] Gen 19.30.
[17] Ex 3.1–10.
[18] Ex 25.40.
[19] Ex 33.11.
[20] Ex 24.12.

these things on Mount Sinai. And when he spoke with Elijah and showed him symbolic visions, he led him up the same mountain.[21] **13** But also when he came to be as we are, putting on our poverty, he revealed most of his mysteries to his disciples on mountains. So if he wanted to call blessed the poor in spirit, and those who mourn, and the meek and the merciful and those who have a pure heart, and all those whom the list of the Beatitudes included,[22] he led his disciples up a mountain.[23] If he wants to teach them how one ought to pray, this, too, he does on a mountain.[24] In the same way, then, when he wants to reveal his divine glory, it is to be expected that he ascend a mountain.[25]

14 But overlooking the other mountains of Palestine, he chooses Thabor. Since Mount Sigor had been the bridal-chamber of illicit marriages (for the daughters of Lot, after they fled from Sodom, got their father drunk and then carried out that bold sexual union with the one who had begotten them[26]), how would it have been right for the mystery of a divine vision to be revealed at the place where wicked deeds had been done? Could he have led them up the mountain of Samaria? Anyone who has read the holy books cannot be unaware that those who were stained with the blood of foreigners hid the abominable idols of the demons in a cave on the mountain, and then persuaded the Samaritans to gaze towards the mountain and to adore them.[27] Therefore that pious woman also said to the Lord, "Our fathers worshipped on this mountain, and you say that one must worship in Jerusalem."[28] How, then, could it be right for the hiding-place of idols to look on the saving mystery of God?   **15** But

[21]III Kg 19.11 (LXX; = I Kg 19.11).
[22]Matt 5.3–11.
[23]Matt 5.1.
[24]Matt 6.5–16.
[25]Matt 17.1; Mark 9.1.
[26]Gen 19.30–38.
[27]IV Kg 17.28 (LXX; = II Kg 17.28).
[28]John 4.20.

you mention Carmel to me! Now that was Elijah's training-ground,[29] and then an excuse would be produced for saying that the vision seen was of Elijah, and they would have suspected that the appearance of the Prophet at that moment was his usual presence on the mountain. The mountain of Galilee and the Mount of Olives were both bypassed, in order to be of service at other times: the one, that he might appear there to his disciples after the resurrection,[30] the other, that he might accomplish from it his ascension into heaven.[31] But why am I elaborating on these things? Do you want me to say what I really think? It had already been symbolically foreshadowed that this illumination would be seen on Thabor; for that reason the Holy Spirit saw fit that this name be given to it (for "Thabor" is interpreted "coming of light"), and from the Spirit this name clearly suggests the mystery of the light that shone upon it.

16   He chooses these three disciples: Peter, the first to be selected, who warmly and clearly confessed him to be Son of God; John, the one who speaks of God, the beloved one; and James, the one with the loudest and most godly-sounding voice. For that was the reason he was considered troublesome and turbulent to the Jews, so that when Herod wanted to gratify them in a significant way, he killed him with the sword.[32] Perhaps, too, it was since these [three] were going to be present with him in the time of his passion. For he took these three when he went on to pray, and perspired drops of sweat in the form of blood, and spoke what seemed to be words of failing courage. And these three, too, were present with him as he was brought to judgment, and saw all the other things that the wicked crowd did to him, in their frenzy of anger:[33] Peter following in order to see the end,

[29]III Kg 18.42 (LXX; = I Kg 18.42).

[30]Matt 28.16.

[31]Acts 1.9–12.

[32]Acts 12.2.

[33]The word Philagathos uses here for "wicked," *atasthalos*, is an archaic term, familiar mainly from the Homeric poems. His word for "act in a frenzy of anger," *epiparoineô*, really means "continue to behave in a drunken way." Clearly he is coloring his references to Biblical scenes with care.

John as one known to the high priest, James sharing his brother's courage. For this reason, it was important that these three should be first-hand witnesses of Jesus' divinity.

17 But next we must investigate what the arrival of the prophets means, and why he set these two next to himself. Because the Jews called him a lawbreaker and an enemy of God, opposed to Moses,[34] he brings these two here, so that his disciples might know that, if he were destroying the Law, the one who formed the Law would not be standing next to him like a servant, nor would the zealous Elijah have put up with accompanying anyone who looks down on the Law. Then, too, since there were differing opinions among people about him, and "some guessed he was Elijah, others Jeremiah or one of the prophets,"[35] the Savior shows that he is not "one of the Prophets" but was actually their Lord, placing them alongside him in lordly fashion by a simple act of the will. And Moses and Elijah were brought there, also, that he might demonstrate that he is the one proclaimed in the Law and the Prophets.

18 It is possible to give a different explanation for why he brought these three disciples and these two prophets to be beside him on the mountain. It is because the world is divided up in three ways. This, after all, is the way David and Paul divided creation. David says, "If I climb up to the heavens, you are there; if I go down into the underworld, you are present; if I takes the wings of dawn, and make my dwelling at the ends of the sea," [you are there].[36] And the Apostle writes, "Every knee shall bend, of those in heaven and on earth and under the earth."[37] Even secular philosophy imagined this kind of division, when it says, "All things are divided in a threefold way."[38] **19** Showing himself to be Master and Lord of the whole

[34]See John 9.16, 9.28.
[35]Matt 16.14.
[36]Ps 138.8–9 [LXX].
[37]Phil 2.10.
[38]Homer, *Iliad* 15.189 (τριχθά πάντα δέδασται).

world, the Savior brought his disciples from the earth, put Elijah alongside him—still living—from heaven, and brought the soul of Moses, with wingless speed,[39] from the underworld. Why are you surprised that only Moses was brought up from the dead below, and that from above only Elijah came down, while from the earth one was not enough, but three? The Lord seems to be suggesting a mystical teaching by these things. For this shows that the things in heaven and under the earth, which we say are souls purified of their connections with bodies, have no share in matter, but are simple and single in form, without the separation in space that bodies have; but the earthy things we perceive here are compounds, measured in three dimensions. Therefore he brings up three from the earth, while individuals come to him from heaven and from Hades single in form.

20 Perhaps we should move straight ahead and lay hold of what comes next, by taking a short-cut; but as I was just speaking, a little notion came into my head about why he put these two prophets next to him, and no others. For God seems to have promised the vision on Thabor, in symbols, long ago to these two, although most people miss the meaning of the riddle. For when life was offered to Moses by himself, on a mountain, apart from all the confusion of public places, the story says that an awe-inspiring revelation of God, brighter than the sun's light, appeared to him at high noon[40]—a different light, breaking forth from some bush. And Moses, amazed by this strange sight, said: "I will go over and see what this great apparition is."[41] But the voice from that light told Moses not to go forward towards the mountain, since he was weighed down by sandals of dead skin, but told him rather to take off the sandals from his feet and so to draw

[39]This is an idiom known in later dramatic literature, a way of expressing almost instantaneous movement.

[40]Here again, Philagathos seems to want to show his literary background: "to him" is expressed by the Homeric dative, οἱ, and the expression he uses for "high noon" (σταθηρᾷ μεσημβρίᾳ), literally "at fixed noon," appears in Plato, *Phaedo* 242a.

[41]Exod 3.3.

near to the bush, which was radiant with divine light.   **21** What is the mystery, then, into which we are being led here? Moses, a man of the highest prophetic gifts, who saw the light of divinity in the flesh of the Only-begotten—to which the bush mysteriously pointed, as if at the end of time—said this in his prophetic fashion: "Let me cross over the intervening time by contemplation, and arrive at that time of the Incarnation,[42] and I shall see this great vision, which is revealed by means of this light." And what did the voice that spoke to him mean? It was a promise to show him the light that shone forth on Thabor. But when? When he is released from the flesh, the garment of skin that is wrapped around our nature; when we have been stripped of it by obeying the divine will. So Scripture says, "when you take off your sandal"—that is, when you are freed from the flesh, "then you will see this vision on Thabor!" Moses made this promise more clear and obvious, when he longed still more hotly to look on God, and said: "Show me your face."[43] And God told him that this was not possible in any other way, but if he were to take shelter first in the rock: so would see his "back parts," signifying the divinized body by means of the rock, and his appearance in the last times by means of the "back parts," all of which reached its fulfillment in the divine Transfiguration.   **22** This, then, was the promise that hinted at a glimpse of God. But when Elijah came to Horeb and was weighed down by distress, God announced to him this apparition on Thabor in typological language, saying, " 'You will stand there tomorrow before the Lord.' And behold, a wind came that destroyed the mountains and split the rocks—but the Lord was not in the wind. And after the wind, an earthquake—but the Lord was not in the earthquake. And after the earthquake, a fire—but the Lord was not in the fire. And after the fire, a voice as from a gentle breeze—and there was the Lord!"[44] For here the text hints at revelations of God

---

[42]Philagathos uses the word *oikonomia*, which in classical Patristic usage predominantly refers to the Incarnation of the Word as the culmination of God's work in history.

[43]Ex 33.18.

[44]III Kg 19.11–12 (LXX; = I Kg 19.11–12).

in time, as also in the [stories of] the patriarchs and in the Law and the Prophets, where he is shown to them faintly and "as if in a mirror";[45] but in the last times the Lord God himself appeared to us. And by the word "tomorrow" it signifies the times that would come afterwards, but by the "gentle breeze" that light, divine, pure body, which has come to be untouched by the weight of sin; and by the "voice," it clearly points to God the Word, associating with us by means of a body. Therefore it adds: "And there was the Lord." On the one hand, the voice commanded Moses, who would be worthy of this vision after death, "First take the sandals off your feet." But it did not command Elijah, since he would see this before laying his body aside. These are the reasons, then, why he brought these two prophets to stand beside him.

23   But on what grounds, then, did the Apostles recognize them? For seeing them did not betray any recognizable marks to their memories, since their physical shapes were completely unknown. How did they recognize them, then, if they had never looked on their features before? Not from their appearance, but from what they said! For the Evangelist says, "And they spoke of the glory which he was going to accomplish in Jerusalem."[46] So when they were conversing about his passion, it seems likely that Moses confessed in response, and said, "I prophesied about you: 'You will see your life hung up on a piece of wood.'[47] Yours is the original, and the representation was the bronze serpent I hung up in the desert."[48] So Elijah, too, by explaining to the Lord all about himself, made known who he was. From this, the disciples recognized the prophets, and what was said made the speakers known. And perhaps the phrase "spoke together" refers to the agreement of the Law and the Prophets with the Gospel: for "speak together" means the same as "have the same meaning."

[45]I Cor 13.12.
[46]Luke 9.31.
[47]See Deut 28.66.
[48]Num 21.9.

For the Lord came not at all to destroy the Law or to overthrow the prophets, but rather to bring them to their fulfillment.[49]

24   Let us investigate, then, also the final puzzle: the insubstantial position put forward by the "Spirit-fighters," the assertion of their distorted minds, upon which—as upon sand—they build their structure, which today the grace of the very Spirit they blaspheme will knock down, through our weak tongue. "If the Holy Spirit," they argue, "is of the same substance with Father and Son, why was he not present with them on Mount Thabor?" But hold your impious and blasphemous tongue in check for a while, O enemy of the Spirit, so that you might learn how the Paraclete was also present along with those who are honored with him. For you must understand that the cloud, which, as you hear, overshadowed the mountain, was nothing else but the Holy Spirit: it was not just a gathering of moist exhalations, but truly something better and more divine.   **25** In many places the Holy Scripture tends to refer to the Holy Spirit in terms of a cloud. What else does that prophetic saying mean, "Behold, the Lord comes to Egypt on a light cloud"[50]? What else was the cloud that guided the people of Israel on their way, as they fled from Egypt?[51] Where, after all, might one locate the activity of that perceptible cloud, since Scripture bears witness that it was miraculous: when the rays of the sun shone hot, it was a protecting screen for the people, shadowing what lay beneath it and moistening the fiery element in the air with light dew; and during the night it became a pillar of fire? But even after [Christ] had completed God's plan on our behalf and made his way back to heaven, "a cloud received him,"[52] and this was the Holy Spirit. And when he comes in glory to judge all things, he will come down from heaven on a cloud.[53]   **26** How can a sensible cloud be formed then, when, as the Prince of the Apostles tells us,

[49]Matt 5.17.
[50]Is 19.1.
[51]Ex 13.21; 14.19–20.
[52]Acts 1.9.
[53]Matt 24.30; see also I Thess 4.17.

"all things will be melted away in fire"[54]? But why should we multiply words, when we can bring forward as witness the Apostle himself, writing to the Hebrews about our ancestors' journey across the Red Sea, "The sea was a type of the water [of baptism], the cloud [a type] of the Spirit."[55] The Holy Spirit is also likened to a cloud because of the rain of charisms, which flows down like a river on those who believe. Since the feeble argument of the "Spirit-fighters" is refuted, then, come, let us examine the text itself.

27 "And he was transfigured before them, and his face shone like the sun."[56] The astonishing miracle of the Transfiguration should be understood in these terms: not that a change or alteration of his features took place, but that, while he remained as he had been before, an additional gift of indescribable light was provided to him. And if the Evangelist compares the brightness of his face to the sun, still that light greatly exceeded the sun's rays; but he compared the miracle to the brightest of the things we see, because he could not find a better point of comparison in the perceptible world. For the fact that the Apostles fell on their faces proves that a light beyond sunlight had broken upon them—no one falls down, after all, because of the sun's brightness! **28** Understood in a more mystical sense, the face of Christ, shining like the sun, is his divinity; the robes that had become like light are the very body he took up. But just as the sun is one thing, and light another—though when they are united they always remain inseparable—so when his flesh is supernaturally united to the divinity, and one composite hypostasis has come into existence, it remains indivisible.[57] As far as his divinity

[54] II Pet 3.12.

[55] This reference to the Letter to the Hebrews is unclear; Philagathos may be thinking of I Cor 10.3, 11.

[56] Matt 17.2.

[57] Philagathos echoes here the classical Christological language of the Second Council of Constantinople and the later theologians who accepted it as normative: that in Christ two utterly distinct natures or substances have been united in "one composite hypostasis" or individual.

is concerned, the text refers to "his face"[58] in the singular, because of his simple and uncompounded person (*prosōpon*); but as far as his flesh is concerned, because of the difference in its elements, "his garments" are mentioned in the plural. And since the divinity of the Word had no temporal beginning, and did not come into being, but his divine flesh is subject to time and is a created thing,[59] it follows that when referring to his face the text does not say it "became" but it "shone," but it says that his garments "became": thus indicating through both terms the uncreated nature of the Godhead and the created beginning of what he has taken up. For the holy flesh of the Word truly became like light, in that it was pure and untouched by any stain. Saint Mark puts this idea before us still more clearly, when he speaks this way: "His garments came to shine brightly, white as snow, in a way no fuller on earth could whiten them."[60] He is calling the prophets and heralds "fullers" here, none of whom was able to "whiten" human nature as the Lord did, making it bright with the light of his divinity. On this point, too, the Psalmist's voice cries out to him, "You have wrapped yourself in light as a garment."[61]

29 "And Peter said to Jesus in reply, 'Lord, it is good for us to be here. If you wish, let us erect three tabernacles—one for you and one for Moses and one for Elijah.'"[62] What are these lowly thoughts, noble Peter? You who previously received the Father's revelation, and called the Lord "the Son of the living God," and raised him above all created[63] nature, now count him among slaves, and make him

---

[58]The Greek word used here for "face" is πρόσωπον, which can mean "face," "mask," "external self-presentation," or "role." Philagathos sees in the Gospel's allusion to the face of Jesus an indication of his single hypostasis or person, as both God and human.

[59]According to Rossi Taibbi's edition, Philagathos here uses the word γεννητός, meaning "begotten." He probably used the very similar word γενητός, however, meaning "brought into being," or "created." The two were often confused in fourth-century debates about the divinity of the Son in relation to the Father.

[60]Mark 9.3.

[61]Psalm 103.2.

[62]Matt 17.4.

[63]In Rossi Taibbi's text, Philagathos again uses the word γεννητῆς, "begotten,"

equal in honor to the prophets! For "Let us make three tabernacles" is a saying suggesting equality of honor—something very different from the oracle your tongue uttered, a sign of carelessness! Or have the lightning bolts of the divinity, breaking on you like hurled missiles, shaken your mind? For when extraordinary events come upon us suddenly, they frequently overturn our reason. Wanting to make this clear to us, the Evangelist says, "Their eyes were weighed down,"[64] signifying, I think, the heaviness that had come upon their spiritual eyes. And the other Evangelist explains this more clearly, adding that Peter uttered this, "not knowing what he was saying."[65]

30 But what was the Prince of Apostles thinking, when he said: "It is good for us to be here"? What is the reason he is ready to accept a life dwelling on the mountain? Why does he reject life in the city, and love the deserted aspect of the mountain more than the trappings of city life? Hear the Lord proclaiming his passion to them openly in advance, and constantly reminding them of what is written about him. Now he says, "Behold, we are going up to Jerusalem, and the Son of Man will be betrayed to the Gentiles and will be put to death";[66] and now, "As Moses lifted up the serpent in the desert, so the Son of Man must be lifted up."[67] At another time, he recalls the example of Jonah, "As Jonah spent three days and three nights in the belly of the whale, so the Son of Man, too, will be in the heart of the earth."[68] When he heard these things, [Peter's] soul was divided many times; his heart was set aflame by grief, anger and despair at the prospect of being separated from the Master; he boiled with rage, thinking of the outrages of the Jewish leaders, and was dizzied by thinking about him, in distress, "Shall I leave the Teacher alone to suffer, or shall I walk along with him towards death?" **31** Divided

rather than γενητῆς, "created." I have assumed the latter is the correct reading (see above, n. 59).

[64]Luke 9.32. This detail is not in Matthew's account.
[65]Luke 9.33; cf. Mark 9.6.
[66]Matt 20 18–19 and parallels.
[67]John 3.14.
[68]Matt 12.40.

by such feelings as these, he did not dare to stop the Lord and keep him from his resolve (for when he tried that once before, he received a sharp rebuke for his rashness, and heard the words, "Get behind me, Satan!"[69]); but seeing the peace of the mountain, and the prophets in attendance, and the cloud overshadowing them, he realized, "If we remain here, we will escape the attacks of the Jews." Perhaps he even said something like this to himself: "Away with you, Judaea! You are full of so much wickedness and contempt! There is malice there, but here there is peace; there they threaten to kill the Teacher as God's enemy, but here the prophets attend on him as Lord; there the crowd maligns him as a deceiver, but here the Father bears witness to him as his beloved Son.   **32** 'It is good for us to be here!' If we remain here, we will escape those who are plotting against us. Let them search for us—they will never find us! And even if they are shameless enough to climb to the mountain's peak, we have strong protection. [Jesus], surely, is patient and is driven on towards his passion, and does not defend himself against those who pursue him; but Moses is here, who could not bear to see God insulted, and brought on all the plagues that he laid on the Egyptians—hail, boils, gnats, dog-flies, locusts, the destroying angel. And if he shrinks back, needing help, we have the zealous Elijah! Let him bring fire down from heaven, and he will destroy both officers and scourging soldiers! So I will hold on to the Teacher, no matter what should happen!" Thinking this, he said, "It is good for us to be here—not knowing what he was uttering." For he wanted to prevent the passion, which was, indeed, the chief event in our salvation and the way the devil has been destroyed!

33   "While he was yet speaking, behold a bright cloud overshadowed them."[70] Long ago, when God came down onto Sinai, the fire in the air, made of pure cosmic brightness, was shaded in darkness, and the whole scene seemed to be clouded by smoke, so that the

[69]Matt 16.23.
[70]Matt 17.5.

mountain became invisible, wrapped on all sides in gloom; but now a bright cloud covered the mountain. Since the Law, which then was given, was covered in obscure signs and dark shadows, that was the reason that the mountain was surrounded by darkness; but the grace of the Gospel is bright and radiant with light and has nothing shadowy or dark in it at all—and the bright cloud witnesses to this.

34   But let us listen to the Father's all-blessed voice, as it openly bears witness to his Only-begotten: "This is my Son, the beloved, in whom I take pleasure."[71] To reveal what is truly real, what has the same substance and is the same in honor, he adds the definite article, so that no one might think he is called "Son" in the same way that Israel is.[72] For he says that without the definite article: "my first-born son Israel."[73] But here he signifies the difference by adding the definite article and the adjective "beloved." For in the former text, the speaker says he is despised by [Israel's] rejecting the one who made them: "I begot sons," he says, "and raised them up, but they have rejected me."[74] But "in whom I take pleasure" means, "In whom I have come to rest, through whom I will that human salvation should come to pass." And by the words "Listen to him," he rouses up the lassitude of the disciples, so that—with the Lord now predicting his own passion—they might not be shaken in their souls. He seems, even more, to be upbraiding Peter for wanting to build tabernacles, and for being eager to talk the Lord out of suffering.   **35** And why, after hearing the voice, did the disciples "raise their eyes and see only Jesus"?[75] So that they might not assume that the witness came from one of the prophets. For this reason [Jesus] let those two go back

[71]Matt 17.5.

[72]The passage in Matthew reads: οὗτος ἐστιν ὁ Υἱὸς μου ὁ ἀγαπητός: literally, "This is the Son of mine, the Beloved." Philagathos contrasts this usage, with the definite article in the attributive position, with passages where Israel is simply referred to as "my firstborn son," without the definite article.

[73]Ex 4.22.

[74]Is 1.2.

[75]Matt 17.8.

again to the places from which they had come, and showed that he was the one to whom this witness was given.

36 Come, then, let us also run up the path of the spiritual mountain of virtue, so that, having arrived with Jesus at the summit of perfection, we might see, as from a broad overlook, that light that has been revealed to those who have followed to the mountaintop. Let us leave behind the hollows of lowly pleasures, shaded by the evil spirits as they might be by hillocks, and let us arrive at that mountain illuminated on all sides by the Father's Cloud. The climb upwards would be easy for us, if we should journey up in the way that Moses, who communicated the Law to us, first showed us in mystical fashion, and that Jesus, who gives the Law to us, later revealed. For Moses, when he led the people to Sinai, commanded that irrational creatures be left behind in the foothills, threatening stoning for anyone who dared approach;[76] but the Savior left the nine disciples behind, and took three with him. **37** What, then, do these two mysteries reveal to us? Since it is characteristic of irrational creatures to be led by the senses alone, without the process of reasoning, Moses legislates through them that we should go beyond the knowledge that comes to us from the senses, in the contemplation of spiritual realities. In harmony with this, the Lord also showed that if the mind does not turn away, and cast down all passionate attachment to the number nine,[77] and does not take the Trinity along with itself as its preferred companion, it will not be strong enough to climb the mountain of true knowledge. But lest we attempt to solve riddles by riddles, let us attempt a more secure explanation. **38** The number nine, containing within itself five and four, signifies sensation by the number five, and the mixture of the four elements by the number

[76]Ex 19.12–13.

[77]Philagathos does not explain the significance of "the nine" here any further, although he will attempt to do so in the next paragraph. It seems here to have some general numerological connection with the sensual beauties of the present world, perhaps because in Greek literature it was the number of the Muses, who inspired the arts.

four. So, then, when the mind becomes superior to bodily things, so that the law of the flesh is no longer at war with it,[78] and is no longer clogged by the senses in the mud of sin, then, at last, having the three parts of the soul as a support in its ascent towards what it longs for, it will be led without any hindrance towards the height of virtue, elbowing the number nine out of the way as it blocks and bars its way upwards. So the mind, leaving behind on earth the cares that beget frivolity in us, and taking along its passionate attachment to God (like Peter), its rationality (like John), and the spirit that leads to courage (like James), is led up to the way of life that is above us, being initiated into the Mystery of the Trinity, and it sees there "Moses and Elijah, speaking with him";[79] for when it examines the Law and the Prophets in a spiritual way, it sees all they contain as being in harmony with the Gospel.

39   And may it happen that we, too, "after six days"—that is, after the consummation of this world, which was created in six days—will be led up the mountain that looms above the heavens, where there is the company of the saints; and may we see the grace that shines out from the Godhead, and be overshadowed by the cloud of the Spirit, and be initiated more clearly and more purely into the Mystery of the Trinity, to whom belongs all honor and glory and praise, now and always and to the ages of ages. Amen.

[78]Cf. Gal. 5.17.
[79]See Luke 9.30.

Neophytus the Recluse

St Neophytus the Recluse (*Neophytos Enkleistos*) is perhaps the best-known monastic writer of Cyprus in medieval Byzantine culture. He was born to a poor family in Lenkara, Cyprus, in 1134, and died sometime after 1214. After entering the monastery of St John Chrysostom, on Mount Koutzouvendes, at the age of 18, he lived there for five years as part of the community, receiving enough education to be ordained a reader. He then left the monastery to travel in Palestine, and when he returned to Cyprus he asked the monastic authorities to allow him to live as a hermit. Although this request was denied at first, he was eventually allowed to retire to a cave as a recluse in 1159; there, his reputation for holiness began to attract disciples, and the local bishop ordered him to receive and instruct them. Eventually a new monastic community, called the Hermitage or *Enkleismos*, grew up around him, and most of Neophytus' spiritual writings were given as homilies or instructions for his disciples there. He drew up at least two versions of a *Typikon* or rule for this monastery. Neophytus' cell—originally decorated at his orders with very simple frescoes—was painted with more elaborate scenes from the life of Christ, mainly from the passion, by Theodore Apseudes in 1183, under the patronage of the bishop of Paphos.

Neophytus' catecheses or monastic instructions, written in his old age, were addressed, as a collection, to his brother John, who had become abbot of the monastery of St John Chrysostom at least by the year 1198, and possibly earlier. Some of the catecheses may well have previously been delivered orally, as instructions for the author's own small community. In his *Testament*, written in 1214, Neophytus refers to the *Catecheses* as already written, so they must have been finished before then. The date of this particular brief instruction, in any case, cannot be determined more precisely. The whole collection, like most of Neophytus' work, remains to be published. This instruction on the Transfiguration interprets the event as a vision of the divine light, radiating outward from the person of Jesus into the world. To perceive this light and to share in its promise, one must free oneself from passion and "ascend" to a life according to the Gospel. Even such a purified life, however, is only an anticipatory sign of the final vision of the radiant Jesus in glory, which we hope for when he comes again.

SAINT NEOPHYTUS THE RECLUSE
Catechesis on the Holy and Radiant Transfiguration of our God and Savior[1]

Please give me your blessing![2]

Brothers and fathers, see: again we have a spiritual festival, a celebration! Again, the eternal light, which comes forth from the eternal light, shines on us. Again "the shining forth of the Father's glory, the form of his hypostasis,"[3] has begun, by God's good pleasure, to illumine us. Again the brilliance of the undying light, the image of God's goodness, has made its home among us. Again the light of "the sun of justice,"[4] that light brighter than the sun, has lightened our world. Again "the true light, which enlightens everyone coming into the world,"[5] has come to be with us. Again the rays of its ineffable light, and the brilliance of its shining, have illumined the souls of believers, and have driven away the darkness of error and lessened the gloom of sin, have driven out the works of darkness and totally

[1] This catechesis has been edited and published by the late archimandrite Paul Benedict Englezakis, from a 13th-century manuscript of Neophytus' catechetical instructions, now in the Bibliothèque Nationale in Paris: Par. Suppl. Gr. 1317, ff. 98–100. See Benedict Englezakis, "An Unpublished Catechetical Instruction by St Neophytos the Recluse on the Transfiguration," in Silouan and Misael Ioannou, eds., *Studies on the History of the Church of Cyprus, 4th–20th Centuries* (Aldershot: Ashgate, 1995) 147–150 [="Ἀνέκδοτος Κατήχησις τοῦ Ὁσίου Νεοφύτου τοῦ Ἐγκλειστοῦ εἰς τὴν Ἁγίαν Μεταμόρφωσιν," *Theologia* 44 (1973) 698–701].

[2] This is a liturgical formula used by a preacher, to ask for the blessing of the presiding minister at a Eucharistic celebration before he begins his homily. The contents suggest the catechesis is being given at a liturgy on the Feast of the Transfiguration, August 6th.

[3] Heb 1.3.

[4] Mal 3.20.

[5] John 1.9.

blinded the spirits of darkness, along with their Prince; [this light] has consigned them to utter darkness, and fully extinguished the shadowy, midnight teachings of godless people, and has caused the arrogance of tyrants to disappear like dust in a windstorm, handing them over to night.[6] It has enlightened the spiritual eyes of faith of our genuinely believing, divinely crowned emperors, and has most powerfully reinforced the might of truth [in them].[7] And it has given light to the mind of the Emperor's high priests, now as in ancient times, to define the teaching of truth correctly; it has endowed the minds of his rulers and prominent leaders with the ability to judge justly and make decisions, in this great abundance [of light]–for Scripture says, "Power has been given to you from the Lord, and domination from the Most High."[8] It has strengthened, too, the divine teaching of [Christ's] Church, and has made the full extent of the earth to be brilliant with the rays of truth.

So now we joyfully celebrate today, as illuminated lovers of Christ, the feast of the divine transfiguration of him who is that great light, so that we, too, might "put off the works of darkness and, clothing ourselves with the armor of light, might walk uprightly as in the day."[9] This, after all, is the reason he calls his holy disciples to a high mountain alone, and makes them witnesses of this great and holy sign. "And he was transfigured before them, and he let his garments shine forth like light, and his face like the sun."[10] His purpose was to show that he had come to bear the world upwards from all that is below, to restore humanity to its original beauty and dignity, and to let no creature be dragged off crawling towards the underworld, forgetting what lies above, but [to lead them to] erect "stairways of

---

[6]Englezakis, the editor, suggests that this may be a reference to the recent presence of Frankish crusaders on Cyprus, and even to their efforts to establish Catholic beliefs and practices (*op. cit.* 147–148 [Greek: 698–699]).

[7]Here Neophytus is clearly referring to the Byzantine Emperor, as the protector of the Church and its official faith. After 1204, the Emperors were in exile in Nicaea, but were still regarded by the Orthodox faithful, even in Cyprus, as their legitimate rulers.

[8]Wisdom 6.3.

[9]Rom 13.12–13.

[10]See Matt 17.1–2.

ascent in the heart"[11] and "to seek what is above,"[12] and to be aware of the day of his ineffable second coming. How shall we sinners, with eyes wretchedly withered by passion, be able to see the divine flashes of that ineffable outpouring of light, when the holy disciples, who had followed Christ for so long, were not able to bear a dim ray of his transfiguration, but fell prostrate on the ground? If they, then, on the mountain, were not strong enough to gaze clear-sightedly at his transfiguration, but fell on their faces, with what eyes, tell me, shall we who live here in sin gaze on him then, when he comes not in transfigured form on a mountain, but comes from heaven in divine glory, and will shake heaven and earth, as it is written? "All at once," Scripture says, "I will shake heaven and earth."[13]

When [he comes] with the sound of trumpets, with heavenly powers, with voices of celebration and hymns to the Trinity, and with indescribable light—when we see him come near us with thousands of thousands, myriads of myriads, of brilliant angels—how shall we then gaze on his glory and his inaccessible light, whose light in the transfiguration the Apostles were not strong enough to gaze on? How shall we sinners be able to see the ineffable glory of his second coming? Scripture says "There is no common sharing between light and darkness."[14] Sin is darkness, and the devil is darkness, as is all he delights in; and it is impossible that this darkness we are speaking of should have any share in the great light of God, and in his Kingdom, which is all light. But if we sinners turn towards the Lord, and produce for him fruit worthy of conversion,[15] I am convinced by his own proclamation of the truth that we shall not simply gaze on his unspeakable glory, but will also, by his grace, rejoice with him in his Kingdom. And perhaps in that precise moment, all the people may say, "Amen! So be it! So be it!"

[11] Ps 83.6 [LXX].
[12] Col 3.1.
[13] Hag 2.6.
[14] II Cor 6.14.
[15] Neophytus touches here on a theme familiar in the long tradition of monastic spiritual writing: that conversion of heart is the prime purpose of the ascetic life, and of monastic observance.

Theoleptos of
Philadelphia

Theoleptos was born in Nicaea in Bithynia, about 1250, and served
as metropolitan bishop of Philadelphia, in Lydia, from 1283 or 1284
until his death in 1322. As a young man, he was married and served
for some time as a deacon; he was also involved in the affairs of the
Church in Nicaea during the last years of its role as imperial capital
of the Byzantine Empire, under the Lascarid dynasty. When still in
his early twenties, he left his wife in order to practice asceticism,
and may have visited the monasteries on Mt Athos briefly; in any
case, in Asia Minor he became acquainted with the former Athonite
monk Nicephoros, one of the early promoters of hesychastic prayer.
Like Nicephoros, Theoleptos was a vocal opponent of the Union
of Lyons with the Catholic church, which the Emperor Michael
VIII Palaeologos had signed in 1274, and which was supported by
Michael's Patriarch, John Bekkos. Theoleptos was summoned to
Constantinople, interrogated, and briefly imprisoned for his opposition to the union, probably in 1275. After his release from prison,
he returned to his eremitical life in the suburbs of Nicaea, and
remained there despite his wife's repeated and vigorous attempts to
persuade him to return home. He soon became much sought after
as a spiritual guide, and continued to oppose any reconciliation with
Rome. In 1283, when the union had collapsed and Michael VIII had
been succeeded by Andronicus II, Theoleptos was ordained bishop
and appointed metropolitan of Philadelphia (present-day Alaşehir),
an ancient city in the Anatolian mountains some 80 miles east of
Smyrna. He later wrote a tract against John Bekkos, the pro-union
patriarch, and exerted an influence on the deposition of Patriarch
Gregory II of Cyprus in 1289.

Despite his opposition to the union of Lyons, Theoleptos was generally a supporter of the new Palaeologan dynasty, and continued to resist the strict "Arsenite" party, who caused much disturbance by refusing to recognize the Emperor Michael's successors. After the dispute was peacefully settled by the Patriarch Niphon in 1310, in what was generally referred to as an *oikonomia* or "deal," Theoleptos continued to reject the Arsenites, considering this new imperial policy of reconciliation a feckless capitulation. He broke off communion with the Patriarch of Constantinople himself, for that reason, between 1310 and 1319, but remained in his see and acted as virtually the chief civil administrator of the city. Philadelphia, at the eastern border of the Byzantine Empire at this stage of history, was heavily fortified, and for a long time played an important role in holding off Turkish incursions from eastern Asia Minor; the bishops of the city were usually important leaders in that defensive role. Widely regarded as a forceful man with unyielding principles, Theoleptos was a close friend of the powerful and learned Choumnos family in the capital, and was the spiritual director of Irene Choumnaia, the daughter of the influential statesman and humanist Nikephoros Choumnos. Vitalien Laurent has characterized Theoleptos as "un prélat de grande classe, qui fut tour à tour pasteur, chef de gouvernement par procuration, condottiere et mystique eminent" ("Les crises religieuses à Byzance: le schisme Antiarsénite du Métropolite de Philadelphie Théolepte [+ c. 1324]," *Revue des études byzantines* 18 [1960] 45).

Theoleptos left a variety of writings, including the series of brief monastic instructions or catecheses, addressed to an unknown community, to which this homiletic piece for the feast of the Transfiguration belongs. It may well date from the years when he was most active as a spiritual director, between 1275 and 1283. For a carefully documented survey of his life, see Angela Constantinides Hero, *The Life and Letters of Theoleptos of Philadelphia* (Brookline, MA: Hellenic College Press, 1994) 11–29.

THEOLEPTOS OF PHILADELPHIA

Catechesis for the Feast of the Transfiguration of our Lord and Savior Jesus Christ[1]

1 The present brilliant day of the Transfiguration, in the grace given us by the transfigured Christ, requires that I place before your Love the mystery of the festival, so that we might learn the meaning of the Mystery, and celebrate the Transfiguration of Christ not only in sacred hymns, but in holy behavior. For this, too, is what it means for us to recognize the gift of which we have been thought worthy, and to reveal its treasure through growth in good works, honoring the festival in life as well as in word.

2 The one who walks on level ground strolls along easily, because of the evenness of the land and the ease he has in walking forward; but the one who goes up a mountain labors, and is drenched with sweat, because the terrain is steep and the result is physical stress. Take the level, hollowed-out land, and the ease of walking there, as an image for the life surrounded by pleasure and luxury and the broad ease of life according to the flesh, because of the relaxed, unresisting character of foolish pleasures; but consider the other as an image of virtuous practice, because of [the importance of] self-control in all things, and the difficulty of training oneself, and the painful need to endure patiently the challenges that meet us.

[1]The Greek text of this catechesis was first edited by H.-V. Beyer, "Die Katechese des Theoleptos von Philadelphia auf die Verklärung Christi," *Jahrbuch der Öster-reichischen Byzantinistik* 34 (1984) 171–198; it has been edited again, with a translation, by Robert E. Sinkewicz, in his collection, *Theoleptos of Philadelphia, The Monastic Discourses* (Toronto: Pontifical Institute of Medieval Studies, 1992) 186–191.

3 The person who lives by self-denial, making his way according to the commands of Christ and keeping tight control over the pleasures of the body, is recognized to be a trustworthy and warm disciple of the Lord, in Peter's footsteps. And the one who puts worldly thinking to death, and represses his fleshly considerations, who makes himself ready to undergo hardships for the Gospel and reproves those who live evil lives, and for truth's sake bears with the evil deeds that come from them, shows the fervor of James. Again, the one who has made his intelligence the dwelling place of the Holy Scriptures, and who is set on fire with concern for divine things, and meditates[2] on the structural principles of nature as a way of understanding the truth, imitates John's way of life. A person like this, who follows after the Lord in body and soul, and always walks the challenging path of virtue, ascends even the intellectual mountain in order to pray without interruption.[3] For in this practice pure prayer is brought to perfection, driving away all thoughts of this present world and forming the whole mind into something radiant, since it is nourished by the oil of divine love and enkindled by outpourings of divine light.

4 When the mind is filled with light by remembering God, and made radiant in knowledge of God through unceasing prayer, and when the body's movements accomplish only pure actions, and words of understanding come forth from the mouth, and the senses wrap themselves in a garment of holy sobriety, then the body's limbs labor to serve [its] good deeds and the whole person becomes focused on light, since the person's soul becomes a lamp, bearing "the true light" of the virtues "that enlightens every person coming into the world."[4]

---

[2]The word Theoleptos uses here, ἀδολεσχέω, usually means "talk foolishly" in classical Greek, but in the Septuagint sometimes carries the meaning of "meditate": see Gen 24.63; Ps 118.15; etc.

[3]Here Theoleptos begins a description of the "ceaseless prayer" of the contemplative, which anticipates in many details the spiritual goal of Palamite monastic prayer.

[4]John 1.9.

5   The one who lives this way and has trained himself to be this "is not conformed to this world,"[5] which changes and is passing away; for he has heard Paul—who gazed on what no one can see—saying that God is "letting the form of this world pass away,"[6] and he does not concern himself with earthly things. He passes by the things that are passing, as being only shapes that have no reality; for as the form that appears suddenly just as suddenly disappears, so the things that presently surround us have nothing firm or stable in them. So, lifting his mind up from the desire for things that decay, and rejecting this life's pleasures as only a shape without substance, he embraces the immortal realities of the age to come, always being transformed by withdrawing into himself day after day, and by renewing his way of thinking hour after hour—the first, by constantly turning away from evil; the second, by constantly turning towards the good, and devoting himself to virtue.

6   These are the kinds of ascents the athlete of the pious life proposes for himself and struggles to attain, as one formed in God's way; he shines out like a star, and stimulates others, too, to imitate his good deeds. With his whole spirit and his whole body he honors Christ's Transfiguration, understanding the mystery of the feast and interpreting it in practice for those who see him. For when Christ was transfigured, he gave a glimpse of the ineffable glory with which he will come to judge all things, and also laid bare the brilliance which those who please him will share; he taught every believer to prepare himself here to be ready to participate in that blessedness that is stored away, preserving, as in wax,[7] that form of activity that will allow us to be gathered up into the divine light.

[5]Rom 12.2.

[6]I Cor 7.31.

[7]A somewhat puzzling comparison. Theoleptos seems to be thinking here not so much of the preservation of the form of what is contemplated by the mind, as a seal leaves its impression in wax, as he is of the wax of a candle providing fuel for the lamp's flame (see secs. 7 and 8).

7   For just as wax , melted by the fire's heat, becomes fuel for the fire because of the fatness that naturally belongs to it—and the light that is nurtured from it radiates on all who come near—so the believer, building up the wax of divine knowledge on himself from the flowers of the virtues, and having all earthly desire melted away by the warmth of divine love, forms himself here into a lamp, and expects—through the law of divine love—to receive, in the revelation of the age we hope for, that divine and ineffable light, and to share fully in that eternal brilliance that radiates outward from it.

8   The act of keeping the commandments of Christ, and the labor of the virtues, which he laid down as the rule for this present age, are the nourishment of divine glory. "For I shall love," he says, "the one who keeps my commandments, and shall show myself to him."[8] And just as sensible fire uses wax for its fuel, so the glory of divine light shines out in those who have made it their own through virtue. "For my food," Christ says, "is to do the will of my Father in heaven."[9] "In his will," says the prophet, "is eternal life."[10]

9   So the one who does good works will live, reaping the reward of his labors by the grace of the guide of our salvation, Jesus Christ, who glorifies those who glorify him. To him all glory belongs, and honor and adoration, along with his Father who knows no beginning, and his all-holy, good and life-giving Spirit, now and always and for the ages of ages. Amen.

[8]John 14.21.
[9]John 4.34.
[10]Ps 29.6 (LXX).

NIKEPHOROS CHOUMNOS

Nikephoros Choumnos, an eminent and wealthy Byzantine intellectual and statesman of the late thirteenth and early fourteenth century, was born in Constantinople between 1250 and 1255, and died there on January 16, 1327. A member of an established and well-connected political family, he studied rhetoric and philosophy under the tutorship of Gregory of Cyprus (c. 1241–1290), the influential writer and intellectual who served as patriarch Gregory II under Andronicus II, from 1283 to 1289. In addition to his literary and philosophical activity, Nikephoros was intensely interested in what we would call the natural sciences; he also held various diplomatic and administrative positions, including being head (*logothētēs*) of a number of imperial departments (*sekrētai*), and finally *mesazōn* or chief minister to Emperor Andronikos II (reigned 1281–1328) from 1293 to 1305. He later also served as governor of Thessalonike (1309–1310). Nikephoros married his daughter Irene—herself a devout patron of monastic life in the capital—to the despot John Palaiologos, and was a close friend of her spiritual director, Metropolitan Theoleptos of Philadelphia, whose catechesis on the Transfiguration of Christ also appears in this collection.

Later in life, Nikephoros used some of his vast wealth to refound the monastery of the "Theotokos Gorgoepēkoos"—"Mother of God swift to help"—which had been founded in the 11th century in the Vlanga quarter of the capital, near the Sea of Marmara, but which had been allowed to fall into ruin during the Latin dominance of the city after 1204. The year before his death, Nikephoros retired to another monastery, one his daughter Irene had founded, that of the "Philanthrōpos Sōtēr," just south of the Hagia Sophia. For details of his life, see Vitalien Laurent, "Une fondation monastique de Nicé-phore Choumnos: ἡ ἐν ΚΠ μονὴ τῆς Θεοτόκου τῆς Γοργοεπηκόου," *Revue des études byzantines* 12 (1954) 32–44; at greater length, Jean Verpaux, *Nicéphore Choumnos: homme d'état et humaniste byzantin (ca. 1250–1255—1327)* (Paris: Picard, 1959).

Nikephoros wrote rhetorical, theological, and philosophical essays on various subjects, and has also left us 172 letters. He was a contemporary, and a political and literary rival, of Theodore Metochites, whom he criticized for the unnecessary complication of his style, even though his own style is scarcely simple or austere. Nikephoros' attempts at subtlety and rhetorical power, in fact, in this present treatise on the Transfiguration, can sometimes simply make his meaning obscure to the modern reader. His language is clearly the language of a highly educated aristocrat, but it is seldom straightforward or simple; the sentences are often long, the syntax complex. A piece that differs markedly in theme and emphasis from the Transfiguration homilies that would soon emerge from the Palamite school, this essay is, as has been observed, "representative of an older piety" based on Patristic tradition (See R. E Sinkewicz, "Gregory Palamas," in C.G. and V. Conticello, *La Théologie Byzantine et sa tradition* [Turnhout: Brepols, 2002] 172). It is also Choumnos' longest essay on a religious theme, and seems to have been cel-ebrated widely in his own time; a letter to Choumnos from a pro-vincial bishop acknowledges it as the most substantial treatment of this Gospel event that the writer had read. It is much less exclusively focused on the Gospel story itself, however, than most of the other homilies or catecheses we have translated here, and reflects widely on a number major events in the history of salvation, including the typological significance of the sacrifice of Isaac and the Exodus in the Pentateuch. Its focus, in fact, is on the meaning of Jesus' sacrifice on the cross, as the central act by which a sinful world is reconciled to God; Choumnos presents the Transfiguration of Jesus, situated in the midst of his prophecies of his passion, as the summary revelation of who Jesus is and of how his sacrifice is for us the fulfillment of all God's interventions in human history.

As chapters 23 and 24 make clear, the work was intended for a female monastic audience, as an invitation to share through discipleship and asceticism in the transfigured life of Christ. Verpaux speculates that it may have been written in 1315–1316, at the start of the Patriarchate of John Glykys, and may have been addressed by Choumnos first of all to his daughter Irene (*op.cit.* 146–147).

NIKEPHOROS CHOUMNOS
On the Holy Transfiguration of Christ[1]

1   When Christ, my savior and God, is transfigured, and a voice
from the Father above bursts from a radiant cloud, saying "This is
my Son, the Beloved"—indeed, crying out and urging us to hear
him—who would not immediately leave everything and run at
once towards the vision and the voice? Who would not desire, even
eagerly rush, to climb Mount Thabor, and to go within the cloud
and become one of those initiated[2] there, since God does not turn
us back but even urges us to come? Who would not wish to reach
out and seize his own cross, as it were—for the one to which Christ
is nailed does not stand far in the distance!—and to lift it on his
shoulders and follow Christ himself, as he encourages us to do?[3]
Who would not love to be himself with James and John, as they go
inside the cloud? Even more, who would not want to drink the cup
which Christ[4] drank on the cross to destroy the bitter taste from
which decay and death have come to us, destroying at the same time
also the judgment passed on Adam, "You are earth, and to earth
you will return"?[5] He ascended the cross himself, and nailed and

---

[1]This homily was first published in a critical text by Nike Papatriantaphyllou-
Theodorides, "Νικηφόρου Χούμνου Λόγος στη Μεταμόρφωση (BHG 1998w)," *Byz-
antina* 18 (1995) 15–38; text 24–38. This is the text we have translated here.

[2]Nikephoros uses the language here of initiation into sacred Mysteries, suggesting that joining the three Apostles in the cloud overshadowing the top of Mount
Thabor, and witnessing what they saw and heard, is a way of participating in a kind
of liturgical action that will unite us to God and empower us to live with new understanding of God's presence and work in creation.

[3]So Lk 9.23.
[4]Matt 20.22.
[5]Gen 3.19.

crucified my sin in himself, and stretching out his hands—those hands whose creature and formation I am, by whose fingers the heavens were formed—called back to himself once again from the earth the one who had turned back to earth and was thus totally shattered, and by the most shameful acts had become useless to himself: shaping him anew and forming him into a new creature by his own blood! O what can I be worth, seeing that all this was for me? What is this great and terrible mystery? How rich are his mercies? What is the great measure of his love for humanity? How does his goodness become reality? Christ was judged by Pilate and by the Jews, judged and sentenced and led away as an evil-doer, without quarreling or crying out, but, like an innocent lamb, sheared and sacrificed for the whole world.

2   All of this, as we have said, happened not long afterwards. For already Judas had received Satan completely,[6] who entered and filled him; spitting out the grace given him and the power of the charisms he had received, he in fact approached the Jews and conspired to hand over the Lord, selling him for thirty pieces of silver. For indeed he wound the halter around himself, made it his own, clung to it as to his betrayal; but the Jews pounced upon what had been promised him, ran to the Sanhedrin, and everything was turned upside-down! So the plot against Christ continued, which had been allowed at the devil's urging!

3   Well, that is what all of *them* did! But my Jesus went up Mount Thabor in the way we have said, leading with him his disciples Peter and James and John. And he placed Moses and Elijah beside him—Moses, for whom he once also wrote the tablets of the law and handed them to him on Sinai. He leads him once again even to Thabor, in order that he [Moses] might be able—not there but here—to

---

[6]For dramatic effect, Nikephoros suggests a chronology for the events of Christ's Passion that is more tightly interwoven than that of the Gospel narratives themselves.

see the one who wrote them. There, [Moses] sought and desired to see him, but did not, and heard that he would be protected by the rock and could see his back parts. Entering that protection, and the shadow it provided, he did not see God's face but his back, because of the shadow—although one must also realize that even the "back parts" of God are his face! But everything that then was shadows and types of what would later be revealed in Christ, Moses is now led to understand by vision itself. Now, apart from anything that might hide him or conceal him or shade him over, Moses gazes on Christ as God, shining forth and glowing in flesh—flesh belonging to him and not at all consumed by the flames, as once he saw him burning in the bush and not in the least burning it away.

Elijah, too, encountered [God] on Mount Horeb in different ways: all of them were types and foreshadowings of what now appeared to him truly on Thabor. And the tablets that were then given to Moses in a particular way—all the Law and everything in the Law—come here to perfection: namely, their fulfillment in Christ. And we may now understand the voice that spoke to them— to Moses and to all who follow Moses, and also to Elijah—rather as urging them to know they are set free; freed from those ancient commands, they should at all times look towards Christ himself, and should, for all time to come, wait constantly for him, and obey his commands.

4 David, too, in saying what he does about Thabor, looks forward to this moment and utters what he perceives about what is now happening. If this is not true, what other reason might there be [for speaking as he does]? But there is nothing—for you would not just invent a reason for saying Thabor will "rejoice in him."[7] In what other name would it be, if not in what Christ always is: the Son of God? For even if this name[8]—which, according to Paul's assertion,

---

[7]Nikephoros is referring to Ps 88.13 (LXX): "Thabor and Hermon will rejoice in your *name*." The "name," of course, he identifies as that of "Son of God."

[8]I.e., Son of God.

is "above every name"[9]—was bestowed on him graciously because of his divine nature and substance, and was inherited in virtue of his timeless, primordial begetting, still Christ himself also clearly reveals it when speaking of baptism. For he says, "Baptizing them into the name of the Father and the Son and the Holy Spirit."[10] And like the name "Father," in the Father's case—and that is what it means to say "I have revealed your name to human beings"[11]—and the name "Spirit" in the Spirit's case, so too the name "Son" in the Son's case is different, with reference to the manner of his being, from all others. For everything else we ascribe to God is surely common to the Father and to the Son himself and to the Spirit, but this [name][12] is proper to him alone, as he is both eternally begotten and exists as eternally perfect in the Father.

5   In this name,[13] then, Thabor now rejoices, as God the Father proclaims it and calls it out, just as Hermon rejoiced earlier when the same verse was fulfilled, at the time of Christ's baptism.[14] One must realize this clearly, if one knows where on this earth Hermon is: it is by the Jordan! Not only this, but at that time,[15] too, the Voice used this name, and affirmed that he is both this [= Son of God] and Beloved, and that all God's good pleasure is fulfilled and rests in him. Now God adds the instruction that we are to "listen to him." At that

[9]Phil 2.9.

[10]Matt 28.19.

[11]John 17.6.

[12]I.e., the title "Son." Nicephoros here summarizes what was by his time the classic Christian understanding of God as Trinity: Father, Son, and Holy Spirit are all fully God; they constitute together a single, unimaginable divine reality or substance; yet each is distinct from the other two, recognized as such by the relationships of origin which we refer to by using their names, "Father," "Son," and "Holy Spirit." Nikephoros is suggesting that "Thabor and Hermon rejoice," in the words of the Psalm, because they were to become the settings for the full revelation of God's Trinitarian Mystery.

[13]I.e., that of God the Son.

[14]For an earlier connection of Christ's Transfiguration scene on Mt Thabor with Mt Hermon, mentioned along with it in Psalm 88.13 (LXX), see the concluding paragraph of Proclus of Constantinople, Homily 8, *On the Transfiguration*: above, pp. 95–96.

[15]At the time of Jesus' baptism.

former time, surely this additional phrase, which we have just mentioned, was also intended. But the words were omitted then, [and added here] because of Moses and Elijah: to suggest [here] that the Law, which came from Moses, had by now grown completely silent; and that all the prophets, along with Elijah (who was still alive), who spoke along with him, realized that the end of what they had prophesied had come upon them, and had reached fulfillment in Christ himself, who is being transfigured on Thabor.

6   Well, then, as we have said, God the Father speaks in this kind of witness, addressing God the Son—[God] proclaims even this. But what do *you* say: you who rest on the Sabbaths and adhere to the law and resist Christ and his miracles; you who release your cow and your donkey from the stall when they are thirsty on the Sabbath, and bring them to water, and who drag up the livestock that has fallen into a pit, without seeing the Law as in any way preventing you, but who in no sense want yourself and the children of Abraham, when they are dreadfully held captive by Satan, to be released at all from those bonds by Christ the Savior, even if it should be necessary to wait the whole Sabbath? You complain against those who have been given the use of their eyes when they had been born blind, and now can see well, by the spittle of the one who once worked the first creation of the human person by breath and mud together—for the creation and shaping of our flesh and all that belongs to it, was from earth; and here the same creative power is revealed, since these people, as we have said, genuinely look on the light that now shines on Mount Thabor, and see everything correctly. And you rebuke even those who bring you here—those who invite you to join the disciples of Christ, to follow the light of life—as you walk miserably in shadow and make your way in darkness, not understanding or grasping the gift immediately, but continuing to abuse and upbraid them for their blind birth. But I believe that this is the reason they were born blind: so that you, who are blind with healthy eyes and vision, deprived of the true light completely and stumbling along in the darkness, might flee the darkness as a result of this great divine miracle, of such magnitude and quality, and might rush forward to the truth.

7   But you claim to be a disciple of Moses, and you say that God has spoken to Moses. If, then, this is a great thing for you—and surely it is a great thing that God has spoken to Moses!—and if the Law is everything to you because it came through Moses, where do you place what is happening now? How much more and how much greater do you think it is that Moses appears along with Elijah, standing alongside Christ and conversing with him? That God the Father speaks from on high, and bears witness, and proclaims that we are to "hear him," and cries out, and commands this as part of his clearly-willed command: you are released from all those things that were said and legislated of old, and are to listen to Christ himself, because he is the beloved Son, and all of the good will from on high that was heralded and pointed out in advance is present in him! How does this not shake everything for you, and knock down all that seemed firm and strong, coming from Moses and the Law, and lead into oblivion everything that comes from Sinai all that was written and spoken there? How does it not call you over, rather, to Thabor, to look on Moses in that situation: to look at him, not hidden again under a shadow or under the rock, but standing next to the inaccessible light–now in flesh and accompanied by flesh[16]—and conversing with the light? What then? When [Moses] heard the Father's voice from above, he immediately realized that the Old Testament as a whole had come to an end along with the Law, and had fallen silent; at the same time Elijah, too, had fallen silent, since he himself knew—and knew with crystalline clarity—whose forerunner he was to be, having been snatched up by a chariot of fire, and whose prophet he now continued to be in safety.[17]

[16] An obscure phrase. Nikephoros may mean that the Son of God, who became flesh, was himself the "inaccessible light" of God (see John 1.7–9), and was surrounded by fleshly companions like the prophets and disciples.

[17] I.e., taken up to heaven, he was no longer persecuted for his witness.

8   So much for them. But you:[18] how can you be what you say you are, a disciple of Moses, when he now teaches you in a different way, yet does not persuade you differently—conversing once again with God, and hearing God once again speaking to him from above? You say that there are six days in which the one who keeps the Law is to work, and you say rightly. But what *is* this work—of what kind do you say it is? Could it really be this: to drive out demons, to put illnesses to flight and cleanse lepers, to give strength to paralytics, to straighten up those bent over and constantly stooped, to make withered limbs healthy again and give freedom of movement to the lame, hearing to the deaf and a voice to the mute, even—to say the ultimate—to raise the dead? If these seem to you to be works that observe the Law, then grant that being able to do these things is certainly given to those led by the Law. But if none of these is possible for anyone at all—at any rate, not for anyone who exists and acts in just a human way—then how is it that what is not possible for anyone at all to accomplish is, as you say, what the Law forbids them to do? In fact, you do not see a good work being accomplished here by acquired skill or any scientific learning, nor by the contrivance of drugs or other inventions, nor by any other of all the devices that have been invented to relieve those burdened by little ills in countless little ways, but [it is done] only by a word and a will—all of which is possible to God alone. If God is offended by these works and actions being done on a Sabbath, from what other source could these people have experienced their effects? But if God is not offended [by them], and if therefore these are God's miracles—performed, indeed, on the Sabbath—why, in the attempt to slander God and deceive us, are you calling on Moses and the Law, which tell you nothing about this at all? How could you have received knowledge that Moses was the first of all legislators, but be unaware of the many varied miracles of God narrated before that, or fail to know the God who both now and then performed wonders in Moses and through Moses?

[18]Nikephoros continues to address the imagined Jewish hearers, who in his view fail to comprehend who Jesus is.

9 If you were persuaded by miracles then to accept the Law, accept now the end of the Law, dissolved by the same and by much greater miracles; accept the fact that the dead rise on the Sabbath, accept that the blind see (as we have said) with renewed eyes and that the woman who was bent over now stands straight again, and all the other things that God is doing—God who has made you, the human person, Lord of the Sabbath,[19] and has not bound you with laws for the Sabbath's sake, but has given the law of the Sabbath for your sake. Why? So that you might realize that he is the shaper of all creation, the one who is able to bring the whole universe into being from what is not—in timeless time, one might say—and to arrange it as it is: so giving glory to himself in six days, as you say yourself, but resting on the seventh, which is the Sabbath. And he gave you the Law for this reason, to know that he is creator of all of these things, as you are led to a vision of the single meaning of this whole time of creation; but that he always has the power to create and bring into operation, and always is acting through the words and modes of the Providence that holds all things together and stabilizes [the creation], and that gives it the ability to remain what it is.

10 If the whole cosmos has itself come to be in six days, and has been made corruptible and impermanent in its nature, how will it be able to endure and remain what it is for the future unless the Creator, who gave it its being at the start, holds it together for the future and controls its flux and disintegration, so that nothing at all should be totally obliterated or corrupted? Therefore what God the Father is constantly creating, the Son is always creating along with him—the Son who is now transfigured and receives the witness of the Father. So you yourself should also listen to this voice of witness; you yourself should join those who believe in these miracles, divine as they are and never performed by anyone else—you must be transformed now, so to speak, from one who does not perceive into one who has received sight and understanding. Let go of the Law and all that the

[19]See Matt 12.8; Mark 2.27.

Law contains to receive God the Father, by receiving the Son, who for your sake and that you might be saved, has worked, along with God the Father, these great deeds which no other person has done.

11   In fact, that all of this—Law and Prophets and whatever there was before the Law—leads the wayfarer to Christ as its goal, ought to be clear anywhere you look.[20] We should consider the Law and the Prophets this way before all else—for clearly this meaning is first before all other things, when we begin in faith: that is the reason that the story of Abraham, and those radiantly supernatural accounts, brimming over with so many miracles, of things that were done for Abraham's sake, have come down to us here, and reach out to the whole world. And since all that concerns us, too, is faith and God's power, this [story] needs no words of demonstration, but is revealed by the whole of perceptible and intelligible creation, which cries out to tell us.

12   When Abraham, then, examined this and grasped its meaning, he dismissed all lower causes, and moving beyond the heavens themselves he found God as the craftsman and wise creator of all things, both sensible and intelligible. And trusting in him, he was never forced away from that goal in any way, never turned to look below, never knew or preferred anything else that exists, but clung to him as his starting point, we might say, and from there kept gazing on all other things, and understanding them, and doing his work. For this reason, too, careful and constant hospitality, and all his earnestness concerning it, characterized him; his memory of God clearly did not fail him in this concern, and his actions raised him up to God himself with a pure mind. For indeed, when no guest appeared of those he hoped to receive at his hospitable table, God himself sat down in the space under the oak tree, seeking to find and nourish [Abraham]. And he did give refreshment to many with his hospitality. How did

[20]Nikephoros emphasizes his main theme here: the unified meaning of the Biblical narrative, and of material creation itself, when seen through faith in Christ.

this happen? God himself loved him for his hospitality, and came to his table. And he came, revealing the fullness of his Godhead, since he is clearly one God in three perfect hypostases, Father and Son and Spirit.[21] That great mystery in which God is known was at that time still hidden, not yet revealed but stored up in Christ; but now it flashes out clearly on Thabor, with the Father speaking from above, the Son shining with light below, the Spirit overshadowing them in the bright cloud.

13   God appears to Abraham in this way, at that time; and he confides himself completely to him, because Abraham believed—giving this, one might say, in exchange and as a repayment for the faith he presented. To us, even here, it is possible to examine the manner in which each was able to show both mercy and hospitality. God leads him forward wherever he wills, and towards the goal that he wills. For when God willed to reveal himself to Abraham, he reveals himself in the very place and at the very table at which Abraham was striving to receive his guests. For this reason, I think, the command of the wise Solomon is a safe policy: "Be merciful, and may pledges of good faith not be lacking to you,"[22]—namely, as you seek and desire to depart from here and rest in the bosom of Abraham.

Consider his boldness; consider also how much he is able to associate confidently with God. For when the entertainment was at an end, and Abraham realized how much God was stirred up against sinners, he fell on his face; and he did not only beseech him, but even dares to test the Benevolent One's benevolence, saying: "Never, Lord! You would never destroy a just person along with an unjust one!"[23] This was the first sign of his familiarity, revealed in

---

[21]Nikephoros' ingenious connection of the story of Abraham's hospitality to his three visitors with the full revelation of the Trinity to Christian faith reminds the reader of Andrei Rublev's famous icon, which seems to represent the Holy Trinity as guests at Abraham's table.

[22]Prov 3.3.

[23]Gen 18.23. Nikephoros presents Abraham's intercession for the citizens of Sodom and Gomorrha as an example of his sense of mercy, which invites mercy from God in response.

his intercession. And when he received all he asked for from God, who approved and granted his request, he immediately changed his whole approach, no longer making his plea and argument on behalf of the just, nor to prevent the just from ever sharing the fruits of the vice and wickedness of sinners, but rather [suggesting] that those who have done evil, base things might escape because of the just and be completely free from judgment. But even here [Abraham] does not balance things out in an equal way, or demand one [person] in return for another or request that the same number be saved as are condemned—[those saved from punishment] measured by the number, in other words, of those who are not held to account in the judgment. What does he ask for, then? He begins with fifty of those found there who are just—if there should be so many. And then, not once but many times lowering the number and making distinctions—and finding God ready to agree—finally coming to ten [people] in number who are recognized for their righteousness, he tries to bring that whole crowd, unsurpassable in their wickedness and impiety—which was an innumerable multitude—to the same outcome: all of them, namely, as many as they were, should be saved together, because of only those ten.

14 And having obtained this, he stopped asking: perhaps because he judged that the number [of the just] would never be found to be fewer than what had already been asked and granted. If he had thought that, perhaps he would have asked that all [be spared] for the sake of one, Lot—and he could have received this. That is, in fact, what happened. Such great deeds of power are revealed when faith is proved by works: in other things, one might say, but certainly in acts of mercy by themselves, and in the pursuit of charity towards one's fellow men and women. And since the realization of such charity has begun with Christ, the full reality of it has shone forth only through faith in him, and in the whole mystery centered on him, as it is understood and has power over those who believe, and are protected by the power of the cross that has now been planted.

[Believers] have overcome the whole world and its rulers, since all visible and invisible powers opposed to them they have trampled underfoot. Demons are overcome by them; fire serves their will; iron withdraws before them, the sea draws back, wild air is tamed. Beasts are friendly towards them, and even if something is deadly, it will never harm them in any way. These are the ones who can dominate all creation, even if it is drawn up against them, rather than being dominated by it.

15   As we have said, then, if we take Abraham as the beginning, all these are ancient symbols of things later brought to fulfillment and brilliantly revealed in Christ. Abraham's wife Sara was sterile; her womb was sealed, and no offspring at all could be hoped for. This continued until quite late in her life. But in her later days, as an old woman, she conceived as had been promised, and according to the promise bore a son: Isaac. After this, Abraham and Sarah received indeed a second, better promise: to look on the stars of heaven and count up the sand of the seas, and to know that the number of Isaac's descendants would be beyond the number of these things. But she did not hear it in this way, nor did she believe—for what was her faith in comparison with the faith of Abraham? But he also had experienced firm assurances from what had previously been promised and fulfilled—something one might find in others, too, who have the courage to look for future things on the basis of what has happened already.[24] So God began now to put him to the test, and told him, "Take Isaac, and go up a mountain to offer him in sacrifice."[25] And Abraham immediately complied with all that was commanded, without thinking or calculating any further. And he took Isaac, brought wood along with him, and led him to the mountain. He seriously set about offering this unspeakable, horrifying sacrifice, without second thoughts. Then he bound Isaac's hands and feet,

[24]Literally, "one who has the courage to expect second events on the basis of first ones."

[25]Gen 22.1–14.

threw him down, held him forcibly with his knee,[26] then turned and drew his dagger and brandished it. But the boy—if nothing more—at least turned and gazed into his father's face; this was such an awful, ill-omened sight, that if wild beasts were the ones who witnessed and saw it, it would have turned them aside, bent them, broken their hearts, to see a son, with his own eyes, watching his father kill him. But Abraham did not turn away his gaze, nor was he shaken at heart, nor did he feel anything in his soul, nor did any of the promises made about Isaac come into his mind. He was not agitated, nor did he relax his hand, nor did the dagger fall from his hand as if his soul were confused; but he pressed on, resolute and keen in intent, as if in a hurry to accomplish the boy's slaughter, even thirsting for his blood. But God, indeed, was still more swift in his intent, arriving a step ahead even here; he restrained Abraham from this resolution and from his quick movement, and with a loud voice he ordered him to do nothing to the lad, whom he seized from Abraham's grip with an invisible hand. What happened then? A ram, who had not been there before, suddenly is seen, caught up in the wood of a bush; he is offered in place of Isaac, and brings the sacrifice to realization, bearing the image and type of Christ, who now is transfigured, and who in a short time will be slain and sacrificed for the whole world.

16 But this is not yet the whole story. Let us, rather, move on, and elaborate on what is disclosed in the symbols, and somehow revealed by the story of Sarah's sterility. For the whole nature of humanity was sterile, unable to conceive children at any point in time. From this it came to pass that, although no one could be produced from this nature,[27] still it was here that all came into being: namely, with a primordial curse attached to our begetting from the start. At the same time, a way out had to be found from the judgment passed on

[26]Literally: "struck him with the knee." Nikephoros seems to be depicting Abraham as holding Isaac down in this way.

[27]Nikephoros sees all humanity as deprived, since Adam, of the ability to reproduce according to God's original plan, and in that sense as unable to hand on life in any significant way.

Adam, and freedom from a life headed for decay and needing to be
lifted once again from corruption, towards the goal for which Adam
had been created: to live free from corruption. In this way, then, our
nature was unable to be productive, and rushed along always on the
road to corruption, completely unable to stand still, without any
hope for salvation—either for those who had once been born and
were now departed, or for those who would come to be and would
also undergo corruption. But at the end of days—or as we might say,
in the old age of human nature itself—so that the whole inheritance
of those who would be saved might be traced back to Abraham,
Christ was born of his seed: completely God, taking up a complete
and full humanity, so that he might save the whole human race.

17   How did he save us? Offering himself freely to the Father as
a holocaust and a spotless sacrifice on behalf of the whole race of
human beings, who had slipped and badly fallen down, and were
unable to do anything at all for themselves, he came for this reason,
to rise again to what humanity was before. He fulfilled this sacrifice
by being fixed to the wood of the cross with nails, just as formerly
the ram, which would be sacrificed in Isaac's place, appeared to
Abraham bound and fixed. So the whole of Isaac's promised birth,
and the promise again made to him, and his killing and the sacrifice
connected with it, and the substitution for him [of a ram], clearly
point to Christ. These were, indeed, a kind of type and advance proclamation of the truth that has now shone forth and been revealed
to us on Mount Thabor, and that soon would be revealed again yet
more brightly and clearly on the cross, when the sun was darkened
and the stars dimmed, the moon turned in its course and the rocks
were split, the tombs were opened, and many who had long lain in
them raised again—righteous people, who appeared to many.[28] In
fact, the curtain of the temple was torn from top to bottom; and

[28]Nikephoros rightly reads these apocalyptic details in the account of Jesus'
death—mainly from Matt 27.51–53—as having eschatological significance for the
community of faith.

because it was torn, there was no longer anything ineffable or hidden in it, or covered over by the veil; Christ, the great and first high priest had already ascended the cross, and had celebrated openly what before had been secret Mysteries—offering up himself, in fact, as the awe-inspiring sacrifice there, on behalf of the whole world, on the cross. He offered this sacrifice to the Father, and with his own blood cleansed the sin of Adam, who first fell, as well as the sin of those who, as descendants of Adam, each shared in it and were held captive afterwards by their own evil actions. This was the reason for the tearing of the curtain, and along with it, everything ordained in the Law to be in the temple; everything which, by the ancient legislation, stood and had its established place there, was torn apart as well.

18   I ask you now: look with me at this lamb, who is the Lamb of God—the one who was offered up and who has cleansed the sin of all the world, whom Moses wrote about and signified beforehand, as the lamb in Egypt. Slaughter him, anoint the doorposts with his blood, protect yourself safely—and indeed the angel of death will pass you by, frightened away by the power of this anointing. The angel will crush all the first-born of the Egyptians, but nothing that is yours will ever perish, because you are protected by the seal of this blood. And if you have the power, seize this[29] from your masters there and take it with you as recompense for the bitter slavery you once endured under their rule. And, girding yourself around the waist, holding the cross as a staff in your hand to lean upon, walk boldly on your way. If Pharaoh pursues you, let not that ever make you afraid. If you come to be in the midst of the Red Sea, surrounded by his chariots, do not fear; for the cloud that now is on Thabor will hover over you and overshadow you and hide you, and completely save you by delivering you from those in pursuit. In fact, since you have been saved in this way and have for that reason the greatest possible grounds for courage from now on, strike the sea with the cross and walk across it. And when you divide it, splitting the waters, and cross through it

[29]Presumably, the "seal of blood" signed on their Egyptian doorposts.

dry-shod, with the water walled up on both sides of you, turn then and strike it again, shaking the walls of the sea with that second blow, and casting them down! All will happen for you as you wish, because the cross is powerful to do this. And now see Pharaoh, along with his chariots and horses and all his forces, overwhelmed by waves and by a mighty wind in the deep. But march on after seeing this, singing a song of salvation to your Savior; make your way through the desert, free of all fear. Those who pursued you have completely perished!

19 If you are hungry, never speak a single word of murmuring! For you will be fed with bread from heaven, since Christ is for you at the same time lamb and sacrifice, at the same time the bread of life who has come down from heaven on us and for us, so that the ancient events—as we have already often said—have become signs and public proclamations of our present life. And if you are thirsty, the rock will be split for you and will gush forth rivers of water, so that you can drink your fill, and so that rivers will then flow forth from within yourself [30]—something that Christ will give: the water of life that endlessly flows and never fails.

20 From there, hurry on to the promised land, which is the land of Eden; Christ calls us there, to become heirs of that land and never to depart from it again. Surely all the old promises are bestowed on us anew, for this reason. [God] gives us the first covenant, in shadows and symbols, as it were, as is clear from all that we have said, but he gives us the second covenant—the one through which we are all saved—no longer in hidden ways, in signs and wrappings, but now on Mount Thabor, in the radiance of ineffable light: the Father and the Son and the Holy Spirit together, the blessed and almighty Triad, so that we might know this rightly and clearly.[31] And soon we will see one of this Trinity, now witnessed to as Beloved Son, on the cross

[30]See John 7.37–39.

[31]Nikephoros recognizes the revelation of God's reality as Trinity, which he sees fully achieved in the Transfiguration of Jesus, as the culmination of the whole narrative of redemption.

fulfilling all things, and dipping his fingers in God's blood to write in red letters and to establish this new covenant—revealed by all these signs to be safe and firm and everlasting.

21   The details of our salvation thus have their beginning in God's plan, and thus also come to their fulfillment in Christ. This is the meaning now, in addition to all we have said, of [Christ's] ascent of Mount Thabor and his transfiguration there: first that when he comes to his passion, the disciples should have no fear at all, because he is God (and his appearance and the voice are signs attesting to this); and even when he is hung up naked on the cross, and the form and beauty of his flesh are taken away, they should not be shaken or disturbed at heart, or abandon their first understandings of him, and their best hopes; nor when he is raised from the dead, should they distrust those who proclaim the good news, or consider the wonder being spread abroad a silly tale, but they should immediately begin running,[32] as if given wings by what they had seen and heard on Mount Thabor.

22   For example, Peter and John ran all the way to the tomb, and going inside they saw; when they had seen, they turned away with joy and believed.[33] I believe, in fact, that what was said to Peter—"and you, when you have turned again, strengthen your brothers"[34]—refers to this: it points to the miracle on Thabor, which Peter and those who had gone up with him then heard they were to conceal and tell to no one, while Christ had not yet risen. So now he turns towards those who had not seen it then and tells them, and persuades them by what he says, and strengthens them by his persuasion.

---

[32]Nikephoros seems here to be referring to the first accounts of Jesus' empty tomb, and to the immediate judgment of the disciples that these were "foolish tales" (see Luke 24.11).

[33]John 20.3–9.

[34]Luke 22.32.

23   As we have said, God has willed this in being transfigured on Thabor, and ordained it for the disciples in advance, for the reasons we have mentioned; but as he ascends to the mountaintop, he also wills that we should be there, and not remain below. We are not to be prisoners of the earth any more, or be dragged down to it by any of those who come from the earth and have turned towards it once again, nor are we to wallow around on it, nor cling to anything there, though it may cling to us. But we are to be light in weight and fitted out for movement, to ascend with alacrity wherever the Lord commands us in our journey towards the heights; we are to set up tabernacles there, not for Moses and Elijah, but for ourselves, and remain in them, established once and for all in what is good. We are no more to bring any shameful thing with us, from what has been produced by sin, nor should we make our beautiful form useless; but being baptized into it along with Christ, we must ourselves be conformed to him. If, then, Christ calls us to go up Mount Thabor along with them, let us not remain below—let us not stand far off from glory! Let us ascend with the one who has ascended; let us all enter within the bright cloud, and share in the radiance that shines from it. God wants us to shine like the sun! As we flee the darkness that pursues us but can never capture us, let us not turn willingly again on our own towards that darkness.

Virgins, brides of Christ![35] Virgins, companions of angels! Virgins, your angelic life is the scourge of the demons! Your way of living is angelic—immaterial in the midst of matter, unfleshly in the flesh, a public representation in the body of the disembodied life! Fleeing from the world, renouncing it and all that belongs to it, come, with your bright and unquenchable lamps[36]—bring your dowry forward, settle it on Christ! For I see these lamps, nourished by the ample oil supplied in your good resolutions and deeds. And when I see this, I rejoice! Go out to meet him! Behold, the bridegroom is "fairest in

[35]Here, near the end of the homily, Nikephoros directly addresses "virgins" in particular: presumably women monastics were the heart of the audience for whom the meditation was written

[36]Matt 25.1–13.

his beauty among the sons of men."[37] All of you, go within the bridal chamber, and join him as he enters the room.

24   And you, Lover of the human race, give your hand in love for us all and betroth us to yourself; protect us for yourself and for your Father, so that no harm of any kind may ever come to us. And at your second appearance, let us stand at your right, sharers in the eternal blessings of your kingdom, "which you have prepared for us since the foundation of the world"[38]—incorruptible, undefiled, everlasting blessings—for the glory of your Father and our God, for your glory as our savior and our God, for the glory of the All-holy Spirit and the God of all of us, to the ages of all the ages! Amen.

[37] Psalm 44.3 (LXX).
[38] Matt 25.34

PSEUDO-JOHN CHRYSOSTOM (SICILY, 14TH CENTURY)

This homily, which is contained only in an early 14th-century Italo-Greek manuscript now in Messina, Cod. Sancti Salvatoris 29 (dated 1307), is attributed there to Saint John Chrysostom, the most celebrated of Greek preachers. The title given in the manuscript is translated: "By our Holy Father John, Archbishop of Constantinople, the Golden-mouthed: Discourse on the Transfiguration of our Lord Jesus Christ." The manuscript collection to which it belongs comes from the monastery of San Salvatore in the harbor of Messina, built under the sponsorship of King Roger II between 1122 and 1132, on land conquered from the Saracens by Roger I in 1061, and populated by monks from the community of the Theotokos Hodigitria in Rossano in Calabria, led by Luke of Messina. (See John Thomas and Angela Constantinides Hero, eds., *Byzantine Monastic Foundation Documents* 2 [Washington: Dumbarton Oaks, 2000] 637–648; the text of Luke of Messina's *typikon* establishing the monastery, no. 26 in the collection, is translated by Timothy Miller.)

The content of the homily is first and foremost Christological. The preacher interprets the disciples' vision on Mount Thabor as a privileged understanding of who Jesus really is: the Son of God, in the human nature that he has made fully his own and that reveals to us in its splendor what Adam and Eve were intended to be before the fall. As a result of their vision, the disciples were later able to see the crucified Jesus in classical Chalcedonian terms: "they realized that he is true God, and the offspring of the true Father; and also a true human being, a single one who is also double and never confused [in nature]" (sec. 6).

Maurice Sachot, who first edited and published the homily, argues, following François Halkin and others, that its language and even its content rule out Chrysostom's authorship. Sachot suggests ("Édition de l'homélie pseudo-Chrysostomienne BHG 1998 [= CPG 5017] sur la Transfiguration," *Revue des sciences religieuses* 58 [1984] 93–93), on stylistic grounds, that it seems to be an Italo-Greek composition, probably of the same period as the manuscript itself, and would thus probably come from the same cultural and religious milieu, perhaps even from the same monastery, as that of Philagathos of Cerami—but two centuries later.

[PSEUDO-JOHN CHRYSOSTOM]
Discourse for the Transfiguration of Our Lord Jesus Christ[1]

1 Master, a blessing!

A holy banquet stands ready before us. For "Wisdom has prepared for us" even now, as Scripture says, "her table,"[2] full of mystical delight; without growing weary, she exerts herself in preparing the dishes, and makes the Church itself ready, adorning each banqueter with the marks of joy and making the entry-doors splendid with ointments and fragrant flowers. Then "she has sent out her servants, with her high proclamation,"[3] inviting all to be converted from wickedness to the fullness of piety, abandoning the way of hardheartedness to turn to the path of salvation. And she tells us to leave behind "the broad and easy way"—I mean the one "that leads all to destruction,"[4]—to spring away from its snares, and with the soul's yearning to seek out God in truth, [by the] "narrow and tightly compressed way that leads to true life."[5] There the spiritual table of God's wisdom is made ready, set before us. For if we will seek out this way with desire, "with all our soul and with all our heart,"[6] we will

[1]This sermon was edited for the first time, and translated into French, by Maurice Sachot, "Édition de l'homélie pseudo-Chrysostomienne BHG 1998 (= CPG 5017) sur la Transfiguration," *Revue des sciences religieuses* 58 (1984) 91–108. This is the text we have used for this translation.

[2]Prov 9.2.
[3]Prov 9.3.
[4]Matt 7.13.
[5]Matt 7.14.
[6]A familiar phrase in Hebrew piety: see Deut 6.5; 10.12; 30.6; cf. also II Kg 23.25; Matt 22.37.

surely find Wisdom and will feast on her fruits and her gifts. For she is unfailingly generous to those who find her.

2   And if we desire to be nourished by these gifts, let us make our way with Peter and John and James, the Apostles of Christ, so that by grasping hold of Christ in faith and worshipping him, we might be worthy to become spiritual companions of theirs on the way, and come to the divine summit, as if on the top of Mount Thabor. At that time, Christ himself went up there with his disciples and revealed himself, by divine power, in a different form, being transfigured as he himself chose, but not changing the body he had made his own. For in its nature he maintained this body as it was; it was not changed by confusion with his own divine nature, nor did it undergo any alteration; by his divine power he preserved the natures that had come together "without change, without confusion," remaining himself "genuinely God and truly human,"[7] even as he was transfigured. Therefore "his face shone like the sun," as the disciples say, "and his garments become white as light,"[8] as far as the disciples were able to see. And why did he appear to them this way? To show them that the Lord of all things had put on the whole Adam and had wiped him clean of sin, and had whitened what had become scarlet[9] in Adam's descendants. And having cleansed him[10] from all stain, he showed him to his own disciples, being transfigured then on the mountain to be as Adam was when he had just been formed. For this is how Adam was before his disobedience, just as Christ appeared in his transfiguration; and this was the reason Christ appeared in this way.[11]

[7]These two phrases are part of the larger formulation of the Christological definition of the Council of Chalcedon (451), which remained the classical norm for conceiving of the complex reality of Christ.

[8]Matt 17.2.

[9]See Is 1.18.

[10]I.e., Adam, whom the Son has "put on."

[11]This interpretation of Jesus' transfigured human form, as a restoration of the original appearance of Adam and Eve before the fall—and thus a full revival of human nature as it was meant to be—appears to be a new theme in the tradition of preaching on this event.

3   And after this, what appeared to them next? "Behold," Scripture says, "there appeared" to the disciples, drawing near and "conversing" with Christ, Moses the Lawgiver, it seemed, with Elijah the prophet who was "jealous [for the Lord]."[12] And "they were conversing with him." [13] How did the Apostles know them, or recognize that this was Moses, whom they had never seen on earth? Or again, Elijah—how did they know him, who had not lived during the time of the incarnation? They would not have recognized them, if not from the words they spoke to Jesus Christ. For the words that they spoke revealed who they were. From this they recognized that these who spoke with him were Moses and Elijah.[14]

4   And what did they say to Christ when they conversed with him? Moses, on the one hand, gazing on Christ made flesh, both God and a human being, was filled with great, ecstatic joy, and falling on his face before him, cried:

"Blessed are you, inconceivable God, whom I glimpsed in the fire of the burning bush![15]

"Blessed are you, who commanded me to lead Israel out of Egypt![16]

"Blessed are you, who gave me the power to work many wonderful signs in Egypt![17]

"Blessed are you, who commanded that I strike the Red Sea with my staff, and it was split into two parts, so that Israel should cross to safety with dry feet![18]

"Blessed are you, who rained down manna and nourished your people in the desert![19]

[12]Matt 17.3; see I Kg 19.10

[13]Matt 17.3.

[14]Philagathos, in his own homily for the Feast of the Transfiguration (Hom 31), asks this same question, and answers it more at length.

[15]Ex 3.2.

[16]Ex 3.10.

[17]Ex 11.9.

[18]Ex 14.16.

[19]Ex 16.33–36.

"Blessed are you, who gave the Law on stone tablets on Mount Sinai![20]

"Blessed are you, whom I begged yearningly, 'If I have found grace before you, reveal yourself to me, that I may see you'[21] and glorify you even more! But I only saw your back, gazing with partial vision through an opening in the rock.[22] For I was enlightened with the back part of knowledge. But now I praise you, because I do not see in part, but I see the same one as complete God and complete human being. And because you have been pleased to become a beggar in this way, I exalt your great mercy exceedingly!"

5   Elijah then used similar words. Crying out in praise to the Lord, he said:

"Blessed are you, God of Israel, who existed as creator before the ages!

"Glory to you, O God, powerful in your acts of will beyond the greatest achievements of all the children of the human race![23]

"Glory to you, Savior whom I love, whom I have so jealously sought to serve![24] For inflamed by jealous zeal for you, Lord, in days of old, when the people of Israel abandoned your commandments and apostatized from you, their creator, I revealed in your name that rain would not fall on the land, nor moisture come, without a word from my mouth. And you, O God, confirmed my words, and brought it about that the heavens were sealed for three years and six months.[25]

"I will glorify you, after all, because you have always given me glory. When I begged from you fire from heaven, I brought it down in three thunderbolts;[26] I divided the Jordan with my

[20]Ex 31.18; 38.15
[21]Ex 33.13.
[22]Ex 33.22–23.
[23]See Ps 66.5 (LXX).
[24]I Kg 19.10.
[25]James 5.17; see I Kg 17.1; 18.1.
[26]I Kg 18.38; 19.12; II Kg 1.10.

sheepskin cloak, and crossed it with unmoistened feet, as if it were dry land.[27]

"And I shall exalt your great power, for you have seen fit to take me up in a chariot of fire,[28] my Lord and King, and so have ordained that I should be preserved in the body which you formed, until I see your coming on earth;[29]and I will resume my jealous zeal for you against your enemy and opponent, when the shameless Satan comes, until the time when you cast him forcefully to the earth and hand him over to eternal fire.[30] For yours is glory and power, for the ages of ages, amen! Therefore I glorify your coming down to be with us."[31]

These were the words that the disciples heard. From them, they recognized Moses, and knew that he was there, from the signs he gave. And [they recognized] Elijah simply from his behavior.

6   Persuaded by this that he would also be in their company, Peter, the leader of the Apostles, spoke in response to the Lord: "It is good for us to be here. If you will, my Savior, let us make three tabernacles here: one for you and one for Moses and one for Elijah, so that we shall always be together."[32] "And while he was still speaking, behold, a cloud of light overshadowed those surrounding the disciples, and behold, a voice came from the cloud itself, saying to them, 'This is my Son, the Beloved, with me from before the ages; in him I am well pleased, as one who shares my throne; listen therefore to him.' And when the Apostles heard these things, they were afraid and fell upon the ground. But the Lord came and raised them, and said to

[27]II Kg 2.8.

[28]II Kg 2.11.

[29]Mal 4.5–6 (= Mal 3.22–23 LXX); Matt 17.10–12. Later Jewish piety expected that Elijah, who was taken directly up to the presence of God at the end of his life, was preserved in life so that he could return to proclaim the coming of the Messiah at the end of time.

[30]See Luke 10.18; Rom 16.20.

[31]The word here translated as "coming down," *synkatabasis*, usually is used in a figurative sense, to mean "condescension" or "adaptation"—"coming down" to the level of one's hearers. The homilist seems, however, to be using it here in a more literal way, to signify the Incarnation.

[32]See Matt 17.4.

them, 'Get up, do not be afraid.' And raising their eyes, they saw no one, except Jesus alone."[33] Then they realized that he is true God, and the offspring of the true Father; and also a true human being, a single one who is also double and never confused [in nature].[34] "And as they were coming down from the mountain, Jesus gave them a precise command: 'Tell no one what you have seen, until the Son of Man has risen from the dead,'"[35] after despoiling death; and you will share with all those who have died incorruptible life and the heavenly Kingdom! And may it happen that all of us attain to this also, in our Lord Jesus Christ: to whom be glory, honor, praise and worship, with the Father and also with the Holy Spirit, unto the ages of ages! Amen.

[33]Matt 17.5–8. It is characteristic of the homilist to embroider slightly the Gospel texts he is quoting.

[34]Once again, the homilist refers to the classical Chalcedonian understanding of the person of Christ.

[35]Matt 17.9.

GREGORY THE SINAITE

Saint Gregory the Sinaite (c. 1265–after 1337) was, with his namesake and fellow Athonite, St Gregory Palamas, one of the most influential spiritual writers of the medieval Greek world. He was born in the village of Koukoulos on the western shore of Asia Minor, near the ancient Greek city of Klazomenai, sometime between 1255 and 1265. After being briefly captured by Turks as a young man, Gregory escaped and entered a monastery in Cyprus. He later moved to the monastic settlement on Mt Sinai, where he made his monastic profession and from which he derived his lifelong sobriquet, "the Sinaite". After disputes, apparently, with other monks there, Gregory moved again briefly, via Jerusalem, to Crete. There he was trained in the contemplative method of hesychastic prayer—the "Jesus prayer" or "prayer of the heart"—by a monastic teacher named Arsenios. Eventually, probably around 1300, Gregory found his way to the great monastic colony on Mount Athos, where he settled in the small, semi-eremitical skete of Magoula. Gregory seems to have exercised influence there as a guide in the ways of contemplative prayer, but after a few decades was forced by Turkish raids on the Holy Mountain to flee again, this time to the mountainous border region in Thrace known as the Paroria, north of Adrianople (Edirne), between the Byzantine Empire and the Bulgarian kingdom. There, about 1330, Gregory founded a new monastic community, dedicated to the Theotokos, on Mount Katakekryomenē, with the support of the Bulgarian Tsar Ivan Alexander, near the present village of Zabernovo, in the environs of Malko Tarnovo. Welcoming both Greek- and Slavic-speaking monks to the community, Gregory became the first teacher we know of, in the Slavic world, of this highly influential approach to contemplation. His pupils in the Paroria included the future Patriarch of Constantinople Kallistos (1350–1363), who wrote Gregory's biography after his death, which occurred at some time after 1337. Although Gregory the Sinaite was an older contemporary of Palamas, the theoretician and defender of hesychastic prayer, it is uncertain whether the two were ever in direct contact with each other.

Gregory was previously known only through Kallistos' biography, and through various collections of short instructions on the ascetical and spiritual life, which have come down to us in the *Philokalia* or anthology of spiritual texts compiled in the 18th century by St Nikodemos of the Holy Mountain. This pre-Palamite homily on the Transfiguration—which, even before the Palamite controversy, clearly witnesses to Gregory the Sinaite's conviction that the Christian disciple is also called, like the three disciples, to see and even to share in the transcendent light of God, which radiated through Christ's humanity on Mount Thabor—was discovered only in 1938, by the British scholar David Balfour, in a 15th century manuscript in the Great Lavra on Mount Athos (Lavra 1201, I 117).

Gregory's language is often unconventional, by classical standards, and uses idioms and grammatical practices not found in most earlier Christian writers; but he is expressive, enthusiastic, and deeply rooted in a sense of the nearness of God in Christ. More than simply a festal homily, this work celebrates in ecstatic, sometimes obscure and allusive, language the divine glory of the holy Trinity radiating on the human race through the humanity of Jesus, and suggests that those who devote themselves to following him and contemplating him are called to share in that brilliant light, occasionally even in the course of this present life. For a thorough discussion of Gregory's life and works, see Antonio Rigo, "Gregorio il Sinaita," in C.G. Conticello and V. Conticello, *La Théologie Byzantine et sa tradition* (Turnhout: Brepols, 2002) 35–130; on this homily, see 87–88.

Discourse of our Holy Father Gregory the Sinaite on the Holy Transfiguration of Our Lord Jesus Christ[1]

1   As many of you as "reflect with unveiled face" the vision of magnificent glory, transfiguring the image of your own nature, in contemplation, "from glory to glory,"[2] just as you are carried from Christ to the spirit of the Godhead, indeed from the divine economy in the world to an understanding of God himself—and as you are mentally transformed, we might say, from flesh to spirit, lifting your perception from the lowliness of sensible things and from the images and appearance of scattered realities—come, let us ascend the spiritual mountain of contemplation, and let us gaze at the view from there, attentively and free from material considerations. Let us gaze and listen! Let us not gaze on Jesus on Mount Thabor on the basis of the great works of creation, which point proportionately to him; but let us gaze immediately on him, from close by, with the eye of the mind, as he radiates light. Let us draw near the light, and, as far as possible, we shall see for ourselves the brilliance of the feast;[3] to speak as the Apostles do, let us gaze on his glory, "glory as of the only-begotten from the Father, full of grace and truth,"[4] filled with the completeness of the eternal light and of the divine brilliance.

[1]The British scholar David Balfour, who discovered this homily in a manuscript of the Great Lavra on Mount Athos in 1938, eventually published it, with his own English translation, in 1981: "Saint Gregory the Sinaite: Discourse on the Transfiguration. First Critical Edition, with English Translation and Commentary," *Theologia* 52 (1981) 631–679. This translation is based on Balfour's edition of that lone Greek manuscript.

[2]II Cor 3.18.

[3]Here and at the end of paragraph 2, Gregory makes it clear that this discourse is a homily for the liturgical feast of the Transfiguration of the Lord, on August 6.

[4]John 1.14.

2   Whoever, then, has grasped the significance of this divine mountain of exaltation, as the great Isaiah commands us, come, let us ascend
to the height of the Lord, and we will see the glory of the radiant
effusion of light from Jesus there, and [we will see] the three chosen
disciples—or rather, let us call together all the lovers of divine vision,
who rejoice ecstatically in such a sight, and although they could not
bear the rays of light coming forth from his face, were completely possessed by it.[5] Let us invite them to be our fellow celebrants, joining us
to realize the purpose of this festival, and let us see how much of that
purpose this Mystery reveals to us, and what its effects are.

3   The mind knows a fourfold sense of this present festival, and
one single sense as its distinguishing mark; that one sense appears
in the lofty ideas that point out its meaning to us, as the feast is
understood and celebrated on four different levels.[6] One is the level
of the law, a shadowy way, although frightening beyond our ability
to bear it, hinting from afar, in a mystical way, at the truth.[7] Another
is that of truth revealed in types, which witnesses to our spiritual
and internal transformation as in a kind of down-payment. A third
is the image and glorious representation of the first, primeval and
archetypal [light], a natural character and beauty, the form and likeness of the image of Christ, who was formed like us and because of
us, and who forms our nature with his divinity. The fourth is divine
and spiritual radiance, which is eternal; God will reveal it, and will
appear and shine upon us, standing in the midst of the circle of his
holy ones, of gods standing around him and of many kings, as he

[5]Gregory seems to be referring to all those who have had some experience of
mystical contemplation, even though they may not have actually had a vision of the
divine light such as the Apostles witnessed on Mount Thabor.

[6]As Gregory develops his thought here, the "four levels" of the Transfiguration
story seem to be: a) that of the natural phenomena, which appear frightening and
recall the phenomena accompanying the revelation to Moses at Sinai; b) that of the
typological significance of these phenomena; c) that of what the story reveals to us
about Jesus and his work; d) that of what it reveals to us about the Mystery of God.

[7]As Gregory will make clear, he means the connection between Mt Sinai, where
the Law was given to Moses, and the mountain of Transfiguration.

judges and distributes the ranks and progressive states of blessed-ness in that place.

4 The godly person, seeing all these things, will surely understand the fourfold brilliance of both,[8] and will be initiated in a passive way into those things being mystically accomplished among the holy ones. For type represented type, each more perfectly than before: the darkness, light; and Horeb, Thabor; and this mountain of virtues, the spiritual, threefold, divine height of glory; and the fearsome storm there, the brilliance of the God-man. There[9] God was seen in the midst of fire, speaking and sending forth lightning, and as a trumpet sounded clearly, crashes of thunder and the crackling of flame [were heard], and the whole mountain smoked, creating fearful threats and dreadful anxiety for the people, showing even in this their unworthiness and their imperfect dignity and rank; revealing to them that God's blessed being could not be contained or approached. These fearful flashes of light, in fact, and the sight of God's "back parts,"[10] and the inaccessible darkness, and the sight of fire, and different positions,[11] were there made available to humans. Here, too, the same one shines forth for us on Thabor, ineffably and lovingly revealing himself in a way that benefits us: in light that communicates God's influence, in thrice-brilliant splendor appear-ing to Moses and Elijah who are there, conversing with him; and surrounding those disciples of his with the rays of his goodness and the flashes of his divinity, he completely overpowers them. For they[12]

[8]Presumably, of both the present liturgical festival and of its significance for mystical prayer and union with God.

[9]At Sinai.

[10]Ex 33.22–23. This picturesque verse, in which God promises Moses only that he will be able to see him from behind as God passes by, was explained in a number of different ways by Greek writers, discussing the possibility for mortals to gain a direct vision of God.

[11]A curious detail. Balfour suggests (p. 647) that Gregory probably is referring to the different places where God allowed Moses, Aaron, and the people to stand during the theophany, in the narrative in Exodus.

[12]I.e., the three Apostles.

could not yet bear the unendurable weight of his divinity, because their purification was still incomplete, and the chief laws of those chosen ones appeared still more powerful and exalted.[13]

And it is no wonder! For those chosen heralds[14] of our adoptive sonship stand out above all others, even if they were shown to be weak in their imperfection; but even if they were pre-eminent [in Israel], and were more godlike than all the more perfect observers of the Law, they were not Apostles, since the spirit of servitude remained in them. And even though they would later be made adoptive children in Christ, it would be a great thing for them if, after death, they should lay hold, in hope, of that which the sons of God in Christ receive through their rebirth, enriched from infancy in that overflowing inheritance of becoming God's children.

5   Of old, Moses and Elijah, chosen to climb Mount Horeb, both were driven to climb it at the proper time—the one, commanded beforehand to enter into the darkness and mist, to receive the Law on tablets, to become a lawgiver and the first of priests, and to be the most mystical witness of symbolic realities, in order to reveal them to others; the other called by a prophetic oracle to go quickly to Horeb, then ordered to go out of the cave,[15] commanded to wrap himself in his sheepskin, and to see the great and mighty wind that crushes those who are led to pursue the way of peace[16]—the earthquake that shakes the heart, the fire that purifies their pow-

[13]I.e., Moses and Elijah, who represented "the Law and the Prophets" to the three Apostles. This seems to Gregory to be the reason why the three Apostles fall on their faces before Moses and Elijah.

[14]Moses and Elijah.

[15]I Kg 19.9–13 (LXX: I Kingdoms 19.9–13). The Greek text of the homily here says he was "commanded to go out of the Magar"; this seems to refer to the Hebrew word for "cave," *ma'ar*, which Gregory seems to understand as a proper noun—although the Septuagint has the normal Greek word for cave, *spēlaion*. David Balfour, in a note to his edition of the text (649, n. 14), suggests Gregory may have heard Elijah's cave referred to as "the Magar" while he was a monk on Sinai, and assumed it was the proper name of the place, rather than simply a word for "cave."

[16]Literally, "who are introduced into what concerns *hesychia* (peace)," apparently a reference to those learning to practice hesychastic prayer, the "prayer of the heart."

ers—and finally allowed to contemplate the "gentle breeze" of light, where God, in a way beyond our nature, becomes knowable to us by participation. God, through the consistent fulfillment of prophecy, guides us mystically along from afar and trains us towards knowledge of him. Now[17] this same pair also became contemplators and witnesses of the brilliance of the Godhead—witnesses also, clearly, of the first and second theophanies,[18] and chosen before all others in accordance with the Law. Standing beside Christ, they are present [here] in a supernatural and immediate way—Christ miraculously summoned the one from among the dead,[19] the other from heaven in a moment,[20] and stood them beside him. The wonder is that he raised the Lawgiver again somehow, though he had already disintegrated. I think myself, as others also do, that the gentle Moses had received, by grace, a symbolic form, and that this is what appeared; it was a body only by way of appearance. But if he was there with his body, "all things are possible to God,"[21] who also thought Elijah worthy to travel through the air, in a way beyond human powers.

6   Of old, Aaron and Hur and Joshua were urged to take their stand on low ground with the others, since they could not yet bear the unendurable effect of the fire and the darkness; but now, he [=Jesus] revealed through the disciples the imperfect state of such things,[22] and that no one still imperfect should be able to see anything of the divine brightness before he or she is purified in hearing and understanding, and makes his or her flesh lean and incorrupt by the cleansing fire of the Spirit. And notice this: the darkness there[23] is a symbol of light; the cloud a sign of this present cloud of the Spirit;

[17]I.e., on Thabor.

[18]I.e., the theophanies narrated in the Old Testament, in Ex 34 and I Kg 19.

[19]Moses, who was understood to have died and been buried in the normal way.

[20]Elijah, who is said in I Kg 2.1–12 to have been taken alive to heaven in a fiery chariot.

[21]See Luke 1.37.

[22]I.e., of such earthly realities.

[23]I.e., at Sinai.

the fire a sign of cleansing; the trumpet a sign of the divine Logos, in its great sound; the thunderclaps a sign of the proclamation [of the Gospel]. Formerly there were flashes of lightning, but now we have the divine illumination that outstrips the sun. The Law was the type of the [new] Law of the Gospel; the mountain of this mountain, in the difficulty of seeing it; the shining light of the ever-clear shining of both revelations of God.[24] And whatever revelatory symbols were given to the Lawgiver on the mountain of darkness, the Lord revealed also now to be a kind of foreshadowing of his own transfiguration, signifying that what had been accomplished there was a figure for our instruction. For he himself is the giver of the Law, he speaks in the Law and is glimpsed there in a symbolic way; he is truly seen, yet naturally invisible; gazed on in the light, essentially shared in through charity towards one's neighbor, and grasped through purity of heart; the fountain of goodness, the abyss of light; both light and the cause of light—one thorough goodness, the other through brilliance. He is light, and is called light, beyond the reach of causality and language.

7   Since he reminded his own disciples—by asking, "Who do people say that I am?" and they answered "Some say Elijah, others Moses, others one of the prophets"—for this reason, he showed this fullness of light on the mountain, and revealed a faint ray of the divinity to them when he appeared: as much as they could bear. The purpose was to show the brilliance of the glory that was to come, and the clear beauty of his own incarnation, since God had truly become human in a way beyond human understanding. Shining forth as God, he is revealed in an outpouring of light, but as a human being he is seen and recognized through his flesh as one with the prophets. As other than human, he is the Word, who is both human and divine; but as the same one, both God and human, he enlightens their mind with the radiance of the divinity, by a most pure light that overpowers the senses of those chosen ones. He overshadows them with the cloud

[24] At Sinai and now on Thabor.

of the Spirit, and with the Father's voice, like a clap of thunder, he strengthens them by his witness. And suddenly he presents the most distinguished, the greatest of the prophets as his witnesses, showing in this, too, that he is not one of those they thought him to be, but that he is himself the God of Law and prophets, appearing miraculously to us in his goodness, wishing to save the human race.

8   And Moses, in those former times, gazed through the darkness on the one threefold God who is—that is on the Father, who gives the Law through the Son in the Spirit, even if he appears to many, including the Jews themselves, to be the Father alone; but here, glimpsing the One who is, one of the Trinity, made flesh on Thabor, transformed by the inaccessible light, and the glory that streams forth through him, [Moses] is filled with joy. And he converses on some mystical themes with Christ himself, in a spirit of amazement and reverence; and speaking in advance of "his exodus, which he was to accomplish in Jerusalem"[25] by suffering, he was overcome by unspeakable joy, gazing on Truth itself as it had come to him and flooded him with light.

9   And Elijah, too, the fire-bearer, who recognized, in fire and a breeze, the God whom he had seen before, today gazes on him on Mount Thabor as he radiates light more brilliant than the sun; amazed by the strangeness of the vision, and of this timeless encounter, he was eager to arouse his zeal against the unbelievers, as we are accustomed to say [of him],[26] but he was restrained by the joy that overcame his anger.

10   In a revealing form, by many kinds of contemplative engagement, the divine writers tell us, it was brought about by God that Moses and Elijah were both seen together with Jesus: of old in darkness, then in light, then here standing next to him. For [the prophets]

[25]Luke 9.31.
[26]I Kg 19.14.

make a distinction between providence itself and judgment, either by distinguishing in their words the patience of God's gentleness from his anger; or else by showing forth the two natures of the Word, or indeed the Trinity itself, as it hypostatically reveals, along with Jesus, that it is triple and single. Even the very outward, perceptible shape of this festival, I may say, is a mystery that reveals the double Triad, revealing the Godhead as twofold and threefold,[27] present above and below and believed to be present everywhere: the divine monarchy that is Trinity, in a way that is more than infinite.

11 How is that? The number of the three disciples is also a type that made it clear the Trinity itself was present here, and would be witnessed to by their preaching in the world, or else it conveyed the triad of virtues—faith, hope and love; or they were themselves also a symbol of the three powers of the soul, so that what is written in the Law would principally be fulfilled, when it says "every word will stand firm with two or three witnesses."[28] For truly, in the midst of their company the Word, creator of every word and form of speech, stands present, and every prophetic saying and law is fulfilled in his coming, by God's plan and in his presence; all Scripture and every word about him is fulfilled, and comes to its end in him, the maker and fulfiller of the Law, as the beginning and the end of the Law and the Prophets.

12 But why did he not take *all* the disciples into that ineffable vision on the mountain, but only certain ones?[29] Because difference was also present among them, in degrees of opinion and faith

[27]Gregory seems to be hinting at the twofold mode in which God's threefold being is understood: as revealed to the human mind, in "kataphatic" or affirmative terms, in the course of history, and as mystically grasped, to some degree, in itself. Or he may simply be anticipating what he says more clearly below (c. 15): that the three disciples represent in their number a type of the Trinity, while the two Old Testament figures represent the two unmixed natures of Christ.

[28]Deut 19.15; cf. Matt 18.16; John 8.17.

[29]Here Gregory begins to interpret the details of the Transfiguration narrative more directly.

and effort and love, even though the grace of the Spirit was one; therefore they received different charisms, even if the Gospel they preached was one. Therefore he took select members of the Twelve and went up Mount Thabor. And indeed, notice what happened: as they looked at him, suddenly "his face shone more brightly than the sun, and his garments became radiantly white as light,"[30] and they became amazed in mind and were fascinated by the divine light. And they fell on the ground—one on his back, the other prone on his face[31]—weighed down by the splendor of the light that gushed forth from him, surrounded and, as it were, frozen by it. And Peter came awake, and seeing his glory, he was struck dumb by the unexpected sight; he said to Jesus, from sheer amazement—seeing the two men, Moses and Elijah, standing alongside him—"Lord, it is good for us to be here."[32] Then he said, "Let us make three tents, one for each,"[33] not knowing what he was saying, because of his mental ecstasy and his drunken state.

13   For when the mind is swallowed up by that ineffable light and comes to exist outside of the real world, it is removed from perceiving relationships, and [God] dulls the senses by the light of his power. Or else just the opposite happens: he separates the mind from the senses, and the senses from their relationships by his light, and makes it be preoccupied by divine love, thrusting away all the attraction that the mind has towards sensible things, through the very operation of the senses.[34]

[30]Cf. Matt 17.2.

[31]This detail does not depend on the Gospels, but is reflected in many standard icons of the Transfiguration scene.

[32]Matt 17.4.

[33]Luke 9.33.

[34]Gregory is speaking here of the experience of ecstatic contemplation, which involves a disruption of ordinary sense experience—either by the senses becoming overwhelmed by God's intervention, or by their heightened operation so that they themselves lead the mind to perceive God and delight in him.

14   See the divine purpose even in these things, so that the very things experienced there receive a symbolic inner meaning that affirms the meaning of this festival, but also so that this interpretation hints in a mystical way at a change in our character.

15   The three,[35] after all, were a symbol of the Trinity and of the truth of the Godhead, for which God offered them as witnesses; but the two[36] were a type of the economy of the one Christ, who is double in nature. God provided both sets of witnesses, in a symbolic way, for the triple and double dogmas of faith.[37] So he bound them together into one, in a wonderful way, and revealed and formed these teachings. Surely in the future, too, Christ will be one reality as coming from the Trinity, even if he differs, as man, in the otherness of his nature. He himself will be the mediator of the Trinity towards us, in all things and in every respect, when he stands as "God in the midst of the gods,"[38] and makes each one recline in glory according to his rank, and coming among them in a godlike way, distributes the charisms.

16   And who is equal to the task of expressing all the hidden symbolic truths that the divine communication of light mystically revealed there, by means of ineffable revelation and knowledge, things formerly revealed in darkness and later shown forth in the light of the Transfiguration? For the symbolic representations of the truth, and the forms and types and reflections of those eternal truths, the parts of eternal wholes, have not afterwards become perfectly clear from these sources in every respect, at their own proper times, to the minds of those who love to contemplate beautiful things. For some of what has happened in the past is gone, and belongs to what

[35]I.e., the three disciples.

[36]Moses and Elijah.

[37]Gregory is suggesting that the two Old Testament figures and three disciples, all present at Christ's self-revelation, are themselves symbolic revelations of who Christ really is, and of what he has shown us about God's being.

[38]Cf. Ps 81.1 (LXX).

lies behind us; other things, present and future, are prologues, also, of a certain condition and state of each individual thing, read from the present before they actually come to pass.

17 The darkness, as we have said, was, on the one hand, a type of the Transfiguration. Both of them now belong to the past, but the Transfiguration is the truth of the appearance of God that occurs in both of them, and is, on the other hand, a pledge of the eternal blessedness of heaven; it will be part of the ineffable outpouring of light, when we shall be made eternal, transfigured in a single light of glory, and be covered, on the spiritual Mount Zalmon,[39] by the grace-filled snow of the light from above that gives us a peace beyond understanding,[40] according to Scripture, and we shall then circle, dancing and singing, around this outpouring of light.

18 "And they were afraid," the Evangelist says, "on entering into the cloud. And a voice came from the cloud, saying, 'This is my Son, the Beloved, in whom I am well pleased.'"[41] For then the Lord Jesus, who is uncircumscribed, truly thundered from the mountain as if from heaven, in a storm of light and in the sound of the glory of his coming; and the Father on high sounded forth his voice—a voice of power from the cloud that radiated light, as Scripture tells us, and said to the disciples:

"This is my Son, the Beloved, the only One, transfigured today on Mount Thabor in his humanity; this is the stamp of my individual being, the radiance of my glory,[42] the unchanging image of my super-substantial being. This is my strong right arm, my all-powerful right hand.[43] This is my personified wisdom and power,[44]

[39]Ps 67.15 (LXX).
[40]Phil 4.7.
[41]Luke 9.34.
[42]Heb 1.3.
[43]Is 53.1.
[44]I Cor 1.24.

through whom I created the ages[45] and brought all things into being from nothing, in whom I am well pleased and through whom I have saved you, through whom I appeared and in whom I shed light on the world and create it anew, in whom I have come to be known and through whom I was glorified, in whom I continue to receive glory and through whom I glorify you and will glorify you again.[46] He is the one who reveals my name among men and women, and I revealed him and bore witness to him and showed him forth at the Jordan; he gave me glory, and I gave him glory today, and will glorify him in the inaccessible light.[47] He lives in me without confusion, and I in him without change,[48] flashing forth in a way that befits a triune God; he is in me singly and I in him in a threefold sense—the first because of the assumption of humanity, the second because of the existence of the divinity. He is the begotten light, I the unbegotten; he the only Son, I the unbegotten Father, source of all things; he is the Word in the beginning, and is God in the beginning, before all ages, I the beginning of the beginning and Father of the Word, the Mind that is above all mind and all substance. He is the light, I am the spring of light; he is the life, I am the cause of life; he is the 'sun of justice'[49] who shines forth in me, I am known in him as the light of three suns, beyond all substance, and in him I shine with 'all the fullness of the Godhead, in a bodily way.'[50] In him I am well pleased, and in him I have willingly chosen you; I remain in him without change, without confusion, without separation, without alteration.[51] I shine out in him, I reveal and foreknow and cleanse and enlighten you, I make you holy in him. In the light of his glory you will see

[45]Heb 1.2.

[46]John 12.28.

[47]I Tim 5.16.

[48]Gregory here is echoing the famous language of the dogmatic formula of the Council of Chalcedon (451), which asserts that Jesus Christ is one hypostasis or concrete individual, existing in two natures, "without confusion, without change, without division, without separation."

[49]Mal 3.20 (LXX).

[50]Col 2.9.

[51]See above, n. 29.

me, the inaccessible light; in him you will recognize me and in me you will see him; the one will happen so that you may be formed, the other so that you may be perfected; or because he dwells in you in this world, and you will be divinized in the next.

"You will see the Son in the Spirit, you will recognize the Father in the Son; in the light of the Spirit you will see 'the shining forth of my glory,'[52] in the image the archetype, and from within yourselves [you will see] what is beyond all substance. And you will see clearly, and know that he remains in me and I in him,[53] and that we are known without confusion, as he himself said to you; he gives light in me, and I perform miracles in him. He makes you new in me, and I bring miraculous works to perfection through him and the Spirit. He speaks in me and acts in me, and does nothing except in me and in the Spirit; and when I speak through him and in him and with him, and remain there, I do these works in the Spirit. He speaks in me in the Spirit, and I speak through him and do all things in the Spirit. Now he flashes forth in me, seen as a single person; but then I will shine forth in him, recognized in threefold form. He is in you, you in him, and I am recognized in a threefold way in him.[54] He is completely in me, without change; he comes from me without flowing away, and is with me beyond time. He does not exist after me, and no other God or Son has come to be besides me or before me. He is always completely in me and in himself, without separation; and I am always complete in him and in myself, without being affected or undergoing separation. And my Spirit is completely from me and in him and in me and in himself, in an unspeakable way. Through him I am known, and I share being with him, and I remain in him and in the Spirit, and I shall make my abode in all of you. No one comes to me, except through him and the Spirit; and no one comes to him, except through me and through the Spirit, as he has made clear among you. And no one can see or know me, unless—as I have

[52]Heb 1.3.

[53]See John 14.11; 17.21.

[54]Although the Father is meant to be the speaker here, he really speaks more as the God of Mystery who is the entire Trinity.

said—he reveals me in the Spirit according to his own decision, to whom he wishes;[55] just as a word reveals the mind hidden within it, and the mind the word that comes forth from it in the spirit."

So [the Father] spoke from above, exhorting them: "Listen to him,"[56] trust in him, follow him, proclaim him, remain in him—and he will remain in you. Receive him, and through him receive me, and he will give you light and will make you holy, and will bestow all things on you as gifts.

19 For as we know speech through the voice and the mind through speech, as something expressed and put into words—for speech naturally has the mind itself as its begetter, and mind naturally has speech itself revealing it—so we have been enlightened to recognize the Son in the Spirit and the Father in the Son. Or to say the same thing in more proper, safer terms: by grace we recognize the Father personally in the Son in terms of nature and substance, and also the Son in the Father in terms of cause, and the Spirit in terms of procession. For the Spirit is given in the Son and through the Son, just as sound comes forth in speech and through speech and with speech, and reveals the word that comes forth from the mind; for sound always accompanies speech, and makes its activity evident, and is called the living activity of speech itself, and belongs to it; it is called the living activity of speech, and brings it to expression, but it is not derived from it, and does not exist as an individual as far as nature is concerned, or for itself. For speech is always recognized as something connected with mind, and is sent out and comes forth in this way; and mind is related to speech, always having speech as part of its substance. And it brings forth language as a mental reality, and knows that it is always producing it, manifesting it in its breath.[57] So that every verbal sound naturally and substantially has mind and language as part of what it expresses. Now we call "mind" not what

[55]Matt 11.27.
[56]Matt 17.5.
[57]The Greek word for "breath," *pneuma*, is the same as the word for "spirit."

is poured out along with speech, but that which exists naturally, as an individual being, in relation to speech; but when we mention "speech," we do not mean what is uttered and dissolved into the air, but the rational faculty which exists, as an individual being, in relation to the mind, and which reasons in a natural way. And when we speak of "spirit," we do not mean the drawing-in and exhaling of air, but the essential, living power itself, which exists in itself and comes forth in speech and makes a sound in the air.

20 It is proven, then, that the human person is created one and indivisible in nature, in substance, and as a concrete being, with regard to mind and reason and spirit; he is the image and glory of the Trinity, and exists in these things, according to the one who has spoken to us. For the Son was never deficient towards Father and Spirit, nor was the Father towards Son and Spirit, or the Spirit towards Father and Son; nor did any one of them ever exist outside of the Word or apart from what is said, even though what is united is distinguished and what is distinguished united, in a paradoxical way, in the manner of their existence and of their substance. But the Trinity is also distinguished in Christ without any addition, in one way by the manner of existence, in the other by the structure of substance, so that the Trinity might not become a quaternity because of the Incarnation of the Son. For the one grace of the Father is brought to fulfillment through the Son in the Holy Spirit, and one divinity and one God is worshiped in the Father and the Son and the Holy Spirit.

21 Those who are eager for knowledge must know clearly that genuine reverence is formed from the use of natural models, especially when they come from our own experience: for they are reliable and are a true tool for demonstration. For the activity of the reason that naturally operates in us is twelvefold, and it comes forth in all of them, and is known and contemplated, in a threefold way. First of all, it is begotten from the mind and the Spirit; then it is freely chosen, when brought to mind, and is distributed along with mind and spirit; next, it comes forth, is understood, written down, sent forth, given, spoken, heard, seen, known, revealed to those who choose it and even to those who do not want to know.[58] It is the same to all, and is identical everywhere, so that as far as nature is concerned reason always has this triadic pattern and never departs from it, everywhere being identified with mind, and alive and active, the same in the midst of change. And the Word of God, begotten from the Father before the ages without passion, is always begotten by the Spirit in those who wish to receive him, according to the great Maximus.[59] For he always comes forth, by divine providence and in a mystical way, for our salvation. After all, he himself bore witness about his eternal generation, by which he is always begotten from the Father in an unspoken way, when he said to the Jews, "You do not know where I come from and where I am going."[60] For he always remains complete in the bosom of the Father, and is complete in us and everywhere, and he comes forth ineffably and comes to us, by which he reveals his activity; yet surely this is to be understood in an ineffable way, as befits the reality of God.

23   The Word, then, who is in the beginning, is begotten from God the Father; then, with the Father and the Son, he arranges by his eternal will the divine economy, which is before time; then he came forth in the end, at the proper time, for our salvation, and he who is completely simple in himself is made composite, shaped in the Holy Spirit. It is written that "the Word," being coarsened, "was made flesh";[61] he was sent from the Father, baptized and witnessed to from above, and became a teacher; the Word is given, in grace, to those

---

[58]Gregory here briefly lists twelve steps by which the understanding generates and communicates to other minds what it knows. It is not clear just what the origin of this analysis might be.

[59]Ps-Maximus the Confessor, *Capita theologica* 3.8. This collection is now thought to have been compiled from the authentic works of Maximus about 1100.

[60]John 8.14.

[61]John 1.14.

who believe; was proclaimed and spoken forth in the world, was heard by those who received him in faith, was seen by the worthy, was known to the pure in mind. And he is known to those who are united to him, who have been chosen "before the foundation of the world,"[62] as has been said. And he has been revealed to those whom he himself knows, and will be revealed at the end of days "in all tribes and tongues."[63] Or to say the same thing in the opposite way, more clearly and emphatically: here is what happens by divine providence in a mystical way for the salvation of each one of us.

23 God the Word, begotten without material outflow from the womb of the Father's substance "before the morning star,"[64] for the salvation of each and every one of us, intercedes with the Father in the Spirit for our sakes and arranges things according to his will. Later, the active Word comes forth in order to renew and transform us, and his seed is given to us and remains with us.[65] As a result, he is connected with our own limbs, and we become his instrument, in a hidden way, to carry out his commandments; for he is the one who "[works] in us both to will and to act for his good pleasure."[66] Then, taking on a body, he becomes the written Word,[67] and the Word then becomes dense and (to speak truly and in an evangelical way) miraculously becomes flesh and dwells among us in the Spirit, making his own what belongs to us. He is always sent in a mystical way into us through the Father's activity, and represents [the Father] because of his goodness; he is given to everyone who believes and carries out the commandments, as the "ingrafted Word that can save

[62]Eph 1.4.

[63]Rev 5.9.

[64]Ps 109.3 (LXX).

[65]Gregory seems to be alluding here to the notion of a "spermatic Logos," a transcendent Logos or Word that is planted within creation as a seed of regular behavior and rationality: an idea found in Stoic philosophy and, in modified form, in some of the second-century Christian Fathers and in later Christian tradition.

[66]Phil 2.13.

[67]See Origen, *Homilies on Leviticus* 1.1; 4.8, who speaks of the Scripture as a kind of written form of incarnation of the Word.

our souls."[68] In the Spirit, the Word is spoken by us in the form of intercessory prayer,[69] since "no one can say 'Jesus is Lord' unless" he is invoked "in the Spirit."[70] He is heard by our spiritual ears, springing up in the heart and "interceding for us" with the Father "with unspeakable groanings."[71] The Word made flesh is seen by the pure in heart in five ways.[72] The Word is truly recognized in the light of glory by those who belong to him, and he himself foreknows those who are his, and is known by them; for "he knows what belongs to him" in reality "and they know him,"[73] since he is united with them, as he himself has said. Then, God the incarnate Word is revealed, and will be revealed in glory at the end of days, when the faithful also are revealed in glory, as it is written, for the shame and the reproach of the faithless and of those who believe wrongly, when "the just too will shine like the sun"[74] in that ineffable transformation and "in the change of the right hand of the Most High,"[75] "transformed from glory into glory"[76] and "from corruption to incorruptibility,"[77] blended with the divine spirit from a state of fleshliness. Then they will become, and will be seen to be, fully spiritual—united

[68]James 1.21.

[69]Gregory may be alluding here to the formula used for the "prayer of the heart" by the monks to whom he is speaking, "Lord Jesus Christ, Son of God, have mercy on me, a sinner."

[70]I Cor 12.3.

[71]Rom 8.26.

[72]In the next few sentences, it is not entirely clear what these five modes of knowledge are, by which "the pure of heart see God" (Matt 5.8); the number five may be chosen because of the five senses, or the five witnesses to Jesus' Transfiguration. However, these ways of knowing God, as set out here in the text of the homily, seem to be: 1) a select number of disciples know him by seeing the light of his glory, here on Mt Thabor; 2) they know him in the historic faith of Israel, as the one who has foreknown them and chosen them; 3) they know him inwardly, by mystical union; 4) they know him in his human, incarnate form as Jesus; 5) they will know him when he appears in glory at the end of history.

[73]John 10.14.
[74]Matt 13.43.
[75]Ps 76.11 (LXX).
[76]II Cor 3.18.
[77]I Cor 15.53.

completely with the Word who exists before the ages, the only God, and made divine in a way beyond understanding.

24 According to the models we have mentioned before, the Paraclete came down in fire; the disciples, enlightened through his purifying power, recognized the Son, and saw him within themselves in the mode of knowledge, whom they had not known accurately before, having received the ability to know perfectly but only partially. And the Son shone forth in a way beyond description on Thabor, in the light of his power; the disciples clearly saw "the Father of lights"[78] because of the voice from above, and the Spirit because of the bright cloud, and recognized the Trinity truly radiating forth in the transformed Christ, as an ever-flowing stream of light and brilliance. Then the mountains, too, celebrated with joy, as Scripture says: "Thabor and Hermon will rejoice in your name";[79] the heavens rejoiced and the whole earth skipped in joy, seeing their own Lord on the mountain, perceptibly and spiritually shining out more than the sun, giving light to all things and making all things holy. The heavens, too, "were telling his glory,"[80] seeing it shine forth as if they were alive; the firmament, by its brilliance, announced the creation by the Father's hands of the most beautiful form of humanity. From up above, the powers saw and shuddered; from down below, the earth trembled in joy and fear. Every creature, then—every nature, "everything with breath,"[81] praised and glorified and magnified, seeing its Master and King, who previously had shone through other things as their creator, now transfigured on the mountain as the world's craftsman; transformed, shining as God more brightly than the sun; glorified by God as a human being and hymned above all human beings; glorified as God, and as a human being glorified through God and with God; shining brilliantly as God, and as a human being shining along with God and drawing his light from

[78]James 1.17.
[79]Ps 88.13 (LXX).
[80]Ps 18.2 (LXX).
[81]Ps 150.6 (LXX).

God; as a human being recognized, and as the God-man intimately known; previously recognized in the flesh, contemplated in the light; recognized as a human being and gazed on as God; transfigured as a human being and testified to from above as the God-man; his face shining more brightly than the sun, and his garments white as snow, radiating light. In any case, the Son himself, a little later on, said to his own Father before his passion: "Glorify me yourself," Father, with yourself, and deify my human mixture "with the glory" of divinity "which I had with you before the world came to be."[82] And therefore the Father spoke to him from above: "I have given glory"—on Thabor, namely, shining with you and bearing witness and overshadowing—"and I will give glory again,"[83] more brilliantly and more perfectly, on the cross. Therefore he said again, more clearly, in the same passage, "Now the Son of Man has been glorified," radiating with the divinity, "and God has been glorified in him," suffering in his humanity. "If God is glorified" now, inviting us in him to wonder, he "will glorify him in himself" in time to come.[84] So he shows that the Lord Jesus is and will be the source of divine grace in all respects: himself recognized as the sun of justice that never sets, the judge of the living and the dead.

25   Let us, then, also glorify, and exalt with a hymn of praise, and magnify the one transfigured today on Mount Thabor:[85] the one who, as God, radiated a light more intense than the sun, who fully assured his disciples, who made the prophets to stand closely beside him by a miraculous vision and meeting. With Moses let us look at him, with Elijah let us ascend; with John let us speak of God, with Peter let us offer our own confession, and with James let us draw

[82]John 17.5.

[83]John 12.28, here interpreted as referring to the revelation of Jesus' divine glory on these two occasions.

[84]John 13.31. Gregory refers to all these passages about God's being glorified in Jesus as if they were taken from the same scene in the Gospel, which in fact is not true.

[85]Gregory now begins the final, hortatory section of his discourse, calling on his hearers to join in praising God who has here revealed his life-giving glory.

near to the light. And we shall "see his glory, as of the only Son of his Father,"[86] as far as possible; because he has himself been seen today "glorified in the council of his holy ones, great and exalted" on Thabor "above all those circled around him,"[87] as Scripture says. He is great and praiseworthy, great and fearsome, great and all-powerful, great and strong and mighty and inaccessible, and "of his greatness there is no limit,"[88] "to his thinking there is no clue."[89] His substance is beyond our understanding, his wisdom cannot be discovered, his greatness cannot be measured, his loftiness is without beginning, his beauty cannot be contrived, his power cannot be described, his life is eternal, his light knows no evening, his Kingdom is without successor and without borders. So worthy of praise, so fearsome, so lofty and powerful and undefeatable, is the one who today shines forth as God, more brightly than the sun, on Thabor!

26 For "who, in the clouds" of angels and prophets, "shall be thought equal to the Lord, who shall be likened to the Lord" in pleasing God and doing his will—"who among those made sons and daughters of God"[90] by the grace of adoption? There is no one! For he is glorified as the great and lofty and fearful God above all others, in the understanding of the saints, as we have already said; and as people who have become filled with God, let us say to him in wonder, in lowliness of spirit:

Lord Jesus, our God, "who is like you, who will be compared to you, who will be thought equal to you";[91] who will rightly glorify you and sing your praise, since you are beyond hymns, beyond divinity, beyond all being? "You are powerful, Lord, and mighty, and the

[86]John 1.14.
[87]Ps 88.8 (LXX).
[88]Ps 144.3 (LXX).
[89]Is 40.28 (LXX).
[90]Ps 88.7 (LXX).

[91]This paragraph and the beginning of the next, an outpouring of praise first to the transfigured Jesus and then to the Father, is a close but expanded paraphrase of Psalm 88.6–13 (LXX).

truth of your divinity radiates outward from you upon all! You rule over the might of the sea" of our passions, in that "you tame its rage from without, and reduce the tossing of both its waves; you humble like a wounded man the haughty one": the enemy and the inner thoughts who rage against us. "With your mighty arm you scatter your enemies," the Jews. "Yours are the heavens," your throne and creation; "and yours is the earth," your house and footstool when you became human. "You have set up this world" and the world to come; you have founded "the harsh north wind" and the uncrossable and boundless sea. Mounts "Thabor and Hermon rejoice" enthusiastically today "in your name," as they see you transfigured in their midst and shining more brightly than the sun!

27 Therefore let us join with David in the following prayer to God the Father, and let us say:

"Your arm it is" that has become human, "in great power"; may your arm, strong in every way, be confirmed in its force, Father on high, beyond all being; and "may your right hand," which today is transfigured among us in wonderful signs, "be exalted."[92] "Blessed is your people"—who we are!—"who know your loud hymn of victory"[93]—the hymn which your faithful ones sing, who have known victory through your Son. Let us, then, make our prayer of intercession, with amazement and with thanks, to the Son in the Spirit:

"Lord, consider us worthy always to walk forward in the light of your face. Today, in the light of your Transfiguration, we shall see you there as the Father's light, which never sets. Enlighten our eyes in the brilliant radiance of your divinity, so that we may not fall asleep in the darkness of eternal death; make the light of joy rise for us—the light of truth and intimate knowledge. O God, you light our darkened lamp, our untended mind; you always lighten the darkness of our ignorance, to gaze on you and sing your praise and your glory. 'Let the light from your face' that shone forth on Thabor

[92]Ps 88.14 (LXX).
[93]Ps 88.16 (LXX).

'be a sign for us';[94] let our minds be transfigured in the light of your glory; intoxicate us from the spring of your love, from which, in the age to come, your saints will be intoxicated with 'the richness of your house.'[95] May we be 'sheltered by the bright cloud of your wings.'[96] May we be enlightened by the brightness of your energies, but may we not be weighed down by that light, due to our own unworthiness. Lead us up onto the mountain of vision; shine on us like the sun, appear before us through your goodness; gather our mind and our voice towards you, as you did Moses and Elijah, and fill them with your glory. Shine on the three powers of our souls with your sparks of brilliant light, as you did on your three disciples, who could not completely endure to look directly at the unbearable beauty of your Godhead, because of the material, earthly character of the corruptibility that still mastered them.

28   "Grant us help from the troubles that surround us. Redeem us, as we are pressed in by them. Crush our enemies to the ground. Protect the Christian religion. Preserve your Church. Strengthen our Orthodox emperors. Judge us worthy of the transfiguration that is yet to come; join us together in glory with the saints who have been made perfect. Show us, in your goodness, unworthy though we are, to be sharers of that stability and order, when you stand in the midst of many gods and kings, Lord, source of all divine grace; and as you shine forth as the sun of justice surrounded by them all—amidst many righteous suns and stars—arrange each of us in divisions according to our worth, but shine your light on all of us, work your divine energy in us, enlighten us (as always) with your grace and your love for us all, which is also the love of our Lord Jesus Christ, with the Father and the Holy Spirit, now and always and to the ages of ages. Amen."

[94]Ps 4.7 (LXX).
[95]Ps 35.9 (LXX).
[96]Ibid. 8 (LXX).

GREGORY PALAMAS

Born in Constantinople of an aristocratic family in 1296, Gregory Palamas was another representative of the profound intellectual, cultural and religious revival that marked the decades after the restoration of the administration of the Byzantine Empire to the capital in 1261, under the leadership of the new Palaeologan dynasty, after almost six decades of the Frankish occupation of the capital. Brought up and educated at the court of the Emperor Andronicus II, and a pupil of the learned layman Theodore Metochites, Gregory probably had rich opportunities for a political career, but chose to become a monk on Mount Athos in 1316, beginning in the monastery of Vatopedi and eventually transferring to the Great Lavra. There he was drawn towards an eremitical life, and moved on to the skete of Glossia, where his solitude was broken only on Saturdays and Sundays by participation in the liturgy of his community. On the Holy Mountain, Gregory was initiated into the hesychastic approach to contemplative prayer by several of his spiritual fathers. This method of prayer, practiced since at least the late fifth century in Eastern monastic communities, emphasized the almost constant repetition of the simple, Biblical invocation, "Lord, Jesus Christ, Son of God, have mercy on me, a sinner," as the focus for developing a steady awareness of living in the presence of God; over time, this refrain becomes as instinctive as breathing for the practitioner, and enables the person to live with his or her consciousness continually centered on God, with an almost physical sense of God's indwelling.

Gregory seems to have become well-known, eventually, as a spiritual guide himself. In 1326, he and a number of fellow monks withdrew to the fortified city of Thessalonica, in the face of Turkish

raids on Mt Athos, but he eventually returned to the Holy Mountain for a brief period as abbot of the monastery of Esphigmenou,
in 1334. He began writing spiritual treatises and letters in the 1330s,
eventually being drawn into controversy with the Italo-Greek monk
Barlaam of Calabria, who had criticized the hesychastic approach
to prayer—which was now growing fashionable in the Byzantine
world, even among lay people—for being too centered on the individual consciousness and on learned practices, and for claiming a
participation in God's life that contradicted the Church's traditional
emphasis on the transcendent otherness and unknowability of
God. In response to Barlaam, Gregory wrote what is perhaps his
most famous work, the *Triads in Defense of the Holy Hesychasts*,
in the late 1330s; in the course of it, he elaborated his famous distinction between the divine essence, which remains completely
beyond the understanding and participation of creatures, and the
divine energies, a web of activity that radiates outward from God's
essence—from God as God is—just as rays come forth from the sun.
Barlaam's criticisms found considerable support among Byzantine
intellectuals, and Gregory, who had returned to Constantinople in
1338 to defend hesychastic theory and practice, was the object of a
good deal of hostility in the capital. In June and August, 1341, two
local synods defended the hesychasts and condemned Barlaam's
position; but after the death of the Emperor Andronicus III, in
1342, the Patriarch John XIV Calecas, who, with several other high
officials, had just staged a *coup d'état* against the *mesazōn* or prime
minister John Cantacuzenus, took up the offensive against Palamas
and his followers once again, apparently for political rather than for
theological reasons. Arrested and imprisoned in 1343, Palamas was
still well enough respected that the Patriach's hostility against him
backfired; another local council deposed John Calecas in 1347, and
rehabilitated both Cantacuzenus and Gregory Palamas, who was
ordained archbishop of Thessaloniki soon after his release from
prison. Gregory served as an exemplary archbishop, championing
the needs of the poor and leading the city to greater internal har-

mony. He died on November 14, 1359, and was recognized officially as a saint by the Patriarch Philotheos in 1368.

Gregory's sixty-three extant homilies date from the time of his ministry as archbishop of Thessalonica. When compared with those of some of his contemporaries, they are simple and straightforward in style, and adhere closely to the Biblical narrative or liturgical feast on which he is commenting. Included among them are these two homilies for the feast of the Transfiguration, on August 6. They clearly go together as a pair, and were probably delivered in the course of an all-night vigil for the feast: the first during the night offices, the second at the liturgy the following morning (see Hom. 1.17). The image of Christ, as the Son of God made fully human and now revealed to the disciples in the heavenly light that is personally proper to him and radiates outward from his person, becomes here a central symbol of the object of the hesychast's prayer and contemplation. By practicing the "prayer of the heart," the hesychast—like the three disciples on Mount Thabor—comes to glimpse the uncreated light that flows from the divine nature and embodies in perceptible form God's "energies" or activities directed outside his own being, and to share in it. A classic expression of Gregory's spiritual theology, these two homilies are really a single, carefully constructed treatise on divinization: the participation of graced and disciplined human followers in the brilliance that shines forth to a unique degree in the humanity of Jesus, but which is rooted in the transcendent, inconceivable being of God. The limits and conditions of that participation, as it is instanced in the story of Jesus' Transfiguration, are the main subject of Gregory's meditation here.

GREGORY PALAMAS

HOMILY 34

On the Venerable Transfiguration of our Lord and God and Savior, Jesus Christ,

in which there is a demonstration that

the light in that event is uncreated[1]

1   Let us, too, praise this great work of God, and let us wonder as
we contemplate it: I mean all of visible creation. Even the sages of
the Greeks praised it and wondered at it, as they searched for its
meaning. But we gaze at creation for the glory of the creator, while
they did so in contradiction of his praise—for they foolishly worshipped creation itself, not its creator. So we, too, will lay out all the
prophetic and apostolic and patristic texts, but for the benefit of our
readers and as a hymn celebrating the Spirit who speaks through the
prophets and Apostles and Fathers.[2] Those, too, who occasionally
appeared as leaders of dire heresies attempted to interpret these passages, but to the injury of those who believed them; they rejected the
truth of piety, using the sayings of the Spirit to contradict the Spirit.
And our divinely wise Fathers have, in a way, smoothed out the very

[1]This translation is based on the edition of Gregory Palamas' homilies by
Panagiōtēs Chrēstou (Thessaloniki, 1985), which is a revision of the seventeenth-
century edition by François Combéfis that appears in PG 151. These two homilies
for the feast of the Transfiguration appear in Chrēstou's edition, vol. 10, pp. 354–406;
Combéfis' edition is most easily accessible in PG 151.424–449.

[2]Gregory emphasizes the normative value of the traditional teaching and exegesis of earlier orthodox authorities. "The Fathers" are placed here alongside Scripture
as giving reliable guidance to the Church's faith in his own time.

narrative in the Gospel of grace—which is lofty, and appropriate for mature abilities to hear and understand—through the words of their own lips, making it accessible also for imperfect hearers like ourselves, just as mothers who love their children chew more solid bits of food to make it serviceable and easily digestible, even for babies still at the breast. And since the moisture in the mouths of bodily mothers becomes nourishment for their children, and the thoughts in the hearts of our divinely wise Fathers become the food of wisdom for the souls of those who listen and obey, so, too, the mouths of wicked and disreputable men drip deadly poison, which, when mixed with the words of life, becomes itself lethal for those who listen without due care.[3]

2   Let us flee, then, from those who do not receive the exegesis of the Fathers, but attempt to introduce opposed doctrines from their own minds, and pretend to discuss what is written in the text, but reject a religious understanding; let us flee from them even more quickly than one flees from a snake! For the snake kills the body prematurely by its bite, separating it from the immortal soul; but these grasp hold of the soul itself in their teeth, and tear it away from God, which is the eternal death of the immortal soul. Let us flee, then, from such people with all our power, and let us run instead towards those who take what is pious and saving as their principles, since these agree with the traditions of our Fathers.

3   I have said all this to your Love[4] now, as a kind of prologue, because we are celebrating the august Transfiguration of Christ on the mountaintop. Today we must also discourse about the light that shone in that event, about which much controversy now rages among the opponents of the light. Come, then—let us briefly set out

[3]Gregory seems to have a heightened sense of the danger of doctrinal controversy and error, perhaps as a result of the recent bitter conflict in Constantinople over the theoretical understanding of hesychastic prayer.

[4]Gregory refers here to his congregation, with a collective title familiar in sermons of both the Greek and the Latin Fathers

the words that were read to us today from the Gospel, to open the Mystery and reveal its truth. "After six days, Jesus took Peter and James and John, and led them up a high mountain by themselves, and he was transfigured before them, and his face shone like the sun."[5] First of all, we must examine this in the Gospel account: from which day does the Apostle of Christ, the evangelist Matthew, count the six days, after which the day of the Lord's Transfiguration occurred? After which day, then? After that day on which the Lord, teaching his disciples, said that the Son of Man would come in the glory of his Father, and added the statement, "There are some of those standing here, who will not taste death before they see the Son of Man coming in his royal power."[6] By the glory of his Father and his own kingly power, he is referring here to the light of his own Transfiguration. The evangelist Luke suggested this, and set it out even more clearly, in saying, "After these words about eight days passed; and then, taking Peter and James and John with him, he went up a mountain to pray. And as he was praying, it happened that the very form of his face became altered, and his robe shone brilliantly white."[7]

4   But how do these authors agree with each other—the one saying clearly that there were eight days between the promise and the epiphany, the other that it was "after six days"? Listen and understand: there were eight [persons] on the mountain, and six were visible! These are three: Peter and James and John, who went up with Jesus; and they saw there, standing with him and conversing with him, Moses and Elijah, so that all of these numbered six. But surely both the Father and the Holy Spirit were invisibly with the Lord, the one bearing witness by his own voice that this was his own beloved Son, the other shining forth through the bright cloud and revealing the Son's singleness of nature and oneness of light with him

[5]Matt 17.1.
[6]Matt 16.28.
[7]Luke 9.28.

and with the Father. For their natural unity is rich, and the degree of their brightness is one. So the six, then, are eight! And just as in these details the number six does not contradict the number eight, so the Evangelists also do not contradict each other, when the one says "after six days," while Luke says "After these words, eight days passed." Rather, through both of these phrases, they gave us a kind of figure of those who were gathered together on the mountain, in a mysterious yet visible way.

5   For one might see, by examining well also the literal sense of the text, that the divine writers agree with one another, in this way: Luke says eight days, not to disagree with him who says "after six days," but including also the day on which those words were spoken and the day on which the Lord was transfigured. Matthew also allows those who examine the text intelligently to understand the days this way. Therefore the one uses the preposition "after,"[8] which signifies what follows on something, while the other omits it; for he [Luke] does not say "after eight days," as the other [Matthew] says "after six days," but "about eight days passed." So there is nothing really different in the historical understanding of the Evangelists.

6   But they also reveal to us, through one another, something great and of mystical meaning in their apparent disagreement. And please pay close attention to what I will say, because it may elude your understanding. For what reason does the one say, "after six days," while the other passed over the seventh day also, and mentioned the eighth? This is the reason: the great vision of the light of the Lord's transfiguration is the Mystery of the eighth day, or of the coming age, after the cessation of the world that came into being in six days; it signifies the suspension of our own form of sensation, which operates in a sixfold way. For we have five senses, but when there is added to them the spoken word that is perceptible, it makes the operation of

[8]Greek: *meta.*

our sensibility sixfold.[9] But the Kingdom of God, proclaimed to the worthy ones, is not only beyond sense perception, but even beyond our powers of reason; so, after the noble inactivity of this sixfold sensibility, when they have come to an end—an inactivity which the seventh day enriches with noble dignity—then on the eighth day the Kingdom of God will appear, by the power of a still greater force. And this power of the Holy Spirit, by which the Kingdom of God is seen by those who are worthy, the Lord—according to St Luke—prophetically revealed to his disciples, when he said, "There are some standing here, who will not taste death until they see the Kingdom of God coming in power."[10] That is, this power will purify them from the fatal and soul-destroying damage, which sin is, by giving those who look on the ability to see what is invisible. And the taste of this sin is the beginning of evil in the mind's reasoning, but those who are purified from it beforehand will not taste the death of the soul, preserved unstained even in their reasoning power, as I understand it, by the power of the coming revelation.

7   "There are some among those standing here, who will not taste death until they see the Kingdom of God coming in power."[11] The King of all things is everywhere, and his Kingdom is also everywhere, so that "the coming of his Kingdom" does not refer to its moving from one place to another, but to the appearance of it in the power of the divine Spirit; therefore he said, "coming in power." And this power does not simply take root in anyone at all, but in those who stand alongside the Lord. This refers to those grounded in faith in him, to those like Peter and James and John—those lifted up beforehand by the Word onto a high mountain: that is, those enabled to cross beyond our natural lowliness. For this reason, too,

[9]Gregory is able to connect the "six days" of Matthew's narrative with the world of ordinary experience by adding the organizing role of language to the perceptions of the five senses. Implied here also seems to be the tradition of interpreting the six days of Genesis 1 as referring to the material, intelligible cosmos.

[10]Luke 9.27.

[11]Mark 9.1.

God is imagined, according to the Orator,[12] on a mountain: in that he comes down from his own point of vantage, and leads us up from our lowliness below, "so that the Uncontainable One might, in some modest way and as far as one safely can do so, be embraced by created nature."[13] This image is not of lesser value than the mind, but much greater and loftier, because it comes into being by the power of the divine Spirit.[14]

8 The light of the Lord's Transfiguration does not come and go, after all, nor is it circumscribed, nor is it subject to our power of perception, even if it is seen by bodily eyes and for a short period of time, and within the narrow space of the mountaintop. But "the Lord's initiates were transferred," as one writer puts it, "from flesh to spirit in that moment, by a change in their sensory powers,"[15] which the Spirit brought about in them. So they saw—in whatever place and degree the power of the divine Spirit bestowed on them—that ineffable light. Those who now do not understand, but blaspheme this light, think that these elect Apostles looked on the light of the transfiguration of the Lord by created powers of perception, and for that reason they attempt to drag down to the creaturely level not only that light, the glory and kingdom of God, but also the power of the Holy Spirit, through which divine things are revealed to the worthy. For they have not heard—or do not believe—Paul when he says, "What eye has not seen, and what ear has not heard, and what has not risen into the heart of a human being—the things that God has prepared for those who love him—these God has revealed to us through his Spirit; for the Spirit searches the depths of God."[16]

---

[12]I.e., Gregory of Nazianzus, known generally as "Gregory the Theologian."

[13]Gregory of Nazianzus, Or. 45.11.

[14]Gregory Palamas is reflecting on the appropriateness of using visual images, like those of ascent and descent, to speak of God's presence.

[15]Maximus Confessor, *Ambigua to John* 7 (PG 91.1125).

[16]I Cor 2.9.

9   But when the eighth day came, as we have said, the Lord took Peter and James and John and went up the mountain to pray. For his constant practice was to withdraw from all, even from the Apostles themselves, and to pray alone—as when he had fed the five thousand along with their wives and children with five loaves and two fish, he immediately dismissed them all and made all the disciples get into the boat, but he himself went up the mountain to pray—or else, taking a few with him, who were outstanding among the rest, as his saving passion was approaching, he said to the other disciples, "Sit down here, while I pray," and he took Peter and James and John with him. Here, then, too, he took them alone and "led them up a high mountain by themselves, and was transfigured before them"[17]—that is, as they looked on.

10   Who is it who was transfigured? The theologian Chrysostom says that he opened up to them a little of his divinity, as he saw fit, and he showed to those who were initiated the God who dwelt within him.[18] "For as he was praying," Luke says, "his form became different"[19]—"shining like the sun,"[20] as Matthew says. "Like the sun," he says, not that one should imagine that light as something perceptible—let us shun the mental blindness of those who cannot imagine anything higher than what appears to the senses—but that we might know that what the sun is to those who live by the senses and see through sense-perception, this Christ, as God, is for those who live by the Spirit and see in the Spirit, and for those in the image of God there is no need of any other light for seeing God. For he is the light of the eternal ones, and there is no other. What need is there, after all, for a second light for those who have the greatest light?

In praying, then, he shone forth light in this way, and revealed in an ineffable way to his chosen disciples that indescribable light,

[17]Matt 14.22.
[18]John Chrysostom, *Homily after the Departure of Eutropius the Eunuch* (PG 52.404).
[19]Luke 9.29.
[20]Matt 17.3.

while the greatest prophets were there with him: to show that prayer is the promoter of that blessed vision, and that we might learn that through nearness to God in virtue and through union with him in mind, that radiance grows in us and is revealed, given to all and seen by those who strive without ceasing for God, through sincere good works and pure prayer. For "true and loveable beauty," as someone has said, "which can only be contemplated by one purified in mind, is what surrounds the divine and blessed nature; the one who gazes intently on its flashes of light and its graces, shares in some of what comes forth from it, as if he himself were changed in color, in his own eye, into a kind of blooming brilliance."[21] So when Moses conversed with God, his face became glorious!

11   You see that Moses, too, was transfigured when he went up the mountain, and so it was that he saw the glory of the Lord. But he underwent transfiguration—he did not bring it about. Someone might say, "In this life, the moderate light of truth brings me to this point: to see and to experience the brilliance of God." But our Lord Jesus Christ had that brilliance from within himself; therefore he had no need for prayer to illuminate his body with divine light, but he revealed it from the same source from which the brilliance of God is bestowed on the holy ones, and in the same way it is made visible to them. For the righteous, too, will "shine like the sun in the Kingdom of their Father,"[22] and so, becoming wholly divine light, as offspring of the divine light, they shall gaze on the one who outshines them in a divine and ineffable way, whose glory, naturally coming forth from his divinity and possessed in common by his body, was revealed on Thabor through the unity of his hypostasis. So it was also through this light that "his face shone like the sun."

[21]Basil of Caesaraea, *Homily on Psalm* 29.5 (PG 29.317), trans. Sr Agnes Clare Way, *The Fathers of the Church* 46 (Washington: Catholic University of America Press, 1963) 220–221.
[22]Matt 13.43.

12   Some people, boasting that we have Greek reason and the wisdom of this world, and choosing not completely to obey spiritual men on the subject of the Spirit's teaching, but even rising up against them, hear of the light of the Lord's transfiguration on the mountain, as it was seen by the Apostles' eyes, and immediately turn it into the perceptible, created light—they turn into this that immaterial light that has no evening, the light that is eternal and is not only beyond perception but even beyond the mind. They themselves live here below, and cannot think of anything beyond what clings to the earth. Yet he who shone forth by this light demonstrated in advance that it is uncreated, calling it the Kingdom of God; for the Kingdom of God is not subject to others or a created thing—it alone, of all things, cannot be mastered or overcome, and lies beyond all time and every age; and God does not permit, they say, that it be dominated or overtaken by ages or times, because it is the Kingdom of God. We believe that this is the inheritance of those who are saved.

13   But since when the Lord was transfigured and shone with light, he revealed glory and brightness and light of that kind, and since he will come again just as he appeared to the disciples on the mountain, did he then acquire a light which he will have in future ages, but which he did not have before? Away with such blasphemy! The person who says this suggests there are three natures in Christ—the divine and the human and the nature of that light. Rather, he revealed this brightness not as a different light, but as what he already had in an invisible way. He had the brightness of the divine nature, hidden beneath his flesh. So, then, that light is the light of the divinity, and it is uncreated—since, according to the theologians, Christ was transfigured not by taking on what he was not, nor by being changed into what he had never been, but by revealing to his own disciples what he was, opening their eyes and making those who were blind now able to see. [23] Do you see that with reference to this light, those eyes which naturally can see were blind? So then, that light was not perceptible

---

[23]See John of Damascus, *Homily on the Transfiguration* 12: above, pp. 220–221.

light, nor did those who saw it simply see with the eyes of sense, but with eyes transformed by the power of the Holy Spirit.

14 They were changed, then, and so they saw the change: not a change that had just now occurred, but the change that took place from the moment [the Son] took on our human composition, a divinely caused change through union with the Word of God. From that moment on, she who had conceived him as a virgin and borne him in an extraordinary way recognized the one born from her as God in his flesh. And Simeon, taking him in his hands as an infant, and the aged Anna, who came forward to meet him,[24] [recognized him also]. For the divine power shone forth as if through crystal membranes, shining on those who have kept the eyes of their heart pure.

15 Why, then, does he take just the leaders of the others and lead them up the mountain, alone and privately? Probably in order to reveal something great and mysterious! How, after all, would a vision of perceptible light be great and mysterious, which those chosen ones had, even before they were led upwards, along with those who were with them and were left below? What need would they have had of the power of the Spirit, and the gift through it of new or changed eyes, to see that light, if it were perceptible and created? Why would light that is perceptible be the glory and kingly power of the Father and the Spirit? Why will Christ come in glory and kingly power like this, in the age to come, when there will be no need of air or light or space or things such as this, but God will take the place of all of them, according to the Apostle?[25] If he takes the place of all things, then surely he will take the place of light! So again, it is demonstrated that this light is the light of the Godhead, since the most theological

---

[24]In using the Greek word *prosypapantēsasa*, Gregory alludes to the accepted name of the feast commemorating this scene in Luke's Gospel, the "Hypapantē" or "meeting."

[25]Gregory seems to have in mind Paul's phrase, "God will be all in all" (I Cor 15.28).

of the Evangelists, John, states clearly in the Book of Revelation, that that city that will come and will remain "has no need of the light of the sun, nor of the moon, to shine in it; for the glory of God gives it light, and its lamp is the Lamb."[26] But did he [= God] not show us clearly Jesus in this passage too, divinely transfigured now on Thabor, possessing his body as a lamp, and instead of light the glory of his divinity shining forth on those who have climbed the mountain with him? But concerning those who dwell in that city,[27] the same author says that "they will have no need for the light of a lamp or the light of the sun, because the Lord God will shine on them, and night shall be no more."[28] What is this light, then, in which "there is no change, nor shadow of alteration"?[29] What is this unchangeable light, without evening? Is it not the light of the Godhead?

16 But Moses and Elijah—especially Moses, who existed as a soul without a body—how could they have been seen and been full of glory by means of perceptible light? For "they appeared in glory at that moment, and spoke about the exodus which he was to bring to fulfillment in Jerusalem."[30] How did the Apostles, who had never seen them before, recognize them, except by the revelatory power of that light?

17 But so that we might not strain your minds any longer, we will save up the rest of the Gospel's words for the time of the most sacred and divine liturgy.[31] Believing, then, as we have been instructed by

[26]Rev 21.23.
[27]The new Jerusalem.
[28]Rev 21.23.
[29]James 1.17.
[30]Luke 9.31.
[31]This remark makes it clear that Gregory's two homilies on the Transfiguration were intended as a pair: this present one was undoubtedly given during the vigil before the feast day itself (August 6), and the second one was given at the Eucharistic liturgy for the feast. This same pattern—often in sets of three homilies by the same preacher, rather than a pair—can be found in a number of the homilies by late Greek Patristic authors for the feast of the Dormition of Mary.

those who were enlightened by Christ, since they alone knew these things accurately (for "my mysteries are for me and mine,"[32] says God through the Prophet), and believing rightly and understanding, as we have been taught, the mystery of the Lord's Transfiguration, let us make our way towards the shining of that light. And loving the beauty of the unchanging glory, let us cleanse the light of our minds of earthly stains, considering worthless all that is enjoyable or superficially beautiful, but which has no permanence. For even if that seems sweet, it is the promoter of eternal sorrow; even if it brings a bloom of beauty to the body, still it wraps the soul in that ugly garment of sin, because of which the one who does not have the robe of incorruptible union is led, with hands and feet bound, to the fire and the outer darkness.[33]

18   May we all be sustained by the illumination and the personal knowledge of the immaterial, eternal light of the Lord's Transfiguration: to his glory and that of his Father, who has no beginning, and of the life-giving Spirit, who possess one and the same brilliance and divinity and glory and kingly power, now and always and for the ages of ages. Amen.

---

[32]Isaiah 24.16 (LXX): this phrase appears in the Hebrew text, and in the Vienna *codex purpureus* of the Septuagint (5th–6th century), but not in other early Greek manuscripts. In Origen, it is marked with an obelisk, as questionable.

[33]Matt 22.13.

[GREGORY PALAMAS]
HOMILY 35
For the Same Transfiguration of the Lord,

in which there is a demonstration that even if the most divine light is, of itself, uncreated, still it is not the substance of God.

1   The prophet Isaiah proclaimed, concerning the Gospel, that "the Lord will give a concise word on the earth."[1] A concise word is one that conveys much meaning in few words. Therefore let us contemplate again today what we have contemplated before of the Gospel's words, and let us add what still remains for our consideration, so that we may be filled now with the pure meaning stored up in them, and may become complete sharers in divine inspiration.

2   "At that time, Jesus took Peter and James and John and led them up a high mountain by themselves, and was transfigured before them; and his face shone like the sun."[2] "Behold, now is the acceptable time, behold, now is the day of salvation,"[3] my brothers—a sacred day, new and eternal, not measured out in intervals of time, not increasing or diminishing, not interrupted by the night. For the sun of justice[4] is the day, "with whom there is no change or shadow of alteration."[5] And when he, by the good pleasure of the Father and

[1]Is 10.23 (LXX).
[2]Matt 17.1.
[3]II Cor 6.2.
[4]See Mal 4.2.
[5]James 1.17.

with the cooperation of the Holy Spirit, shone on us in a loving way, he "led us out of darkness to his wonderful light,"[6] and extended the time that is always with us by shining down on us, since he is himself the sun that never sets.

3   Being the sun of justice and of truth, he does not allow himself to appear, or to be truly known, to those who circulate lies, or who speak extreme injustice or demonstrate it in their deeds. Rather, he appears to those who work righteousness and love the truth, and is believed in by them, and he gives joy to them by his bright rays. This is what Scripture says: "Light has risen for the righteous man, and his companion is good cheer."[7] For this reason, too, the Psalm-singing prophet sings to God, "Thabor and Hermon will rejoice in your name,"[8] prophesying the joy that will later come to be in the hearts of those who witness that illumination on the mountain. And Isaiah says, "Break every bond of injustice, loosen all the ties of violent agreements, tear up every unjust contract!"[9] And what next? "Then your light will break forth early, and your healing will rise quickly, and your righteousness will go before you, and the glory of God will cover you."[10] And again, "If you take away the bond from your midst, and pointing with your finger, and words of grumbling, and if you give bread to the hungry from your heart and fill up the heart that is laid low, then your light will rise in the darkness and your darkness will be like midday."[11] For he will make those on whom this sun clearly shines into other suns: "For the just shall shine like the sun in the Kingdom of their Father."[12]

[6] I Peter 2.9.
[7] Ps 96.11 (LXX).
[8] Ps 88.13 (LXX).
[9] Is 58.6 (LXX).
[10] Is 58.8 (LXX).
[11] Is 58.10 (LXX).
[12] Matt 13.43.

4   "Let us then put away the works of darkness," brothers and sisters, "and let us do the works of light,"[13] so that we may not only walk nobly, as in this present day, but may also become "children of the day."[14] Come, then, let us climb the mountain where Christ shone forth, so that we may see what is there; or rather, the Word of God himself will, in due time, lead us up [the mountain], since we have become people of this kind, worthy of such a day. So now focus and raise the eye of your mind, I beg you, towards the light of the Gospel message, so that you may be "transformed" in this time, "by the renewal of your minds";[15] in this way, clinging to that brilliant vision above, you will become conformed to the likeness of the glory of the Lord, whose face shone on the mountain today like the sun.

5   Why "like the sun"? There was a time when this sunlight was not contained in the vessel of this disk; for the light was the first thing to be created, but he who brought all into being formed the disk on the fourth day, joining the light to it and so giving concrete existence at once to the star that marks and brightens the day. In the same way, too, there was a time when the light of the Godhead was not[16] in the body of Christ, as in a vessel; for the one existed beforehand, without beginning, but the additional part, which the Son of God took from us, was brought into being later for our sakes, receiving the fullness of the Godhead into itself, and so the star began to shine that makes others divine, and that radiates divine light. So "the face of Christ shone like the sun, and his garments became white as light."[17] But Mark says, "They shone very white, like snow, such as no fuller on the earth could whiten them."[18]

[13]Rom 13.12.

[14]I Thess 5.5.

[15]Rom 12.2.

[16]Gregory here echoes the famous phrase of Arius from the fourth century, coined to suggest the Son is a creature: "There was when he was not." Gregory uses these words in the restricted sense that the humanity of Christ was not co-eternal with his divine being.

[17]Matt 17.2.

[18]Mark 9.2.

6   Both that adorable body of Christ and his garments, then, were radiant with the same light, but not in an equal measure. For his face "shone like the sun," but his garments, since they were near his body, became radiant, too, and through them he revealed what the robes of glory are like, which those who are close to God will put on in the age to come, and what the clothing of sinlessness is, which Adam took off by sin—after which he was seen to be naked, and was ashamed.[19] Saint Luke says, "His form became different, and his clothing shone forth white,"[20] seeing all that happened there without making any comparison. But Mark gives us a concrete picture of his clothing; and when he says that they were "shining very white, like snow,"[21] he too is providing images and inadequate comparisons for what those garments looked like. For snow is white, but it does not shine; and it always has an uneven appearance, since it is always composed of delicate, tiny bubbles, because of the mixture of air that is in it. For the cloud is not perfectly formed, and is not able to squeeze out the air that is caught up within it, but it becomes hard because of the extreme cold; so the snow falls and bears the air with it, having an appearance something like foam in its whiteness and, at the same time, in its unevenness.

7   The whiteness of snow, then, was not sufficient to express the delight of that vision, and "gleaming" was added; so, through these words, the Gospel writer is showing us that that light, through which those garments became brilliantly white, was supernatural. For it is not in the power of light to make things illuminated white and gleaming, but to reveal them as whatever they are in color; but this

---

[19]Gen 3.7. For the widespread ancient notion that Adam and Eve were clothed in light at creation, and only became naked when they lost these original, glorious garments through sin, see Gary Anderson, *The Genesis of Perfection. Adam and Eve in Jewish and Christian Imagination* (Louisville: Westminster John Knox 2001) 117–134 .

[20]Luke 9.29.

[21]Mark 9.3 (following the "koinē" or Byzantine and "Western" recensions, which are not normally followed in modern editions).

light, it seems, covered over[22] their color, or rather changed it, which it is not the property of perceptible light to do. And what is still more mysterious, even though it changed their color, for the time being it kept [the garments] unchangeable, as will be shown shortly. How can this be a property of the light we know? Therefore when the Evangelist points out not only the exceeding brilliance and beauty of the face of the Lord, but also the supernatural loveliness of his clothing, he distinguishes both of them from what is naturally beautiful, connecting gleaming to the whiteness of snow. And since art seems to be able to add a certain beauty to nature, he adds that reference to artificial beauties, and says, "a whiteness such as no fuller on the earth was able to cause."

8   But surely the eternal Word, who became flesh for our sakes, the personalized Wisdom of the Father, also bears the word of the Gospel proclamation in himself. And just as the letter is his garment, white and clear, it is at the same time glowing and radiant, like a pearl, even godlike and divine, to those who see the things of the Spirit in their own spirit; they are the ones who can interpret the sayings of Scripture in a divine way, and can show that these words of the Gospel proclamation are such as "no fuller on earth"—that is, no person wise in the ways of this age—can explain them. And why do I say, "explain"? For one cannot know them deeply if someone else attempts to clarify them. "The unspiritual person,"[23] as the Apostle says, "does not receive the things of the Spirit, nor is he able to know deeply."[24] Therefore he makes the mistake of taking the spiritual illuminations, which are above the mind, and divine and spiritual, in perceptible terms, "entering into things he has not seen, foolishly puffed up by the mind of the flesh."[25]

[22]Reading here, with Combéfis, *epekalypse*, "cover, conceal," rather than Chrēstou's *apekalypse*, "reveal."

[23]Literally, "the psychic person (*psychikos*)": the person whose life is dominated by natural reason, rather than by the enlightenment of the Spirit, as the life of the "spiritual person (*pneumatikos*)" is.

[24]I Cor 2.14.

[25]Col 2.18.

9   But Peter, illuminated in his intelligence by that most blessed vision, and inflamed towards a greater divine love and longing, wishing no longer to be at a distance from that light, said to the Lord, " 'It is good for us to be here. If you will, let us make here three tabernacles—one for you, one for Moses, and one for Elijah'—not knowing what he was saying."[26] For the moment of the restoration[27] had not yet arrived, but when the time does come, we will not have any need for tabernacles made by hand. Also, one should not equate the Lord with his servants by means of similarity of dwelling places; for Christ, as genuine Son, is in the bosom of the Father; but the prophets, as genuine sons of Abraham, will dwell, in turn, in the bosom of Abraham. As Peter, then, without understanding, was saying these things, "Behold, a bright cloud overshadowed them,"[28] interrupting Peter's words and revealing what the tabernacle is that befits Christ. But what was this cloud, and how, being full of light, did it "overshadow" them? Might this not be the inaccessible light in which God dwells, which "wraps him in light like a garment"?[29] As Scripture says, "He makes clouds his stepping-stones,"[30] and "uses the dark as his hiding-place, his tent about him."[31] And yet, as the Apostle says, "he alone has immortality, dwelling in unapproachable light,"[32] so that in this instance, light means the same thing as darkness, overshadowing us with its excess of brightness.

10   But what was formerly seen by the eyes of the Apostles is now identified by the holy theologians as something inaccessible. "For today the abyss of inaccessible light," one of them writes, "today the limitless outpouring of divine radiance, shines on the eyes of the

---

[26]Luke 9.33.

[27]Greek: *apokatastasis.* Cf. Acts 3.21, referring to the coming end of history, in which God will "refresh" Israel and "restore" the original order of the universe.

[28]Matt 17.5.

[29]Ps 103.2 (LXX).

[30]Ps 103.3 (LXX).

[31]Ps 17.12 (LXX)

[32]I Tim 6.16.

Apostles on Mount Thabor."[33] The great Dionysius, too, observing that the inaccessible light, in which God is said to dwell, is darkness, says, "Everyone who is counted worthy to know and see God comes to be within it."[34] So it was this same light that the Apostles first saw, shining from the face of the Lord, and which later overshadowed them as a bright cloud. Earlier it had shone more dimly, and made it possible to see; but shining much more fully later, it was invisible to them because of its excessive brightness, and so it "overshadowed" Christ, the sun of righteousness, the spring of divine and ever-flowing light. After all, even with the sun we perceive, the same light both makes seeing possible, through its rays, and again takes away our ability to see, when someone looks directly into it as it is; for its brightness is out of all proportion to our eyes.[35]

11 But the sun of our sensible world appears as it naturally is, not as it wills nor to those whom it chooses. But Christ, the sun of truth and righteousness, possesses not simply a nature, and natural brightness and glory, but also corresponding freedom of choice; he shines, by his own decision and in a saving way, only on those he chooses, and to the degree he chooses. Therefore he willed to shine like the sun and to be seen by the Apostles' eyes, and he did this not at a great distance; then, willing to shine more powerfully still, he became invisible to the Apostles' eyes because of an excess of brightness, entering, as it were, into a "bright cloud." But a voice came from the cloud: "This is my Son, the Beloved, in whom I am well pleased. Listen to him!"[36] If, then, when the Lord was baptized in the Jordan, the heavens were opened and the same voice spoke—surely from

[33]John of Damascus, *Homily on the Transfiguration* 12, above p. 206.

[34]Ps.-Dionysius, *Letter 5*.

[35]Ancient theories of visual perception, although they varied in detail, imagined that the eye itself generates some form of light, which is projected outward onto the objects of the world around us, and the encounter of that ray with the light of the external world, reflected back from the object towards the eye, was understood to be what causes vision. In the case of our gazing into the sun, Gregory observes here, the inequality of these two forms of light makes the sun virtually invisible to us in itself.

[36]Matt 17.5.

that same glory, which Stephen later gazed on and saw, when the
heavens were opened to him, and he had been filled with the Holy
Spirit—now it came from the cloud, which overshadowed Jesus. So,
then, this cloud is the same as the glory of God, which is above the
heavens! How, then, could this super-heavenly reality be perceptible
light?

12   The Father's voice from the cloud taught us that all those things
that occurred before the coming of our Lord and God and Savior,
Jesus Christ—the sacrifices, the legislation, the adoptions—were
incomplete, did not happen perfectly according to the guiding will
of God, but were permitted because of this presence and appearance
of the Lord that was to come. He is the one in whom the Father is
well pleased, on whom he rests, and in whom he perfectly delights;
therefore he commands us to hear him and to obey him. And if he
says, "Enter by the narrow gate, because the way leading to destruction is broad and wide open, but the road leading to life is narrow
and compressed"[37]—listen to him! And if he says that this light is
the Kingdom of God, listen to him and believe him! And make
yourselves worthy of such a light!

13   But when the bright cloud appeared, and the Father's voice
sounded from the cloud, Scripture says that the disciples fell on
their faces.[38] It was not because of the voice, since this had sounded
often enough at other times, also—not only at the Jordan, but also
as the saving passion was drawing near in Jerusalem. For as the Lord
prayed, "'Father, glorify your name,' a voice came from heaven, 'I
have glorified it and I will glorify it again.'"[39] And all the crowd
heard it, but none of them fell down. Here, however, there was not
only a voice, but boundless light burst forth with the voice. Probably because of this—not just because of the voice, but because of

[37]Matt 7.13–14.
[38]See Matt 17.6.
[39]John 12.28.

the unique, supernatural character of the light—the inspired writers realized that the disciples fell on their faces. And before the voice sounded "they were afraid," as Mark says,[40] surely because of that manifestation of the divine.

14 But since, because of all these things, that light appears to be divine and supernatural and uncreated, what will they feel who are overly absorbed in secular and psychological categories, and cannot recognize here the things of the Spirit? They will be swept onto the other shore, and they will say that this is not divine glory, or the Kingdom of God or its beauty or grace or brightness, as we have been taught by God and the theologians, but they will insist that this is the *substance* of God, which previously they had said was some perceptible, created thing. But the Lord, in the Gospels, says that this glory is not just common to him and the Father alone, but also to the holy angels, as Saint Luke writes: he says, "Whoever is ashamed of me and my words in this generation, of him will the Son of man be ashamed when he comes in his glory, and in that of his Father and the holy angels."[41] Those, then, who contend that this glory is something substantial, are saying that the substance of God and that of the angels are the same thing, which is the ultimate in impiety!

15 Not only the angels, but also holy human beings share in the glory and the Kingdom. But the Father and the Son, along with the Holy Spirit, share the glory and the Kingdom by their nature, while holy angels and human beings have a share in this by grace, receiving their light from that source. Moses and Elijah, too, appearing with him in glory, illustrate this for us. Moses did not only appear as a partaker in divine glory now, on Thabor, but also when his face was so radiant with glory that the children of Israel could not bear to look steadily at it. A writer confirms this when he says that Moses received in his mortal face the immortal glory of the Father; to Eunomius,

[40]Mark 9.7.
[41]Luke 9.26.

who argued that "the glory of the Almighty One could not be shared even with the Son," he replied that even if the discussion were about Moses, he could not accept such an argument as this![42]

16   This glory and kingly power and brilliance, then, are one and the same, common both to God and to his holy ones. Therefore "let the glory of God be upon us,"[43] the psalmist prophetically sings; but no one, up to now, has ever dared to say that the substance of God and that of the saints is one and the same. The divine brilliance, common to the Godhead of the Word and to his flesh, has just appeared to us on the mountain; but to say that the substance of Godhead is shared in common with the flesh is something Eutyches and Dioscorus[44] would say, but not those who wish to speak reverently. All will see this glory and brilliance when the Lord appears, "from the East even to the West,"[45] and those who ascended with Jesus have seen it even now, but there is no one who has taken his stand within the substance and essence of God, or has seen or declared God's nature. This divine light is given by measure, and more of it or less is received according to the merit of those who receive it, distributed without being divided. And the proof lies here at hand: the face of the Lord shone more brightly than the sun, and his garments became bright, and white as snow. And Moses and Elijah appeared in the same glory, but neither of them at that time shone like the sun; and

[42]Gregory of Nyssa, *Refutatio Confessionis Eunomii* 120 (ed. W. Jaeger, *Gregorii Nysseni Opera* 2 [Leiden: Brill, 1952] 363.6–9). Gregory of Nyssa is here refuting the late "Arian" Eunomius' argument that everything associated with the transcendent being of God, including God's glory, cannot be shared with creatures because of the infinite gulf in substance between them.

[43]Ps 89.17 (LXX).

[44]In the debates of the late 440s, leading up to the Council of Chalcedon (451), the archimandrite Eutyches of Constantinople was criticized for holding that the divine nature of Christ and his flesh formed one new, shared nature, after the union of God and humanity in the Incarnation. Dioscorus, bishop of Alexandria at the time, defended Eutyches from charges of heresy, at a synod he called at Ephesus in 449 and later at Chalcedon. Gregory here alludes to them as classic proponents of an indiscriminate "mixing" of the divinity and the humanity of Christ.

[45]Matt 24.27.

the disciples themselves saw something of that light, but were not able to gaze on it.

17   So it is given by measure, and is distributed without being divided, and this light admits of more and less—one aspect of it is known now, another will be later on. That is why Saint Paul says, "Now we know in a partial way, and prophesy in part."[46] But the substance of God is completely without parts and beyond conception, and no substance admits of more or less.[47] It belongs to the accursed Messalians, for instance, to think that the substance of God is visible to those whom they consider saints.[48] But we reject unorthodox thinkers, of past and present, and believe—as we have learned—that it is possible for holy people to see and to share in the kingly power and glory and brilliance and ineffable light and grace of God, but not in God's substance; and we will make our way towards the shining of the light of grace, so that we may experience and worship the Godhead in triple form, shining forth with a single ineffable brilliance from a single nature in three hypostases. And we will strain the eye of our mind towards the Word, now enthroned with his body over the triumphal arch of the heavens.[49] He is seated, as befits his Godhead, "at the right hand of the Majesty,"[50] and addresses to us this word, as if from a great distance: "If anyone wishes to stand in the presence

[46]I Cor 13.9.

[47]In the classical understanding of the terminology of substance, going back to Aristotle's *Categories*, a *substance* is what a thing is: it specifies a thing's identity, but not its quantity or grade. Accidents and other characteristic qualities can be possessed by an individual to a greater or lesser degree, but the thing either is or is not the substance that it is said to be.

[48]A fifth-century spiritual movement about which little is known directly, the Messalians were considered heretical by later Orthodox writers for believing that humans could come literally to see and experience God directly by cultivating constant prayer.

[49]Gregory may be evoking here a comparison of the glorified Christ with the representation of him in the famous sixth-century mosaic in the apse of the church of Osios David in Thessaloniki. His reference to "the heavenly triumphal arches" has, in any case, an architectural ring.

[50]Heb 1.3.

of this glory, let him imitate, as far as possible, the way and the form of life that I have shown on earth, and follow it."

18   Let us contemplate, then, with our inner eyes this great vision: our own nature, now co-existing forever with the immaterial fire of the Godhead. Taking off our "garments of skin,"[51] which we put on after the fall—our earthly and fleshly thoughts—let us stand on holy ground, each of us demonstrating through our virtue and our eagerness for God that our own ground is holy. So we will gain in confidence, dwelling in the light of God; and we shall be filled with light even as we press forward. And we shall share in his eternity, as we are filled with light: to the glory of that brilliance that is utterly single in its power, yet formed of three suns: now and always and for the ages of ages. Amen.

[51]Gen 3.21. This image fascinated many rabbinic and early Christian commentators. For most Christian interpreters, it referred to the coarsened condition of human nature, and its mortality—suggested by dead animal skins—which became characteristic of humanity after the fall. See, for instance, Gregory of Nyssa, *Catechetical Oration* 8 (GNO III, 4.30).

ST VLADIMIR'S SEMINARY PRESS
1-800-204-2665 • www.svspress.com